TELEVISION AS
DIGITAL MEDIA

CONSOLE-ING PASSIONS
Television and Cultural Power

Edited by Lynn Spigel

TELEVISION AS
DIGITAL MEDIA

EDITED BY JAMES BENNETT AND NIKI STRANGE

Duke University Press   Durham and London   2011

© 2011 Duke University Press

All rights reserved

Printed in the United States of America on acid-free paper ∞

Designed by Heather Hensley

Typeset in Scala by Tseng Information Systems, Inc.

Library of Congress Cataloging-in-Publication Data appear
on the last printed page of this book.

FOR OUR PARENTS

CONTENTS

ACKNOWLEDGEMENTS

We are very grateful to Ken Wissoker, Leigh Barnwell, Court-
ney Berger, and Danielle Szulczewski at Duke University
Press for their belief in the project and for their guidance in
bringing it to fruition. We would also like to thank Lynn Spigel
for her invaluable advice and comments throughout the process. Our contributors themselves have been fantastic to work
with. We thank them for all of their efforts, responses to criticisms and comments, and for so generously sharing their insights in this collection.

The Communications, Culture, and Media Research Capability Fund at London Metropolitan University has provided
James the time and space to help bring this collection together.
Thanks must go to his colleagues, particularly Anna Gough-
Yates, Bill Osgerby, Paul Cobley, Mike Chopra-Gant, Paul Kerr,
Gholam Khiabany, as well as James Walters and Tom Brown
who have been excellent sounding boards and sources of advice throughout the process. A debt is also owed to the University of Warwick Film and Television Department, which
at different moments shaped our experience of television
and television studies, particularly via the help, support, and
friendship of Charlotte Brunsdon and Rachel Moseley.

We would like to thank our families for their love and encouragement throughout the process. Finally, our greatest
thanks go to each other for making the co-editing of this book
as enjoyable and rewarding as it has been.

Television as Digital Media

In December 2007 the BBC launched its online streaming and download service, the iPlayer (see figure 1). By the end of 2009, over 729 million requests to view programs had been made via the service, which offers U.K. viewers a chance to watch programs screened on the BBC's television channels in the last seven days or listen to radio broadcast over any BBC radio station over the same period via their computer or a range of mobile media devices.[1] Advertising for the service featured the tagline, "Making the unmissible, unmissible," calling our attention to the way the service converges television and radio's broadcast form with the computer. Similarly, in the United States services like Hulu present television along with film under the simple banner, "Watch your favorites. Anytime. For free." In this context, television programs become merely a form of audiovisual content—to be watched whenever and wherever users demand, on whatever device they choose. Removed from the structure of television's scheduled flow, the program as content on these services calls our attention to its embedding in a new, digital media context: instead of flow, here we have an interface, hyperlinks, and a database structure experienced via broadband rather than broadcasting. Moreover, where such services allow downloading or are available on a variety of digital media platforms, such platforms bring their own distinct viewing protocols to bear on the experience

FIGURE 1 Services such as the BBC iPlayer dislocate programs from the scheduled flow of television, drawing our attention to their status as content in a digital media context.

of content—from the commuter cradling an iPod, to the office worker grazing content across multiple browser windows, to the student sharing clips on a mobile phone—a relaxed enjoyment of this content on computers or portable devices in comfortable domestic or public spaces. The iPlayer and Hulu provide an experience that promises the freedom to decide what to watch and when to watch it and, in so doing, fragment the previously mass audience of television into a series of personalized choices. Welcome to television as digital media.

By the end of 2010, the United States, Germany, Finland, the Netherlands, Denmark, and Sweden will experience television solely as a digital media, while in the United Kingdom, Japan, and France, penetration of digital television services will be well in excess of 80 percent as each country closes in on switchover dates set for the coming three years. These penetration rates and switchover programs—focused as they are on the digital transmission of signals by cable, satellite, or terrestrial technologies—speak to a traditional understanding of television as the "box in the corner." Arguably, they therefore tell us only half the story. Television as digital media must be understood as a non-site-specific, hybrid cultural and technological form that spreads across multiple platforms as diverse as mobile phones, games consoles, iPods, and online video services such as YouTube, Hulu, Joost, and the BBC's iPlayer, as well as computer-based mediaplayers such as Microsoft's Windows Media Player and Apple TV. Equally pertinent to producing a fuller understanding of digital television, therefore, is to note the rising penetration of broadband services and mobile media devices, such as figures that show broadband take-up at 62 percent of all U.S. households and 57 percent in Japan, while in the United Kingdom there was "nearly one broadband connection for every four people" by the end of 2007—an approximation that calls up the nuclear family household traditionally addressed by television.[2] The penetration of mobile phones has risen even more starkly, with the U.K. market standing at a staggering 129 percent take-up, while in the United States and Japan the figure stood at 85 and 79 percent, respectively.[3] Although these technologies might not be television as it is traditionally understood, they represent just some of the new technologies on which television is experienced, produced, and regulated.

Figures from official switchover programs, however, call our attention not only to some of the not-so-radical shifts that television's digitization engenders, but also to the fact that such transformations occur within specific national and local configurations. As *The New York Times* reported of the U.S. switchover to digital in June 2009, "for most viewers, the transition amounted to a minor hiccup at most," one focused primarily on retaining existing channels and services rather than a massive expansion of new technologies and screens or interactive and customizable options.[4] Elsewhere, while the Audiovisual Media Services Directive in the European Union may have promoted a universal approach and deadline for switchover, individual E.U. members are in varying states of preparedness.[5] Although a variety of international contexts might all promote the digital switchover by emphasizing the benefits that digital TV will bring consumers (increased choice, interactive options, Internet services, high-definition television) and governments (increased revenue from the sale of analog spectrum), the experience of digital TV differs greatly according not only to geography, but also to economic and cultural factors that speak to the role television has had in defining modernity. Thus, as suggested by a *New York Times* headline from 2009 that warned "Millions Face Blank Screens in TV Switch," even this seemingly minute change in the technological form of television transmission posed a potentially profound shift in what television is in the digital age.[6] Behind the *New York Times* headline lay a set of assumptions about television's role in modern Western societies: a central, universally available (whether by way of advertiser-supported content or license fee), defining element of everyday life. Implicit in these assumptions is a view of television as a *mass medium* that has helped define the social collective experience—the rhymes and routines of the working day, month, or calendar year; shared national or international moments—and digital television as a fragmenting experience in which we must all make our own choices, self-schedule, download, and fend for ourselves. As William Uricchio has recently noted, "While not yet individualized . . . we inhabit a moment where the steady erosion of the mass viewing public has created anxiety in political terms regarding the future of television as a collective mode of address."[7]

Such issues in relation to television's digitization remind us that nothing about television is ever *just* about television. Key theorists such as Roger Silverstone, Lynn Spigel, and David Morley have demonstrated the way television emerged in the postwar era as a symbol of modernity that has functioned to define everyday life, particularly in the way it has structured the routines of daily life and the relationship between public and private space.[8] As Silverstone argues, drawing on Anthony Giddens's notion of ontological security, "in its spatial and temporal significance; in its embeddedness in quotidian patterns and habits; as a contributor to our security . . . television is part of the grain of everyday life."[9] Television as digital media, to some extent, threatens to upset assumptions taken for granted not only about the medium, but also the organization of everyday life, forms of sociality, and culture. Taken in this light, the transition to television as digital media is about the rise of a digital culture that increasingly both networks and atomizes society. Michael Curtin addresses this transition in relation to a turn to "matrix media," which are "characterized by interactive exchanges, multiple sites of productivity, and diverse modes of interpretation and use." Such matrix media, he argues, "increasingly thrive in an environment where distinctions between production and consumption blur, where television seasons give way to an evergreen cavalcade of content that is made use of by audiences on flex-time schedules."[10] Curtin's analysis points to the changes in time, spatial, economic, and cultural relations engendered by the shift to digital media, whereby television's live schedule no longer orders and structures daily life on a mass level.

This shift challenges long-held and fundamental assumptions about television, such as its position as a "window on the world." As Anne Friedberg suggests in an excellent history of the virtual window in Western society, "The window's metaphoric boundary is no longer the singular frame of perspective—as beholders of multiple-screen 'windows,' we now see the world in spatially and temporally fractured frames, through 'virtual windows' that rely more on the multiple and simultaneous than on the singular and sequential."[11] Friedberg's analysis of the fragmentation of the media window speaks of the increasingly personalized experiences, the multiplicity of options, and the changing modes of address and engagement offered by digital television. This is not to suggest that we are experiencing a simple shift from "broadcasting" to "narrowcasting," community to individual, or window to portal. Digital television's screen does not simply replace the window; rather, it repurposes, remediates, and constantly recalls and recirculates television's window-on-the-world positioning in the digital era. As often as we are promised the convenience of the television experience "anytime, anywhere," we are equally invited to participate in communities, share television moments, watch live now, come home to television, and structure our daily lives around TV.[12]

This collection of essays addresses digital television's position within the wider digital culture of matrix media and multiple windows, producing understanding of television as digital media as a complex interplay of sites, screens, technologies, industries, economies, aesthetics, national and global contexts, domestic and public viewing spaces, citizenship and consumer functions, community and fragmentation, as well as new and established production, user, and audience practices. Treating television as digital media includes understanding the continued importance of the role of television as the "box in the corner," which continues to answer the rhythms and routines of day-to-day life—including the desire to simply sit back on the couch and *not* choose, interact, or download—what John Ellis has termed the nexus between "time famine" and "choice fatigue."[13] Yet as Jason Jacobs argues in his essay, in relation to the forms of attention cultivated by digital television, we need to interrogate how this seemingly long-held and ordinary role of television and its viewing practices is experienced in the digital landscape. The essays contained here suggest that television as digital media is a significant shift in television's cultural form, requiring new ways of thinking about and studying it. To be sure, an overarching concern is to interrogate the everydayness and ordinariness that has structured television's position in modern and postmodern society. As essays from Roberta Pearson and Julian Thomas remind us, this is no radical break from television's analog past: the practices and technologies of digital television have long been established within television and its associated industries. Nor has the future arrived with digital television: the medium of television remains one in transition. As Lynn Spigel has remarked, discussions that explicitly position television as "in transition" hark back at least as far as Phillip Drummond and Richard Paterson's 1986 collection, *Television in Transition*, with a range of collections and monographs emerging periodically ever since with the same or similar titles. Equally prevalent has been what Spigel describes as the inclusion of the "future chapter" in classic texts on the medium; such chapters can be traced back to Raymond Williams's foundational *Television: Technology and Cultural Form*.[14] In many of these works it is the digitization of television that represents the future, yet this process is well underway and television's form as digital media is already shifting, as industry and audience alike look for new modes of engagement.[15]

Seeking to capitalize on the buzz around Web 2.0, the BBC has already announced that the iPlayer will be radically overhauled to marry Internet video with social media, in what Anthony Rose (BBC head of online media) has described as "Broadcast 2.0."[16] Beyond the hyperbole of such proclamations, statements like Rose's speak of both the continual technological and cultural renewal as well as the hybridity of television, which increasingly connect television to not just the computer but also digital culture.[17] Moreover, such discourses demonstrate the industry's attempts to position itself at the heart of digital culture, against the competition posed by new digital media forms. As Jean Burgess argues in this volume, understanding digital television requires a double mastery of such discourse: "it is not enough to go around 'debunking' the hype because, for one thing, hyperbole is a constitutive force in the field of study." Thus while Graeme Turner's essay suggests we be wary of claims that television's digital incarnation is changing viewing patterns in the context of surveys revealing viewers spend an average of only six minutes watching online video each day, Max Dawson's chapter suggests that such a limited viewing time might sit perfectly well with new forms of TV, such as the digital short. Elsewhere in the collection, Jeanette Steemers argues that preschool children are already downloading, sampling, and experiencing content across multiple platforms—or at least fantasized as such by the industry—with real economic and cultural effects within the sector's production ecology. In treating television as digital media, therefore, the essays in this collection move beyond the now familiar question of "What's new about new media?" and develop approaches that are sensitive to the specificities of digital television and its analog history while continuing to consider the implications for the future of television, its convergence and divergence with other digital media and role in everyday cultural life. As a collective, the essays seek to form a new critical paradigm for thinking about television in the digital era.

Television's digitization explicitly makes a new media form out of a technology that has often been positioned as the old media technology par excellence. So, finally, then, what is television as digital media? The answer is that as television has always been, television as digital media is a hybrid media form. In Jason Jacobs's excellent history of early television, he suggests that one of three key discourses—together with intimacy and mobility—to emerge around the invention of television in British public life was hybridity, whereby the value of television was placed on its relay ability: to act as a hybrid of other media forms, such as opera, newspapers, and national events, by allowing the viewer live access to them through television's window.[18] Raymond Williams's much-quoted description of the experience of television flow draws our attention explicitly to such hybridity, describing it as "having read two plays, three newspapers, three or four magazines, on the same day that one has been to a variety show and a football match. And yet in another way it is not like that at all, for though the items may be various the television experience has in some important ways unified them."[19] That we can now watch both YouTube on our TVs via a games console and television programs on YouTube via channels accessed on our iPods suggests that this hybridity is merely underscored rather than radically new. The more challenging aspects of this hybridity in the digital age ask us to understand television as dispersed across a range of screens, sites, and devices that mix it with the properties from digital media—such as software, code, interfaces, social networking, broadband, peer-to-peer file sharing, intellectual property, and technological design—and, at the same time, recognize that the experience is still somehow television. "What is television as digital media?" is a question for which each of the essays in this volume, in different ways, seeks to provide answers—and to which I shall return at the conclusion of this introduction—as I now want to turn more directly to the epistemologies that might help us understand how to go about studying television as digital media.

STUDYING TELEVISION AS DIGITAL MEDIA:
TELEVISION STUDIES AND NEW MEDIA STUDIES

If digital television is a new media formation of television, then, to paraphrase Charlotte Brunsdon, what is the digital television of television studies?[20] Brunsdon's inquiry into the television of television studies in 1998 examines how, as an object of study, television has been constituted differently by separate bodies of academic work. Brunsdon eschews policing the fields of what is and isn't television studies, instead drawing our attention to the fact that it is the hybridity of television studies that makes it exciting. Telling the story of television studies in six "anthologies," she traces the field's emergence from the traditions of critical journalism, literary/dramatic criticism, and the social sciences through the influence of feminism and film and cultural studies. Charlotte Brunsdon and Lynn Spigel—in Spigel's overview of the field in the introduction to *Television after TV*, and each author's subsequent revisitation of the issue in *Cinema Journal*—have mapped the contours of television studies, helpfully periodizing its study, demonstrating the diverse range of disciplines that have influenced its construction, and setting out some of the key debates, problems, and generative assumptions that television studies faces (and brings with it) as it engages with television as digital media.[21] Given such excellent histories of the field, it is not my intention here to trace a history of television studies, nor television itself, for that matter. Instead I want to engage explicitly with what both Brunsdon and Spigel regard as the present moment of transition, which connects television's long hybrid form no longer with radio, newspaper, or cinema, but the computer and digital media more generally.[22] To ask "What is the digital television of television studies?" is to suggest that there is an urgent and pressing need to consider a new anthology in television studies history, one that draws explicitly on new media studies in order to constitute television as digital media as its object of study. In this section, therefore, I want to map the relationship between television and new media studies.

As Spigel suggests, the main debates within television studies regarding culture, ideology, and audience have largely shifted elsewhere, predominantly to a focus on new media. It is not that these older debates have been resolved or forgotten, but that the pace of digital media development seems to produce an urgency in engaging with new technologies as embodiments of the future itself.[23] Arguably that debate has often unfolded around the democratic, liberatory potential of new media—with utopian and dystopian views equally evident.[24] Where the debate divides into polar opposites, Spigel argues, "this is new media studies at its worst. At its best . . . [it offers] a critical engagement with what is actually going on."[25] The essays here fully engage in these debates, suggesting that while television's era of mass audiences may be increasingly called in question, its digital formation continues to facilitate new and important forms of community.

Tiziana Terranova suggests that such an engagement is provided by new media studies' "key concern of . . . [examining] the causal relation between technology and society."[26] Reviewing a range of works that might broadly be understood as new media studies, Terranova argues that it is this concern that has both most distinguished the discipline from earlier paradigms of media studies—mass communications, British cultural studies, and political economy—and "unsettled the consensus . . . [which] emphasized the absolute primacy of cultural and social agency over technological determination."[27] As attested to by Henry Jenkins's invocation of Ithiel del Sola Pool as the "prophet of convergence," technological determinism is something that has remained contested in media and new media studies.[28] Terranova unpicks these debates by focusing our attention on the work of three key scholars: Marshall McLuhan, Raymond Williams, and Michel Foucault. Demonstrating McLuhan's influence on the emergence of mid-1990s new media scholarship that celebrates new technologies' capacity to increase individual freedom "discursively associated with . . . the notion of the free market," Terranova suggests, "many cultural theorists . . . returned to . . . Raymond Williams' critique of McLuhan . . . to show that media technologies are only provisional outcomes in more complex social processes." Outlining the criticisms of Williams's own work, which have concentrated on the absolute authority ascribed to human agency, Terranova suggests that a great deal of new media studies has therefore turned to Foucault, and to a lesser extent Gilles Deleuze,[29] to "understand technical machines as part of larger social *dispositifs* which express mutations in the organization of power relations."[30] As Terranova sets out, Foucault's work has proved so influential in studying new media because of the networked, hyperlinked, and surveillance-oriented nature of digital media technologies.

Given television studies' debt to Raymond Williams's work, it is unsurprising, both in the essays here and those elsewhere that address television as digital media, to find that technological determinism is eschewed within television studies. While work by scholars such as William Uricchio and William Boddy has considered the status of television as new media at different historical epochs, these scholars are a priori concerned to demonstrate the social forces that have shaped its technological form.[31] Equally, Foucault's influential position within cultural studies has informed studies of television as digital media, such as excellent accounts of the relationship among reality television, digital media, citizenship, and surveillance by John Caldwell, Laurie Ouellette and James Hay, and Mark Andrejevic.[32] Essays in this volume draw fully on these heritages, with Daniel Chamberlain's, William Boddy's, and my own essay utilizing Andrejevic's work to call attention to power relations in forms of digital television that track and survey their audience and users. Equally, essays by Boddy and Thomas in the first section demonstrate the argument for the "social shaping" of technology, with a number of other essays all examining the cultural milieu within which television as digital media is constructed.

And yet television's status as new media sits uneasily with many of the approaches and rhetoric found within new media studies. Leah Lievrouw and Sonia Livingstone have criticized new media research in cultural studies and media arts and design for often taking a "technologically deterministic tone," citing the works of Lev Manovich, Mark Poster, and Allucquére Rosanne Stone as evidence. In contrast, they assert: "new media researchers in the social sciences are virtually united in rejecting accounts in which technological innovation is the cause and society is the effect."[33] Insofar as work such as William Merrin's and David Gauntlett's (which calls for a "Media Studies 2.0") is indicative of the continued trend for technological determinism in arts-based studies of new media, their criticism would appear to ring true.[34] However, while the approach that Lievrouw and Livingstone set out for new media studies avoids the pitfalls of technological determinism and its associated neologisms generated in the digital theorization land rush — providing instead empirical and close analytical scrutiny to issues of political economy, democracy, audience practices, and regulatory debates—it also largely fails to engage questions of the aesthetics or texts of digital media.

Television studies' textual tradition clearly has a place in drawing on the insights new media studies brings to such issues, but also in refocusing our attention on screen form, ideology, and culture.[35] However, as many of the studies here suggest, the textual study of television as digital media extends beyond the place of texts in the simple production-text-audience triumvirate and instead can yield valuable insights into the study of audiences and producers. Furthermore, as I have suggested elsewhere, television studies' attention to texts and aesthetics may allow the discipline to "act as something of a corrective to the strand of new media studies that pays attention to aesthetics only insofar as they are demonstrative of links to cinema as 'high art.'"[36] Jason Jacobs's essay proves such an antidote here, bringing close critical attention to the nature of pollution and interruption in digital media to yield important insights about the nature of digital media. Moreover, as evidenced by many of the essays in this volume, such an approach to the text also avoids the technological determinism associated with such accounts, addressing the productivity of texts as urgently as the political economy of their production. Thus Karen Lury discusses the animation and reanimation of time in digital television as an aesthetic, economic, and ideological construct, while Max Dawson demonstrates the formation of new aesthetic tropes in the digital short in relation to the business practices, labor disputes, and production cultures of television. Such analyses respond to Brunsdon's criticism of the textual emphasis in television studies over and above attention to political economy and "an understanding of the production of texts, as opposed to their productivity."[37] Ten years on Brunsdon rightly criticizes a continuation of such "productivity" studies of television: "It is no good to say 'well, no one has ever looked at this program before, and I'm going to show you why it's interesting,' because many people have looked at a great many programs."[38] Brunsdon refers to television studies as "somehow smaller and more repetitive," a point starkly echoed by Paul Kerr, who, returning to academia after twenty years of working in the production of television, found "how little seems to have changed," with Brunsdon's call seeming "to have gone largely unheard."[39]

While collections such as that of Vicki Mayer, Miranda J. Banks, and John Caldwell and studies such as David Hesmondhalgh's, Georgina

Born's, and John Caldwell's point to the emergence of a field of "production studies" that addresses this blind spot, Brunsdon's and Kerr's arguments point to significant issues within television and media studies.[40] As Brunsdon has recently noted, "traditions of British public service broadcasting . . . were much more significant to the formation of television studies than has been previously recognized."[41] Most problematic about the repetitive nature of studying texts has been, for Kerr, "lack of synchronicity—between the 'issues' absorbing academics and those of concern to many television workers and indeed viewers," particularly regarding attention to the pressing policy and other issues concerning broadcasters. This point is reiterated by Brunsdon's observation that TV scholars have been noticeably absent in the defense of the license fee and the future of the BBC and public service broadcasting in the United Kingdom.[42] The developments of the Media, Communication and Cultural Studies Association policy network and the prominent role of academics in the establishment of the Citizens' Coalition for Public Service Broadcasting are welcome developments in this regard.[43] Niki Strange's essay here addresses the continuing importance of intervening in such debates. Written from the perspective of both scholar and digital media insider, Strange provides an account of the BBC's practices that demonstrates the complexities of the corporation's role in the digital television era, setting out how some of its strategies fulfill public service remits in the digital age, but also what some of the limitations to supporting its extension into digital media might be. Such debates about public service broadcasting have obvious connections with the way digital media have been studied in terms of their democratic and communal potential. While some see the fragmentation of television's mass audience by the development of nichecasting and multiplatform media entertainment as the death of citizenship—replaced by the ubiquity of consumer choice and commercial exploitation—others have stressed both the way digital media provide for new modes of democratic engagement and the cultural creativity of consumer practices. John Caldwell's essay demonstrates the way such debates can be understood as calls for intervention and understanding of labor relations in the television industries, which increasingly require us to pay attention to the practices of audiences as well. As he has argued forcefully elsewhere, studying "television's 'production of culture,' is simply no longer entirely convincing if one does not also talk about television's 'culture of production.'"[44]

New media studies itself owes a large debt to the traditions of study-ing audiences in television and cultural studies, with Henry Jenkins's pioneering study of fans regularly invoked to study the communities that build around digital and online spaces.[45] Similarly the legacies of John Fiske and John Hartley inform studies of the activity and produc-tivity of fans, leading Axel Bruns to describe the digital era as one of "produsage," while elsewhere the influence of feminism and its impact on the study of TV audiences is felt in analyses of identity online, such as Sherry Turkle's *Life on the Screen* and Donna Haraway's "manifesto for cyborgs."[46] As with television studies, the impact of feminism in new media studies has been extended to other identity practices in virtual and online worlds, such as Lisa Nakamura's analysis of race in cyber-space.[47] Arguably the mixing of feminism with studies of fandom can go too far, leading Toby Miller to accuse much of this work of studying audiences only "insofar as they are populist delegates for analysts' own fandom."[48] Burgess's essay here calls for a return to central questions in audience studies from television and cultural studies through empirical analysis of the increasingly public activities of the audience, which, as she suggests, are more often ordinary and everyday than profound and revolutionary.

Texts, aesthetics, ideology, culture, audiences, and production prac-tices—television studies' approach to digital television, as I am repre-senting it here, appears a happy utopia of perfect analysis. Obviously this isn't true. For example, questions of identity are, not for want of trying, largely neglected in this volume but gestured toward in a series of spaces for other scholars and students to pick up. Elsewhere, how-ever, the study of television as digital media has addressed such issues, with Anna Everett and Priscilla Peña Ovalle making important contri-butions to this debate.[49] Equally, while Caldwell's call for studying the cultures of production is heeded by a number of scholars here and else-where, there remain limits to the abilities to conduct such research, which, despite the textual traces such production cultures increasingly leave open to us all, often requires well-funded, large-scale, and care-fully negotiated access to be truly valuable. Where we still might make greater connection between television studies' humanities tradition and issues of policy, political economy, and regulation is in the area of legal studies. One such example is Andrew Kenyon's *TV Futures*, which brings together legal analysis and media and cultural research, including new media studies, to examine the ways copyright and intellectual property are shaping the political economy of the digital television industries. Kenyon's call for greater analysis of issues such as "media's symbolic power, the generation of subjectivity in mediated societies, changing production practices with multi-platform digital communication companies, and media representations of citizenship," at the intersection of interests between legal and media scholarship, is one we must heed.[50] As Daniel Chamberlain argues here, industrial struggles for emergent TV practices often take shape in the form of copyright and patent lawsuits, as well as surveillance systems that raise pressing questions of privacy. Similarly, Julian Thomas's chapter suggests that the proprietary interests involved in shaping our current experience and definition of digital television may result in a system that is "less usable" than the first forays into digital TV during the late 1970s. Elsewhere Lawrence Lessig has pioneered the study of the way law, technology, media, and society intersect, which scholars such as Tarleton Gillespie have drawn upon to examine how systems such as DVDs and the "broadcast flag" in the United States are designed to effectively frustrate user rights, having important implications for our cultural life.[51]

Television studies, therefore, has much to learn from new media studies, but it also brings its own important generative assumptions and methodologies to the study of digital media. It is equally true to say that new media studies has much to learn from television studies in analyses of television as one of the most ubiquitous forms of digital media. While much of the rhetoric and engagement with digital media as new media coalesced around the explosion of the Internet in the late 1990s, when the dot-com bubble burst at the start of the millennium, media companies and conglomerates often looked for safer spaces from which to mount forays into the digital mediascape: television. Television has responded to the threat online and new media posed by colonizing digital media, offering discrete services such as Hulu and the BBC iPlayer, spreading video virally across YouTube and MySpace, and providing content via live streaming or for download to mobile media devices. The development of such services has not necessarily secured the future of all television companies. Indeed, the position of the U.K. public service broadcasters' funding models appears particularly precarious—Boddy's and Chamberlain's pieces here speak of a corporate schizophrenia that television companies must master as they develop online and digital distribution platforms that maintain network brand while simultaneously investing in a number of new services that directly compete and undercut that brand. The success of television's old media practices and formations suggests, however, that the newness of digital media is perhaps its least interesting facet.

Overall the essays in this volume do not treat television as new media but rather—and hopefully in a less loaded sense—as digital media. They suggest that digital media are increasingly less "new" and increasingly more "ordinary"—much as television itself has been conceived for most of its history. Indeed, television's digitization perhaps most starkly puts such matters into relief, demonstrating the confluence of regulatory, policy, and legal frameworks with the everyday cultures of production and reception, both within the industry and its audience, as well as the very ordinariness of the digital experience.

CHAPTER SUMMARIES AND ORGANIZATION

Television as Digital Media is separated into four parts: history, production, aesthetics, and audiences. Essays in each part range across the traditional media studies triumvirate of producer-text-audience relations, with the final part paying close attention to audiences as producers whose activities are manifest in the texts of digital television. The opening part considers these relations in respect to technological and historical change. Similarly essays in part 2 (on production) consider the textual strategies of producers as well as the audience practices that inform them, while those in part 3 (on aesthetics) consider political economy as an integral part of textual analysis. Each part is concerned with a fundamental problematic. Part 1 considers what digital television is in relation to the industrial, national, technological, regulatory, economic, and cultural forces that have shaped its meaning and form. Part 2 engages with how producers are negotiating the digitization of television, seeking to close some of the gaps between the way producers and academics talk about and understand television. Part 3 asks what are, and how do we approach, the aesthetics of digital television as a convergence and fragmenting media form. Finally, the essays in part 4 are concerned with how effectively the production-text-audience model of the study, industrial practices, and assumptions of television function in a digital landscape.

As I have noted above, digital television continues to be informed by national contexts, and this is true of the essays here, which generally focus on European, Australasian, British, and American experiences of the medium. In turn, these locations inflect the contributors' essays—most obviously by the way ideals and notions of public service broadcasting inflect essays from many of the u.k. and Australian scholars. And yet the digitization of television has forced each contributor to interrogate assumptions about the medium and question what role digital television plays in the formations of the everyday and the social and, in turn, to what extent these cultures are nationally specific. Nevertheless, there is an orthodoxy to this collection that reinforces the Anglo-American paradigm of television and media studies, and we must be aware of the contingency of the theories and understandings offered here. Elsewhere, Graeme Turner and Jinna Tay's collection, *Television Studies after TV*, admirably works toward redressing this balance—as have other collections such as Shanti Kumar and Lisa Parks's *Planet TV: A Global Television Reader*[52]—providing essays on what Turner and Tay describe as "the peripheries of television studies," such as the television experiences of China, Central Europe, Latin America, and the Middle East.[53] At their best, such accounts provide rich understandings of the global mediascape and challenge the hegemony of Western media studies—providing what Shanti Kumar describes as a "dialogical engagement" that aims "not to *teach* but to *learn*, not to rescue the 'other' but to understand the 'self' through the incommensurability of irreducible differences one encounters in the dialogue."[54] I hope the essays here avoid such a fate and encourage dialogue about what digital TV means in different national contexts. At the same time, we have avoided international comparison for the sake of it. It is much better, as Turner suggests in this volume, to understand the conjunctural and contingent nature of television that is shaped by social, cultural, political, and industrial factors. This collection pays attention to the place of television as digital media within digital culture as a key site of such contingency, change, and contestation.

Essays in part 1 examine the switchover process to digital television from technological, regulatory, aesthetic, and industrial perspectives that range across the globe, from the United States to the United Kingdom, Europe, and Australasia. In chapter 1, Graeme Turner brings a "conjunctural analysis" to historicize the process of switchover in a global context. He questions the perceived dominance of U.S. television industry models of the digital future, particularly the way fragmentation of the mass market supposedly produces personalized, individualized digital television services that distract from and deter the formation of communities, both national and otherwise. As a result, he suggests that while the digitization of television takes place under umbrella conditions of globalization, understood as a drive toward deregulation and marketization, the meaning of digital television will always be felt locally. In chapter 2, Julian Thomas charts a much earlier phase of television's digitization to suggest that the proliferation of remote-controlled devices that households accumulate attests to the inability of the industry to provide ready technological means of controlling how viewers access content, leading to a range of responses at the consumer end: from the development of universal remotes to sticking notes onto equipment to more sophisticated software responses. Thomas sets out some of the complex battles around controlling content, which refocuses our attention on the intersection of copyright and conditional access systems, and television hardware and software, which structure our use and experience of digital television. William Boddy closes part 1 by engaging with understandings of television as continually in flux, pointing to the extent of this flux by examining the way in which television's digitization has disrupted one of the fundamental features of TV as a broadcast regime: advertising. In so doing, his chapter speaks of a crisis felt globally within not only the TV industry, but also the wider advertising economy of media entertainment, caused by the fragmentation of the mass audience. This crisis produces a range of responses that Boddy details, most particularly pointing to an investment in out-of-home media and surveillance models of targeted advertising. What emerges is a disturbing trend, that the glance of the viewer at such fleeting out-of-home media sites as billboards, elevator television channels, and shopping carts is returned by a steadier gaze of surveillance that monitors, tracks, and measures consumer behavior. However, in returning to the question of whether such advertising practices are "TV yet," Boddy draws our attention not so much toward how far these new advertising forms, screens, sites, and practices are or are not television, but rather how they impact the funding, practices, and aesthetics of the television industry.

Overall the essays in part 1 point to complexities in terms of both what digital television means and how we historicize this present moment. Various attempts to periodize television's development and coin an understanding of digital television's relationship to broadcasting have emerged recently, from John Ellis's account of British television as a series of eras, moving from scarcity to availability to plenty, that speak to the public service broadcasting context of the United Kingdom's broadcast history; to the use of TV1, TV11, and TV111 by Mark Rogers, Michael Epstein, and Jimmie L. Reeves and others to describe the historical continuities and changes in U.S. network television; to Lisa Parks's use of the term "post-broadcast" and Amanda D. Lotz's description of the current U.S. television landscape as "post-network."[55] The essays in this section demonstrate that there is good reason for the range of these terms to coexist, enabling us to pay attention to the specifics of particular national, regional, or local contexts. If, as I hope the collection of essays here serves to, we can unload the term "digital television" from its revolutionary connotations, it is this description that might most aptly describe our current experience of television.

Roberta Pearson's historical account of cult television provides a fitting opening to part 2, where essays focus on the economic and production practices of digital television. Calling on a wealth of archival research, Pearson sets out how shows like *Star Trek* have consistently been at the cutting edge in areas of political economy, production strategies, and inspiring cult audiences that respond to, and make commercially viable, these originalities. Tracing U.S. network television's transition from TV1 to TV111, Pearson demonstrates how radical production and financing practices often associated with particular epochs have been long established as profitable in cult television forms. Neither reducing fans to the position of dupes exploited by the industry nor celebrating their activity as "redactors" or "produsers," she provides a compelling study in the way technological and cultural change is negotiated at the level of production practices.[56] Niki Strange analyzes the texts and production strategies that have emerged as broadcasters implement multiplatform television strategies. Focusing on the BBC, she examines how the corporation's adoption of 360-degree commissioning and program-making practices addresses the double bind faced by public service broadcasters in the digital landscape who are at once charged with building digital television but threatened by the seemingly unlimited choices offered to viewers, now repositioned as consumers. Strange addresses this bind by detailing how the BBC's adoption of a "public value" test attempted to reimagine the audience as "co-producer"—newly empowered in the interactive, digital era. Far from a truly dialogic or interactive engagement, however, such a strategy speaks of wider industrial attempts to harness the productivity of audiences, as well as herd and manage user flows across multiple platforms in the service of particular objectives.

Jeanette Steemers picks up on this issue of broadcaster dominance to examine how the adoption of such multiplatform commissioning imperatives have impacted the economic and production practices of children's television in the United States and United Kingdom. As Steemers sets out, the children's television sector proves to be a particularly important area of study because it "affords us some insight into the ways in which the industry is trying to capture the interest of children, who are growing up as 'digital natives.'" Despite broadcasters' panic and cries for help in the face of losses from advertising revenue in a fragmenting mediascape, Steemers demonstrates that it is the independent production sector that is most affected by these changes, with multiplatform distribution and content creation representing an increased cost rather than additional revenue. Together with Pearson's and Strange's essays in this section, Steemers's study suggests that traditional television broadcasters may continue to dominate the way in which television is made, distributed, and experienced in the digital era for some time to come.

In part 3, the focus shifts to issues of aesthetics in digital television. While scholars such as Christine Geraghty, John Corner, Karen Lury, Jason Jacobs, and others have suggested that the increasing attention paid to issues of aesthetics attests to the growing maturity of television studies as a discipline, the essays here engage with how television's digitization already throws such work into question.[57] Karen Lury's chapter opens this part by suggesting that the animation of time on digital television has led to the loss of the contingent, undermining some of the vital social and cultural functions that television has traditionally performed. In her polemical essay she argues that as new industrial and aesthetic tactics emerge to capture viewer attention in the digital landscape, a new economy of contempt has replaced the common culture of empathy and community television once provoked. Next, Max Dawson investigates television's relationship to time and aesthetics on digital media platforms, providing the first critical study of digital shorts—the ancillary short-form texts that are produced and circulated by the television industry on digital platforms. While recognizing their promotional branding function for the program or network, Dawson argues that paying attention to the digital short can yield valuable insights into the conditions of digital television production, consumption, and distribution, enabling him to discuss labor disputes, economic rationalization by the U.S. networks, and ways production and consumption activities and discourses increasingly overlap.

Daniel Chamberlain draws our attention to the way interfaces not only structure our experience of digital television content but also discipline our interactions, their interactive scripted spaces providing the illusion of consumer choice and free will that hides the different masters and metrics they serve. Chamberlain suggests how the ontology of digital television alters spatial relationships with content and control, providing fertile ground for further consideration of the complex interplay of industrial design, computer programming cultures, and the structuring logics of computer code, copyright law, and digital rights management systems. Jason Jacobs provides a fitting close to part 3 by questioning whether there is anything distinctive in televisual form in an era of convergence. Jacobs sets out how television's commodity form in the digital era allows viewers to remove traces of the traditional schedule, leaving only occasional marks that exist as "pollution." By focusing on how the texts of digital TV are experienced within the milieu of the everyday and seemingly banal, Jacobs shows what television studies can bring to the study of digital media while simultaneously recognizing that television itself may lose some of its distinctiveness as a digital medium.

In the final part, essays engage with the changing position of the audience from a range of different perspectives that question and complement assertions that in the digital era the "audience is dead," replaced by users and active "produsers" in a digital age of participatory culture. While not refusing the positions set out by observers such as Henry Jenkins and John Hartley, who are concerned with a seemingly newly empowered audience, the chapters here generally strike a more cautionary tone, engaging with how such audiences are produced, harnessed, and commodified by the media industries.[58] In so doing, they most radically speak to the study of collapsing distinctions between producer and user, examining the production cultures, texts, and audience practices of user-generated content (UGC) in order to understand its role in digital television's cultural, economic, and industrial form. John T. Caldwell examines digital television through the lens of production labor's interaction and intermingling with the audience. Building on his earlier calls to study television's production culture in order to understand television more fully, Caldwell suggests that such a study must recognize how "inadequate the old categories are that cleanly separate producers and media workers from audiences and consumers."[59] He thus charts the changing workflows of labor in digital television's economy, examining not only how media conglomerates crowdsource and bootstrap the unruly practices of UGC into mainstream media practices, but also how workers in the labor sector respond to such practices. Via the telling and retelling of highly ritualized trade stories and the practice of disseminating unauthorized accounts of industry practice, termed "worker-generated content," Caldwell demonstrates how workers broker digital culture and point to future modes of production that will become increasingly viral and nonlinear.

Jean Burgess similarly resists the notion that UGC is a radical inversion of industry/audience roles and instead argues that the practice of creating content on sites such as YouTube may well be more commonplace but that it is best understood as part of a longer lineage of audience practices. Drawing on an empirical study of the site, Burgess shows that far from the radical "remix" or "mashup," YouTube's "common culture" is built around such ordinary practices as the "bedroom video." Away from the hyperbole of interactive audiences, she shows that YouTube operates as a site of community and vernacular creativity, producing cultural value as an archive of popular memory—a position complicated by the site's proprietary and economic concerns.[60] My own essay continues to concentrate on the relationship between digital television and the ordinary, using fame as a locus to explore the position of the audiences and users of new forms of television. By engaging in debates about the supposed democratization of celebrity through its extension to a range of "ordinary people," I examine how such discourses intersect with those surrounding participatory culture in digital media. In so doing, I argue that the ability to produce do-it-yourself (DIY) celebrity through Web 2.0 technologies does promise more control, but this does not necessarily produce a more democratic ethos of participatory culture or celebrity. Instead, an analysis of Kevin Rose as the "architect of participation" on digg.com suggests that both fame and the commodification of one's own user community is increasingly ordinary in digital culture. The essays in part 4 therefore move beyond a simple dichotomy that often positions amateur or fan practices of UGC as good—offering spaces for resistance, play, and self-expression—and their cooption by media conglomerates as bad—such as News Corporation's purchase of MySpace—and instead speak of the complex and contradictory roles of producers and audiences in the digital television era.

Just as we learned to live with television, we are learning to live with digital television. The essays in this volume provide a number of different approaches for understanding this shift and studying digital TV. In treating digital television as a confluence of production practices, industrial strategies, aesthetic markers, audience practices, everyday cultures, and historical antecedents, they extend our understanding of what digital TV is beyond the "box in the corner" and the switchover programs and schedules that are in operation around the globe. Rather than provide a definitive account of what digital television is, therefore, these essays provide new insights into the emergence of contemporary digital culture. By focusing on the hybridity of television—or what Milly Buonanno has defined as its status as an "open medium"[61]—these contributions suggest that it is perhaps less helpful to try to draw lines in the sand of the digital landscape that say this is or isn't television—although no doubt some readers will object to the way in which the term is applied to such a diverse range of experiences and technologies in this book. There are, of course, limits to what we might term "television," but as Caldwell's provocative discussion on the "viral future of cinema" as television suggests, what these limits are is increasingly unclear.[62] It is more productive, therefore, to ask what studying digital media as television can bring to understanding our contemporary media experience. Perhaps what unifies the diverse range of interests I have discussed above—from political economy to public service broadcasting, iPlayer to YouTube, ideology to cultural practices, podcast to digital short—is a more simple question: "What is television for?" This becomes a more pressing question, for industry, audience, and the academy alike, when considering television as digital media.

NOTES

My thanks to Tony Bennett and Lynn Spigel for their helpful comments and advice.

1. "Top Gear Is Most Watched Show on iPlayer," BBC, December 23, 2009; http://news.bbc.co.uk/1/hi/entertainment/8428096.stm.
2. Ofcom, *The International Communications Market Report: Key Points*, November 2008; http://www.ofcom.org.uk/research/cm/icmr08/keypoints.

3. Ofcom, *The International Communications Market Report* (London: Ofcom, 2008), 285–300.

4. Brian Stelter, "Changeover to Digital TV Off to a Smooth Start," *New York Times*, June 14, 2009, A16; http://www.nytimes.com/2009/06/14/business/media/14digital.html?_r=1&scp=2&sq=digital%20tv&st=cse.

5. See Petros Iosifidis, "Digital Switchover in Europe," *Gazette — The International Journal for Communication Studies* 68 (2006): 264.

6. Stephen Labaton, "Millions Face Blank Screens in TV Switch," *New York Times*, June 6, 2009, B1.

7. William Uricchio, "The Future of a Medium Once Known as Television," in *The YouTube Reader*, ed. Pelle Snickars and Patrick Vonderau (Stockholm: National Library of Sweden, 2009), 35.

8. Roger Silverstone, *Television and Everyday Life* (London: Routledge, 2006); Lynn Spigel, *Make Room for TV: Television and the Family Ideal in Postwar America* (Chicago: University of Chicago Press, 1992); David Morley, *Media, Modernity and Technology: The Geography of the New* (London: Routledge, 2007).

9. Silverstone, *Television and Everyday Life*, 19–22.

10. Michael Curtin, "Matrix Media," in Graeme Turner and Jinna Tay, *Television Studies after TV: Understanding Television in the Post-Broadcast Era* (London: Routledge, 2009), 13–19.

11. Anne Friedberg, *The Virtual Window: From Alberti to Microsoft* (Cambridge, Mass.: MIT Press, 2006), 243.

12. See, for example, James Bennett, "'Your Window on The World': The Emergence of Red-Button Interactive Television in the UK," *Convergence* 14, no. 2 (2008): 161–82.

13. John Ellis, *Seeing Things: Television in the Age of Uncertainty* (London: I. B. Tauris, 2000), 169–73.

14. Lynn Spigel, "TV's Next Season," *Cinema Journal* 45, no. 2 (2005): 86. See, for an example of a "future chapter," Jamie Sexton, "Case Study: Television and Convergence," in *Tele-Visions: An Introduction to Television Studies*, ed. Glen Creeber, 160–68 (London: BFI, 2006).

15. See, for example, Jeanette Steemers, ed., *Changing Channels: The Prospects of Television in a Digital World* (Luton: John Libbey Media, 1998); Jens Jensen and Cathy Toscan, eds., *Interactive Television: TV of the Future, or the Future of TV?* (Aalborg, Denmark: Aalborg University Press, 1999).

16. Rose quoted in Tim Anderson, "How iPlayer Will Become Our Player for Your Friends," *Guardian*, December 11, 2008, T5; http://www.guardian.co.uk/media/2008/dec/11/interview-anthony-rose-iplayer.

17. Max Dawson's work demonstrates how such discourses often attempt to "repair" the damage done by understandings of television as a pacifying and antisocial force; see *TV Repair* (forthcoming).

18. Jason Jacobs, *The Intimate Screen: Early British Television Drama* (Oxford: Oxford University Press, 2000).

19. Raymond Williams, *Television: Technology and Cultural Form* (London: Routledge, 1992), 95.

20. Charlotte Brunsdon, "What Is the Television of Television Studies?" in *The Television Studies Book*, ed. Christine Geraghty and David Lusted, 95–113 (London: Hodder Arnold, 1998).

21. Charlotte Brunsdon, "Is Television Studies History?" *Cinema Journal* 47, no. 3 (2008): 127–37; Lynn Spigel, "Introduction," in *Television after TV: Essays on a Medium in Transition*, ed. Lynn Spigel and Jan Olsson (Durham, N.C.: Duke University Press, 2004), 1–34; see also Spigel, "TV's Next Season."

22. Brunsdon, "Is Television Studies History?" 131.

23. Spigel, "Introduction," 11.

24. See Henry Jenkins and David Thorburn, eds., *Democracy and New Media* (Cambridge, Mass.: MIT Press, 2004).

25. Spigel, "Introduction," 12–13.

26. Tiziana Terranova, "Cyberculture and New Media," in *The Sage Handbook of Cultural Analysis*, ed. Tony Bennett and John Frow, London: Sage, 2008).

27. Ibid., 596.

28. Jenkins's book, *Convergence Culture*, is undoubtedly an important, influential, and useful analysis of digital culture. However, despite his attempts to balance utopian accounts of the digital future that spring from technological determinism with grounded empirical analysis, ultimately the book can't escape the legacy it draws upon in calling up Sola Pool, whose "prophecy" "understood convergence not as some bringing together of different devices in one, but also the way one medium might not be produced in several different physical ways" (*Convergence Culture: Where Old and New Media Collide* [Cambridge, Mass.: MIT Press, 2006], 10).

29. See Chamberlain in this volume; see also Jo T. Smith, "DVDs and the Political Economy of Attention," in *Film and Television after DVD*, ed. James Bennett and Tom Brown (London: Routledge, 2008), 129–48.

30. Terranova, "Cyberculture and New Media," 596–97.

31. William Uricchio, "Old Media as New Media: Television," in *The New Media Book*, ed. Dan Harries (London: BFI Publishing, 2002), 219–30; William Boddy, *New Media and Popular Imagination: Launching Radio, Television, and Digital Media in the United States* (Oxford: Oxford University Press, 2004).

32. Caldwell arguably provides the most coherently theorized position of television as digital media by examining the way in which media conglomerates employ "second-shift aesthetics" in the digital age to herd, aggregate, and otherwise seek to control the migratory patterns of users. This account bears the influence of Foucault's account of the cyclical flow of power. John Caldwell, "Second Shift Media Aesthetics: Programming, Interactivity and User Flows,"

in *New Media: Theories and Practices of Digitextuality*, ed. Anna Everett and John Caldwell, 127–44 (New York: Routledge, 2003); Laurie Ouellette and James Hay, *Better Living through Reality TV* (Oxford: Blackwell, 2008); Mark Andreje-vic, *iSpy: Surveillance and Power in the Interactive Era* (Lawrence: University of Kansas Press, 2008).

33. Leah A. Lievrouw and Sonia Livingstone, "Introduction to the Updated Student Edition," in *The Handbook of New Media*, ed. Leah A. Lievrouw and Sonia Livingstone (London: Sage, 2007), 4.

34. See William Merrin's blog, Media Studies 2.0.

35. See John Caldwell's pioneering study of television screen form in *Televisuality: Style, Crisis, and Authority in American Television* (New Brunswick, N.J.: Rutgers University Press, 1995).

36. James Bennett, "Television Studies Goes Digital," *Cinema Journal* 47, no. 3 (2008): 162.

37. Brunsdon, "What Is the Television of Television Studies?" 110.

38. Brunsdon, "Is Television Studies History?" 131.

39. Paul Kerr, "Channel 4 Dossier: Introduction—Thinking outside the Box," *Screen* 49, no. 3 (2008): 321.

40. Vicki Mayer, Miranda J. Banks, and John Thornton Caldwell, *Production Studies: Cultural Studies of Media Industries* (London: Routledge, 2009); David Hesmondhalgh, *The Cultural Industries*, 2nd ed. (London: Sage, 2007); Georgina Born, *Uncertain Vision: Birt, Dyke and the Reinvention of the BBC* (London: Vintage, 2005); John T. Caldwell, *Production Cultures: Industrial Reflexivity and Critical Practice in Film and Television* (Durham, N.C.: Duke University Press, 2008).

41. Brunsdon, "Is Television Studies History?" 131–32.

42. Kerr, "Channel 4 Dossier," 318–19; Brunsdon, "Is Television Studies History?" 131.

43. See http://www.publicservicebroadcasting.org.uk.

44. John T. Caldwell, "Convergence Television: Aggregating Form and Repurposing Content in the Culture of Conglomeration," in Spigel and Olsson, *Television after TV*, 45.

45. Henry Jenkins, *Textual Poachers: Television Fans and Participatory Culture* (New York: Routledge, 1992).

46. Axel Bruns, *Blogs, Wikipedia, Second Life, and Beyond: From Production to Produsage* (New York: Peter Lang, 2008); Sherry Turkle, *Life on Screen: Identity in the Age of the Internet* (London: Simon and Schuster, 1997); Donna Haraway, *Simians, Cyborgs and Women: The Reinvention of Nature* (London: Routledge, 1991).

47. Lisa Nakamura, *Cybertypes: Race, Ethnicity, and Identity on the Internet* (London: Routledge, 2002).

48. Toby Miller, "Turn Off TV Studies," *Cinema Journal* 45, no. 2 (2005): 99.

49. Anna Everett, "Double Click: The Million Woman March on Television and the Internet," in Spigel and Olsson, *Television after TV*, 224–47; Priscilla Peña Ovalle, "Pocho.com: Reimaging Television on the Internet," in Spigel and Olsson, *Television after TV*, 324–41.

50. Andrew Kenyon, "Changing Channels: Media Studies, Copyright Law and Communications Policy," in *TV Futures: Digital Television Policy in Australia*, ed. Andrew T. Kenyon (Melbourne: University of Melbourne Press, 2007), 8.

51. Lawrence Lessig, *Free Culture: The Nature and Future of Creativity* (London: Penguin, 2004); Tarleton Gillespie, *Wired Shut: Copyright and the Shape of Digital Culture* (Cambridge, Mass.: MIT Press, 2007).

52. Shanti Kumar and Lisa Parks, eds., *Planet TV: A Global Television Reader* (New York: New York University Press, 2002).

53. Graeme Turner and Jinna Tay, "Introduction," in Turner and Tay, *Television Studies after TV*, 5.

54. Shanti Kumar, "Is There Anything Called Global Television Studies?" in Kumar and Parks, *Planet TV*, 147.

55. Ellis, *Seeing Things*; Mark C. Rogers, Michael Epstein, and Jimmie L. Reeves, "The Sopranos as HBO Brand Equity: The Art of Commerce in the Age of Digital Reproduction," in *This Thing of Ours: Investigating The Sopranos*, ed. David Lavery, 42–57 (London: Wallflower Press, 2002); Amanda Lotz, *The Television Will Be Revolutionized* (New York: New York University Press, 2007); Lisa Parks, "Flexible Microcasting: Gender, Generation, and Television-Internet Convergence," in Spigel and Olsson, *Television after TV*, 133–56.

56. Cult television has been an important site for the investigation of fan practices, as well as developments in televisual narrative form, branding, and issues of representation; for example, see the following: Henry Jenkins's analysis of fans and digital culture, *Fans, Bloggers and Gamers: Exploring Participatory Culture* (New York: New York University Press, 2006); Catherine Johnson's discussion of branding in "Tele-Branding in TVIII," *New Review of Film and Television Studies* 5, no. 1 (2007): 5–24; Derek Johnson's examination of *Lost*'s transmedia storytelling in "Inviting Audiences In: The Spatial Reorganization of Production and Consumption in 'TVIII,'" *New Review of Film and Television Studies* 5, no. 1 (2007): 61–80.

57. Christine Geraghty, "Aesthetics and Quality in Popular Drama," *International Journal of Cultural Studies* 6, no. 1 (2003): 25–45; John Corner, "Television Studies and the Idea of Criticism," *Screen* 48, no. 3 (2007): 363–69; Karen Lury, "A Response to John Corner," *Screen* 48, no. 3 (2007): 371–76; Jason Jacobs, "Issues of Judgement and Value in Television Studies," *International Journal of Cultural Studies* 4, no. 4 (2001): 427–47.

58. Jenkins, *Convergence Culture*; John Hartley, *Television Truths: Forms of Knowledge in Popular Culture* (Oxford: Blackwell, 2008).

59. See also Caldwell, "Convergence Television"; Caldwell, *Production Cultures*.

60. As such, Burgess's discussion connects with an increasing awareness of the importance of television archiving practices. See Rachel Moseley and Helen Wheatley, "Is Archiving a Feminist Issue? Historical Research and the Past, Present, and Future of Television Studies," *Cinema Journal* 47, no. 3 (2008): 152–58; see also John Ellis, Catherine Johnson, and Rob Turnbock's "Video Active" project on archiving European television online, http://videoactive .wordpress.com.

61. Milly Buonanno, *The Age of Television: Experiences and Theories*, trans. Jennifer Radice (Bristol: Intellect, 2008), 41.

62. John Caldwell, "Welcome to the Viral Future of Cinema: Television," *Cinema Journal* 45, no. 2 (2005): 90–97.

Historicizing the Digital Revolution

CONVERGENCE AND DIVERGENCE

The International Experience of Digital Television

At the end of her account of American television, *The Television Will Be Revolutionized*, Amanda D. Lotz provides a telling demonstration of the cultures of use that have developed around the new technologies of production, delivery, and consumption that constitute television in the so-called digital age. Once, Lotz reminds us, the use of television "typically involved walking into a room, turning on the set, and either tuning in to specific content or commencing the process of channel surfing." Now, however, it is not so simple: "My DVR is set to automatically record *The Daily Show* Monday through Thursday and keeps two episodes. Typically, I automatically record only one cable series (set a Season Pass in TIVO vernacular), because I often forget when they are on and I usually take advantage of a late night replay of episodes so that I can record something on a broadcast network during the prime-time airing."[1] And so on. It takes Lotz several pages to detail the practices that have become necessary as a means of appropriately dealing with the range of choices available to her.

I live in Australia, where there has been a reasonable degree of media convergence: broadcast, cable, satellite, and online forms of video are available in most locations, and the U.S. market is routinely regarded as the model for the media market's development and thus for the regime of policy settings required. However, many of the options available to Amanda

Lotz remain unavailable to me.[2] At the time of writing, TiVo has only just arrived in Australia, although there has been an analogous device, iQ, marketed by the cable company Foxtel to its subscribers for some time. I know very few people who have a DVR; DVRS are in the early stages of their take-up in Australia and are still relatively expensive: AUS$700 for the base model, AUS$1,500 for one that can record onto a DVD. Currently, these work only with free-to-air television, not pay TV. The wider industry context is different as well. Network television still dominates, with cable capturing up to 30 percent of the sets in use, but the television audience is declining under competition from other forms of entertainment. Pay TV has been in place for a decade and a half, but the selection of channels is more limited than that available in the United States, and thus we don't yet have the range of choices Lotz must navigate in constructing her personalized menu of television.[3]

The point I am making here is that although most of us talk about "television" without any qualifying prefix such as "Australian" or "American," the fact is that, especially since the digital revolution and notwithstanding the processes of globalization, "television" involves such varying forms, platforms, and content in its different national and regional locations that it is increasingly implausible for one set of experiences to be regarded as representative. As part of a wider research project with Anna Pertierra and Jinna Tay, this chapter examines and attempts to capture some of those differences in the international context of postbroadcast television. Within Anglo-American media and cultural studies, it has become something of an orthodoxy to see the current formations of television as enmeshed within a process that has the medium moving from regulation to deregulation, from a mix of public and private ownership to overwhelming commercialization, and from broadcast and cable into broadband. This chapter questions how comprehensively such an account covers the various formations of television today, while also considering what kinds of social and cultural roles television now plays within the nation-state, the local community, or the transnational geolinguistic region.

While there is certainly a dominant view that foregrounds the "death of broadcasting," on the one hand, and the rise of user-generated "alternative" content online, on the other, it would be wrong to say that there is anything like a consensus within the international fields of media, television, and cultural studies about the possible futures of post-broadcast television. Indeed, there are some extremely stark contrasts among the opposing points of view in the international literature.

In a recent article, for instance, Axel Bruns presents an account of the growth of online video and, in particular, forms of "produsage" (do-it-yourself [DIY] or user-generated content [UGC]) that proposes them as the core, rather than the periphery, of the development of the future of television—or what he calls "audiovisual distribution." Bruns argues that "conventional television technology constitutes only a second-rate, impoverished version of (live) streaming media, providing only the 'creaky and unreliable technology of audiovisual distribution' of the analogue, mass media age." The range of options now available on digital platforms—to "request, play on demand, pause, restart, rewind, save, share, or retransmit content"—leaves television behind.[4] "What becomes obvious here," says Bruns, "is that the technologies and processes of television—once constituting an effective and powerful network for widespread content distribution—have now been outclassed by the Internet."[5]

In what is admittedly a polemical and speculative piece, Bruns doesn't say how he has come to the conclusion that television has been "outclassed," but he is far from alone in making such claims—both about the death of broadcast television and about the potential of online platforms for DIY content distribution. These claims need, however, to be tested against others. Joseph Straubhaar, for instance, in his account of "world" television, insists that it is still true—and will be true for many years to come—that most of the people in the world who watch television do so via broadcasting networks. Some have a choice but others do not: "Many of those concerned about impacts of satellite and cable television technology fail to recognize that most people in the world do not have access to them either because they cannot afford them, because governments like China restrict access to them, or because they are sufficiently satisfied with broadcast television that they choose not to pay for access to them."[6] Straubhaar is clearly concerned to hose down some of the rhetoric used to boost the significance of the multiplication of digital platforms of delivery by reminding us how uneven their distribution and take-up have been.

It is little wonder that those within the television industries required to deal with the pace and effects of these changes should have difficulty in sorting out how they might influence the future shape of a post-broadcast global television industry. In 2008, the conference of the National Association of Television Programming Executives (NATPE)—the primary industry marketplace for television in the United States—was thoroughly focused on digital technologies but undecided about their significance for the future.[7] On the one hand, the conference heard Michael Eisner, the former head of Disney and now an independent producer of for-mobile TV soap operas, claiming categorically that the future of television lay in online and mobile services rather than in cable or broadcast. On the other hand, Bruce Leichtman of the Leichtman Research Group provided a reality check on such claims in his presentation. Leichtman reported that while it was certainly increasing steadily, online video usage remained a relatively minor component of the U.S. media landscape. According to his research, among respondents who watched any online video in the month surveyed, the average time per day spent doing so was only six minutes. While constituting a significant increase from the previous year, this is still pretty inconsequential when compared to the 3.5 *hours* per day that consumers spend, on average, watching cable or broadcast television in the U.S. market. The comparison is even more pronounced when Leichtman includes the whole survey sample: the mean time spent watching online video for the sample population as a whole is 3.5 minutes per day.[8] The implications of these figures contrasted dramatically with the conference presentations from the online entrepreneurs such as YouTube, Yahoo, and Joost.

We don't stop at online video, of course, when we talk about the likely uses of post-broadcast television. There are also those who would argue that television's future lies in the social networking capacities exploited by Facebook, MySpace, and, to a lesser extent, YouTube. Media and cultural studies academics such as John Hartley have long explored this potential through their focus on user-generated content. The role television plays in constructing a community is a topic to which I want to return in the final section of this chapter, but it does seem as if there is a prima facie case for investigating whether this capacity—something television always claimed it possessed—is in the process of migrating from television's traditional platforms into the online environment.

That said, it is also important to acknowledge the presence of what I might call "convergence skeptics" within media and cultural studies, who respond to the projections about shifts in the current mediascape by pointing to the lessons to be learned—from the histories of technological change, to the fallacies of technological determinism, and finally to the undeniable fact that it will be the currently existing commercial and regulatory structures that will exercise the most influence on how all of these developments play out. Although there may be some reason to hope that the potential capacities of digital technologies will open the media up to new players, there are many commentators who point out that, notwithstanding the proliferation of choices available to consumers today, the major media corporations have retained their dominance. Furthermore, projections of technological change are often—indeed notoriously—short of substantial evidence. Milly Buonanno warns of the "imprudence" of regarding the behavior of the "early adopters" as "representative of possible mainstream trends,"[9] a tendency that has always plagued projections about the media industries. Others simply query the empirical basis for the excitement about convergence. Des Freedman quotes evidence that reveals how few sites are actually consulted by Internet browsers and how infrequently (one survey to which he refers reports that 42 percent of users pass through five or fewer sites per week).[10] From Freedman's point of view, the possibility that convergence will drive significant change is limited by factors such as "control of distribution networks by familiar multinational companies," "relatively narrow media consumption patterns of the majority of the online population," and the fact that new technological possibilities of the Internet are, in the end, still "constrained" by the same old "economic imperatives of the media business."[11] Rather than accepting the claims made for the interactive and DIY potential of media convergence, David Morley describes its celebration as "born-again techno-determinism" and quotes Freedman's description of the global history of the Internet as a process through which the platform has been transformed "from being a mainly non-commercial instrument of information exchange into a highly commercialized tool of mainly private and business transactions."[12]

In the following section, I want to explore these issues a little further by looking at examples of some of the divergent ways in which the future of digital TV is unfolding, before using the final section to discuss how what many would describe as an increasingly individualized mode of consumption manages to construct its communities.

Over the years, both the academy and the entertainment industry have acquired the habit of seeing the development of television as an evolutionary process that more or less assumes there is a trajectory that all systems in all locations are bound to follow—or if there are aberrations, that it is not hard to spot them and therefore discount their broad significance or applicability. As Jinna Tay and I have discussed elsewhere, the dominant evolutionary model for most Western regulatory jurisdictions is the American experience of television.[13] It seems to be taking quite a while, even in the current circumstances where there are so many provocations, for industry insiders and observers alike to accept what the evidence should be telling them: there are no longer grounds for thinking about television like that. With the multiplication of platforms, formats, production centers, and distribution systems, it is abundantly clear that the precise configuration of any nation's or region's experience of television is going to be the product of the complex interplay among a number of specific conjunctural factors—and only one of these will be technological.

The historical specificity of such factors, as well as the motivated contingency of their interplay in any one location, is a dimension that television studies methodologically has tended to overlook. This is especially true of Western analyses of the rise of digital media. Even as the digitization of television platforms and systems of delivery unfolds across much of the world, there is no guarantee (or even much likelihood) that the technology will produce the same effects in every case. Even in the United States, where so many have argued that digital convergence will see the end of broadcasting and maybe even of cable, there remains a strong possibility that digitization will actually have rescued some local broadcasters after the analog signal was switched off in 2009. The added spectrum will enable the local stations to broadcast more than one channel, thus providing many local markets with a significant number of additional free-to-air channels—thereby reducing the demand for subscription services in those markets.[14]

One area where there are quite dramatic contrasts in the take-up and application of digital television platforms around the world is in the production and consumption of television content distributed via mobile phones—what Michael Eisner insisted at NATPE was the real future of the medium. The mobile or cell phone has itself quite a complicated history of adoption with short message service (sms), for instance, a widely used capability in Asia but notoriously slow to attract users in the United States. Mobile television, at the time of writing, remains relatively unimportant in Europe and relatively undeveloped in the United States — although it is certainly a prime target for future projections there. The use of mobiles for Internet access, video distribution, music downloads, news services, and so on is certainly growing in the United States, but to nothing like the extent that it has, for instance, in parts of Asia. Cheng Liu and Axel Bruns report that the growth of mobile newspapers has been a significant feature of the digital revolution in China.[15] They also report that the growth in the numbers of Chinese consumers who use their mobiles to connect to the Web is faster than the growth in the numbers connecting via personal computers. These seem to be quite distinctive aspects of the Chinese adoption of digital technologies, and Liu and Bruns argue that mobiles are at the leading edge of convergence there in much the way that Internet-enabled computers and broadband have been in the West. They speculate that the situation in China may mirror that in Japan, where the national enthusiasm for mobile communication has led to mobile-based Internet access outstripping Internet access through other means.

Some researchers have been brave enough to attempt to relate such variations to their cultural origins. Jaz Hee-jeong Choi, for instance, connects shifts in the take-up and deployment of mobile phone technology in East Asia to social, contextual, and even teleological determinants.[16] While it is now commonplace for media analysts to relate the Japanese affective investment in the mobile phone to the indigenous ke-tai culture, which fetishizes cute shiny objects, Choi's article suggests that particular aspects of the functionality of the mobile phone intersect with cultural aspects of what it means to be a subject in South Korea, China, and Japan. By using James Carey's distinction between transmission and ritual models of communication, Choi situates much East Asian use in the ritual mode because of its emphasis on sharing, participation, association, fellowship, and the like:[17] "Korea, China, and Japan share a traditionally collective, interdependent and high-contextual culture, as opposed to individual, independent, and low-contextual cultures, which are predominantly evident in the West. As East Asian nations, they are heavily influenced by Taoist, Buddhist, and Confucian ideologies and therefore often embrace rigid social hierarchy or class distinction, conformity and dedication to one's duties within one's position."[18]

Choi then outlines three cultural characteristics that she argues play particularly crucial roles in making East Asian cultures unique. The polychronic conception of time, in which the harmonious maintenance of selective relationships is valued over prompt time management, leads, Choi says, to forms of interaction that "are eminently dissimilar to those that occur in monochronic societies" (the individualist West, in this formulation).[19] The other two characteristics she discusses are interdependent self-definition—analogous to the idea of a network—and facework (in collective societies, this is about saving the face of others as well as one's own, so, again, it is about networked interdependencies). There is a fine line between properly recognizing the cultural determinants involved and presenting what might be read as an essentialist analysis (and Choi is perfectly aware of this). However, Choi's work deserves recognition for confronting the need to explain why such dramatic variations might occur in a world that tends to assume the inevitability of the impact of technological change on the production of culture without considering the role of particular formations of culture in influencing change.

Cultural change is, of course, the product of multiple factors, and some accounts of convergence have overestimated the momentum generated by the application of new technologies. Nevertheless, we can point to a relatively common set of industrial effects consequent upon television's digitization. Digital technologies reduce the cost of production, as well as the cost—both in capital and in terms of the quality of the product—of copying and reproduction. The digital revolution has also enabled the integration of low-cost television production with computer technologies, bringing television production within the reach of "ordinary people," not just the professional industry. The pattern of global content production is shifting toward the new "media capitals";[20] geolinguistic regional markets in East Asia and Latin America, for instance, have developed production capacities on a scale that enables them now to convincingly compete with the Americans.[21] They do not merely export their local content to diasporic, regional, or other markets, but in some cases they have also found ways to "de-globalize," or localize, the media they import. In his book *Global Capital, Local Culture*, Anthony Fung analyzes this process in order to argue that while it may look like globalization, China's strategic engagement with the global media companies is among the primary means through which the state is modernizing its local media.[22] I will discuss this further in the last section of this chapter.

In recent years the literature on media globalization has been peppered with contributions from those who wish to significantly complicate what was initially a comparatively univocal view. Now there are very few who see media globalization operating as a one-way street, and most would recognize that the particular economies of digital media production and distribution have played a significant part in complicating, and even reversing, the transnational flows in media content and strategic investment over the last decade.

It is important to acknowledge that much of this has been driven by the vigorous commercialization of the global media, which has in turn been assisted by a highly supportive political environment. Since the early 1990s, the climate of deregulation and marketization, which has been prosecuted to a greater or lesser degree and in various ways around the globe, has been a significant factor in the remaking of the media in general, not just those sectors involved in digital television. Neoliberal economic and communications policies have reformed national media systems, breaking up public broadcasting sectors and expediting the proliferation of commercial broadcasting and other media companies.[23] Many of these new players are the convergent media enterprises serving markets that previously did not exist.

As the prevailing climate of commercialization has become more widespread, increasingly, if gradually, the cost of television has been transferred from the advertiser or the state to the consumer. The task for entrepreneurs in the post-broadcast market is to sell their services to consumers who are already receiving a free broadcast service. Even in the most affluent markets, there are limitations to the extent to which these entrepreneurs can succeed because the capacity to absorb the cost (and this cost is for entertainment, after all, not the necessities of life) is unevenly distributed. Not only does this create an international "digital divide," but it is also creating differentiated corridors of access within nations. As John Sinclair argues,

> Television is becoming stratified, with convergent services for the
> elite who can afford them, and free-to-air for the masses who can't.

Since this division corresponds to real socio-economic differences in the population, it is most acute in developing world regions. In Latin America, for example, globalized elites can enjoy direct-to-home subscription television, while *la gente corriente*, the ordinary people, watch more traditional fare on the national networks. All over the world, such stratification and fragmentation of national audiences is presenting complex challenges for the television we have known.[24]

Such details indicate the difficulty in drawing conclusions about the market consequences of digital television and indeed what digital television will actually turn out to *be* for its stratified audiences, in most places. The variations are simply too many and the objects too close for us to see them as a whole. In the final section I discuss some of the questions about what digital TV might be able to do in terms of its social function—what kinds of experience it might offer, how it might construct community, and how these potentials might differ from those we identified with earlier, mass communication models of television.

THE POLITICS OF CONSUMPTION

In an engaging piece (posted, appropriately, by way of the online journal *Flow*) Karen Lury has registered her sense of having been "disenfranchised" from television as she learns to live in a "post-TV world." Despite the fact that she earns her living as a television studies academic, she confesses to no longer watching network or scheduled television any more—in fact, to not watching a television screen at all but rather preferring to access video content via her computer:

> [Television] has, or used to have, a public role that was not just about "knowing something" but feeling. Television engages the private me— us—with public life, with a "structure of feeling," to use Raymond Williams' well-worn phrase. . . . Television used to mediate—however imperfectly—between private and public selves. As production and reception are privatised and tailored increasingly to individuals, that sense of the audience as a "public," rather than a heavily invested community of fans or as a "demographic," has eroded. The common culture of "public concern" and "public sentiment" articulated by "old TV" tried to secure "public opinion" and in reality this was often met by a healthy mixture of participation, resistance and scorn; nonetheless it meant that "we" had something in common. In a post-TV world

I no longer need to watch television that is "not for me" and is no longer about "we": in fact I might just as well read a book.[25]

Amanda Lotz raises a similar point, but in a slightly different way, by framing it as a conceptual question for the field of media studies. The changes that have shaped the multichannel environment, she says, obviously have "manifold consequences" for the study of the media and their role in society. However, so far the focus has been much more on mapping the technological and market shifts rather than broader questions—such as "the significance and repercussions of the erosion of the mass media, or how audiences exercising choice and control require us to revise fundamental ideas about media and culture."[26] We need to rethink the role of television as digital media, then, not just to map its shifts and permutations, but also to understand what it might do and how it will do it. This is related, as Lotz suggests, to questions about to what extent the media are any longer the "mass media." If the media are no longer "mass," if they no longer gather a heterogeneous national audience into a community, then what kinds of broad community function can they perform, and how might what she describes as their "emancipatory potential" be realized?

First, few would contest the proposition that television consumption is significantly changed by the digital environment because of its proliferation of choices and platforms and the way these choices are offered to consumers. Teresa Rizzo has written an interesting piece on the possibilities that are emerging—and it is worth emphasizing that it *is* the emergent we are describing here—where she uses the playlist as the model for the way post-broadcast television audiences must organize their behavior. This audience now constructs its priorities from a menu of options that enables not only the choice of content but also its scheduling and the format of delivery. The playlist, Rizzo suggests, is now the normative mode of organizing our personal media consumption, generating a particularly high degree of "personalisation, customisation and individualisation" that constitutes a "key point of differentiation from broadcast television."[27] Such a mode of consumption, doing away with "appointment viewing," fundamentally changes the relation between the audience and its selection of content.

The playlist mode implies an intensity of engagement, however, that I would argue is not yet (and may never be) typical of the average viewer of television. In fact, as Joshua Green points out, the ideal addressee of digital television is the fan.[28] Green acknowledges that this label leaves a lot of other categories of engagement out of the mix—in particular, the original addressee of broadcast television, the family. The traditional model of television was not only addressed to the family, but it also implied a particular site of consumption: the home. In many markets where digital TV has arrived, both the importance of the family and the implied domesticity of the discursive regime within which the medium addresses its audience have declined. Even though the family audience remains a major target for advertisers, there is arguably less evidence of that in the patterns of scheduling and programming. Furthermore, the increase in out-of-home viewing in Western markets and mobile television in the Asian markets has had an impact on the dominant characteristics of the medium; it is no longer so overwhelmingly domestic, fixed, or national.[29] All of that said, however, it is highly unlikely that the majority of consumers will engage with television, in any of its forms, through the modalities of fandom.

As a result, the fan-consumer has limited provenance as a model for transactions in the future. Instead, it seems that consumers will face an assemblage of media choices that will generate different kinds of engagement, involving different modalities of subjectivity, perhaps, in addition to those currently on offer. Milly Buonanno picks up Horace Newcomb's notion that the model of consumption that now describes television has changed from the open forum of broadcasting to a more private, despatialized, and socially asynchronous model—comparable to that of reading a book in a library (Lury's suggested default activity). The parallels with the rows of DVDs lined up on people's bookshelves are obvious, but more important, the comparison highlights the fact that this model of consumption is not exactly new. Further, Buonanno argues that "reading is inseparable from a sense of sharing and connection, even though it is completely detached from simultaneousness."[30]

This returns us to the question of how post-broadcast television, consumed like this, is going to construct its communities. An observation one could make about the tendencies underpinning both Rizzo's and Green's accounts of the television of the future is that the practices they predict are so highly individualized that they will fail to provide the experience of community so fundamental to the broadcast era—not just the process of constructing citizenship but also the more banal and everyday social engagement implied in industry nostrums about the water cooler effect. However, as Rizzo points out, while the playlist model is indeed highly personalized, the playlist is also one of the things—just like one's favorite book—that is most likely to be shared through social networking sites. As a result, she argues, the fact that the personal playlist can be and is routinely shared with others means that it does "not result in social isolation, but rather the opposite: [it] encourage[s] sharing and tap[s] into the desire for communities."[31] Lotz makes a similar point, but perhaps more strongly, arguing that while network-era television created communities by "watching common shows at a common time," post-network communities are defined by interests that bridge geographical constraints. Picking up a term used by Chris Anderson, she discusses the sharing of favorites and self-produced content that enables viewers to self-organize in a highly positive way as "tribes of affinity."[32]

Up to a point, I am persuaded by the argument that there is a logic that leads from the personalized playlist to the creation of community around the choices inscribed and that is facilitated by the technologies involved. In such a context, television in its various forms becomes a category of content that is drawn down in order to construct social and personal identities—much as outlined by Bruns's essay. In the post-broadcast era, I have noted elsewhere, television has become increasingly involved in the production of identities.[33] The fact that these are increasingly described as personal rather than national identities is a point of differentiation between the functions of post-broadcast television and those of the broadcasting era during which it was widely argued that television was engaged in the production of citizenship (see Hartley's work during the 1990s, for instance).[34] As the term *mass media* becomes a less appropriate descriptor for some digital media, the function of constructing national identities—of defining modes of citizenship, belonging, and participation—declines in importance as well. These broader national identities will not disappear, of course, but it is not yet clear precisely how they will be rearticulated to the mediascapes of Western democracies in the near future. Indeed, in some of these locations, there is an emerging policy orientation that challenges the objectives of such a process. In the European Union's "Television without Borders" initiative and in some of the debates about the construction of Canadian television, the notion of national identity is resisted as a spurious and inappropriate means of constructing a sense of belonging; in its place,

Bart Beaty and Rebecca Sullivan argue, in relation to Canada, that there should be a stronger sense of belonging to the region, on the one hand, and to a transnational community, on the other.[35]

There are limitations, though, to the broad application of the arguments in the previous paragraph. While they might constitute an uncontroversial line to argue in relation to most Western democracies, there is plenty of evidence that it is not so elsewhere. It is a mistake to regard individual media market formations as purely the effect of the technologies involved, rather than as the products of specific conjunctures of social, cultural, political, and industrial conditions. Emerging nation-states such as those in the Balkans or in the Middle East continue to make routine use of television programming (drama, reality TV, soap opera, and news) as an explicit technique of nation formation. In China, the capacities provided by digital media, especially their replication of capitalist market economies' access to global entertainment products, are promoted by the state and welcomed by its citizens as evidence both of the new freedom attached to Western-style cosmopolitan consumption and of the nation's successful modernization.[36] Indeed, Anthony Fung argues that the processes of media globalization have been so successfully harnessed by the Chinese state that it has led, paradoxically, to the formation of a "nationalised popular culture." Fung describes the consequences of a partnership between the Chinese state and global media capital as a form of "neo-nationalism," in which the new forms of individual consumption provided by (among other things) digital media are directly linked with the promise of China claiming its place as a modern global superpower. The audience's new cultural freedoms, then, to do with the released constraints upon the consumption of entertainment rather than their participation in politics, are duly incorporated into the service of the state.[37] Many Western television viewers will have seen evidence of this during the coverage of the Beijing Olympics in the very precise, and repeated, articulation of the Chinese people's enthusiasm for the event. The success of the Beijing Olympics as a national media, technological, and entertainment spectacle was offered to the rest of the world as a conclusive demonstration of China's achievement of modernity.

In such a context, then, it is worth thinking about the political potential of the new modes of media consumption (not to mention the possibilities of "produsage"). Where the state maintains firm control over media, including the Internet, in order to ensure that their content does not dislodge government agendas, the political potential of digital media is necessarily compromised. In Singapore or China, for instance, the increased media choices now available through online social networking sites, video aggregators, blogging, and all the other accoutrements of the digital era certainly do provide the basic materials for the construction of personalized and individualized identities for particular sectors of the society. In both states, however, these materials are nonetheless regulated, their availability carefully articulated to the construction and renovation of national identities. In China, the precise structure of this articulation has been negotiated directly between the digital provider and the state as part of the price of entry into the market. At the time of writing, in order to gain access to the Chinese market, for instance, providers such as Google had signed up to formal agreements on Internet practice, which installed local filters for the Chinese market and dramatically changed the way in which Chinese users created and posted user-generated content. Furthermore and in conformity with that agreement, Google monitored Chinese users' behavior and provided this information to the Chinese government on occasion.[38]

China's political regulation of its citizens' use of the Internet is colloquially referred to as the Great Chinese Firewall and has been the subject of international news stories over some time.[39] It became more widely controversial, however, during the Beijing Olympics, when the international media objected to limitations on their use of the Internet, which seemed to breach agreements between the International Olympic Committee (IOC) and the Chinese government. As it turned out and just as Google had to do, the IOC had to accept limitations on its customary freedoms in order to operate within China. As a result, journalists found that they were not able to search the Internet using terms such as "Falun Gong" or "Tibetan independence."

A feature of much of Western media studies' discussion of post-broadcast television, convergence, and the emerging capacities of the online environment is the politics of consumption so often attributed to the changing environment. Implicit in the coinage of terms like "produser," in the vigorous interest in the phenomenal growth of UGC or DIY content, and in the focus upon the new time-shifting and playlisting opportunities with digital video is a conviction that the digital revolution tips the balance of power away from the media corporations (or the state) and toward the (inter)active consumer. This complex of developments is seen as benefiting the user, not the corporation.

I am not suggesting that this notion is unique to those who most welcome the expansion of digital television and digital media in general. Indeed, the politics behind this privileging of the interests of the user is consistent with the ethical objectives of what I referred to above as conventional accounts of the emancipatory potential of mass communication. However, among the attributes customarily seen as fundamental to the emancipatory potential of the electronic media of mass communication was universal access. By and large, information in the mass communication era was free; in the digital era, that is not quite so categorically the case, and the political consequences are significant. In Latin America, as we have seen already, and in China, there are internal and economically entrenched digital divides that skew media access toward the more affluent urban elites.[40] Even in the United States there is debate about the extent to which the benefits of the new media platforms will be accessible to everyone. The optimistic politics attributed to the expansion of the Web and other interactive media are qualified significantly if there remains "great uncertainty. . . about how many would or could adopt new technologies and ways of using television even once content became available" as a result of differentials in the capacity to pay.[41]

There are other uncertainties that make a persuasive reading of the politics of media consumption in the current circumstances quite difficult. These include the fact that the commercial nature of so many of the convergent media developments can't help but undermine the much-valued privileging of the user and the construction of community. Kylie Jarrett's discussion of the future of YouTube draws out the contradictions at the heart of the enterprise. On the one hand, she says that YouTube attracts its loyal following as a result of its investment in the "broadcasting of the self," the construction of personal identity through active participation in the site. For its participants, YouTube promises to construct a community that is not contained by the corporate media. On the other hand, Jarrett points out that the site is also a trademark, located within "regimes of property rights, copyright ownership and commercial interests." Ironically, even while it wants to maintain the idea that it enables "resistant identity practices" that challenge "established media relations," YouTube is a valuable piece of commercial real estate, and it is directly connected to the conventional economy.[42] Moreover, if YouTube wants to maintain the quality and volume of its menus of content, it cannot rely solely on user-generated material. There has to be a significant, probably a growing, amount of commercially produced content, and for that YouTube has to enter into agreements with commercial providers.

There is a further, and slightly more worrying, line of attack against the optimistic politics of consumption described above. Mark Andrejevic argues that much of the labor that goes into generating the attraction for the online DIY video and social networking sites comes from the fans themselves. While "broadcasting themselves" and creating communities, he says, they are also helping to monetize the site by contributing to its content. He argues that this unpaid labor is subsumed into the marketing for the site and therefore seamlessly integrated into normal media relations, eventually ending up "reinforcing social and material relations" rather than challenging them.[43] Andrejevic points this out in order to question what he regards as an overly naïve assessment of the politics of interactivity in these media formats. Addressing precisely the complex of political assumptions I have been detailing here, he argues for a greater specificity and contingency in discussing this politics. To assume that interactivity per se necessarily embodies a progressive politics is, he argues, problematic: "It is one thing to note that viewers derive pleasure and fulfillment from their online activities and quite another to suggest that pleasure is necessarily either empowering for viewers or destabilizing for entrenched forms of corporate control over popular culture."[44] Such are some of the limits to the cases that are made and the assumptions that have been allowed to develop in relation to shifts in technologies and their uses if we are to properly understand the social and cultural capacities of this new television landscape.

As we have seen, it is possible to describe aspects of the new modes of digital consumption and the purposes they serve; it is possible to think about the effects on the construction of community; and it is possible to examine the likely issues to arise from television's increasing engagement in the construction of personal identity. What is less possible, however, is to assess the likely politics of this digital media environment because we can read the same developments from quite contradictory points of view. To some extent, these contradictions underline the importance of the point I made above that big, overarching models of mass media production and consumption no longer appear to be as inclusive, comprehensive, or applicable as might once have been the case. Nor are the developments I chart mutually exclusive, with a success for one necessarily resulting in a disaster for another.

The digital transformation of television has introduced a significant complication to what in retrospect seems to have been a relatively simple paradigm of mass communication—that is, a communication system focused on institutions or organizations more or less closely articulated to the operation of the state, freely accessible to all, concerned with the production of the citizen as a national subject, and taking as their potential audience the whole of the population of the nation-state. This paradigm has not disappeared, of course, and in many places it is still well and truly in place. But its function and provenance are changing. Even this may be reversible; we may find that there are ways in which the mass media will be re-embedded into our social, cultural, and institutional systems. James Bennett and Niki Strange's article on how a particular set of BBC strategies has led their audiences through the Web into an engagement with the operation of citizenship is a useful demonstration of how that might occur.[45] At this point, though, it is probably more important to emphasize the fact that once the mass media lose their "massness" in the ways I have been discussing here, they become much more radically conjunctural, much more volatile and contingent in response to the precise configuration of the forces of change in particular sociohistorical circumstances. We need to be responsive to that volatility in our accounts of what is going on as television becomes digital.

NOTES

1. Amanda Lotz, *The Television Will Be Revolutionized* (New York: New York University Press, 2007), 241–42.
2. Jinna Tay and Graeme Turner, "What Is Television? Comparing Media Systems in the Post-Broadcast Era," *Media International Australia* 126 (2008): 71–81.
3. It is also worth making the point that at the time of writing, DVR penetration into U.S. households was still only around 25 percent. So my situation is probably not dissimilar to that of the remaining 75 percent.
4. Axel Bruns, "Reconfiguring Television for a Networked, Produsage Context," *Media International Australia* 126 (2008): 83.
5. Ibid., 86.
6. Joseph D. Straubhaar, *World Television* (Thousand Oaks, Calif.: Sage, 2007), 21.

7. I should acknowledge that my attendance at this conference was made possible by a NATPE Educational Foundation Faculty Fellowship; I am very grateful to NATPE and to the program director, Greg Pitts, for providing me with this opportunity.

8. The Leichtman Research Group publishes regular "Research Notes" on its Web site, www.LeichtmanResearch.com, and also sells full research reports to clients. The results I cite are reported in issue 3Q2007 of the "Research Notes" under the headline "Six Minutes to Glory."

9. Milly Buonanno, *The Age of Television: Experiences and Theories*, trans. Jennifer Radice (Bristol: Intellect, 2008), 67.

10. Des Freedman, "Internet Transformations: 'Old' Media Resilience in the 'New Media' Revolution," in *Media and Cultural Theory*, ed. James Curran and David Morley (London: Routledge, 2006), 287.

11. Ibid.

12. David Morley, *Media, Modernity and Technology: The Geography of the New* (London: Routledge, 2007), 241.

13. Tay and Turner, "What Is Television?"

14. In a recent post to the media comment blog TV Board, Frank Maggio reported on his installation of the new set-top box that U.S. consumers will need to convert their analog sets to digital reception. "I have seen the future—and it is free!" he exclaimed; he now had access to sixteen broadcast channels in high definition, with an onscreen program guide and so on. Partnerships between local broadcasters and existing cable companies would also enable the former to compete directly with the range of choices available on cable. "TV Board for Friday, May 2, 2008"; http://blogs.mediapost.com/tv_board/?p=307.

15. Cheng Liu and Axel Bruns, "Convergence on the Fast Track: The Rapid Restructure of China's Media"; Visiting Scholar Research Project QUT, 2007, unpublished paper.

16. Jaz Hee-jeong Choi, "Approaching the Mobile Culture of East Asia," *M/C Journal* 10, no. 1 (2007); http://journal.media-culture.org.au/0703/01-choi.php.

17. It is notable that this runs against the grain of some of the Western accounts of the social function of mobile phones—or even the technical descriptor "cellular" that is used in most locations, which metaphorically foregrounds the mobile phone's personal, individualizing, attributes.

18. Choi, "Approaching the Mobile Culture of East Asia."

19. Ibid. This distinction effectively replicates the collective versus individualist model outlined in the previous quotation. Choi does not explicitly define each term in the polychronic/monochronic dichotomy in her article.

20. Michael Curtin, "Media Capitals: Cultural Geographies of Global TV," in *Television after TV: Essays on a Medium in Transition*, ed. Lynn Spigel and Jan Olsson (Durham, N.C.: Duke University Press, 2004), 270–302.

21. Straubhaar, *World Television*, 72.

22. Anthony Fung, *Global Capital, Local Culture* (London: Peter Lang, 2008).

23. Dai Yong Jin, "Transformation of the World Television System under Neoliberal Globalization," *Television and New Media* 8, no. 3 (2007): 179–96.

24. John Sinclair, "Into the Post-Broadcast Era," in *Contemporary World Television*, ed. John Sinclair and Graeme Turner (London: BFI, 2007), 45.

25. Karen Lury, "Confessions of a Television Academic in a Post-TV World," *Flow* 7, no. 7 (2008); http://flowtv.org/?p=1150.

26. Lotz, *The Television Will Be Revolutionized*, 247. Lotz goes on: "Questions such as how cultures and subcultures come to know themselves and each other without widely shared programming and how this affects perceptions of difference in society require new thinking. Many assumptions of the 'mass' nature of media undergird theories postulating the emancipatory potential of media. Even as the new norm of niche audiences eliminates some of these imagined possibilities, it may create others."

27. Teresa Rizzo, "Programming Your Own Channel: An Archaeology of the Playlist," in *TV Futures: Digital Television Policy in Australia*, ed. Andrew T. Kenyon (Melbourne: University of Melbourne Press, 2007), 112.

28. Joshua Green, "Why Do They Call It TV When It's Not on the Box? 'New' Television Services and Old Television Functions," *Media International Australia* 126 (2008): 103.

29. On the other hand, we also need to acknowledge an opposing, but not necessarily related, trend—the rise of the home theater and the gradual penetration of the DVR beyond the North American markets.

30. Buonanno, *The Age of Television*, 70.

31. Rizzo, "Programming Your Own Channel," 114.

32. Lotz, *The Television Will Be Revolutionized*, 246.

33. Graeme Turner, "The Mass Production of Celebrity: Celetoids, Reality TV and the 'Demotic Turn,'" *International Journal of Cultural Studies* 9, no. 2 (2006): 153–66.

34. John Hartley, *The Uses of Television* (London: Routledge, 1998).

35. Bart Beaty and Rebecca Sullivan, *Canadian Television Today* (Calgary: University of Calgary Press, 2006); see also Serra Tinic, *On Location: Canada's Television Industry in a Global Market* (Toronto: University of Toronto Press, 2005).

36. This connection is actually quite widespread, and the modernizing capacity of technology is put to work for a variety of ideological causes. See, for example, Zala Volcic and Karmen Erjavec, "Technological Developments in Central-Eastern Europe: A Case Study of a Computer Literacy Project in Slovenia," *Information, Communication and Society* 11, no. 3 (2008): 326–47, for a discussion of this trope.

37. Fung, *Global Capital, Local Culture*.

38. See, for example, Paul Wiseman, "Cracking the 'Great Firewall' of China's Web

Censorship," *USA Today*, April 23, 2008, n.p.; http://www.usatoday.com/tech/news/techpolicy/2008-04-22-internetBandits_N.htm. While Google has subsequently changed its approach to China, moving its servers to Hong Kong as a result of security attacks on Google's architecture, national configurations of censorship and surveillance laws remain important conjunctural factors that shape user behavior—including the kinds of user-generated content created.

39. Ibid.

40. Yuezhi Zhao, "Who Wants Democracy and Does It Deliver Food? Communication and Power in a Globally Integrated China," in *Democratizing Global Media: One World, Many Struggles*, ed. R. Hackett and Yuezhi Zhao (Lanham: Rowman and Littlefield, 2005), 70.

41. Lotz, *The Television Will Be Revolutionized*, 251.

42. Kylie Jarrett, "Beyond Broadcast Yourself: The Future of YouTube," *Media International Australia* 126 (2008): 135.

43. Mark Andrejevic, "Watching Television without Pity: The Productivity of Online Fans," *Television and New Media* 9, no. 1 (2008): 43.

44. Ibid.

45. James Bennett and Niki Strange, "The BBC's Second-Shift Aesthetics: Interactive Television, Multi-Platform Projects and Public Service Content for a Digital Era," *Media International Australia* 126 (2008): 106–19.

JULIAN THOMAS

WHEN DIGITAL WAS NEW

*The Advanced Television Technologies of the
1970s and the Control of Content*

The digitization of television broadcasting is familiar as a focus
of contemporary media policy and politics, but the digitization of television is an altogether more obscure, older, longer-
running, and more diffuse cluster of transitions. It began with
a sequence of advanced television technologies that appeared
decades before the new channels of the millennium. The sequence includes teletext systems, games consoles, laser disc
players, remote controls, and programmable vcrs. These devices were not all successful, and they have their own particular geographies and trajectories, producing not a singular sys-
temic change but a plurality of histories. They did create, in
the 1970s and 1980s, new forms of television that anticipated
and in some ways preempted the digital broadcast media of
the new millennium. The old "new television" was an analog
and digital hybrid. What it achieved, in essence, was exactly
the underlying aim of digital broadcasting today: an extraordinary increase in the amount and diversity of information
accessible for ordinary viewers through a television set. The
point of this chapter is not simply to show that certain aspects
of the current digital environment were anticipated in an
earlier period, but also to underline the extent to which some
of the most contested, intractable, and unresolved aspects
of contemporary digital television systems—those concern-

ing the capacities of viewers and users to record, copy, appropriate, and share content—are directly connected to a longer history of transformation. If, from the point of view of the present, we may now think of content as the software of television—understood as both computer *and* TV program—then struggles over the hardware—the machines and the codes and standards that they employ—turn out to play a critical role in shaping our experiences and uses of this volatile medium.

The new television technologies of the 1970s appeared without a great deal of planning or coordination and with little in the way of national policy sanction. They were taken up on the fringes of regulated television systems, on what we would now describe as the user-controlled edges of media networks. They were adaptive innovations, working around the limitations of a broadcast system to offer something different. That meant they were not controlled by broadcasters, and they were the object of intense commercial struggle. It also resulted in a certain amount of difficulty and complexity, which stayed with objects such as vcrs for their entire life.

The new television of the 1970s and 1980s brings some key features of contemporary digital television into sharp relief. It was in that period that television and broadcasting began to diverge, leading to the volatile codependency that is now familiar. The dynamism at the fringes of the broadcasting system generated new, domestic audiovisual economies on the boundaries of the household and the market, and the movement of content around the domestic economy became increasingly contested. This chapter considers one device from this period, the remote control, an underestimated but nevertheless essential element of the new television of the 1970s and 1980s. When the bandwidth of television systems increases, as happened then and is now happening again, the user interface becomes a critical problem. The remote was the first way of managing the proliferation and expansion of television content. Far from being a simple accessory, it was a distinct, proliferating, and disruptive technology for media use.

The remote therefore has an important place in the continuing attempts of users to organize and control television. In a recent essay William Uricchio uses Raymond Williams's familiar terminology to suggest that the remote enabled "viewer-dominated flow" to replace "programming-centered" flow. Uricchio notes the remote control's "synergetic relation to the increase in broadcast channels, the availability of cable service, and the introduction of the VCR."[1] My argument in this chapter is more specific. The remote played a further critical role in changing television, one that continues to have consequences today: it contributed to the detachment of television from broadcasting of all kinds. From the simple integration of function and content in early television receivers, the hardware and software of television have diverged into a multiplicity of boxes, applications, and sources of content. This divergence was preceded and made possible by the gradual physical disconnection of the remote from the television set; it was not until the 1980s that wireless remotes became standard items in Western households. The remote also has a history that is distinct from broadcast television, both predating it and extending beyond it. Considered not as an attachment to another machine but as a machine in itself, the remote is notable as an early example of a tactile, handheld media device, closely related to mobile phones, personal music players, and other media machines that share this warm proximity to people.[2] At the same time, the remote is interesting as a technology that never entirely succeeded, despite its apparently simple capacities and proliferation. Its failures and frustrations are as telling as its triumphs. Remotes have had a major impact on new forms of television but still cannot simply and effectively control it.

It is not novel to suggest that the remote control is an important element in the experience of television; extensive debates were generated in the 1980s and 1990s by the diffusion of the television remote control and its related technologies, especially videocassette recorders. Rather than revisit those arguments, this chapter offers a sequel to them. The research of that period was oriented around the problems presented by the remote as a social and economic instrument operating within a broadcast environment dominated by free-to-air television, cable or satellite, and the VCR. The prevailing analysis at the time was that the freedom the remote offered viewers in an era of cheap VCRs and proliferating services was likely to be transitory: governments had encouraged a consolidation of media industries, and real choices for viewers were likely to diminish.[3] That issue is vitally important and reappears below in this chapter, but first we need to reconsider the idea of the remote as a mediating technology between viewers and broadcasters. The remote control did indeed become functionally integral to broadcast television, allowing users to navigate programs and channels in new ways. However, it also became the means by which viewers could switch between different sources of audiovisual content, including free-to-air; subscription and pay-per-view broadcast content; packaged media such as DVDs; and user-recorded, user-downloaded, and user-generated content. For some time, the TV remote control has not been a device functionally dedicated to navigating and selecting broadcast programs. There are therefore two vital, and related, trajectories to understand. The first connects the diffusion and popular take-up of the remote to its gradual disconnection from the television set. The second is the equally gradual disconnection between the software, or content, of broadcast television and the hardware that presents it to its viewers.

The two lines of development converge around the question of control over content, something the remote has made challenging for both users and media industries. That problem is the central theme of this chapter. Attempts to reestablish control over content in the current digital era depend upon new technologies that aim to reintegrate the hardware and software of television creating new domestic audiovisual systems dedicated to the most valuable forms of content. At the same time, however, the dynamic of divergence continues, creating new opportunities for viewers on the edges of the television system.

THE SCIENCE OF THE REMOTE: AUDIENCE STUDIES AND INDUSTRY STRATEGY

In the scholarship of the new television technologies of the 1980s and 1990s, the remote control was interesting because its use gave researchers something that they could clearly observe audiences doing. It could be monitored as a series of actions over time. It therefore helped create a body of scholarship that, in John Hartley's words, constituted television as a kind of behavior, rather than a form of communication.[4] How often were remotes being used and in what ways? Who clicked the clicker? How did the remote control change the family viewing experience? How did it change the way people watched television, especially when it was combined with the VCR? Did viewers watch programs or channels? In the language of television research in the 1990s, the remote was interesting because it allowed viewers to do new things: "zipping" (fast-forwarding through recorded content), "zapping" (switching channels), and "hopping" or "grazing" (creating a mix of content from a sequence of sources). Gauging the impact of these activities in a rigorous way turned out to be a difficult research problem, with very few studies able to provide a fine-grained picture of what a significant number of viewers actually did with remotes. Counting the number of channel changes or the number of ads zipped has not proved particularly informative, and results are hard to interpret because researchers have used many different ways of measuring remote control use. In *Television and the Remote Control* (1996), U.S. television scholars Robert V. Bellamy and James R. Walker produced a comprehensive survey of what we might now call the "science of the remote," the accumulated academic and industry literature on remote control effects. Bellamy and Walker's overall analysis of dozens of studies led to several broad conclusions about user activity. Viewers with remote controls changed channels much more frequently than those without; some commercials were zapped much less often than others; zipping ads in recorded programs was very frequent; and the more television technology there was in a household, the more likely viewers were to use it to avoid ads.[5]

As an aggregate picture, findings of this sort could both reassure and unsettle broadcasters. We now know that none of these activities seriously compromised the broadcasting business model. Zipping was not a profound problem because only a small minority of viewers actually used VCRs to record a substantial amount of content—a result that could be attributed both to growing broadcast choices in this period and to the famous usability problems of VCRs. Zapping also was not a disaster: it turned out that although viewers changed channels more often, that did not mean they watched significantly more channels or that they zapped frequently in the middle of programs.[6]

Even so, as Uricchio notes, for industry analysts, broadcasters, and scholars, remotes were and remain a source of deep ambivalence, a symbol of uncertain media futures.[7] For Bellamy and Walker, the new paradigm of the remote was best understood as a "second-generation" television audience, enabling passive viewers to become active users, albeit in a terrain that was still a "vast wasteland."[8] Remotes clearly added to the overall pleasure of watching television—at least for the viewers who got to click the clicker—and probably increased the amount of time people spent watching TV. In the marketing of consumer electronics, remotes were presented as both marvelous and mundane, saving viewers the trouble of getting up to change the channel or turn down the volume.

They thus contributed both to the much-celebrated empowerment of viewers and to their much-worried-about immobilization. In academic research and media industry commentary, there was also a double edge of this sort to much of the analysis. Remote controls were taken to be "subversive technologies," shifting the balance of control from advertisers and broadcasters to viewers, with the qualification that some viewers, especially men, were likely to want to control the remote much more than others. In a 1999 study, David Gauntlett and Annette Hill quoted a knowing thirty-eight-year-old self-employed caterer: "As the male of the family I believe it is my right and duty to monopolize the remote control."[9]

On the one hand, the remote, together with the VCR, was often presented as potentially undermining the broadcast business model by enabling the viewer to avoid advertisements. On the other, these devices sparked new business models and new ways of engaging audiences. Even without a time-shifting revolution in viewing, the VCR had dramatic and wide-ranging effects on audiovisual trade, opening up new markets and breaking down old territorial boundaries.[10] Further, the remote and other new television technologies encouraged innovations that increased both the density and velocity of programming and production: fewer breaks between programs, strong lead-ins to "front load" drama, and the simultaneous running of credits with previews, creating the split-screen division of channels. The remote encouraged all sorts of experiments and stratagems on the part of broadcasters, advertisers, and program makers to attract viewers' interest and then keep them watching.

One of the real challenges for this body of knowledge was the instability of the television environment and its user base. Remote controls have changed and multiplied over the last twenty years (and are continuing to change), so studies concerned primarily with channel changing or zipping no longer describe some of the key things that people may now do with them—control DVDs and other storage media, navigate electronic program guides, or pause broadcast television. A retail market for "universal" remote controls has emerged, encouraging adaptations such as online setup and software updating; lighting controls; larger, color screens on the remote itself; and user-defined "favorites" buttons. These are labeled as "His" and "Hers" on one current model, suggesting that the gendering of the remote control persists.[11]

In order to better understand the remote controls of the 1970s, we need to go back a little further. The home entertainment remote control has a history of its own, predating that of television. Before the TV version, there was the radio remote control. Like many other aspects of contemporary domestic comfort and technology, the appearance and early development of the remote are part of the extraordinary between-wars diffusion of radio. From the late 1920s on, wired devices were available that gave listeners "armchair control" over the living room radio set. These controls were essentially small electric motors, connected to a receiver through a flat ribbon control cable that could sit beneath rugs and furniture. They could switch on or off the receiver and speakers, and they offered "automatic tuning," the capacity to cycle through selected stations in a fixed sequence. These devices were clearly well adapted to the living room experience of multichannel 1930s radio, but they were also expensive and cumbersome in many ways—they were hard to "fine tune"; they had to be attached to the receiver; the connecting wire could easily be damaged; and once positioned in a room, they were not easily moved. Nevertheless, these early devices were clearly the creatures of active radio listeners and are the precursors of both the remote controls for today's home audio systems and those that we use now for television. From 1938 to 1941, the U.S. electronics firm Philco produced the "Philco Mystery Control," a wireless radio remote with eight station presets and two volume controls organized around a dial with finger holes, like a rotary dial telephone. The Mystery Control was designed as an accessory for the best Philco radios and transmitted radio signals to a special receiver box in the radio cabinet.[12]

Although they were not widely adopted until much later, television remote controls appeared early in the history of the medium, not from the mainstream television industry but from its periphery. Louise Benjamin's account of early U.S. remote controls suggests that from the late 1940s to the mid-1950s there was a first generation of simple remotes designed or sold by independent entrepreneurs or electronics enthusiasts. In 1953 one U.S. advertising executive was marketing the $2.98 "Blab-Off," a muting device that, with the twenty-foot cable supplied, could be attached to a television loudspeaker, enabling the viewer to "select the advertising he wants to hear, and he can get away from the commercials he dislikes."[13] Electronics, radio, and television magazines instructed their hobbyist readers in the construction of similar devices. This pattern of somewhat subversive innovation from the margins has long been an element in the development and application of remote technology—the Blab-Off has a recognizable descendant in today's $19.99 "TV-B-Gone," a key ring–sized, high-powered universal remote that can turn on or off most television sets by cycling through the various codes used by leading manufacturers. The TV-B-Gone was designed to combat the diffusion of television in public places such as airports, bars, restaurants, and laundromats. Its inventor, Mitch Altman, says you can use the TV-B-Gone "to control access to television for philosophical or practical reasons, or simply to have fun!"[14]

The early television remote control is interesting not so much as a rather rare curiosity or as a technical breakthrough, but because it foreshadowed continuing arguments around television viewers and their relationship to the medium. The Blab-Off raises immediately the business implications of viewer control. By 1955 a second generation of more polished remotes had appeared, with television manufacturers beginning to sell and vigorously promote their own devices. The U.S. manufacturer Zenith is generally credited with the development of the first wireless remotes. Zenith's founder, Eugene F. McDonald, known to all as "Commander" after a career in the navy, believed that free-to-air, advertising-supported television could not achieve consumer acceptance, and he asked Zenith engineers to develop a convenient and reliable device to help viewers circumvent advertising. Zenith's innovations emerged in the context of extensive debate and commercial rivalry around the television business. At the time Zenith was developing new remotes, McDonald was seeking Federal Communications Commission (FCC) approval for "Phonevision," an early model of what was then called "pay-as-you-see TV," where a scrambled terrestrial signal could be unlocked by a code sent through the telephone system. Phonevision had been a project at Zenith since the mid-1940s; by the mid-1950s, other parties were also interested in the area, although the basic mechanics of how to deliver a paid-for service were not yet clear. Paramount Pictures was working on the technology through a subsidiary, International Telemeter, as was a firm called Skiatron, which used a decoder box and IBM punch cards.[15]

In the 1950s, television remote controls of many kinds were widely

FIGURE 1 Advertisements during the 1950s for early remote controls emphasized the gift of controlling television "from where you sit." (Advertisement published in the *Melbourne Age*, December 19, 1957.)

advertised in newspapers and magazines. The remote control of the 1950s was presented as an artifact from an imaginary future, a world characterized by short working hours, diminishing household labor, and, axiomatically, miraculous technological control over the domestic environment. The idea of "automatic" control or the capacity to control machines simply by pressing buttons—a physical action without effort or any mechanical relation to its outcome—was clearly enormously attractive. Advertisements for early remote controls emphasized the gift of controlling television "from where you sit." In December 1957, just one year after licensed television broadcasting began in Australia, an advertisement in the *Melbourne Age* announced that "Yes, now, for the first time in Australia, you can control your TV set COMPLETELY from wherever you are sitting. You can switch the set on and off, change programs and adjust tuning, simply by pushing buttons beside your chair."[16] A smaller and simpler device, with the capacity to control only volume and picture contrast, was advertised under the heading "Don't bother to get up": "Every owner of an H.M.V. 21-inch Receiver can now stay relaxed in an easy-chair and make adjustments for comfortable looking and listening."[17] Before it became a problem for public health, the combination of sedentary relaxation and electronic control was a positive selling point. Cecelia Tichi's study of early U.S. television culture shows how the "relaxed" viewer would quickly come to be seen as pathologically inactive and immobilized, but before that transition, there was the "La-Z-Boy" and, to go with it, Zenith's early remote, the "Lazy Bones."[18]

PROLIFERATION

The extraordinary flowering of the new television technologies of the 1970s gave TV viewers access to an exponentially greater amount of information. It did so not only by giving viewers greater control over broadcast material, but also by providing alternative sources of content. Totally different and much more powerful user controls were necessary. Devices such as VCRs, games consoles, and laser disc players demanded a level of user attention and interaction that could be achieved only through something like a keyboard, and they all initially relied upon wired keypads. BBC's "Ceefax," launched in September 1974, is a case in point. Ceefax was an early teletext service, transmitted in analog TV's vertical blanking interval. The underlying technology was first developed as a way of displaying captions to hearing-impaired viewers, but the system grew into a news and information service that was independent of BBC's regular programming. At its launch, Ceefax was promoted as "the up to date way of keeping up to date" and "dial-a-page news and information on your TV screen": "BBC Ceefax offers you another way to enjoy television. It lets you browse through magazines of pages which you can read on your screen whenever you choose, any time that BBC Television is on air. . . . To see a particular page you just dial a simple number on a push button pad and in a few seconds it's there."[19]

The U.K. Post Office's "Prestel" and the French "Minitel" were other initiatives from the same era, all bearing distinct signs of their origins in state-run broadcasting, post, and telecommunications systems.[20] Ceefax pages had a three-digit number, so decoders included a wired remote "page selector unit." A simple television remote capable of nothing more

FIGURE 2 Ceefax was promoted as "the up to date way of keeping up to date," but the apparent simplicity and ease of use of the service belied the engineering and cultural challenges and complexities it heralded. (*Ceefax: Browse through a New Magazine* [London: BBC, 1974].)

than cycling through channels could never usefully manage the volume of content, just as a calculator-style keypad would also become necessary for multichannel cable television. Teletext services such as Ceefax were probably the first forms of digital broadcasting. Turning them from engineering concepts into generally affordable and available devices was a major challenge, and several multinational electronics businesses were closely involved in developing receivers. The U.S. firm Texas Instruments was the first to produce an inexpensive chip set for Ceefax decoders. The U.S. conglomerate ITT, formerly International Telephone and Telegraph, appears to have led the development of the infrared alternative to ultrasonic remotes, which had developed around the use of radio frequencies. Infrared remotes used light-emitting diodes (LEDS) to transmit a series of digital signals to a receiver and decoder built into the Ceefax set-top box. The signals were encoded according to a simple protocol that allowed for a large number of possible functions, enabling far more complex operations than ultrasonic remotes. But navigation was only one of the tasks of the new infrared remotes. The Ceefax remote had to include a particularly important new capacity: viewers needed the capacity to switch between Ceefax and regular broadcast content. The button for switching back to broadcast programs was labeled "TV." So there were now two things: TV and something else, "a new way to enjoy television." Television's software was beginning to separate from the hardware.

CONSEQUENCES: COMPLEXITY AND CONTROL

Infrared remotes were successful because they were well adapted to domestic applications. By the late 1970s they were relatively simple and cheap to manufacture—infrared emitters had been the earliest of the LED semiconductors to be invented and developed, and they had the further advantages of being very energy efficient, long lasting, and—unlike some radio frequency–based alternatives—well contained within rooms because they were blocked by walls. But although they were rapidly adopted, no general industry standards developed for the codes they used; individual manufacturers invented or adapted their own versions of the various communication protocols that were developed. Although the basic technology of the infrared remote was almost standardized, the devices themselves fragmented and proliferated.

We've seen that remote controls were available from the early years of television broadcasting. Take-up for at least the first two decades of broadcasting seems to have been low, given the expense of the available technologies and their practical shortcomings, especially the inconvenience of wired remotes. Because remote controls are usually seen as accessory devices and are sold with many kinds of audiovisual equipment, it has always been more difficult to track the diffusion and take-up of the television remote control than for other consumer electronic technologies, such as DVD players. The diffusion of remote controls can in part be deduced from the extraordinary take-up of devices supplied with them, such as VCRs, television decoders, media servers, and DVD players and recorders. But unlike these devices—which if successful must reach a point of market saturation—the acquisition of remotes does not have a natural end point. Households continue to accumulate remote controls with every additional device. The dynamics of innovation in the consumer electronics industries means that there are always options of new devices offering new possible uses for audiovisual content, and the new device will always entail a new remote, tailored to some specific set of functions but not necessarily operating consistently with all the others. Thus a small population of remote controls grows around every television screen: the display, the decoder, the games consoles, the media players and recorders. They all connect to something, but they are not connected to each other.

This brings us back to the detachment of television from broadcasting and what I have referred to as their "volatile codependency." Over fifty years, television receivers have gradually evolved into video displays; they are no longer functionally dedicated to content of a particular sort or origin. Like the word processors of the early 1980s, TVs were once designed around essentially one application, in this case the reception and selection of a limited number of VHF and UHF broadcast channels. A single radio frequency input socket enabled viewers to plug in an aerial and nothing more. Hence the complexity of early VCRs, which could be attached to a TV only through that socket and therefore had to pretend to be television transmitters accessed through a specially designated channel. Television sets are now designed as aggregating displays for an ever-increasing amount and diversity of home audiovisual content, whether it be broadcast, streamed, purchased, user-generated, stolen, or shared. Current televisions include support for an increasing range of video sources, as well as the capacity to connect to personal computers.

New devices, such as Apple TV, are supposed to help viewers use the TV to draw together and navigate some or all of this proliferating material; others, like the Slingbox, find ways of retransmitting that material beyond the TV onto home computer networks and the Internet. Where does the remote belong in this scene? Remotes are now the means of user control for home audiovisual equipment. Sliders, buttons, and dials have vanished from the surfaces of the components that display, store, and process information, reappearing as arrays of buttons on a remote or as options on remote-controlled onscreen user interfaces. Remotes are now designed as embodiments of corporate brands. They are complex, they speak different languages, and in the main they are designed around specific uses. This means that despite the marketing rhetoric, they are not created in any simple way for the viewer's convenience.

Take one example: pay TV broadcasters supply remotes that are dedicated to functions of the subscription service that create value for the broadcaster, such as interactive content, electronic program guides, and pay-per-view content. In Australia, the Foxtel "IQ" remote is an instance, identical to the "Sky Plus" unit provided by a related News Corporation broadcaster in the United Kingdom. The IQ decoder incorporates a DVR, so recording and program navigation buttons are also prominent, enabling viewers to time-shift easily, to navigate among recorded programs, and then to play back and fast-forward. Colored buttons control certain additional features of the IQ so that programs may be easily scheduled for recording, readily deleted once recorded, and linked for recording as a series. The remote is designed to embody a carefully crafted set of technological and commercial compromises, enabling the viewer certain degrees of control over the content available but restricting certain critical options. The viewer can fast-forward through advertisements but cannot jump past them. In order to better control the distribution of digital content, the IQ is a time-shifting rather than an open-ended recording device, so the remote, together with the screen interface, is organized around the temporary storage of content—recording and deleting are both functionally prominent, although the "Box Office" button is more so. But the most salient feature is what is missing or obscured: there is no obvious way of accessing another source. The remote wants to convey the idea that this subscription service provides the complete television environment. There is no clearly identified way of switching to an alternative, competing content source or storage destination, such as a DVD or games console.

A remote may control a specific task well, but it is designed to do so in a particular way that may benefit some uses but not others. It will do so in the absence of standard protocols and certainly without an overall operating system that manages all the different things that people do with television sets. Firms such as Microsoft seek to fill this gap with "media center" software—with mixed success so far. The result for now is a level of complexity and difficulty that falls short of the old mid-century dream of effortless "space command." Jakob Nielsen, an expert on the usability of Internet applications, has written in this vein about the "anarchy" and "overwhelming complexity" of the remote control.[21] Like many television viewers, Nielsen was attracted to the idea of a modest home cinema, involving a connection between his television display, pay TV decoder, audiovisual devices such as a DVD player and VCR, and his audio system. Controlling all this involved using six remotes with 239 separate buttons, many of them with confusing or completely obscure labels, inconsistent colors, and four different numeric keypad layouts. The remotes all looked rather similar, making it hard to tell them apart in a dim room, and they all did things differently. But the most difficult aspect of remote control anarchy was the absence of interoperability among the remotes.[22] While many remotes can perform some universal functions, specific devices (for example, DVD recorders) sometimes require some particular controls accessible on only one remote. Other general, very basic functions, such as volume control, may also be managed on more than one remote but often with inconsistent effects that may actually make managing the overall system more difficult.

Earlier remote control scholars were optimistic about universal remotes being able to control the full gamut of devices. These remotes have a growing market, but they remain relatively expensive (especially for consumers who perceive remotes as accessories), they can be difficult to set up, and they cannot on their own resolve the complex relationships among the various machines that need to be combined to do something. It must be a sign of considerable design failure when viewers stick pieces of paper on the side of a TV set setting out the sequence of steps required to watch a video tape or attempt to disable confusing buttons on the remote with electrical tape—my parents do both. One response is for the universal remote to take on the task of providing something like an audiovisual operating system. Instead of providing dizzying numbers of buttons devoted to arcane technical functions, the remote provides controls for "watching a movie," or "watching TV." These controls activate a series of commands directed at a range of devices, but the user has no need to follow the specific steps in the process, just as a graphical user interface conceals a sequence of technical operations from the user. A system like this, however, still depends on a fixed configuration of complex hardware, probably arranged by the emerging professional service industry of domestic audiovisual installers and system integrators.

AFTERMATH: CONTENT CONTROL AND AUDIOVISUAL CODE IN THE NEW DIGITAL AGE

Navigating post-broadcast television raises difficulties extending well beyond the scope of this chapter. Without an easy integration of the diverse elements of the domestic audiovisual economy, services on the periphery of a broadcast or cable platform risk losing visibility. Should a content provider make an arrangement with a dominant platform such as a cable or satellite network simply in order to avoid requiring a viewer to use another decoder, and therefore another remote control, to access the provider's content? This takes us back to the question of control in the digital media environment, and the anxiety expressed over a decade ago by Robert Bellamy and James Walker, that the freedom offered by the remote could rapidly evaporate in an increasingly concentrated media landscape.[23] There is now another issue to be added to their concerns about diversity: if remotes are above all about controlling content, then efforts by media businesses around the world to restrict the capacity of consumers to store, share, and modify content need careful attention, especially in the light of new provisions in national copyright laws that aim to prevent users from working around technological protections of copyright material, such as conditional access systems and encryption.

There are several key features of this new field of digital content control. First, there is a reassertion of the spatial dimension of audio-visual content distribution. At a geographical level, national and regional boundaries continue to be one of the most important ways media businesses spread risk and segment their consumer markets, despite the promise of the borderless Internet—and, in its day, the vcr. Geo–Internet Protocol systems, for example, use the Internet addressing system to identify the physical location of users so that the bbc can prevent non-u.k. access to programs freely offered through the broadband iPlayer. At a domestic level, as we shall see in the discussion of Apple tv below, the definition of proximity—or local space—is also critical: because Western households increasingly contain a profusion of imaging, receiving, playing, recording, and networking devices, distinctions need to be made between the movement of content among those domestic machines and distribution over wider networks and the public Internet.

A second aspect of digital content control follows from the first point: a complex relationship is evolving between digital broadcast technologies and those that manage content over networks. Digital *communication* among devices is the issue. The idea behind concepts such as the U.S. "broadcasting flag" proposal is that transmission signals should include information that activates controls in the reception device over whether or not a program may be recorded, stored for any period of time, or burned to a dvd. The fcc mandated the inclusion of broadcast flag technology in U.S. receiving devices, a decision subsequently reviewed and disallowed by the U.S. Court of Appeals. The flag has since been part of various proposals for legislation promoted by the U.S. entertainment industry, generating extensive controversy. Critics of the flag are concerned in particular about the limitations it places on the use of material already in the public domain and more generally about its apparent failure to accommodate existing exceptions in copyright law.[24] These are criticisms that have been applied, in varying degrees, to attempts at digital rights management more generally. In Europe, the powerful DVB (Digital Video Broadcast) standards group has devised its own technical "content protection and copy management" system, known as CPCM.[25] The flag and CPCM differ in important ways, but both are striking examples of broadcast technologies that are presented as "anti-piracy" measures. In fact both go far beyond attacking the illegal trade in audiovisual content, seeking instead an overall form of control over what viewers may do with material after the fact of transmission and reception. It was precisely this feature of the flag that led to its failure when challenged in the courts by the American Library Association, a major user of broadcast content. The D.C. Circuit of the U.S. Court of Appeals found that the FCC's authority to regulate audiovisual devices was limited to those engaged in the actual reception of the broadcast transmission and could not extend to those involved in any subsequent redistribution of that content.[26]

The DVB group's CPCM system, on the other hand, is not an attempt at regulatory rule-making. Instead it seeks to embody negotiated agreements among the content production, distribution, and information technology sectors. Legal and policy frameworks form a necessary context for these agreements but cannot prescribe them. The outcome of CPCM, like other copy protection technologies, is intended to take the form of code: a system of rules and principles that will determine what users can actually do. Much of this is about reasserting spatial controls over the circulation of digital content. At the level of the household, CPCM attempts to reconceptualize the domestic proliferation of audiovisual devices into "local" and "managed" or "authorized" domains. Within these domains, viewers will have varying capacities to record or copy broadcast content.

These broadcast protection technologies can be compared with those used for stored digital media, such as DVDs. There are also emerging systems for managing the movement of audiovisual content across household networks, irrespective of its source. Here a third aspect of the new digital environment is important: the emergence of mainstream consumer markets for high-definition (HD) digital content beyond the "standard-definition" material offered on DVDs and the first wave of digital TV channels. High-definition television takes advantage of the falling costs of large, flat-panel displays and surround-sound audio. It connects to the old idea of the "home cinema": a domestic exhibition space that promises to replace the clutter of casual media consumption with a more immersive personal audiovisual experience. But it is worth remembering that the cinema was a bitterly contested and tightly controlled distribution medium, and "home cinema" is subject to equally intense industry pressures. While content owners must now be reconciled to viewers' comparatively unhindered access to standard-definition content from DVDs and broadcast sources, they see high-definition material as another matter. The CPCM system, for example, is focused on controlling the recording and copying of HD material, with an assumption that viewers should always be able to make a standard-definition copy.

However, a new way of connecting electronic devices, known as HDMI, or high-definition multimedia interface, points to the tensions surrounding high-definition distribution. HDMI is intended to replace both digital DVI connections and older analog standards, such as composite video (used in the European SCART system) and component video. It has been rapidly adopted among digital television manufacturers and is beginning to appear in computers and consumer electronics but may or may not prove successful in the wider consumer electronics universe; in this field, there are always competing technologies. HDMI is at the heart of new devices like Apple TV, a set-top box that combines commercial, free, and user-generated content in an interesting way. The box is set up so users can buy or rent movies and TV shows from the popular iTunes online store; see YouTube, podcasts, and Flickr galleries from the Internet; and access music, video, and photos stored on other computers over a home wireless network. HDMI has received less attention from scholars and policy activists than the flag, mainly because it has appeared in the somewhat less regulated space of consumer electronics and personal computing and has been promoted by a group of electronics manufacturers rather than broadcasters or semi-official standards setters. It is, however, potentially more significant than a broadcast technology as an attempt to govern the flow of content around and beyond domestic space.

The appeal of HDMI is that it appears to offer viewers some attractive advantages over older, analog connections: it can provide the bandwidth needed for the highest current resolutions of audiovisual content, and it includes a control channel, which means that, in theory at least, one remote can be used for every connected device, whether it's a set-top decoder, a display, a personal computer, an audio receiver, an optical disk player, or a games console. The promise is an end to the proliferation and confusion of remotes. But the corollary of this consumer convenience is greater control for rights owners—and the inconvenience of viewers who may not be able to see material they have legitimately acquired. HDMI supports a content protection system known as HDCP, or High-Bandwidth Digital Content Protection, which seeks to establish secure, encrypted connections among devices. HDCP therefore works alongside and in addition to systems for encrypting broadcasts or DVDs: it encrypts communication rather than stored data. Such a system involves a reordering of the domestic audiovisual ecology into a new network topology. HDCP devices are categorized variously as "sources," such as DVD players, which transmit content; "sinks," which render content for human consumption, such as a television display; and "repeaters," which may receive, decode, process, encode, and then retransmit the content. An example would be a receiver or amplifier used in a home cinema.[27] The idea is that an HDCP display—the sink—and an HDCP DVD player—the source—will exchange secret keys and then encrypt the transmission of audiovisual content in a way only the other device can decipher. These keys function as certificates of authenticity, verifying that the sink is to be trusted with the protected content. In this "trusted system," no other device should be able to eavesdrop on this communication, and the audiovisual content should never be exposed to the risk of further copying or distribution.[28] In the case of Apple TV, high-definition movies, purchased by the viewer and downloaded onto the box through a wireless Internet connection, can then be securely displayed on an HDMI-equipped TV.[29]

Apple TV, and devices like it, are signs of a remarkably complex new environment. Like the early, consumer-driven forms of digital television, these technologies move well beyond the reach of traditional, national domains of media or communications law and policy. For consumers, this may not always be a bad thing, as the failure of the FCC's broadcasting flag mandate suggests. HDMI and its competitors fall within the evolving, and still incompletely understood, field of "audiovisual code." Here "code" does not refer to the encryption of the signal in these systems but rather to the capacity of software to become a kind of law, a point emphasized by Lessig.[30] The rules built into audiovisual code are not the subject of public policy debate. Instead they are presented as technical elements within "industry standards." Such standards are based upon negotiations among technology developers, consumer electronics manufacturers, and content rights holders, and because they involve a collective pooling of intellectual property rights that might otherwise stand in the way of a new product or service, they can help kick-start new markets.[31] But such standards are also often much more than technical decisions about how devices may connect and communicate. They are commercially driven strategies that attempt to bind all parties to a certain model of how the technology should work; they use anti-circumvention provisions in copyright law and, in some cases, confidential licensing agreements, to protect those models and they then depend on the positive feedback effects that characterize network markets to overwhelm rival models.[32]

The fate of RealNetworks's REALDVD software appears to illustrate this point. REALDVD is an application that enables users to copy DVDs to a hard drive and play them back. The software does not modify files and preserves their encryption. To make it work, RealNetworks licensed encryption and authentication technology from the DVD Copy Control Association. The company was then sued by the Motion Picture Association of America for infringements of U.S. anti-circumvention laws, with the DVD group claiming that RealNetworks had breached "hidden and secret contractual terms" in its licensing agreement.[33]

The risk here is that the new digital television, for all its promise, may end up less usable than the old. The domestic circulation of content first made possible by the new television technologies of the 1970s is now the focus of a wave of reactive innovation. William Uricchio suggests that filtering and searching system engineers may take over from remote-control-wielding viewers as the next generation to dominate the "flow" of television.[34] He envisages predictive, taste-shaping tools such as those that offer book recommendations on Amazon.com. Search in particular is likely to be a vital part of television's new information infrastructure. But this chapter points to other possible futures for the digital medium of television, based on a different reading of the remote control's history. I have emphasized that the remote is not only about managing an ever-increasing array of broadcast content; by making it easier for viewers to access alternative sources of audiovisual content, it has also contributed to the proliferation of audiovisual sources and the divergence of television from broadcasting. What is envisaged in HDMI and HDCP is a model for managing that proliferation, reordering devices according to a new network topology and establishing new rules for controlling the flow of content. HDMI, in essence, attaches specific audiovisual content to specific devices. The idea of HDMI is the reintegration of the hardware and software of television, uniting the profusion of household devices into one logical machine and thereby returning us to the more manageable era of the stand-alone TV. In such an environment, if it can sustain an aggregated media platform, filtering is indeed likely to become increasingly important.

On the other hand, there remains the curious, persistent, and infuriating "anarchy" of remote controls and the plethora of machines they do not always manage. The case of Apple TV, again, is instructive: independently of any traditional television network, it offers a remarkable array of different kinds of content, some of it traditional TV fare, while other elements are quite new. Of course Apple TV tries to integrate these into an accessible, easy-to-use interface, which will also direct traffic and transactions to Apple. In this respect Apple TV is already an effective platform for the kind of engineering Uricchio describes. But it is also a platform that can be adapted, fairly easily, for other purposes. Since Apple TV appeared, enthusiastic users have worked out ways of using its storage, connections, and processing capacity to access a much wider range of content. Apple CORE LLC, a Colorado-based developer, provides aTV Flash, a software package that opens Apple TV to almost any digital video format, including ripped DVDs, and almost any kind of Internet-sourced video. It makes it possible for users to install a regular Web browser and to attach basic peripherals such as additional hard disks, keyboards, and mice.[35] Users can then access almost any online search engine or Internet-accessible source of content.

Technology may never succeed in protecting Hollywood movies from the pirates and the file sharers. Developers are designing new ways of controlling media with personal computers, and open-source personal video recorders such as MythTV and Freevo are already in wide use. In other words, the long legacy of digital disruption at the edges of the television network is still with us. A chaotic plethora of devices and communication standards frustrates viewers, but control is likely to prove just as elusive for those who most wish to manage television.

NOTES

A number of people helped me with the research that informs this chapter. I would like to thank Louise Goebel and Jason Bosland at the ISR; Louise North, Ben Green, and Andrew Cotton at the BBC; and Andrew Kenyon at the University of Melbourne. Thanks especially to Diane Hamer for her enthusiasm and support.

1. William Uricchio, "Television's Next Generation: Technology/Interface Culture/Flow," in *Television after TV: Essays on a Medium in Transition*, ed. Lynn Spigel and Jan Olsson (Durham, N.C.: Duke University Press, 2004), 168–72.

2. This is a topic for another paper, but we can note here the functional resemblance between radio telephones and remotes. Early remote controls for radio and television, such as those made by Philco in the United States and Redifusion in Britain, employed rotary dials very much like telephones of the period and worked by transmitting radio signals to a special receiver in the main cabinet. The Apple iPhone supports a number of remote control applications for television and audio using WiFi networks.

3. Robert V. Bellamy and James R. Walker, *Television and the Remote Control: Grazing on a Vast Wasteland* (New York: Guilford Press, 1996).

4. John Hartley, "From Republic of Letters to Television Republic? Citizen Readers in the Era of Broadcast Television," in Spigel and Olsson, *Television after TV*, 387.

5. Bellamy and Walker, *Television and the Remote Control*, 24–45.

6. D. A. Ferguson, "Measurement of Mundane TV Behaviours: Remote Control Device Flipping," *Journal of Broadcasting and Electronic Media* 38 (1994): 35–47; W. R. Neuman, *The Future of the Mass Audience* (Cambridge: Cambridge University Press, 1991).

7. Uricchio, "Television's Next Generation."

8. Bellamy and Walker, *Television and the Remote Control*.

9. David Gauntlett and Annette Hill, *TV Living* (London: Routledge with British Film Institute, 1999), 243.

10. Tom O'Regan, "From Piracy to Sovereignty: International VCR Trends," *Continuum: The Australian Journal of Media and Culture* 4, no. 2 (1991): 112–35.

11. For specifications of current leading Logitech and x10 models, see http://www.logitech.com and http://www.x10.com (icon remote).

12. The most informative account of the Philco Mystery Control can be found at http://www.philcorepairbench.com/mystery/history.htm.

13. Louise Benjamin, "At the Touch of a Button: A Brief History of Remote Control Devices," in *The Remote Control in the Age of Television*, ed. James R. Walker and Robert V. Bellamy, Jr. (Westport, Conn.: Praeger, 1993), 17. Adjusted for inflation, the Blab-Off would have been worth $22.86 in 2007; http://www.westegg.com/inflation.

14. Mitch Altman, "TV-B-GONE," n.d.; http://www.tvbgone.com.

15. See John Chamberlain, "Pay-As-You-See TV?" *Barron's National Business and Financial Weekly*, May 2, 1955, 3, 23–24. Robert V. Bellamy provides a useful account of the failure of Phonevision in "Constraints on a Broadcast Innovation: Zenith's Phonevision System, 1931–1972," *Journal of Communication* 38, no. 4 (1988): 8–20.

16. "Control Your TV Set COMPLETELY," *Melbourne Age*, December 19, 1957.

17. "H.M.V. 21-Inch Receiver," *Melbourne Age*, November 18, 1957, 3.

18. Cecilia Tichi, *Electronic Hearth: Creating an American Television Culture* (New York: Open University Press, 1992). Lynn Spigel discusses the La-Z-Boy, the remote control, and *The Seven Year Itch* in *Welcome to the Dreamhouse: Popular Media and Postwar Suburbs* (Durham, N.C.: Duke University Press, 2001), 53.

19. BBC, *Ceefax: Browse through a New Magazine* (London: BBC, 1974).

20. A further discussion of the role of state broadcasters in developing new television technologies can be found in Bennett, "'Your Window on the World.'"

21. Jakob Nielsen, "Remote Control Anarchy," comment posted June 7, 2004, on http://www.useit.com.

22. Ibid.

23. Bellamy and Walker, *Television and the Remote Control.*

24. For a general discussion of the broadcast flag proposal and the debate around it, see Angie A. Welborn, Congressional Research Service, "Copyright Protection of Digital Television: The 'Broadcast Flag'"; CRS No. RS22106, May 11, 2005; Debra Kaplan offers a wide-ranging policy critique in "Broadcast Flags and the War against Digital Television Piracy: A Solution or Dilemma for the Digital Era?" *Federal Communications Law Journal* 57 (2005): 326–44.

25. For a comparison between the U.S. and European systems and their prospects, see Andrew T. Kenyon and Robin Wright, "Television as Something Special? Content Control Technologies and Free-to-Air TV," *Melbourne University Law Review* 30, no. 2 (2006): 338.

26. Matt Jackson, "Protecting Digital Television: Controlling Copyright or Consumers?" *Media and Arts Law Review* 11, no. 3 (2006): 252–71.

27. HDCP is controlled and licensed by Digital Content Protection, LLC, a subsidiary of Intel Corporation. The firm's Web site, http://www.digital-cp.com, provides useful information about the system.

28. On HDMI and HDCP, the official knowledge base is very useful; see http://www.hdmi.org. HDCP has been the subject of extensive discussion in software security and intellectual property circles.

29. Fundamental weaknesses in the design of HDCP are described in Scott Crosby, Ian Goldberg, Robert Johnson, Dawn Song, and David Wagner, "A Cryptanalysis of the High-Bandwidth Digital Content Protection System," presented at ACM-CCS8 DRM Workshop, May 11, 2001. Problems have occurred in establishing and maintaining secure connections among devices so that a TV may cease to display images from a PlayStation or high-definition decoder.

The fix, apparently, is to unplug the device and plug it in again, forcing a new exchange of keys between the sink and the source. See "Zonk," "The Dark Side of HDCP—Why Is My PS3 Blinking?" comment posted January 18, 2007, on Slashdot.org; http://games.slashdot.org/article.pl?sid=07/01/18/197212.

30. Lawrence Lessig, *Code and Other Laws of Cyberspace* (New York: Basic Books, 1999).

31. For a discussion of these aspects of standard setting with particular reference to the information technology sector, see Mark A. Lemley, "Intellectual Property Rights and Standard-Setting Organizations," *California Law Review* 90 (April 2002): 1889–2002.

32. For examples of these network effects, including their role in the introduction of color television in the United States and subsequently HDTV, see Carl Shapiro and Hal R. Varian, *Information Rules: A Strategic Guide to the Network Economy* (Boston: Harvard Business School Books, 1999), 173–225. Tarleton Gillespie's *Wired Shut: Copyright and the Shape of Digital Culture* (Cambridge, Mass.: MIT Press, 2007), an extended analysis of the successes and failures of digital rights management in the creative industries, makes the following point: "The real power behind DRM is not the rise and embrace of encryption itself, but the institutional negotiations to get technology manufacturers to build their devices to chaperone in the same way, the legitimation to get consumers to agree to this arrangement, the political machinations to get the government to authorize these rules for building the technology according to the specs, and the legal wrangling to make it criminal to circumvent" (254).

33. See Jacqui Cheng, "RealNetworks Court Loss a Reminder about Limits of 'Fair Use,'" *Ars Technica*, August 12, 2009; http://arstechnica.com.

34. Uricchio, "Television's Next Generation."

35. See the ATV Flash Web site at http://www.atvflash.com.

WILLIAM BODDY

"IS IT TV YET?"

The Dislocated Screens of Television in a Mobile Digital Culture

Several recent developments in the U.S. television and film industries, including the increased prominence of digital signage and out-of-home media, the growing digital distribution and exhibition of theatrical films, the proliferation of handheld display devices, and the growing popularity of Internet-based video distribution (IPTV), suggest the need for media scholars to reassess the place of television as an industry and social practice. This chapter will explore some of the emerging nondomestic reception sites and protocols of the digital media landscape and examine the ways in which existing media firms have attempted to respond to new challenges and opportunities beyond the setting of traditional broadcasting. The contemporary vision of the platform-indifferent ubiquitous circulation of electronic imagery across cell phones, computer monitors, digital billboards, and cinema screens belies the uncertain longer-term implications of such proliferation, both for the financial fortunes of specific media firms and for the fragmented and mobile audiences targeted by advertisers.

Major actors in the traditional media industries, including broadcast networks, advertising agencies, sponsors, and hardware and software manufacturers, have responded to the new dispersed media audiences in complex and sometimes contradictory ways. In addressing the new strategic imperatives of ubiquity, mobility, and interactivity, media firms face uncertainties about the viability of competing platforms while they attempt to devise appropriate programming and advertising forms for emerging applications and test the limits of public appetite for, and resistance to, the ever-greater penetration of advertising into public and domestic spaces.[1] Amid the improvisation and uncertainty, the contemporary Internet advertising model of audience surveillance and accountability has provided a consistent aspirational yardstick for competing media platforms, venues, and corporate players in the emerging out-of-home media market. The contemporary film and television industries are struggling to avoid the fates of both the record industry (in the face of pervasive file sharing) and of the newspaper business (in the face of Google's command of the online advertising market).[2] Meanwhile, advertising agencies are fearful that their traditional role mediating client and platform will be usurped as Google and Microsoft move beyond the Internet advertising world.[3] For media scholars, the dispersal of video screens, from massive displays in public cinemas and sports stadiums to interactive screens in streets, shops, bars, elevators, shopping trolleys, and handheld devices has provoked a proliferation of distinct textual forms, business models, and viewing practices that collectively challenge traditional notions of television as medium and cultural object as much as its centrality as an advertising medium.

INDUSTRY IDENTITY CRISES

By 2006 a new tone of uncertainty and introspection was emerging in trade shows across the industries of broadcasting, motion pictures, consumer electronics, event staging, and video gaming as event organizers and industry leaders debated the implications of technological change. Such public venues provide important staging grounds for product launches, industry alliances, and corporate rebranding efforts across the digital media. One lesson from the recent trade conventions has been the systematic blurring of industry boundaries; for example, 40 percent of the National Association of Broadcasters (NAB) convention space in Las Vegas in 2006 was taken up by equipment exhibits aimed outside of broadcasting, and the NAB's chief executive warned in his keynote address that "we cannot afford to be an organization that is perceived as protecting the status quo. . . . Broadcasters must move quickly to increase the number of distribution channels and platforms for our content. Broadcast signals must be everywhere in the culture. Our signals must go everywhere . . . to everyone . . . through every device."[4] *Milli-meter* magazine's report on the 2006 NAB convention (attended by over one hundred thousand visitors and generating an estimated $30.4 billion in business deals)[5] concluded that "for the first time, a whole new networked world of telcos, wireless, and IPTV companies, and manufacturers of streaming gear and codec cards made it clear that it really might be time to change out 'broadcasters' for 'bitcasters' in the NAB acronym."[6] The decision in 2006 of the world's second-largest broadcasting trade show, the International Broadcasting Convention, to drop any reference to "broadcasting" altogether in the organization's name and event in favor of the generic acronym IBC literalized the broadcast industry's rebranding to a post-broadcast sector. The four themes of its show in 2007 included digital cinema, IPTV, HDTV, and mobile video, all outside the traditional parameters of the broadcast industry. Likewise, at the Consumer Electronics Show (CES) in 2006, CBS President Les Moonves proclaimed his network's plan "to evolve from a one-way content-distribution and content company into being a sort of new thing—an audience company."[7] Moonves told his audience that "there's no such thing anymore as old media. We're just media. Whether programming means *CSI* or C++ [a computer language], we're all playing on the same big digital field."[8] Equally, as *Advertising Age* reported from the CES, "If media companies are trying to become 'sort of new things,' telecom giants Verizon Communications and AT&T are trying to become media companies," using the CES to announce live mobile video services and content deals.[9]

A similar tone of introspection and uncertainty pervaded less prominent trade venues in 2006 as well. On the eve of the InfoComm convention in May 2006, an event for the AV installation, live event, and video conferencing industries, the executive editor of *Rental and Staging Systems* wrote the following in a special editorial: "We ask, what business are we in, anyway? AV? Staging? Rental? Rental and Staging? Digital Signage? The answer should be: We are in the message business."[10] Later that year across the Atlantic, Britain's *Computer Reseller News* noted the convergence of the industries of audio-video and computer networking; the trade magazine quoted an industry executive who predicted "turbulence, market confusion and merger and acquisition activity between the AV and IT communities, as the lines continue to blur and both sides race to bring the two worlds together."[11]

The commitment to the goal of strategic ubiquity expressed by CBS's Moonves at the CES was also evident among other leaders of the new digital economy, exemplified by the presence of Microsoft's Bill Gates at the Electronic Entertainment Expo in 2006; it was his first appearance at the video game industry's convention, then in its twelfth iteration. Microsoft's decades-long quest to get a piece of all manner of content-delivery and e-commerce services is reflected in a range of current company projects, including the XBOX 360 game console as Internet portal, high-definition DVD player (albeit for the now obsolete HDDVD format), and home entertainment server; the new Vista operating system featuring Microsoft's "Live Everywhere" initiative, linking PC, TV set, and mobile devices; and the development of proprietary compression and encryption software for digital cinema, high-definition DVDs (for both HDDVD and Blu-ray formats), and IPTV.[12]

The interest of Microsoft and others in pursuing increasingly fragmented and mobile media audiences and advertising targets, and the attendant proliferation of business models and dissolving of traditional industry boundaries, have only become more emphatic since 2006. In 2008 Microsoft consolidated its advertising services into a new subsidiary, Microsoft Advertising. Microsoft advised advertisers that "the prospect of trying to gain a foothold in a fast-moving, constantly-shifting media landscape . . . can be daunting" and warned that "consumers have grown more sophisticated, discriminating and discerning, learning to tune out all but the most relevant, ingenious or attention-grabbing ads."[13] Such warnings from within the advertising community about the increasingly sophisticated and recalcitrant consumer have been a staple of twentieth-century trade discourses, typically used to justify ever-bolder assaults on public consciousness by marketers. As we shall see, while Microsoft's extension of Google's context-sensitive advertising model into traditional and emerging advertising media provides a blueprint for countless contemporary digital media firms, large and small, it also speaks of a wider industry crisis. Indeed, the sprawling operations of Microsoft, as well as "old media" companies like Technicolor—a brand once emblematic of the traditional single-minded feature film industry but now also invested in video games, video conferencing, television, and out-of-home screen media—across the myriad venues of digital media suggest the identity crisis of many traditional media forms and sectors.[14]

Part of this strategy of diversification among leaders in the traditional broadcast, software, and film industries is clearly defensive in nature, reflecting an attempt to pursue audiences beyond the traditional domestic television setting. The fragmentation of network TV audiences has deep historical roots, going back to the sustained decline of network audience share already underway in the 1970s. Many commentators have attempted to discern the cultural and ideological implications of the decline of the traditional broadcast pillars of the electronic mass media. Cultural critic David Marc, in his elegiac essay from 1996 titled "What Was Broadcasting?" outlined the decline of network television hegemony at the hands of multichannel cable and the VCR since 1980. Marc lamented the cultural loss in the transition from broadcasting's "nation-as-audience" to the post-broadcast era's "nation-of-audiences," characterized by both the expansion of cultural options and the "contraction of democratic values and institutions," promised, if rarely fulfilled, in broadcasting's technological egalitarianism.[15]

However, other contemporary cultural critics have greeted the end of the broadcast era of undifferentiated mass audiences and mass markets with unequivocal ideological delight. By the early 1990s, the technophilic and policy discourses around HDTV, the information superhighway, and virtual reality frequently cast the model of non-interactive, analog, and top-down TV broadcasting in opposition to the shiny new world of digital media, an opposition that persists today.[16] In this scenario, the introduction of the digital video recorder (DVR) in the late 1990s marked a crucial intervention of the ethos of the personal computer into the television economy and viewing experience, serving as a prefiguration of the introduction of digital regimes of surveillance and audience quantification across contemporary out-of-home media. For example, Michael Lewis's article for *The New York Times Magazine* in 2000 offered the date of August 4, 1997—which marked the launch of TiVo's DVR—as "the beginning of the end of another socialistic force in American life: the mass market," calling the DVR "really just a fantastically powerful accelerator of the fragmentation of markets that has occurred in response to cable television and the Internet." Indeed Netscape founder Marc Andreessen claimed that TiVo represented a "Trojan horse for the computer industry to gain control of the entertainment industry."[17]

Describing the mass market itself as "a collective" where "people who watch commercials subsidize people who don't," Lewis argued that "this little pocket of socialism came into being at least in part because the technology did not exist that could measure, and put a price on, the attention of individual consumers." According to Lewis, the DVR not only provides the means for viewers to avoid TV's traditional thirty-second advertisement but, equally crucially, enables perfect surveillance of viewer activity. Together, these promise to overthrow both the fundamental business practices of commercial television, the twentieth century's quintessential mass medium, and the entire mass market that supports it and was made possible by it: "The television is the mass market. . . . If television ceases to be a mass market, the mass market largely ceases to exist."[18] Lewis predicted that the rise of individually targeted media messages would reinforce the customization of consumer products themselves as marketers sought to match slightly remixed or repackaged goods to more carefully defined market segments.

The shift to tailored branding and more targeted marketing strategies is widely viewed as undermining traditional television's long-term financial prospects. A report by marketing firm Profitable Channels in 2006 included a chart, "The Lifecycle of Marketing and Communication Channels," which plotted several traditional and emerging media platforms according to their growth rates in 2005 along an evolutionary time-line stretching from "Incubate," "Grow," and "Harvest" to "Decline" and "Retire." While "New Digital," "Interactive Media," and "Out-of-Home" media platforms all occupied places along the "Grow" and "Harvest" portion of the spectrum, the advertising media of "Broadcast TV" and "Newspaper" barely escaped the "Retire" end of the scale.[19] However, while the television industry desperately searches for new revenue streams via multiple channels, high definition, and Internet distribution, it faces new competition from screens beyond the home, in the form of advertising-supported digital cinema, digital signage, and mobile video.

OUT-OF-HOME MEDIA

Responding to the perceived threats to the mass market and television's centrality within it, the U.S. television networks have recently signaled their interest in energetically pursuing the out-of-home advertising market, including the CBS purchase of SignStory, a company that distributes programming and advertising to retail venues, for $71.5 million in September 2007. Relaunched as CBS Outernet, the firm reaches over 80 million viewers monthly at 1,500 locations, including "grocery stores, pharmacies, medical waiting rooms, taxis, gas stations, and other places where people shop, eat, travel and gather."[20] A list of the firm's venues includes "American Airlines, the Automotive Broadcasting Network (car dealership/service center waiting rooms), AutoNet (automotive and tire service center waiting rooms), Atlanta's MARTA commuter trains, Gas Station TV (gas station pump tops and convenience stores), the Healium Network (doctor and dentist offices), Indoor Direct (quick service restaurants) [and] the Mall of America."[21] Sumner Redstone, CEO of Viacom—the corporate owner of the CBS television network, as well as cable television and radio networks and a billboard company—explained: "What advertisers buy is platforms to get their brand promoted, and we've got four platforms for them—broadcast TV, cable TV, billboards, and radio. . . . We're everywhere, because in this day and age you have to be where the advertisers need to be."[22] Likewise, in what *Advertising Age* called "a sign of the emerging power of out-of-home video," in January 2008 NBC announced its first national advertising presentation on behalf of the company's digital outdoor services across ten distinct out-of-home venues; the network's out-of-home division, called "NBC Everywhere," claimed to reach 3 billion consumers in 2007.[23]

An article in *The New York Times* in March 2007 pointed to over thirty-seven thousand screens in out-of-home locations in the United States, including 20 percent of grocery stores and 11 percent of all office buildings.[24] The so-called digital signage industry encompasses existing out-of-home video networks (also called "captive audience networks") located in airport lounges, medical offices, sports venues, retail locations, and even more site-specific services like the health club, grocery store, and elevator networks.[25] Traditionally characterized by small firms, imprecise audience measurement, and a skeptical reception among advertising executives, the digital signage industry in 2006 experienced the fastest growth rate of any advertising medium outside of Internet advertising, though it still represents less than 2 percent of what is spent on network TV advertising.[26] The out-of-home market was boosted in September 2005 when Procter & Gamble announced that it was shifting up to 33 percent of its advertising budget from TV commercials to point-of-sale advertising, and one market research firm predicted that the North American digital signage industry would grow from $102.5 million in 2004 to $3.7 billion in 2011.[27] Advocates of out-of-home media point to the value of location and opportunity, especially for point-of-sale video networks; as one marketing consultant told *The New York Times*, "People aren't thinking about toilet cleaner during the Super Bowl. . . . But when they're waiting in line at the supermarket, thinking 'did I get everything on my list,' that's probably the one time they want to think about it."[28]

Consisting of everything from small screens in elevators and shopping carts to enormous public billboards, the business of digital signage has been transformed by the rapidly falling cost of displays, the increasing use of networked programming, and the ability to offer interactive features. Each out-of-home niche market reflects the relentless pursuit of media audiences, who are seen as increasingly fragmented, peripatetic, and resistant to traditional mass media advertising. Thus, the Adspace Mail Network, America's largest in-mall video network, points out on its Web site that "after home and work, the average American spends more time in the mall than anywhere else," and Gannett's Captivate Network—which programs 8,200 elevator displays in twenty-three U.S. markets to 2.4 million viewers—promises advertisers that "because we deliver your message to a captive audience in a focused, distraction-free environment, we have an average ad recall rate that exceeds that of most other media."[29] Unlike the recalcitrant domestic television audience, increasingly adept at evading traditional thirty-second spots via the DVR, video-on-demand, and IPTV, out-of-home networks like Captivate can claim that "our audience is actually eager to watch—actively looking for information and entertainment to fill the dead air and social void of an elevator ride. That's why 96% of our viewers regularly watch Captivate and 88% of them watch virtually every time they ride the elevator."[30]

Figure 1 highlights another highly visible sector of the out-of-home media industry: the global launch in 2007 and 2008 of a Microsoft-powered interactive shopping cart equipped with a twelve-inch touch screen, voice recognition, product scanner, and radio frequency identification (RFID) navigation system was received enthusiastically by many in the trade press and elsewhere. *The New York Post* announced that "Microsoft's new souped-up supermarket shopping carts may do for the grocery list what GPS did for driving directions,"[31] and *Advertising Age* happily announced that "the shopping cart as ad medium, a so-far elusive

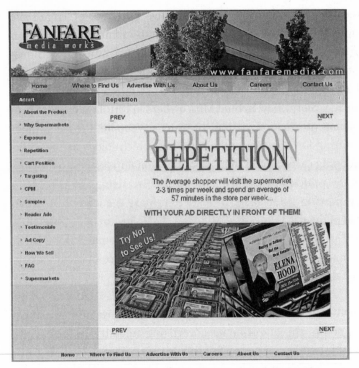

FIGURE 1 MediaCart's location monitoring capability allows advertisers "to leverage the immediacy of the actual shopping experience." (Screen capture from fanfaremedia.com.)

dream . . . may finally have found its killer app."[32] Linked to a customer's store loyalty card, the new interactive shopping cart can display personalized shopping lists, volunteer recipes, provide store directions to spoken queries, and be programmed to sound an alarm if the cumulative fat content of the items placed in the basket is excessive. Beyond its use as a screen advertising medium, RFID technology's ability to track the cart's store location, accurate within a foot, provides advertisers "measurement data akin to that offered by online-search advertising," according to *Advertising Age*: "MediaCart tracks and analyzes how many shoppers stay in the presence of in-store ads and for how long."[33] Moreover, the cart's location monitoring capability allows advertisers "to leverage the immediacy of the actual shopping experience" with each store shelf RFID tag triggering specific product ads, "even," according to *The New York Post*, providing "the potential to give the shopper an opportunity to second guess his or her choice after it is made—'Don't buy brand X, try brand Y instead.'"[34]

Another demonstration of the interactive potential of large-scale digital signage was recently offered by the auto manufacturer BMW on behalf of its Mini Cooper; the company launched a campaign reminiscent of Steve Martin's mentally unstable Los Angeles weatherman, who adopted a magical interactive billboard as a life coach and relationship adviser in *L.A. Story*. BMW invited Mini owners in four U.S. cities to provide personal information via the company's Web site; the car's radio-signal-emitting key fob (using the same RFID technology as the interactive shopping carts) would then trigger personal messages to the car's owner as the vehicle approached a billboard advertising the Mini, such as "'Mary, moving at the speed of justice,' if Mary is a lawyer, or 'Mike, the special of the day is speed,' if Mike is a chef." A Mini USA spokesman told a U.S. radio reporter that the campaign was "about making them feel that this is a brand that really cares about them and really treats them special."[35]

Beyond these specific out-of-home case studies, recent years have seen growth and consolidation, along with new efforts at media measurement across the out-of-home advertising industry. In 2007, ten major U.S. networks formed the Out-of-Home Video Advertising Bureau, and another trade group, the In-Store Marketing Institute, made a deal with the Nielsen ratings service to measure out-of-home audiences for the first time.[36] At a recent U.K. trade seminar titled "2007: Digital Outdoor's Big Bang," one advertising executive predicted that "ultimately, I guess all outdoor will probably be digital in some shape or form," and governmental restrictions in the United States and elsewhere on the number of public billboards within a specific area have encouraged the transformation of traditional billboards into digital signs, which generate six to eight times the revenue per installation.[37] Many of the most striking recent digital signage campaigns have taken place in London and the United Kingdom, where the head of Britain's Outdoor Advertising Agency estimated in early 2007 that digital screen revenue would increase nearly fourfold over the next five years.[38] In 2006 Viacom Outdoor announced plans to install 2,200 large video screens in London's Underground system, reaching 335 million annual viewers, "an advertising impact equal to running a commercial during every episode of *Coronation Street* . . . for a year," according to Tim Beakley, managing director of Viacom Outdoor in Britain.[39] Viacom's London Underground campaign includes digital escalator panels, GPS-equipped bus displays, large ticket hall LCD screens, and "cross-track projections at 150 sites in 24 Tube stations."[40] At the same time, it is important to recognize the modest size of the relatively young digital outdoor market; indeed, the £30 million allocated to Viacom's London Underground campaign alone was equivalent to the revenue of the entire digital screen sector for 2007.[41] One advertising executive told *Revolution*, "As soon as you start thinking about the amount of technology and the amount of sites that need to be digitised to create a significant product, you realise what a huge task it is," and the journal concluded that "even as the momentum builds, it is clear that this is a long-term shift with a long-term time-table."[42]

Underscoring the dream of public ubiquity and interactivity of the out-of-home advertising sector in a very different application, a Dublin-based firm, Adwalker, in 2004 introduced a mobile interactive display consisting of a personal computer, DVD player, digital display, cell phone, and keyboard, all worn by an ambulatory cyborg-looking backpacker (usually female — "Girls are less threatening when approaching people," explained an Adwalker executive; see figure 2).[43] The company's aim, as stated on its Web site, is "to establish Adwalker as a de facto Media standard alongside Television, Radio, Press, Outdoor and Online." The firm, listed on the London Stock Exchange since 2005, offers services in six hundred U.K. rail stations with one billion annual passengers, Premiership Soccer and Rugby venues, seventy British shopping malls, and U.K. British Airport Authority (BAA) airports (with eighty-seven million annual passengers), as well as U.S. locations in Times Square in New York (seventy-seven million annual footfalls) and over two hundred American shopping malls (with over two billion in annual footfalls).[44] One British ad agency executive who contracted with Adwalker in an Irish city center bluntly explained the service's rationale from the agency's perspective: "We want to interrupt people in their daily lives."[45] The History Channel used Adwalker's "brand ambassadors" to promote its *Ice Road Truckers* TV series to forty thousand NASCAR fans at Dover speedway in 2007, where promotional content was downloaded to nearby iPod users on the fly.[46]

Adwalker has been variously described as "wearable media," "sales cyborgs," and even "live Teletubbies without the plush or the girth."[47] *Duty-Free News International* worried that "while Adwalkers with their packs may be construed as having an overbearing presence at the air-

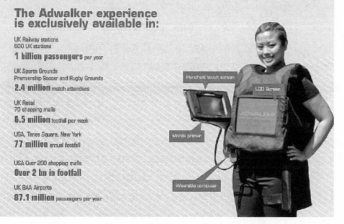

THE ADWALKER EXPERIENCE

LCD Screen: audio visual screens to convey your brand message
Wearable computer: store multiple variations of your brand message
Handheld touch screen: for consumer interaction - competitions, games, data capture
Mobile printer: instant personalised information, ticketing, coupons and consumer reward

The Adwalker experience is exclusively available in:

UK Railway stations
600 UK stations
1 billion passengers per year

UK Sports Grounds
Premiership Soccer and Rugby Grounds
2.4 million match attendees

UK Retail
70 shopping malls
6.5 million footfall per week

USA, Times Square, New York
77 million annual footfall

USA Over 200 shopping malls
Over 2 bn in footfall

UK BAA Airports
87.1 million passengers per year

Handheld touch screen
LCD Screen
Mobile printer
Wearable computer

FIGURE 2 Adwalker has been variously described as "wearable media," "sales cyborgs," and even "live Teletubbies without the plush or the girth." (Adwalker brochure, n.d.)

port," it quoted the company's European sales director's reassurance that "we try to make sure that Adwalkers are friendly and the screen that they wear usually displays the brand they are promoting."[48] A skeptical editor at *Marketing* magazine in the United Kingdom confessed, "my reservation is that I think the national psyche is such that you are not likely to go up to one of these people and start interacting with their body pack."[49] Despite such public security fears, one marketing journal's discussion of Adwalker concluded optimistically that "with most interactive systems still in their infancy, this combination of screen technology and human interface might prove to be one of the most effective—and, ultimately, profitable."[50]

Despite the hopes represented in the diverse array of emerging out-of-home moving image technologies, from scolding shopping carts to electronic sandwich-women, the fundamental questions of sponsor appeal, consumer resistance, and appropriate program forms remain unresolved. The proliferation of public screens provoked journalist Neal

Weinstock to predict skeptically that "eventually, with video screens ubiquitous throughout the public environment, somebody will figure out moderately compelling programming to put on them."[51] As suggested by the title of Weinstock's 2006 survey of the medium ("Digital Signage Fails Over and Over Again Until . . ."), there remain significant pitfalls for would-be leaders of the post-broadcast television industry.

WATCHING THE CONSUMER

Complementing and underwriting the hardware, content, and advertising industries' dreams of mobility, ubiquity, and interactivity are new devices and services to provide comprehensive passive monitoring of media exposure and consumer behavior in and out of the home.[52] As a page-one *New York Times* article argued in 2008, "In advertising these days, the brass ring goes to those who can measure everything—how many people see a particular advertisement, when they see it, who they are. All of that is easy on the Internet, and getting easier in television and print."[53] In July 2006 a U.S. start-up firm called Integrated Media Measurement (IMMI) began offering free cell phones for two years to teenagers and adults up to age fifty-four; the phones automatically capture ten seconds of audio from the user's environment every thirty seconds. The sampled audio is compressed and uploaded continuously to IMMI servers, where the fragments are matched against the digital signatures of advertising-supported, audio-based media, including radio, television, DVRs, game consoles, CDS and DVDS, and cell phones, as well as public sporting venues, cinemas, and concert halls (figure 3). Echoing the marketing mantra of the expanding digital advertising media, the company's CEO boasted, "The simple way to think about us is that we're doing for broadcast media what Google did for the Internet."[54]

The IMMI-supplied phones are also equipped with a so-called Bluetooth beacon, which allows the firm's clients to match commercial message exposure to specific consumer purchases in retail stores (à la Tom Cruise's visit to the Gap in Steven Spielberg's *Minority Report* of 2002); the beacon also indicates whether the sampled audio was captured inside or outside of the home. The firm's ten initial clients included NBC and ESPN, and IMMI has enlisted three thousand users, with plans to add two thousand more and provide the ability to monitor Web page use as well. The young company has already provided a steady stream of striking behavioral nuggets from its research sample, reporting that 10 percent of

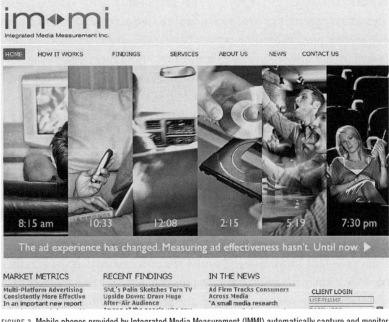

FIGURE 3 Mobile phones provided by Integrated Media Measurement (IMMI) automatically capture and monitor users' media consumption, providing the industry dream of comprehensive passive monitoring of media exposure and consumer behavior in and out of the home. (Screen capture from immi.com.)

the audience of NBC's *Heroes* watched it over the Internet, not on television, a larger figure than the network had anticipated. In the summer of 2007 IMMI drew attention to other early research findings with press releases titled "Parents Set to Watch More Media Than Kids in 2007" and "Democrats Twice as Likely Than Republicans to Use DVRs When Watching Television News."[55]

Responding to critics expressing privacy misgivings, an IMMI executive offered reassurances that the company's cell phone sampling system did not preserve uploaded audio files but merely matched digital fingerprints of overheard commercial messages: "If you're planning a bank robbery while listening to a radio all day long, all we know is what radio station you're listening to," the executive told *The New York Times*. Noting that "many people may find its technology an intolerable intrusion into their privacy," *Technology Review* editor Jason Pontin argued that "IMMI's research could precipitate a turbulent, unpredictable era in broadcasting." Citing the economic havoc Google's advertising model has had upon the traditional print media, he wondered, "Who knows what a similar revolution will bring to broadcast media?"[56] Already the IMMI Web site suggests that traditional advertising-supported broadcasters might alter programming practices based upon the service's more precise viewer monitoring inside and outside the home, promising that the technology would provide answers to questions like "What songs cause radio listeners to change stations? What programming causes TV viewers to change channels?"[57] Mike Gruss, a columnist at the Norfolk *Virginian-Pilot*, described Nielsen's attempt to recruit him to IMMI's new cell-phone measuring service: "'You don't have to do anything,' read a flier on the company's Web site. . . . The online brochure has a great cartoon of people dancing with their cell phones in front of the television." Gruss confessed that he was "not so worried about the loss of privacy or personal data or anything like that. We gave up a lot of that stuff a long time ago," but, he protested, "I can't afford more effective advertising. . . . I don't need the continual temptation of another television show. I don't have the money for a litany of new products. I need more less-effective advertising, like people dancing in front of their televisions with cell phones."[58]

The single-minded pursuit of increasingly dispersed media audiences, together with the appeal of the marketing efficiency of Internet advertising, have only reinforced the long-term trends toward increased advertising exposure and more complete consumer monitoring inside and outside of the home. One recent striking extension of the Internet advertising model into the world of out-of-home media can be seen in competing schemes to enable public billboards to provide real-time surveillance of their audiences; as *Popular Mechanics* explained in 2008, "Internet advertisers have pioneered the 'pay-per-click' advertising model, but now a similar concept is ready to make the jump into the real world, with billboards that watch you watch them."[59] The concept has been independently developed and marketed by three international firms (Xuuk, developed at Canada's Queens University Human Media Laboratory; Paris-based Quividi; and TruMedia, a Jerusalem-based firm whose "technology is an offshoot of surveillance work for the Israeli government," according to *The New York Times*).[60] Xuuk's $999 EyeBox 2 device allows Web-linked advertisers to monitor billboard spectators from up to ten meters away; the company's marketing slogan, "Sell Your Stuff . . . by the Eyeball," contrasts with the slightly more ominous marketing tag from TruMedia: "Every Face Counts." While the EyeBox 2 device merely counts spectators and notes dwell time in front of the billboard, both the Quividi and TruMedia devices analyze facial features to assess spectator gender and age. Via a single standard webcam, Quividi provides continuous real-time measures of opportunities to see, number of actual viewers, attention time, presence time, position, and demographics of anyone located in front of any technologically equipped public billboard; *The New York Times* reported that "so far the companies are not using race as a parameter, but they say that they can and will soon."[61] Quividi, which started up in 2006, has operated demonstration projects in Ikea stores in Europe, in McDonald's restaurants in Singapore, on street billboards near Columbus Circle in Manhattan, and in a commuter train station in Philadelphia. Again invoking the ideal of Internet advertising efficiency, *Wired* magazine explained that "Until now, methods of measuring the traffic and reach of billboards and plasma displays have been limited to human-conducted site surveys using notepads and tally-counters. . . . [The new devices promised] Google-like measurement metrics that real-world advertisers could only dream about until recently."[62]

All three firms have taken pains to address privacy concerns, assuring skeptics that, like IMMI's cell phone devices, only quantitative templates, not raw recordings, are collected. Xuuk's founder reassured *Newsweek* magazine in 2007 that "people have to get used to technologies. . . . I think we'll look at this very differently in 10 years' time."[63] However, some observers of the new surveillance technology remained troubled. Journalist Vinay Menon wrote in the *Toronto Star* in June 2008 that "the long-standing relationship between humans and billboards used to be clear: We stared at them. They did not stare at us. But . . . this is about to change."[64] A senior staff attorney for the Electronic Frontier Foundation argued that "a big part of why it's accepted is that people don't know about it. . . . You could make them conspicuous . . . but nobody really wants to do that because the more people know about it, the more it may freak them out or they may attempt to avoid it."[65]

Shortly after its Columbus Circle Quividi-equipped billboard installation, A&E received even greater press attention from another technologically advanced billboard application in Manhattan, this one using a device that beams narrowly focused ultrasonic audio waves inaudible to anyone outside the targeted area. The *Gazette* of Montreal explained that the technology works by beaming waves of sound at a frequency that is undetectable by the human ear. The waves continue until they smash into an object such as a person's body. The waves then slow, mix, and recreate the original audio broadcast. If the person steps out of the waves, they are no longer obstructed and they are rendered inaudible. Using the technology, marketers can target an audio message at one person in a crowd of hundreds, leaving everyone around that person unaware.[66] Holosonics Inc., maker of the so-called Audio Spotlight, proudly explained the installation's operation and rationale in a press release in December 2007 aimed at potential advertisers: "In the sea of billboards and advertising that is Manhattan, it is becoming increasingly difficult to send a message to the public. . . . Mounted above the billboard, the system projects an isolated beam of sound down onto a targeted area of the sidewalk—from seven stories up! . . . Passersby entering the beam hear the sound immediately, and very clearly, which captures their attention. This is an extremely effective method of making your message stand out in a sea of advertising."[67]

The 2007 Holosonics billboard in Manhattan's Soho neighborhood was part of a $5 million advertising campaign for A&E's supernatural-themed television series *Paranormal*; the audio portion consisted of a woman's voice whispering, "Who's there? Who's there?" and, after a pause, "It's not your imagination." As Holosonics founder and president Joe Pompei boasted to the press, "The whole point of it was to be creepy. . . . It does sound like it's next to you or inside your head. But that's truly an illusion your ears create."[68]

As with the responses to the billboards-that-look-back technology launched around the same time, the uncanny ability to beam individual audio messages into public crowds provoked concern and scorn from critics in the press. The media Web site *Gawker* posted an account of the Soho billboard under the headline "Schizophrenia Is the New Ad Gimmick," which wondered "How soon will it be until in addition to the Do-Not-Call list, we'll have a 'Do Not Beam Commercial Messages into My Head' list?"[69] The original post provoked a number of striking reactions online; one reader who had experienced the Soho billboard noted that "one thing the article fails to mention is that the hypersonic sound beams actually have a tactile effect on the body as well. . . . It literally felt like I got felt-up by the billboard lady while she was whispering wierd [sic] nothings into my ear. Pretty cool for an ad."[70] Another *Gawker* reader worried, "I imagine the creative brainiacs who came up with this idea don't realize that about 10% of New York City pedestrians are marginally medicated paranoid schizophrenics who can barely handle stimulation like blinking traffic lights. I can't wait until they start reacting en masse to REAL fake voices in their heads. It'll make the zombie invasion look like your average rush hour."[71] A third *Gawker* reader joined the Holosonics billboard thread to offer reassurance to those concerned about the potential danger of the otherworldly audio advertising media with, "Jeeze. Relax, people. Nothing a tinfoil hat can't handle."[72]

THE GOOGLE MODEL

Beyond the advertising industry's perennial struggle to break out of its self-created cacophony and clutter, the disorderly and sometimes improbable collection of emerging out-of-home moving image and audio technologies is united by the twin goals of continuous consumer surveillance and advertising ubiquity. Google's ability to deliver context-sensitive advertising messages linked to an individual user's search terms or e-mail text continues to inspire attempts to extend the goals of targeting and accountability to all media, old and new. Many within the computing industry, from major players like Microsoft and large Internet service providers (ISPs) to small start-up firms, are feverishly working to replicate Google's model across emerging out-of-home media. For example, at the same trade conference in May 2008 where Microsoft announced plans for its interactive shopping carts, the company also unveiled plans to extend display advertising capabilities to handheld devices via its Windows Live Messenger and Windows Live Hotmail services. This included ongoing field tests of "engagement mapping," which "allows firms to track back through all previous interactions consumers have had with advertising and marketing messages across multiple sites and channels culminating in the sale."[73] Microsoft also described two new projects from adLabs, its new "digital advertising technology incubator," including "'LifeStages,' a new technology that segments users of Windows Live Spaces into different life stages—for instance, recent college graduates or newlyweds—based on their public blog entries or photo captions," and the use of speech recognition software to deliver customized advertisements based upon the video clips users are watching.[74] In another application of the Google model, in late 2007 Silicon Valley start-up firm Pudding Media began offering free voice over Internet protocol (VOIP) telephone service in exchange for displaying on-screen advertisements tailored to the content of the user's conversations monitored by the service.[75]

These and other recent efforts to extend Google's targeted advertising model have encountered resistance from industry observers and public officials. One recent application, called "deep packet inspection," allows Internet service providers to sell advertisements based upon all forms of individual customer online activity—"every Web page visited, every e-mail sent and every search query entered," according to *The Washington Post*.[76] In mid-2008 approximately one hundred thousand U.S. customers of several smaller ISPs were already subject to such surveillance, and ISPS serving 10 percent of American subscribers had considered or tested the service.[77] *The New York Times* earlier reported that NebuAd, the firm brokering the targeted ads in the United States, offered participating ISPS several dollars per subscriber a month.[78] At the same time, *The Economist* reported that Britain's three largest ISPS (accounting for approximately 70 percent of the national market) had partnered with a technology company to introduce the application, "offering the prospect of working out what web surfers are thinking, perhaps even before they know themselves." It is clear that many firms within and beyond the computing industry have coveted Google's extraordinary economic success.[79]

However, in June 2008, after consultations with elected officials in Washington, Charter Communications, the nation's fourth-largest ISP, abruptly suspended plans to test the surveillance technology in four U.S. cities. Representative Edward J. Markey, chairman of the House Energy and Commerce Subcommittee on Telecommunications and the Internet, responded to the firm's decision by telling *The Washington Post*, "The fact is that it would have allowed profiling of an individual—where they were going and what they were doing online, and there was no guarantee that this information could not ultimately be compromised. . . . They made the right decision in halting their test."[80] Jeff Chester, director of the Center for Digital Democracy, told the *Post*, "Charter isn't a fool— they got the message." Its proposal, according to Chester, "crossed a digital line in the sand that up till now hadn't been challenged. Congress had accepted targeted Internet marketing, but the fact that ISPs were going to do it clearly had the potential of creating a firestorm."[81]

Despite talk of digital lines in the sand, debates over the appropriate limits of advertising in domestic and public spaces clearly did not begin with the recent proliferation of digital tools of audience surveillance and advertising display. Indeed, as Raymond Williams noted in 1960, public complaints that advertisers "have gone about as far as they can go" date back at least to the mid-eighteenth century.[82] However, to some observers, contemporary digital technologies have brought with them a qualitative shift in the role of advertising. As media critic Michael Lewis concluded in 2000, "The process of getting inside a consumer's mind so that you can then get inside his wallet sounds invasive, and perhaps it is. But it's nothing personal."[83] For Lewis, the decline of the mass media and the mass market spelled the end of "Market Man" himself. Devices like TiVo allow advertisers to match marketing plans to individual viewing behavior, not traditional demographic categories.

Via diverse and increasingly ingenious technical means, advertisers have extended their ability to monitor consumer behavior, from computer keystrokes to gazes on public street corners, and the feedback effect of such individually tailored advertising messages on consumer activity and identity is unknown. For example, one of the unexpected effects of Pudding Media's voice recognition system, which delivered advertisements matched to the content of users' VOIP phone conversations, was, according to the company's CEO, that the screen ads began to determine the course of the conversation itself: "The conversation was actually changing based on what was on the screen. . . . Our ability to influence the conversation was remarkable."[84] Michael Lewis raised the larger question in 2000: "What happens to people when the market view of them is different from the one they have of themselves? Do they come to see themselves as the market sees them? . . . Will they come to think of themselves not as white or young or female but as Positivists or Relativists or whatever other types get dreamed up in response to the data generated by the black boxes?"[85]

William Uricchio has noted the growing sophistication and pervasiveness of adaptive intelligent agents that mediate the television viewer's negotiation of the flood of video programming available in the home. Such digital gatekeepers and artificial intelligence devices (marketed as the "Television Fairy" in Germany) conjure up an implicit psychic and social avatar continuously reconstituted by the sum total of the users' every media interaction.[86] Given the expanding subtlety and pervasiveness of such surveillance regimes in public and private spaces alike, the urgent policy questions become who will design the architecture of these new identities and determine the ends to which they are put.

Collectively the emerging technologies of digital display and surveillance reposit the ways in which electronic communications traverse and define the spaces of production and consumption, of the public and the private. The new technology enables the market to redefine the consumer along significantly different lines. Instead of grouping him according to observable traits over which he has little or no control—age, race, gender, and so on—the new market will know him by the decisions he has made about how to spend his time, each and every moment of which is recorded by his black box. Media scholars have been intensely concerned with these issues since Raymond Williams developed the concept of "mobile privatization" in the 1970s in relation to early broadcasting.[87] For example, cultural studies scholars in the 1990s considered the ways in which the Sony Walkman portable music player made it possible for users to carve out a privatized media sphere within public space.[88] However, as Mark Andrejevic argues, the ongoing refinement of the instruments of monitored mobility represent a deepening of the logic of industrial production and the consumer society, not their refutation.[89]

While we are considering the implications for public policy and political economy of the expanding regimes of mobilized media consumption and surveillance, it is important to remember that the artifacts and experiences constituting the electronic media have always been powerful tools in the construction of personal and social identities, long associated with the uncanny and magical as much as the functional and quotidian.[90] The elusive psychic meanings of such everyday public encounters with digital media devices will undoubtedly help determine the fortunes of the various business and regulatory models, textual forms, and social practices associated with new digital media. In the meantime, the most urgent questions facing both leaders of the broadcast television industry and scholars in the only recently consolidated field of television studies will revolve around the place of traditional domestic television—with all its characteristic program forms, viewing habits, and industry practices—in this new world of mobilized screens and fragmented audiences.

NOTES

1. On the reception of television beyond the domestic space, see Anna McCarthy, *Ambient Television: Visual Culture and Public Space* (Durham, N.C.: Duke University Press, 2001).

2. Richard Pérez-Peña, "Papers Facing Worst Year for Ad Revenue," *New York Times*, June 23, 2008, c3.

3. Eric Pfanner, "Ad Leaders See Web's Threat and Promise," *New York Times*, June 23, 2008, c3.

4. Quoted in Fiona Williams, "4K Rules, OK," *Encore Magazine* (Australia), June 1, 2006, n.p.

5. Lee Alan Hill, "Content Delivery a Big-Draw Topic," *Television Week*, April 24, 2006, 29.

6. S. D. Katz, D. W. Leitner, Dan Ochiva, and Jan Ozer, "NAB 2006," *Millimeter*, June 1, 2006, 45.

7. Quoted in Alice Z. Cuneo, "Consumer Electronics Show Draws Full House; 140,000 Swarm Sin City to Ogle . . . Content, Not Just Gadgets and Gizmos," *Advertising Age*, January 15, 2007, 26.

8. Ibid.

9. Ibid.

10. David Keene, "What Business Are We In?" *Rental and Staging Systems*, May 1, 2006, 4.

11. Chris Carr, director of video markets at Masergy Communications, quoted in "A Technology Marriage Made in Heaven," *Computer Reseller News UK*, August 28, 2006.

12. Ibid.

13. "Microsoft Highlights Innovation, Growth and Momentum at Advance08 Event," found at http://www.microsoft.com.

14. As the Web site for Technicolor's digital signage services promises, "Any platform. Any Media. Anywhere"; http://www.technicolor.com/Cultures/En-Us/OutOfHomeMedia (accessed July 31, 2008).

15. David Marc, "What Was Broadcasting?" Reprinted in *Television: The Critical View*, ed. Horace Newcomb, 6th ed. (New York: Oxford University Press, 2000), 640, 629.

16. See William Boddy, *New Media and Popular Imagination: Launching Radio, Television, and Digital Media in the United States* (Oxford: Oxford University Press, 2004), esp. ch. 5.

17. Michael Lewis, "Boom Box: The End of the Mass Market," *New York Times Magazine*, August 20, 2000. Andreessen quoted in Lewis.

18. Ibid.

19. Profitable Channels, *Adding Out-of-Home Digital Advertising Networks to the Marketing and Media Mix*, August 2006; http://www.profitablechannels.com/document.

20. CBS Outernet, available at http://www.cbsouternet.com/company.

21. Ibid.

22. Quoted in Anthony Bianco, "The Vanishing Mass Market," *Business Week*, no. 3891 (July 12, 2004): 60.

23. Brian Steinberg, "NBC Readies New Upfront as Video Goes Out-of-Home," *Advertising Age*, January 7, 2008.

24. Louise Story, "Away from Home, TV Ads Are Inescapable," *New York Times*, March 2, 2007.

25. Neal Weinstock, "Digital Signage Fails Over and Over Again Until . . ." *Television Broadcast*, July 1, 2006, 44.

26. "Forecast 2007: Out-of-Home," mediaweek.com, January 1, 2007.

27. Ronald I. Gross, "Retail Signage Primer," *Sound and Video Contractor*, December 1, 2006, 52.

28. Quoted in Louise Story, "Away from Home, TV Ads Are Inescapable," *New York Times*, March 2, 2007.

29. Adspace Mail Network, available at http://www.adspacenetworks.com/advertise_research.php.

30. Previously available at http://www.captivate.com/why-captivate/why-captivate.asp (accessed July 31, 2008).

31. Jeremy Olshan, "Hey, Check Out Smart Carts," *New York Post*, January 15, 2008.

32. Jack Neff, "A Shopping-Cart-Ad Plan That Might Actually Work," *Advertising Age*, February 5, 2007, 10.

33. Ibid.

34. Jeremy Olshan, "Hey, Check Out Smart Carts," *New York Post*, January 15, 2008.

35. "Mini's Billboards Zoom in on Drivers," *Marketplace* radio program, January 29, 2007; transcript available at http://marketplace.publicradio.org.

36. Louise Story, "Away from Home, TV Ads Are Inescapable," *New York Times*, March 2, 2007.

37. "Forecast 2007: Out-of-Home," mediaweek.com, January 1, 2007.

38. Darren Davidson, "Out-of-Home Advertising Set for Digital Boost in 2007," *Brand Republic News Releases*, January 19, 2007.

39. Quoted in Eric Pfanner, "Digital Video for the Tube," *International Herald Tribune*, August 14, 2006, 8.

40. "Long Road for the Great Outdoors," *Revolution*, February 1, 2007, 40.

41. Ibid.

42. Ibid.

43. Andrew Cawte, chief executive of Adwalker Asia Pacific, quoted in Sidney Luk, "Batteries Included with Next Generation of Walking Advertisements," *South China Morning Post*, November 17, 2005, 4.

44. Available at http://www.adwalker.com.

45. Quoted in Catherine O'Mahony, "New-Tech Walking Ads on PCs Will Woo the Voters," *Sunday Business Post*, May 30, 2004.

46. Lunda Haugsted, "History Pounds the Pavement," *Multichannel News*, July 9, 2007, 16.

47. The Teletubbies reference is found in Diane Holloway, "They Walk among Us, Bellies Aglow with Promos for cw," *Austin American-Statesman*, August 22, 2006, E1.

48. In Tina Milton, "The Digital Board Walk: Interactive Digital Sandwich Boards Are Touted as the Advertising Media of the Future," *Duty-Free News International*, October 15, 2006, 183.

49. On the national psyche, Jeremy Lee, the news editor for *Marketing* magazine, is quoted in Fergus Sheppard, "These People Really Are Walking Advertisements," *Scotsman*, July 27, 2006, 40.

50. "Screen Media—Location, Location, Location?" *Promotions and Incentive*, January 1, 2007, 4.

51. Neal Weinstock, "Digital Signage Fails Over and Over Again Until . . . ." *Television Broadcast*, July 1, 2006, 44.

52. On the implications of emerging forms of media surveillance, see Mark Andrejevic, "The Work of Being Watched: Interactive Media and the Exploitation of Self-Disclosure," *Critical Studies in Mass Communication* 19, no. 2 (2002): 230–48.

53. Stephanie Clifford, "Billboards That Look Back," *New York Times*, May 31, 2008, 1.

54. Quoted in Jason Pontin, "Are Those Commercials Working? Just Listen," *New York Times*, September 9, 2007, c4.

55. See the press release available at http://www.immi.com/pdfs/DVR.pdf.

56. Jason Pontin, "Are Those Commercials Working? Just Listen," *New York Times*, September 9, 2007, c4.

57. IMMI information about "How It Works" available at http://www.immi.com.

58. Mike Gruss, "Effective Advertising Campaigns Can Come at a Price," *Virginian-Pilot*, August 6, 2007, E1.

59. Alex Hutchinson, "10 Tech Concepts You Need to Know for 2008," *Popular Mechanics*, January 2008.

60. Charles Mandel, "Eye-Catching Ad Campaign? Prove It," *Globe and Mail*, June 28, 2007, B9; Stephanie Clifford, "Billboards That Look Back," *New York Times*, May 31, 2008, 1.

61. Stephanie Clifford, "Billboards That Look Back," *New York Times*, May 31, 2008, 1.

62. Dan Skeen, "Eye-Tracking Devices Let Billboards Know When You Look at Them," *Wired*, June 12, 2007; http://www.wired.com.

63. Quoted in Jenna Crombis, "Eyeball-Tracking Signs Bring Click-Counting Out of Doors," *Newsweek*, November 26, 2007.

64. Vinay Menon, "Billboard Puts Readers on the Spot," *Toronto Star*, June 5, 2008, A2.

65. Quoted in Stephanie Clifford, "Billboards That Look Back," *New York Times*, May 31, 2008, 1.

66. Vito Pilieci, "Sound Is Getting Personal: 'Hypersonic' Beam Heard only by Target," *Gazette*, May 12, 2008, A11.

67. Holosonics, Inc., "A&E's Manhattan Billboard Whispers at Passersby with the Audio Spotlight," press release, December 10, 2007; http://www.holosonics.com/PR_AE.html.

68. Quoted in Andrew Chung, "Your Ad Here; and Here and Here . . . ," *Toronto Star*, February 17, 2008, D1.

69. Joshua Stein, "Schizophrenia Is the New Ad Gimmick," *Gawker*, December 2007; http://gawker.com/news/the-future/schizophrenia-is-the-new-ad-gimmick-329133.php.

70. Poolboy300, comment on "Schizophrenia Is the New Ad Gimmick," *Gawker*, comment posted February 19, 2008; URL in note 69.

71. SarahHeartburn, comment on "Schizophrenia Is the New Ad Gimmick," *Gawker*, comment posted December 4, 2007; URL in note 69.

72. Adorkable, comment on "Schizophrenia Is the New Ad Gimmick," *Gawker*, comment posted December 4, 2007; URL in note 69.

73. "Microsoft Highlights Innovation, Growth and Momentum at Advance08 Event."

74. Ibid.

75. On Pudding Media's plans, see Louise Story, "Company Will Monitor Calls to Tailor Ads," *New York Times*, September 24, 2007; Henry Blodget, "Today's Terrible Idea: Pudding Media," *Silicon Alley Insider*, September 24, 2007; http://www.alleyinsider.com/2007/09/todays-terrible.html.

76. Peter Whoriskey, "Internet Provider Halts Plan to Track, Sell Users' Surfing Data," *Washington Post*, June 25, 2008, D1.

77. Ibid.

78. Saul Hansell, "Charter Will Monitor Customers' Web Surfing to Target Ads," *New York Times*, May 14, 2008.

79. "Watch While You Surf," *The Economist*, June 5, 2008.

80. Quoted in Peter Whoriskey, "Internet Provider Halts Plan to Track, Sell Users' Surfing Data," *Washington Post*, June 25, 2008, D1.

81. Ibid.

82. Raymond Williams, "Advertising: The Magic System," in Williams, *Problems in Materialism and Culture* (London: Verson, 1980), 172; for a discussion of debates over advertising limits in other recent media contexts, see Boddy, *New Media and Popular Imagination*.

83. Michael Lewis, "Boom Box: The End of the Mass Market," *New York Times Magazine*, August 20, 2000.

84. Louise Story, "Company Will Monitor Calls to Tailor Ads," *New York Times*, September 24, 2007.

85. Michael Lewis, "Boom Box: The End of the Mass Market," *New York Times Magazine*, August 20, 2000.

86. William Uricchio, "Television's Next Generation: Technology/Interface Culture/Flow," in Spigel and Olsson, *Television after TV*, 163–82.

87. Raymond Williams, *Television: Technology and Cultural Form* (London: Routledge, 1992 [1975]).

88. See Rey Chow, "Listening Otherwise, Music Miniaturized: A Different Type of Question about Revolution," in *Doing Cultural Studies: The Case of the Sony Walkman*, ed. Paul du Gay et al. (Thousand Oaks, Calif.: Sage, 1997), 135–40.

89. Mark Andrejevic, "Tracing Space: Monitored Mobility in the Era of Mass Customization," *Space and Culture* 6, no. 2 (2003): 136.

90. On the associations of electronic media and the uncanny, see Jeffrey Sconce, *Haunted Media: Electronic Presence from Telegraphy to Television* (Durham, N.C.: Duke University Press, 2000), and Boddy, *New Media and Popular Imagination*.

PART 2   PRODUCTION STRATEGIES IN
THE DIGITAL LANDSCAPE

ROBERTA PEARSON

CULT TELEVISION AS DIGITAL TELEVISION'S CUTTING EDGE

Some New Yorkers may first have seen Captain Kirk not on a television screen but in an advertisement for a television. On Wednesday, August 24, 1966, the day before *Star Trek*'s first-ever TV appearance as part of an NBC fall season preview night, *The New York Times* ran an advertisement that touted three of the "full color" network's new shows and the new Magnavox color television, available from Macy's department store (see figure 1). *Tarzan* would deliver tigers, elephants, and Cheetah the Chimp; *The Hero* would feature an actor smoothly gunning down the bad guys on a movie set; and *Star Trek* would show "exciting missions to worlds beyond imagination." The twenty-one–inch Magnavox color TV consolette would deliver a "265 sq. in. viewable area," "automatic degausser," and "automatic gain control," all for the price of $459.50 (worth $2,993.92 in 2007).[1] A montage photo included images of all three new series, but the screen on the product photo showed a medium close-up of William Shatner as the heroic *Enterprise* captain.[2] On April 22, 1968, two months after NBC responded to fan protests by renewing *Star Trek* for a third season, *The New York Times* ran another Macy's advertisement mentioning the program: "Imagine yourself luxuriating in a bath of bubbles, martini in hand, television tuned into *Star Trek*."[3] This might sound "out of this world," but the new Pearlwick hamper, combining clothes bin, built-in TV, radio, clock, telephone, bar, book compartment, electric razor, and jewel hide-

FIGURE 1 Some New Yorkers may have encountered Captain Kirk not on television but in an advertisement *for* television. (*New York Times*, August 24, 1966, 14.)

away, would make all this possible for a mere thousand dollars ($6,146.84 in 2007).[4]

Although its signature Peacock debuted in 1956, NBC did not become the "full color" network until 1965, at a time when the high cost of color receivers kept ownership to around 6 percent of American families.[5] Penetration figures for Pearlwick hampers aren't available, but I think we can safely assume that even fewer than 6 percent of American families could have afforded, or would have wanted, a bathroom entertainment center featuring a "jewel hideaway." Nevertheless, Macy's had chosen its demographics well, aiming both advertisements at well-educated and affluent *New York Times* readers inclined to be technologically savvy early adopters and to watch shows such as *Star Trek*, subsequently labeled cult television. Associations among desirable demographics, cult television, and technology drive the multiplatform distribution and promotion strategies of TVIII, but these two advertisements show that TVI also forged such connections.

The distinctions among TVI, TVII, and TVIII rest broadly on notions of channel scarcity versus channel abundance and of broadcasting to a mass audience versus narrowcasting to niche audiences. In the United States, TVI, dating from the mid-1950s to the early 1980s, is the era of channel scarcity, the mass audience, and three-network hegemony. TVII, dating from roughly the early 1980s to the late 1990s, is the era of channel/network expansion, quality television, and network branding strategies. TVIII, dating from the late 1990s to the present, is the era of proliferating digital distribution platforms, further audience fragmentation, and, as Rogers, Epstein, and Reeves suggest, a shift from second-order to first-order commodity relations.[6]

This consensual periodization marks the coming of age of television studies; like film scholars, we can now situate texts, producers, and audiences within their respective industrial contexts. But like film scholars, we must be aware of the dangers of a teleological perspective that posits a linear historical process with clear demarcations between eras. Matt Hills makes a similar point when he says that "discussions of 'TVIII' (or other rival periodisations) [are] themselves working to foreclose and delimit 'TVI' and 'TVII' as stable discursive objects."[7] Useful as they may be, periodizations cannot contain history's multiple complexities and contradictions, which can be fully understood only through a detailed analysis of the historical archive. As my opening paragraphs indicate, many of the characteristics we now associate with TVIII can be seen, in at least nascent form, in TVI. This chapter uses cult television, focusing on *Star Trek* as a case study, to reveal the complexities of the industrial transformations of American television from TVI to TVII to TVIII. I explore, in particular, three factors: first, the producer brand; second, niche audiences; and third, multiple channels, all of which are seen as characteristic of TVII and TVIII but all of which have roots in TVI.

PRODUCER BRAND

Channel proliferation and audience fragmentation have led to a strong emphasis on the branding of networks in TVII and TVIII.[8] As I have argued elsewhere, these factors have also led to increased significance of the producer brand, as the move from a flow to file model causes audiences to pay less attention to distributors and more attention to content.[9] J. J. Abrams, Chris Carter, Steven Bochco, David E. Kelley, Aaron Sorkin, and other writer-producers associated with quality/cult television have become household names, at least in households of dedicated television watchers, their imprimatur lending their products distinction in a crowded field. But in the sixties, despite the fact that American television has always been considered the producers' medium (in contrast to u.k. television, in which the writer has often had a controlling hand), the conventional wisdom has it that TVI producers kept a low public profile; it was the shows and the studios that mattered, not the show runners. Frank La Tourette, in his foreword to Muriel Cantor's 1971 book, *The Hollywood TV Producer: His Work and His Audience*, said the television producer "prefers to turn the publicity spotlight away from himself so that it may shine fully on the program or the series he produces. He welcomes a secondary role and would embrace even anonymity if that would help his program achieve a higher Nielsen rating."[10] But at least two TVI producers, Rod Serling and Gene Roddenberry, sought higher Nielsen ratings by turning the spotlight—and in Serling's case even the camera—on themselves.[11] Their celebrity status, to reference P. David Marshall, served to structure meaning, crystallize ideological positions, and provide "a sense and coherence in a culture. . . . The concept of the celebrity is best defined as a *system* for valorizing meaning and communication."[12] Both Serling and Roddenberry occupied similar ideological positions, contrasting their artistic integrity and social conscience with the commercial degradation of mainstream television, in so doing establishing a template for the creators and show runners of the future.

Serling transformed himself from a writer of early television's New York–based live anthology formats to writer-producer of TVI's Los Angeles–based filmed episodic formats. Serling, together with Paddy Chayevsky and Reginald Rose, was one of the best-known writers of the so-called Golden Age of live television, winner of three Emmy awards for his scripts for *Patterns*, *Requiem for a Heavyweight*, and *The Comedian*. The pages of *The New York Times* attest to his reputation among the East Coast elite. In April 1956, an article titled "Author Who Arrived" said that Serling had sold over one hundred scripts in the past six years.[13] In November 1957, Serling himself penned a lengthy article for the *Times* magazine, in which, as the subhead put it, "A prize-winning video writer states the case for live television but does not rule out the possibility of the filmed show as an art form."[14] Serling stressed the connection between artistry and public recognition: "The writer of the filmed television play was never and is not now an identifiable name in terms of the audience. This is in sharp contrast to the New York television writer who has been granted an identity, an importance and a respect second only to the legitimate playwright."[15]

Serling himself was about to defect to canned drama but wished to retain the public recognition, importance, and respect he had garnered from the live drama by publicly asserting his control of the new project. Less than two months after his article appeared, the *Times* announced that Serling, "a leading exponent of live television," was "preparing to co-produce and write a filmed television series in association with the Columbia Broadcasting System."[16] An article from March 1959 gave further details, saying that the new series would be called *The Twilight Zone*, noting that "Mr. Serling will write at least half the scripts and possibly more" and that "an executive producer for the show will be appointed by cbs."[17] Later that year, however, the *Times* ran an article titled "A Playwright at the Controls." Serling said, "I'll have a say in taste and policy. . . . Nobody will be able to change the lines by going to the executive producer, because I am the executive producer." But Serling, well known as an outspoken critic of sponsor censorship, added, "I'm not writing any material that lies in the danger zone. There won't be anything controversial in the new series."[18]

Serling assumed a similarly conciliatory attitude in a televised interview with Mike Wallace (on cbs of course). His decision to leave live television in favor of *The Twilight Zone* resulted, he said, from no longer being willing "to battle sponsors and agencies. . . . I don't want to have to compromise all the time, which in essence is what the tv writer does if he wants to put on controversial themes." But Serling emphasized that abandonment of the live drama didn't entail abandonment of artistic integrity. "We [the sponsor and Serling] have a good working relationship wherein with questions of taste, questions of the art form itself, questions of drama, I'm the judge. In 18 scripts we have had one line changed." Conflicts with the sponsor were unlikely, however, because *The Twilight Zone* was "strictly for entertainment. Because [the shows] deal in the areas of the imagination and of fantasy and of science fiction, there's no opportunity to cop a plea or chop an ax or anything."[19] As we now know, while allaying sponsor concerns by dismissing *The Twilight Zone* as "strictly entertainment," Serling used the fantasy/science fiction format to address many of the most controversial issues of the 1960s—prejudice, the Cold War, individual conscience, and the like. Post–*Twilight Zone*, Serling, no longer having to placate sponsors, was free to admit this. "I found that it was alright to have Martians saying things Democrats and Republicans could never say."[20] In retrospect, he reclaimed the mantle of angry young man and staunch opponent of censorship shed for a time to accommodate the realpolitik of TV I. Those metaphoric Martians did Serling a favor as, in an ironic twist worthy of one of his own scripts, the public identity he so craved now rests securely on the canned rather than the live drama. Only television historians remember *Requiem for a Heavyweight*, but *Twilight Zone* fans old and new still happily recount their favorite episodes. Serling's producer brand as perfectly suits the sensibilities of TV III as it seemed alien to those of TV I.

In contrast, Gene Roddenberry had no public reputation to lose or preserve when he created *Star Trek*, the show that would enshrine him alongside Serling in the pantheon of cult television gods.[21] Roddenberry started his television career as a freelance writer in the mid-1950s before serving as head writer on CBS's *Have Gun, Will Travel*. In 1963, he formed his own company, Norway Productions, and produced *The Lieutenant* for ABC. Roddenberry, like most TV I writers and producers, remained unknown outside the industry, his only mention in *The New York Times* in this period being a credit for his *Kaiser Aluminum Hour* script, "So Short a Season," a "drama of the old West."[22] But *Star Trek*, and its creator's alleged zeal for self-publicity, would give Roddenberry a public reputation and a fan base to rival, and eventually surpass, Serling's; in 1985 the former became the first television writer to be honored with a star on the Hollywood Walk of Fame, while the latter, despite his preeminence during the Golden Age, had to wait another three years for similar recognition.

Roddenberry, or Desilu/Paramount/NBC publicists, or some combination thereof, immediately began crafting the *Star Trek* myth, seeking cultural legitimacy through many tactics. Claims to scientific accuracy seemed intended to liberate *Trek* from the kiddie-TV associations of most previous televised science fiction. The show's initial publicity foregrounded Roddenberry's consultations with personnel from the Rand Corporation, NASA, and Caltech to obtain the latest scientific opinions on space travel and spacesuit/starship design.[23] At the end of the show's first season, *The Los Angeles Times* reported that Roddenberry would attend formal presentation ceremonies at the Smithsonian Institution to donate the pilot, still pictures, and descriptive material that the institution had requested.[24] By the end of the second season, Roddenberry was claiming that "over a hundred high school science classes assign *Star Trek* as credit" and that "even educational journals ask students to analyze the show."[25]

Publicity also stressed psychological realism, implicitly contrasting *Trek*'s realist characters with its kiddie-TV predecessors' cardboard cutouts. At the start of the second season, Burt Prolutsky wrote in *The New York Times* that "Science fiction has been notably unsuccessful on TV. [*Star Trek*'s] success must be attributed to creator-producer Roddenberry and his insistence on the credibility factor. For this reason, he urges his writers not to get too wrapped up in the wonder of it all. 'People aren't going to stop eating, sleeping or getting dressed in a few hundred years. We're trying to imagine . . . what they'll most likely be eating or thinking or wearing.'"[26] Like Prolutsky, many critics spoke of *Trek* in terms now associated with quality television. For example, reporting that local station KCOP had been the first to acquire *Trek* syndication rights, Don Page of *The Los Angeles Times* referred to "this beautifully mounted science-fiction drama."[27]

Claims for social relevance also contrasted *Star Trek* with mainstream television, which, as Serling had constantly pointed out, shied away from controversy for fear of offending sponsors. Said Roddenberry in that second-season *New York Times* article, "The point we'd like to bring home is that we on earth have the choice of living together or dying together." The *Times* noted that Roddenberry would "attempt to stress this point by introducing . . . a Russian character as a crewman aboard the ship" (this at the height of the Cold War).[28] Less battle-scarred and thus perhaps less wary than Serling, Roddenberry made explicit *Trek*'s metaphoric interrogation of contemporary mores. In another article after the end of the show's first season (and at the height of the Vietnam War), *The Los Angeles Times* noted that "Because *Star Trek* takes place in the 21st century [*sic*], Roddenberry finds it easier to take on subject matter which, if it were pinned on contemporary characters and situations, would probably be tossed out by the network as too controversial. For example, war between the planets on *Star Trek* can be condemned. Here on earth in 1967, TV would rather not make a comment on war."[29] On that same date, the paper featured an interview with Roddenberry, quoting him as saying, "We did shows last year about sex, bigotry, unionism, racism and religion. We even did one on Vietnam—disguised of course." The reporter's comments indicate the contemporary status of mainstream, commercial television even in its "hometown" newspaper. "You are justifiably surmising that we were talking with the producer of an educational or closed-circuit TV project or an experimental lab in some small eastern university. . . . [But Roddenberry] was discussing stories he released over normally gutless, non-commital, play-it-safe, fun-and-games commercial television."[30]

This comment reflects a culturally prevalent assessment of television in the 1960s, echoing as it does FCC commissioner Newton Minow's famous characterization of the medium as a "vast wasteland." Cultural critics like Minow and Serling routinely criticized the dominant medium's timidity and sameness. Opposition to the putatively gutless mainstream, a hallmark of cult and quality television in TVII and TVIII, was a significant aspect of Roddenberry's producer brand at the height of TVI. After Star Trek's cancellation, Roddenberry assiduously cultivated the image of himself as valiant David against NBC's oppressive Goliath. In 1973, The Los Angeles Times reported that Roddenberry "still grows darkly angry at NBC's cavalier treatment of Star Trek."[31] His ingenious end-runs around network censorship figured prominently into his narrative. In the run-up to the release of Star Trek: The Motion Picture (Robert Wise, 1979), the first of the Trek feature films, The New York Times once more interviewed Roddenberry. "TV was so tightly censored that science fiction was the only way to escape the taboos in politics, religion or anything else that was considered controversial. I thought of 'Star Trek' as a 'Gulliver's Travels.'"[32]

Some have called into question Roddenberry's denigration of NBC. Herbert Solow, vice president of production at Desilu and closely involved in the development and production of Star Trek, defended the network in an interview in 2005, asserting that it had done everything possible to support what was, by the standards of the times, an underperforming series: "NBC should be applauded. . . . I feel that NBC has been totally misjudged and maligned by Star Trek fans. . . . Gene set about making NBC the heavy, the villain with regards to everything: schedule, ratings, program practices, publicity, etc., thus playing to the fans. He felt that the fans were more important than the network. He cast himself as the god and NBC as some demonic force from the other side."[33]

As Solow indicates, Roddenberry's brand did not necessarily reflect the realities of the production process. Similarly, Catherine Johnson argues that there has been a "mythologisation of Gene Roddenberry as [*Star Trek*'s] maverick creator who used the 'cloak' of science fiction to disguise the treatment of contemporary socio-cultural issues."[34] Johnson says that the series should not be understood "as a uniquely innovative programme enabled by Roddenberry's ingenious use of science fiction" but as a response to the "needs of commercial U.S. television," offering both conformation to standard production processes and differentiation from the standard action-adventure series format.[35]

Nonetheless, contemporary journalistic accounts demonstrate that Roddenberry successfully created a producer brand consonant with the period's fascination with space travel and anxieties over the cultural status of television. His championing of *Trek*'s scientific credentials and quality nudged the hitherto devalued science fiction genre on a path toward respectability that eventually led to *The X-Files* and *Battlestar Galactica*. However self-serving, Roddenberry's championing of artistic innovation and social conscience in television was a legacy to his (and Serling's) spiritual heirs, the hyphenate auteurs of TVII and TVIII who similarly position themselves against the putative artistic wasteland of network television. Many of these high-profile hyphenates produce for HBO, whose slogan, "It's not TV. It's HBO," specifically defines the quality of its programming in opposition to the networks' standard fare. Consciously or not, these writer/producers frequently echo HBO's branding discourses. Says Alan Ball, executive producer of *Six Feet Under*, "At the networks every decision is second-guessed by every single executive. At HBO, they leave you alone for the most part and trust your instincts."[36] *The Sopranos*'s David Chase, who had a long career in network television, nonetheless expresses disdain for its programs, dismissing the entire medium in favor of the supposedly superior medium of cinema. "I loathe and despise every second of it."[37] "I don't watch television. Not a single other show. Just *The Sopranos*. I much prefer to go to the movies."[38] Cult auteur Joss Whedon expresses similar sentiments about the networks' obtuseness: "There will always be shows the networks don't get."[39]

The audience fragmentation of TVII and TVIII now causes both HBO and the four major networks to trade heavily on the value of their producer auteurs, but such was not the case in TVI. Roddenberry's cultivation of his producer brand during the initial *Trek* years did not immediately aid his career; after the show's cancellation he was "perceived as the guy who made the show that was an expensive flop and I couldn't get work."[40] Although Roddenberry did find work again in television, he would never personally produce a show that equaled or even approached *Trek*'s impact on popular culture. And while the growing value of his producer brand in TVII required his continued association with the *Trek* franchise, he was fairly quickly reduced to marginal participation in both the feature film series and *Star Trek: The Next Generation* [TNG]. But if Roddenberry himself was a liability, the significance of the Roddenberry brand dictated that his sidelining be kept quiet. In 1992, *California Business* quoted TNG producer Rick Berman to this effect: "'The fans never knew that Gene Roddenberry's active involvement in *The Next Generation* diminished greatly after the first season,' admits Berman, copping publicly to something Hollywood insiders knew well."[41] The Roddenberry brand, if not the man himself, continued to gain value in the reconfigured industrial conditions of TVII and TVIII. Despite his lack of active involvement, Roddenberry receives a credit as the "creator" on all episodes of all four spin-off *Trek* series. Even after Roddenberry's death in 1991, two new series were developed based on his concepts and notes, *Gene Roddenberry's Earth: Final Conflict* and *Gene Roddenberry's Andromeda*. As *The New York Times* put it in an editorial the week after Roddenberry's death, "His imagination continues to beam."[42] But that imagination would have beamed for a far shorter period had not legions of loyal viewers turned *Star Trek* into such an unlikely success story.

NICHE AUDIENCES

Niche audiences and narrowcasting have become increasingly central to industry business models in the transitions from TVI to TVII and, most particularly, TVII to TVIII; but, as with the producer brand, such clear historiographic demarcations mask complexities. The conventional wisdom has it that CBS's 1970s youth-oriented sitcoms—*All in the Family* (1971–1979), *The Mary Tyler Moore Show* (1970–1977), and *M*A*S*H* (1972–1983)—pioneered niche audience strategies that became dominant from the early 1980s onward with quality dramas such as *Hill Street Blues* (1981–1987). But as Mark Alvey argues, these sitcoms signaled the culmination of "more than a decade of research and rhetoric" not only at CBS but at the other two networks as well.[43] Elana Levine shows how, during the 1960s, ABC used daytime programming to brand itself as the "young, unconventional network" through shows aimed at young audiences: the gothic soap *Dark Shadows* (1966–1971) and the Chuck Barris game shows, *The Dating Game* (1965–1973) and *The Newlywed Game* (1966–1974).[44] Aniko Bodroghkozy says that from 1967 onward "broadcasters and advertisers tended to fall back on the 18-to-49 demographic as the general age composition they wished to attract" but "continually tried to refine and further limit the age range in attempts to figure out what the audience really wanted."[45] But as Alvey clarifies, "As the 1970s wore on, mass ratings maintained considerable importance."[46] Jason Jacobs sums up: "Throughout the 1970s and into the 1980s, the 'big three' broadcast networks alternated between long-held strategies for mass-ratings success and newer ideas for attracting more demographically specific audience segments."[47]

Clearly the roles of niche audiences, demographics, and narrowcasting in TVI require further investigation; this section makes a small contribution by providing evidence about a specific 1960s niche audience: *Star Trek* viewers. Due to its often poor performance in the overall ratings in the period, NBC was an early champion of demographic thinking. Alvey tells us that the vice president for research, Paul Klein, who joined the network in 1961, flaunted "his network's demographic superiority at every opportunity, citing it as the criterion for leadership." By 1963, NBC's Research Bulletins began to emphasize the "quality" of the audience, characterizing NBC as the "leading network for upper income, upper educated young adults."[48] These claims continued throughout the mid-1960s with phrases such as "number one network among young adults," "the leading network among the better marketing groups," and "the preferred network among college-educated adults" showing up in the bulletins. But while NBC used demographic analysis primarily to defend poorly rated programs, it had "negligible" influence on programming decisions. By 1967, however, demographics "began to play a role in the retention of programs with marginal audience share (twenty-eight to thirty-one)."[49] In an article that year in *Television* magazine on programs in this "vast gray belt," Klein said that audience "quality" might justify renewing shows despite relatively poor Nielsen numbers. "A quality audience—lots of young adult buyers—provides a high level that may make it worth holding onto a program despite low over-all ratings," said Klein, specifically citing this as a key motivation for *Star Trek*'s renewal after a first season in which its poor ratings would normally have portended cancellation.[50] As Klein told *TV Guide* in a later interview, *Star Trek* was retained after a second season of poor ratings "because it delivers a quality, salable audience," in particular "upper-income, better-educated males."[51]

Judging from the contemporary press, *Trek*'s quality audience seems to have formed a main talking point in the network's publicity for the show. *The Los Angeles Times*'s Hal Humphrey reported halfway through the first season, "So much of its mail is from scientists and clergymen that the NBC sales department has been able to use that fact in making its sales pitch to particular potential sponsors."[52] The article also mentions another cult favorite, saying that the heavy mail protest against canceling *The Avengers* (1961–1969) caused ABC to bring the program back to replace the canceled *Custer* (1967). *The Avengers* and *Trek* viewership probably overlapped (it certainly did in my case); some of those who wrote to ABC to save the former may well in a few months' time have written to NBC to save the latter. Reporting NBC's decision to renew *Trek* for a third season, *The Washington Post* said that the show drew "more mail from upper educative viewers than any other program on NBC." The article characterized *Trek* as having "relatively low ratings and high prestige."[53] The network could well, and most probably did, say the same of a show that would not debut for another thirteen years—Hill Street Blues, the origin of quality television dramas' association with niche audiences.

Perhaps aware of their network's views on the subject, *Trek*'s producer and stars also emphasized their show's appeal to demographically desirable viewers. Roddenberry told Hal Humphrey that *Trek* received four thousand letters a week during its first season, "a lot of it . . . highly literate," from "graduate students at Harvard and from astrophysicists."[54] A *Los Angeles Times* profile of Shatner said that *Trek* was "extremely popular in the intellectual community, especially among scientists and rocket engineers." Shatner had toured Cape Kennedy the previous spring and discovered that "the people at the Cape are out of their minds about the show. . . . [They] enjoy [it] because it gives an insight on what the future will be like."[55] In a *New York Times* interview, Shatner indicated that *Trek* amalgamated several niche audiences: "It has action-adventure . . . so the kids like it. On another level, we deal with a philosophical concept— that what's alien isn't necessarily evil—so we reach their parents. Many of our episodes deal with scientific concepts, so our program entertains the technicians and space scientists. And with the hippies, we have a far-out show. They think we're psychedelic."[56]

Leonard Nimoy (who played First Officer Spock), also speaking to *The*

New York Times, added teenagers to the mix. The article said that "teenagers avidly follow Nimoy-Spock in the fan magazines and bid at auction for his foam-rubber ear-tips at science fiction gatherings." Nimoy thought that teenagers appreciated the fact that Spock, "in spite of being an outcast, being mixed up, looking different . . . maintains his point of view."[57] Like any TVII or TVIII show aimed at a niche audience, *Star Trek* most probably appealed to a combination of smaller audiences, ranging from disaffected teens to rocket scientists. For example, Susan Murray says that *Buffy the Vampire Slayer* (1997–2003) would not have succeeded had it appealed only to teenagers since that age cohort watches less television than others; network executives know that teen shows must target multiple demographics even in the age of narrowcasting.[58]

As Roddenberry's reference to four thousand letters a week shows, *Star Trek* viewers were not just a demographically desirable audience, they were also a highly active audience. Frequently invoked by Roddenberry and Trekkies/Trekkers as evidence of the show's unique status, the campaign that reputedly prevented cancellation after the second season has long contributed to *Trek* mythology, but the pages of *The Los Angeles Times* corroborate the protest's impact: "When news of the rumored cancellation of NBC's *Star Trek* reached the hinterlands, it started the biggest rumble since Tony Galento fought Max Baer. On the surface it appears that the series has more fans than Lawrence Welk. Even a large contingent of Caltech students will protest with a torchlight parade over the weekend."[59] The paper subsequently reported that three hundred students marched to NBC's Burbank studios.[60] On March 1, 1968, over the end credits of the episode "Omega Glory," NBC officially announced that the program had been renewed for a third season. *The Los Angeles Times* ran follow-up articles in July and August. The first spoke of a "rare showing of candor" from NBC, which "admitted that [the fan protests] had an 'influence' on saving the series. The turn of events was so startling that it began to sound like a far-fetched science fiction story."[61] The second included an interview with Roddenberry, who told the reporter that a "subculture . . . supports cultist publications, known as fanzines," which included "lengthy critiques of the shows, some of them very helpful."[62]

Even those NBC suits familiar with *Star Trek*'s demographics might have been surprised by the show's ability to get the youth audience, the most elusive of all viewers, marching in the streets. As *Variety*'s Les Brown said of demographic thinking in 1969, "To speak of an 18–49 viewership is to obscure the fact that 18–25 scarcely exists—for television. . . . It isn't that American youth will not watch television, but rather that it doesn't watch it very often. . . . And with three networks and any number of independent stations trying with all their might to capture that single element of the audience, it is necessarily being splintered to almost negligible size."[63] Yet hundreds, perhaps thousands, in this age category were so committed to sitting in the front of the set during *Star Trek*'s hour that they were willing to write, petition, and march to keep doing so. This was at a time when, according to Bodroghkozy, traditional programming practices of attracting mass audiences with "sit-coms, westerns, cop shows, variety shows, and the like" were alienating both "younger and highly educated viewers."[64]

In another parallel to TVIII developments, this panic over missing younger viewers echoes recent industry discourse. Max Dawson says that the archetypal figure of the "Lost Boy" has featured prominently in discussions of TV ratings since 2003: "This figure has come to function as a convenient and . . . crucial shorthand within ratings discourse for members of the male eighteen to thirty-four demographic. For the beleaguered broadcast networks, the Lost Boy is at once a profoundly alluring and deeply worrisome figure, one who both inspires and personifies anxieties about the limits of their ability to know their viewers at a moment when new technologies of distribution and reception shake their faith in dominant conceptualizations of their audiences' tastes and behaviors."[65] In the 1960s, as in the early twenty-first century, young male viewers watched less television than others, their elusiveness making them a highly valuable target to advertisers. Given the educational demographics of the period, many of the Harvard graduate students who wrote letters and many of the Caltech students who marched in the streets were undoubtedly male. Then, as now, it's the cult shows that attract the Lost Boys.

Star Trek's famous reprieve has provided inspiration to generations of fans trying to save their own favorite shows, but it also raises more questions than I have time to research or space to answer. The above evidence indicates that *Star Trek* was much better suited to the industrial configurations of TVII than to those of TVI; *The New York Times* said as much in 1986: "The 28 percent of the audience who watched *Star Trek* in 1966 would be enough to make the show a hit today when dozens of channels and millions of video cassette recorders are competing for a viewer's attention."[66] But did the palpable evidence of a demographically desirable, active audience have any immediate impact on industry programming decisions? The fact that *Star Trek* was canceled after a third season of poor ratings indicates the contrary. Not until the early 1980s, during the transition from TVI to TVII, does it seem to have become standard practice to renew shows with relatively low ratings but high prestige—that is, the right viewers.

Could the fierce loyalty exhibited by *Star Trek* viewers be engendered only by a show with what we would now term a cult sensibility? Other post-hoc designated cult shows did have loyal fan followings. In its time, *The Twilight Zone* received five hundred letters a week and had fan clubs in thirty-one states.[67] Rod Serling claimed to have received "several thousand letters of protest" when CBS canceled the show in 1962.[68] And, as noted above, ABC brought back *The Avengers* in response to viewer letters. Evidence of such intense viewer loyalty may well have influenced TVII producers who specifically designed shows for the cult niche (for example, *Twin Peaks* and *The X-Files*), knowing that these avid viewers would not only watch every week but also purchase ancillary products such as DVDs. As Hills details in relation to cult TVIII series, "DVDs of shows such as *Futurama* and *Family Guy* garnered sufficiently high sales to their relevant fan bases (and extended their followings through this medium) that they in fact became viable broadcast shows again, despite having previously been cancelled."[69]

Hills's examples are but one indication of media industries' increasing dependence on the fan base. The Trekkie phenomenon of the 1960s and '70s, which showed that fans constituted a highly desirable and engaged audience, was an early manifestation of the reconfigured relationship between television producers and viewers in the TVII and TVIII eras of narrowcasting. In Henry Jenkins's terms, this might be understood as a form of participatory culture; the active audience "is now taken for granted by everyone involved in and around the media industry."[70] Derek Johnson makes such an argument for understanding TVIII's television producer/audience relationships.[71] Johnson's gloss on a *Time* magazine article on *Lost* illustrates the widespread realization of the increasing economic importance of the fan audience: "Going to great lengths to get people who already like a show to like it more would have been a waste, incompatible with the undifferentiated audiences of mass marketing in the twentieth century. But in relying upon and catering to passionate fan audiences in the twenty-first century . . . television could 'turn passion into money.'"[72] Johnson argues that if in TVII fans figured as crucially important consumers, in TVIII they also figure as producers: "If so-called 'TVII' gave rise to the industrial cultivation of fans for television content, those strategies have more recently accelerated the dissolution of boundaries between that content, its production and those audiences. Audiences are not just cultivated as fans, but also invited in, asked to participate in both the world of the television text and the processes of its production."[73]

Many of those 1960s/'70s Trekkies whom I've discussed above produced texts ranging from fiction to videos, actively participating in the world of the television text, albeit without producer sanction. But Gene Roddenberry did issue limited invitations to those "hundreds of fanzine people" who he said had visited the studio. And some of the most ardent *Trek* fans went on to become the very producers who now invite a younger generation of fans into the production process; one of the most prominent among them is J. J. Abrams, creator of *Lost* and director of *Star Trek XI* (2009), the critically well-received and box-office smash film that may reboot the *Trek* franchise. Historical causality cannot be conclusively established, but circumstantial evidence points to the crucial contribution of early *Trek* fans to the participatory culture of TVII and TVIII.

MULTICHANNELS

Star Trek struggled along on impulse power during its NBC first run but took off at warp speed in off-network syndication, a surprising success that led directly to the establishment of the once vast and powerful *Trek* franchise. This franchise produced *Star Trek: The Next Generation* ([TNG], 1987–1994), the most successful drama series in first-run syndication to date and launched a new channel, UPN, centered around the flagship *Star Trek: Voyager* (1995–2001). Since the original series, no *Trek* television show has appeared on a major network; the story of *Trek* television is in concise form the story of the collapse of the three-network hegemony. *Trek*'s off-network triumphs presage two key aspects of the TVII/TVIII business model: first, cult shows targeting specific demographic categories, and second, marginal ratings performers achieving profitability in subsequent release windows (initially with *Trek* syndication and then the home video market, into which it was an early entrant with both cassettes and DVDs). And it is therefore possible conclusively to demonstrate *Trek*'s impact on the emergence of the multichannel mediascape.

Off-network syndication is the rerunning of old network shows by individual stations; from the early 1960s onward it became an increasingly significant aspect of the television marketplace.[74] The syndication market received a considerable boost from the FCC's All-Channel Receiver Act, which required all television sets manufactured from 1964 onward to receive channels broadcasting on the UHF spectrum and which immediately began to increase the number of independent stations needing content.[75] This proved extremely serendipitous for *Trek*. In 1967, while the original series was still on the air, Paramount Television Syndication struck a deal with Kaiser Broadcasting, which owned a number of major-market UHF stations—in Philadelphia, Boston, Cleveland, Detroit, and San Francisco. Kaiser, aware of the series's demographic profile, scheduled the show every night against its competitors' 6 p.m. newscasts, "gambling that young males were not heavy viewers of television news programs," as Herbert Solow (and his co-author Robert Justman, associate producer on the original *Trek*) later put it.[76] Not only UHF stations followed this narrowcasting strategy. In the autumn of 1969, WPIX, one of three New York City VHF independents, scheduled *Star Trek* against the network news, hoping to emulate the success that fellow independent WNEW had had in stripping *I Love Lucy* (1951–1957) in the same slot. WPIX president Fred Thrower said that "the station . . . is banking heavily on *Star Trek*."[77] Thrower, like Kaiser Broadcasting, may have been motivated to acquire the show by virtue of its proven appeal to niche audiences, particularly those desirable young males.

Judging from *Trek*'s performance elsewhere, Thrower's investment undoubtedly paid off. In the first year of syndication, *The Los Angeles Times* reported that the show continued to "acquire the most enviable ratings in the syndication field."[78] Two years later the same paper reported that *Trek* was now seen in more than sixty countries and one hundred U.S. cities. Most important, the show was still working its magic on those elusive younger viewers. "The time-slots for the reruns, usually late afternoon or early evening, make it an attractive lure for the young audience." And, as always, that audience was fanatically loyal and active. By the mid to late 1970s, the *Star Trek* phenomenon was streaking along at warp ten. University students were allegedly halting "their studies to watch the 50th re-run of *Star Trek* episodes on television"[79] and, having "become addicted to continuing *Star Trek* re-runs on non-network stations," flocking to *Star Trek* conventions.[80] Advertisers were reportedly lining up to "get into the *Star Trek* time slot at premium rates." Mary Barrow, publicity director for KTLA in Los Angeles, which in 1977 was airing *Trek* seven days a week, said that it was "one of KTLA's hottest shows. . . . And it has gotten hotter as it has grown older."[81] Two years later another KTLA spokesperson was still singing the show's praises. "It's as good now as it was the first day we ran it"; by that time, episodes had "been seen 30 to 40 times in many markets."[82] But contrary to usual industry practice, in which "shows usually get cheaper the longer they've been around," Randy Reiss of Paramount Television said that "we're now getting more for *Star Trek* and when the movie comes out it will get even better."[83] Even by 1986, twenty years after *Star Trek* premiered on NBC and seventeen years after its cancellation, it was still the fifth-highest-rated one-hour show in syndication, seen in 140 national markets covering 90 percent of the nation.[84] The show was also continuing to perform well in overseas markets, already by 1977 being seen in 120 countries.[85] It may be the case that *Trek*'s famously multicultural—or, more accurately, multiplanetary—cast played a role in its overseas success; were this the case, *Trek* could be seen as the harbinger of yet another TVIII trend: international casting specifically intended to appeal to foreign markets, as with *Lost* and *Heroes*. As *California Business* reported, Paramount certainly had an eye overseas with the first *Trek* spin-off, *The Next Generation*: "Paramount is smart enough to see that *Star Trek*, with its cosmopolitan, interplanetary cast of characters, travels well overseas. *Next Generation* is not just a domestic phenomenon; the overseas market is extremely lucrative."[86]

But it was the domestic phenomenon of the original series syndication that gave birth to TNG. Said Kerry McCluggage, president of Paramount Pictures Television in 2002, "The original *Star Trek* . . . became a hit and a phenomenon when it was sold into syndication. There were only seventy-nine episodes, but they were stripping it five days a week, and it became immensely popular. And it was the popularity of that show in off-network syndication that spawned *The Next Generation*."[87]

The key phrase here is "off-network"; the original series, syndicated at a time when the mass audience model still dominated network thinking, proved that a show aimed at the younger male audience could be very profitable. Paramount specifically designed TNG to exploit this market niche; according to *Daily Variety*, Paramount's "syndie prez" Steve Goldman said that the three major networks' prime-time programming (with the exception of sports) had ignored the 18–49 male audience at which TNG was targeted. TNG did "surpass network series in the key selling demo" but also proved "a household success," showing that it, like the original series, amalgamated demographic segments.[88] TNG became as hot in first-run syndication as its predecessor had been in off-network syndication, pioneering business practices that became standard in TVII and TVIII and contributing to the weakening of the established networks.

First-run syndication—that is, programs first aired in syndication rather than on the networks—had been a major component of early television programming, encompassing a range of genres, but faded in importance as the networks, in concert with a small and closed circle of producers, took over origination of the vast majority of television content.[89] By the late 1980s, first-run syndication had for a long time been the exclusive province of *Wheel of Fortune*, *Entertainment Tonight*, and similar fare, with "fictional first-run syndication finally returned to prominence in the late 1980s through the late 1990s (after an effectual twenty-five year absence) led by . . . [*Star Trek: The Next Generation*]."[90] A rapid growth in the number of independent stations during the 1980s, increasing from 100 in 1980 to 328 in 1986, facilitated fictional first-run syndication's rebirth. These independents had "thrived by using a new method of financing called barter syndication" to acquire first-run programs.[91] Rather than paying an upfront acquisition fee, stations gave up a certain percentage of commercial time to the syndicator, who then sold it on to national advertisers.

Paramount decided to use this business model for TNG, the earliest fictional first-run series to be distributed on this basis. In a decision aimed at both short- and long-term profitability, the studio bypassed all four networks (including the fledgling Fox, which wanted to use the show to help launch its Saturday night slate)[92] and offered the show to the 145 stations (including 98 independents) that were broadcasting the original series.[93] Following the standard deficit financing model and licensing the show to a network for a fee that barely covered production costs would have required Paramount to wait for off-network syndication to make money. Barter syndication made TNG profitable much sooner. Long-term profitability resulted from making a fictional program for first-run distribution, as senior industry analyst Doug Lowell explained. "Because everyone else got so fearful of cable and worried about the bottom line they stopped making expensive programs for syndication. The attitude is: If it's cheaper to do an Oprah Winfrey or a live action cop show, then why run this big deficit financing if we don't have to? And suddenly, you have a zillion Geraldos. This is a big mistake because such a show has no library value—no one is going to want to watch it five or 10 years from now. But what Paramount did . . . is to continue to make the kind of TV programs that do build a library."[94]

TNG became a syndication phenomenon, outperforming first-run stalwarts like The Wheel of Fortune, as well as network hits like Cheers, LA Law, and Monday Night Football,[95] and consistently ranking in the top ten of hour-long dramas.[96] Its biweekly airings attracted an estimated 20 million viewers, including many of those sought-after affluent young males.[97] TNG's rating triumphs so disconcerted the established networks that they joined together to dispute Paramount's claim that TNG (and the studio's other first-run shows, Star Trek: Deep Space Nine and The Untouchables) were delivering higher ratings among 18- to 49-year-old men than top-rated network shows. The networks said Paramount's figures were gross average audience ratings, based on multiple airings of the same episode, and therefore not comparable.[98] But as Paramount's Goldman put it, the networks were unable to stop the "first-run monster" that caused affiliates to preempt the network feed in favor of first-run syndication shows like TNG.[99] TNG's stellar ratings showed that a first-run show could beat the networks at their own game, while Paramount's innovative business practices made the first-run market potentially more profitable. As Electronic Media reported, Paramount's taking TNG into first run, with "several innovative marketing twists—including double runs, an aggressive seven/five barter advertising split, and upfront sales of back-end repeats," established "industry standards."[100] Trey Paul, writer for King Features Syndicate, credited TNG with "the current presence of so many fantasy hour dramas in syndication ('Babylon 5,' 'Robocop,' 'Time Trax,' etc.)."[101] Kompare adds Hercules: The Legendary Journeys, Xena: Warrior Princess, Forever Knight, and Highlander: The Series to the list.[102] Arguably TNG's demonstrable "library value" in reruns and home video could have influenced the rise of non-network original programming, with players ranging from HBO to the rather unlikely AMC and its hit *Mad Men*.

Paramount's gamble with TNG and first-run syndication paid off to the tune of tens of millions of dollars. But ten years before TNG's debut, the studio had contemplated an even greater risk and an even more direct challenge to network hegemony that again reveals the complexities hidden beneath historical periodizations. In 1977, Paramount tried to launch a fourth network, the Paramount Television Service, on the strength of *Star Trek*'s syndication success. In June of that year, *The New York Times* announced that "*Star Trek* will return to airwaves as part of a television service being established by Paramount Pictures."[103] Paramount planned to revive the original series with the original cast (minus Leonard Nimoy, who was in dispute with the studio over revenues from licensed products bearing his image) as *Star Trek: Phase II* (ST:PII). In conjunction with made-for-TV movies, ST:PII would have formed a "three hour block of expensive original programming one night a week" to be offered to independent stations.[104] But come November, Paramount announced that ST:PII, which had been scheduled to air in April 1978, would not now be shown until September at the earliest. The studio said that although stations covering 57 percent of the country had expressed interest, recent falls in advertising rates had negatively impacted the proposed network's economic viability.[105] As we know now, we had to wait another ten years for more *Star Trek* television and another eighteen years for a Paramount network. Once again, the studio used *Star Trek* as a lure to pull in independent stations, which, to get the new *Voyager*, had to agree to initially carry four hours of Paramount programming from 8 to 10 p.m. Mondays and Tuesdays.[106] *Voyager*'s ratings never equaled those of its first-run predecessors; the last (to date) *Star Trek* series, *Enterprise*, managed a feeble four years before cancellation in 2005; a year later UPN met essentially the same fate, merging with the WB to form the currently struggling CW netlet. Does the death of *Enterprise* signal the end of the *Trek* franchise's innovative run, or will *Star Trek XI*, for which a sequel has already been announced, revivify it? Whatever the answer, the counterfactual history of a 1970s fourth network shows yet again that developments strongly associated with TVII and TVIII have roots in TVI.

The *Star Trek* television franchise contributed to the weakening of network hegemony and the advent of the multichannel environment in three ways: (1) the unprecedented syndication success of the original *Trek* demonstrated that the hard-to-reach younger audiences that avoided network fare could be lured to the medium through cult programming; (2) TNG offered a new model of financing while showing that first-run off-network programming could be extraordinarily successful; and (3) the franchise served to launch a direct competitor to the established networks in the form of UPN. As I argued in this chapter's first two sections, the *Star Trek* franchise also played a major role in the development of the producer brand that was to become so significant in TVII and TVIII and to the growth of a fandom that would become an important component of all media industries. Overall this chapter has sought to reveal the key innovations pioneered by *Star Trek* and other cult television shows in the political economy and production strategies of the American television industry.

NOTES

My thanks to the editors for their very helpful input.

1. Inflation calculator available at http://www.westegg.com/inflation.
2. *New York Times*, August 24, 1966, 14.
3. Advertisement, *New York Times*, April 22, 1968, 24.
4. Inflation calculator available at http://www.westegg.com/inflation.
5. Mark Alvey, "'Too Many Kids and Old Ladies:' Quality Demographics and the 1960s U.S. Television," *Screen* 45, no. 1 (2004): 40–62. Alvey says that NBC knew that its "leadership in colour programming . . . gave it an undeniable edge in attracting more desirable demographics." For more on *Star Trek* and color, see Catherine Johnson, *Telefantasy* (London: BFI, 2005). Johnson notes that RCA, having learned from Nielsen research that *Star Trek* was the highest-rated color series on air, used the show in a promotional campaign for its color sets (85–86).
6. Mark C. Rogers, Michael Epstein, and Jimmie L. Reeves, "The Sopranos as HBO Brand Equity: The Art of Commerce in the Age of Digital Reproduction." In *This Thing of Ours: Investigating the Sopranos*, ed. David Lavery (London: Wallflower Press, 2002), 42–57.
7. Matt Hills, "From the Box in the Corner to the Box Set on the Shelf," *New Review of Film and Television Studies* 5, no. 1 (2007): 44.
8. See, for example, Amanda Lotz, *The Television Will Be Revolutionized* (New York: New York University Press, 2007).
9. See Roberta Pearson, "*Lost* in Transition: From Post-Network to Post-Television," in *Quality: Contemporary American Television and Beyond*, ed. Kim Akass and Janet McCabe, 239–56 (London: I. B. Tauris, 2007).

10. In Muriel G. Cantor, *The Hollywood TV Producer: His Work and His Audience* (New York: Basic Books, 1971), vii.

11. Of course, other TVI producers, such as Alfred Hitchcock and Desilu's Lucille Ball and Desi Arnaz, had prominent public profiles, but their prominence derived from other fields of production, in Hitchcock's case film directing and in Ball's and Arnaz's, television acting. The public profiles of significant TVI producers such as Stephen J. Cannell, Aaron Spelling, Norman Lear, and Quinn Martin bear investigating. For more on television producers see Michael Saen, "Producer in Television," *The Encyclopedia of Television*; http://www.museum.tv/archives/etv/P/htmlP/producerint/producerint.htm.

12. P. David Marshall, *Celebrity and Power: Fame in Contemporary Culture* (Minneapolis: University of Minnesota Press, 1997), x.

13. John P. Shanley, "Author Who Arrived," *New York Times*, April 22, 1956, 123. See also Gilbert Millstein, "Patterns of a Television Playwright," *New York Times*, December 2, 1956, SM13.

14. Rod Serling, "TV in the Can versus TV in the Flesh," *New York Times Magazine*, November 24, 1957, 49.

15. Ibid., 56

16. Oscar Godbout, "Serling to Film CBS TV-Series," *New York Times*, January 17, 1958, 47.

17. Val Adams, "TV-Radio News: A Rod Serling Series," *New York Times*, March 8, 1959, X11.

18. John P. Shanley, "A Playwright at the Controls," *New York Times*, September 20, 1959, X19.

19. Mike Wallace interview, *60 Minutes*, 1959; for a transcript see http://www.rodserling.com/mwallace.htm.

20. Quoted in John J. O'Connor, "Next Stop, the Sight and Mind of Rod Serling," *New York Times*, November 29, 1995, C13.

21. "The Gods of Cult TV," *Cult Times Special*, Special # 15.

22. "On Television," *New York Times*, February 12, 1957, 55.

23. "Star Trek's Crew Travels in Future," *Los Angeles Times*, September 11, 1966, SFB10; Hal Humphrey, "A Flight Plan for Star Trek," *Los Angeles Times*, October 2, 1966, A2.

24. "Smithsonian Seeks TV Pilot," *Los Angeles Times*, June 13, 1967, C19.

25. Don Page, "Enterprising Star Trek Taps TV's Potential," *Los Angeles Times*, August 13, 1968, G10.

26. Burt Prolutsky, no title, *New York Times*, October 15, 1967, 14.

27. Don Page, "How about 'Kumaon?'" *Los Angeles Times*, August 25, 1969, D31.

28. Burt Prolutsky, no title, *New York Times*, October 15, 1967, 14.

29. Hal Humphrey, "Star Trek's Upward Flight," *Los Angeles Times*, August 13, 1967, A39C.

30. Don Page, "Enterprising Star Trek Taps TV's Potential," *Los Angeles Times*, August 13, 1968, G10.

31. Cecil Smith, "Roddenberry Sires Son of Star Trek," *Los Angeles Times*, February 16, 1973, H1.

32. Quoted in M. L. Stein, "At Last, All Systems Are 'Go' for 'Star Trek," *New York Times*, January 21, 1979, D13.

33. Interview and e-mail exchanges with Herbert Solow, April 2005. For more on *Star Trek* and NBC, see Maire Messenger-Davies and Roberta Pearson, "The Little Program That Could: The Relationship between NBC and *Star Trek*," in *NBC: America's Network*, ed. Michele Hilmes, 209–23 (Berkeley: University of California Press, 2007).

34. C. Johnson, *Telefantasy*, 91.

35. Ibid., 75–80.

36. Quoted in Polly LaBarre, "Hit Man (Part 2)," *Fast Company*, September 2002, 90.

37. Quoted in Allen Rucker, *The Sopranos: A Family History—Season 4 Update* (New York: New American Library, 2003).

38. Quoted in Stephen Armstrong, "Analyse This," *Sunday Times*, September 9, 2007, 16 ("Culture" section). My thanks to my student, Anthony Smith, for the quotes from Chase.

39. Quoted in Michael Patrick Sullivan, "Interview with Joss Whedon"; http://www.ugo.com/channels/filmtv/features/firefly/josswhedon.asp.

40. Roddenberry quoted in David Schonauer, "'Star Trek' Sails Boldly On," *New York Times*, March 27, 1988, H37.

41. Michelle Logan, "Star Trek: Paramount's $1 Billion Enterprise," *California Business*, November 1, 1992, 20.

42. "Topics of the Times: A Stargazer's Playground," *New York Times*, October 29, 1991, A2.

43. Alvey, "'Too Many Kids and Old Ladies,'"44.

44. Elana Levine, *Wallowing in Sex: The New Sexual Culture of 1970s American Television* (Durham, N.C.: Duke University Press, 2007), 26.

45. Aniko Bodroghkozy, *Groove Tube: Sixties Television and the Youth Rebellion* (Durham, N.C.: Duke University Press, 2001), 201.

46. Alvey, "'Too Many Kids and Old Ladies,'" 58.

47. Jason Jacobs, "Experimental and Live Television in the U.S.," in *The Television History Book*, ed. Michele Hilmes (London: BFI, 2003), 89.

48. Alvey, "'Too Many Kids and Old Ladies,'" 45–47.

49. Ibid., 48–51.

50. Walter Spencer quoting Klein, quoted in ibid., 51.

51. Richard K. Doan quoting Klein, quoted in ibid.

52. Hal Humphrey, "TV Networks Get Mail from Home," *Los Angeles Times*, December 7, 1967, D23.

53. Laurence Laurent, "Star Trek Is Rescued," *Washington Post*, February 20, 1968, D11.

54. Hal Humphrey, "Star Trek's Upward Flight," *Los Angeles Times*, August 13, 1967, a39c.

55. Don Page, "Adventure, Shatner Seek One Another," *Los Angeles Times*, July 25, 1968, E27.

56. Quoted in Burt Prolutsky, no title, *New York Times*, October 15, 1967, 14.

57. Digby Dieh, "Girls All Want to Touch the Ears," *New York Times*, August 25, 1968, D17.

58. Susan Murray, "I Know What You Did Last Summer: Sarah Michelle Gellar and Crossover Teen Stardom," in *Undead TV: Essays on Buffy the Vampire Slayer*, ed. Elana Levine and Lisa Parks (Durham, N.C.: Duke University Press, 2007), 19.

59. Don Page, "Rumors Galore: Have You Heard about Star Trek?" *Los Angeles Times*, January 5, 1968, c14. Roddenberry himself repeatedly denied instigating the "save *Trek*" campaign, but others have said otherwise. See Dave Hipple, "The Accidental Apotheosis of Gene Roddenberry, or, 'I Had to Get Some Money from *Somewhere*,'" in *The Influence of Star Trek on Television, Film and Culture*, ed. Lincoln Geraghty, 22–40 (Jefferson, N.C.: McFarland, 2008).

60. Jerry Ruhlow, "Cosmic Issue—TV Series," *Los Angeles Times*, January 8, 1968, 3.

61. "All Systems Are 'Go' for Star Trek," *Los Angeles Times*, July 7, 1968, A31D.

62. Quoted in Don Page, "Enterprising Star Trek Taps TV's Potential," *Los Angeles Times*, August 13, 1968, G10.

63. Les Brown, quoted in Bodroghkozy, *Groove Tube*, 202.

64. Ibid., 202–3.

65. Max Dawson, "The Lost Boys," paper presented at the Society for Cinema and Media Studies Annual Conference, 2008. My thanks to the author for sharing the paper with me.

66. Aljean Harmetz, "New 'Star Trek' Plan Reflects Symbiosis of TV and Movies," *New York Times*, November 2, 1986, H31.

67. Marc Scott Zicree, *The Twilight Zone Companion* (Beverly Hills: Silman-James Press, 1989), 134.

68. Val Adams, "News of Television and Radio—Rod Serling," *New York Times*, April 29, 1962, 135.

69. Hills, "From the Box in the Corner to the Box Set on the Shelf," 49.

70. Henry Jenkins, *Fans, Bloggers and Gamers: Exploring Participatory Culture* (New York: New York University Press, 2006).

71. Derek Johnson, "Inviting Audiences In: The Spatial Reorganization of Production and Consumption in 'TVIII,'" *New Review of Film and Television Studies* 5, no. 1 (2007): 61–80.

72. Ibid., 62.

73. Ibid., 63.

74. For an excellent history of syndication, see Derek Kompare, *Rerun Nation: How Repeats Invented American Television* (New York: Routledge, 2005).

75. Ibid., 76.

76. Herbert F. Solow and Robert H. Justman, *Inside Star Trek: The Real Story* (Darby, Penn.: Diane Publishing, 1999), 418.

77. Quoted in Fred Ferretti, "Independents Fight for Growing TV Audience Here," *New York Times*, August 4, 1969, 70.

78. Don Page, "Gentry Special Due," *Los Angeles Times*, February 13, 1970, C21.

79. Ben Bova, "Why Hollywood Finds Profits Out of This World—SF Now Very Popular," *New York Times*, November 13, 1977, D1.

80. Paul Grimes, "Fantasy Boom: The Profits Are Real," *New York Times*, May 30, 1976, 213.

81. Quoted in Ronald L. Soble, "'Star Trek' Still Grounded," *Los Angeles Times*, April 28, 1977, F1.

82. "Best, Worst, Oddballs," *Los Angeles Times*, October 28, 1979, W7.

83. Quoted in Joe Saltzman, "Syndication—Pot of Gold at End of the TV Rainbow," *Los Angeles Times*, October 28, 1979, W6.

84. Lewis Beale, "'Star Trek' at 20: A Universal, Enigmatic Success," CT, September 14, 1986, A3.

85. Ronald L. Soble, "'Star Trek' Still Grounded," *Los Angeles Times*, April 28, 1977, F1.

86. Michelle Logan, "Star Trek: Paramount's $1 Billion Enterprise," *California Business*, November 1, 1992, 20.

87. Interview with Kerry McCluggage, Maire Messenger-Davies, and Roberta Pearson, January 2002.

88. Jim Benson, "Comp Fight Not Preempted: NATPE Sesh Shows Some Affils Still Upset over Issue of Cuts," *Daily Variety*, January 27, 1993, 43.

89. See Kompare, *Rerun Nation*, ch. 3.

90. Ibid., 133.

91. Aljean Harmetz, "New 'Star Trek' Plan Reflects Symbiosis of TV and Movies," *New York Times*, November 2, 1986, H31.

92. Thomas Tyrer, "Paramount Placing Trust in 'Voyager' to Launch Network," *Electronic Media*, May 16, 1994, 53.

93. Aljean Harmetz, "New 'Star Trek' Plan Reflects Symbiosis of TV and Movies," *New York Times*, November 2, 1986, H31.

94. Quoted in Michelle Logan, "Star Trek: Paramount's $1 Billion Enterprise," *California Business*, November 1, 1992, 20.

95. Ibid.

96. John Kessler, "Star Trek Boldly Going . . . Going . . . Gone," *Denver Post*, May 25, 1994, F-01.

97. Michelle Logan, "Star Trek: Paramount's $1 Billion Enterprise," *California Business*, November 1, 1992, 20.

98. Joe Mandese, "Fox, Big 3 Unite against Paramount," *Advertising Age*, April 5, 1993, 32.

99. Jim Benson, "Comp Fight Not Preempted: NATPE Sesh Shows Some Affils Still Upset over Issue of Cuts," *Daily Variety*, January 27, 1993, 43.

100. Thomas Tyrer, "Paramount Placing Trust in 'Voyager' to Launch Network," *Electronic Media*, May 16, 1994, 53. This "seven/five split" meant the syndicator could sell seven minutes of advertising time compared to the stations' five-minute allocation (Kompare, *Rerun Nation*, 162n32).

101. Trey Paul, "Stellar Finale: Last 'Next Generation' Episode Becomes a Major Television Event," *Seattle Post-Intelligencer*, May 21, 1994, C1.

102. Kompare, *Rerun Nation*, 141.

103. "'Star Trek' Will Return," *New York Times*, June 18, 1977, 12.

104. "New Star Trek Debut Postponed," *Los Angeles Times*, November 9, 1977, F20.

105. Ibid.

106. William LaRue, "Stations Compete for New Trek," *Post-Standard* (Syracuse, N.Y.), May 30, 1994, B4.

NIKI STRANGE

MULTIPLATFORMING PUBLIC SERVICE

The BBC's "Bundled Project"

This chapter discusses the changing production practices of the television industry in relation to the emergence of multiplatform television. In this context, multiplatform television can be understood as a commissioning and production imperative that increasingly requires practitioners to produce and exploit content for screens and sites away from the traditional TV screen and schedule, including the production of online content such as Web sites, interactive television applications, mobile phones, and other portable media devices. I take the BBC as a specific locus to explore these developments, examining the corporation's practices, policies, and texts of multiplatform television, not only in terms of its public service remit but also in terms of the BBC's status as an important—indeed, some might argue, dominant—market player in the U.K. and global TV marketplace. In particular I am concerned to examine the development of multiplatform television between 2001 and 2006, as the BBC moved from traditional linear broadcaster to position itself as the "UK's number one digital destination," aiming for ubiquity through developing a presence on all emerging platforms.[1] Finally, such a focus enables a consideration of these developments as part of the BBC's strategic positioning of itself in relation to ongoing debates about the future of its status as a public service broadcaster funded by the compulsory license fee.

Addressing the Royal Television Society in late 2003, Tessa Jowell, then culture secretary, launched the u.k. government's review of the BBC's Royal Charter and License by describing it as "the biggest ever public debate on the future of the BBC."[2] The following summer, by way of presenting findings from the Department of Culture, Media and Sport's (DCMS) public consultation, Jowell stated, "People believed that the BBC should keep up-to-date with developments in new technology and should be a lead partner in the new markets. . . . [But] there was also strong opinion, and voiced particularly by industry respondents, that the BBC should not assume automatic rights to colonise every new platform and market that might emerge."[3]

Jowell's comments speak to the double bind faced by the BBC as the corporation seeks to reposition itself within a digital landscape—between positive growth and "colonization," between publicly funded innovation and anti-competitive skewing of the market. As I shall go on to set out below, however, such a tension also exists between the new modes of engagement from audiences in a digital, multiplatform television landscape and the production practices that have developed in relation to such audience behaviors. As Jane Roscoe has argued, multiplatform event television developed as a production practice that was designed to mimic changed patterns of media consumption and new modes of communication among audiences.[4] While Roscoe asserts that such expansive production strategies have been driven largely by a desire among broadcasters to capture a (youth) demographic whose patterns of media consumption were beginning to shift in favor of such platforms, the experience of television away from the domestic "box in the corner" is an increasingly common experience.[5] This is particularly true in the United Kingdom, which boasts not only one of the highest penetrations of digital television at 85 percent of households, but also recorded the second-highest use of online TV on-demand services behind the United States.[6] Moreover, the BBC in particular has been charged with "building digital Britain" as part of its current license fee obligations, taking a key responsibility for driving take-up of new platforms and consumption patterns among a wide-ranging demographic.

This remit to "build digital Britain" is arguably at the heart of the BBC's dilemma in the digital age, forming part of a changed remit for the corporation set out as a result of the above review. While the BBC had previously received license fee funding for fulfilling its remit to "inform, educate, and entertain," in the digital television landscape this traditional function was deemed "no longer sufficient." Instead, six core purposes were set out by the DCMS:

Sustaining citizenship and civil society
Promoting education and learning
Stimulating creativity and cultural excellence
Representing the United Kingdom, its nations, regions, and communities
Bringing the United Kingdom to the world and the world to the United Kingdom
Building digital Britain.[7]

While "inform, educate, and entertain" remains the mission statement of the BBC, these public purposes will be judged against criteria of high quality, level of challenge, originality, innovation, and engagement across all genres, services, and output. This means that all programs, output, and services should display at least one of these criteria. Moreover, in light of the BBC's controversial coverage of certain aspects of the Iraq War, which had led to the resignation of both its chairman and director general in January 2004, such a changed remit was accompanied by a significant institutional reshuffle that saw the BBC's board of governors replaced by a new "BBC Trust," responsible for ensuring the independence, rigor, and proper purpose of BBC activities. One of the key elements introduced as part of this reshuffle was the adoption of a "public value" test to judge the merit of any new service planned by the BBC in line with not only the criteria outlined above but also, more significantly, against market impact. The focus on the public value test as a "mechanism for weighing public value against market impact" was indicative of the broader concerns and criticisms concerning the BBC's potentially damaging effect on the market in the digital, multiplatform television landscape outlined by Jowell above.[8]

Such concerns about the BBC's place in a digital market were further exacerbated by the controversy surrounding the Hutton Report, which investigated the circumstances surrounding the death of Dr. David Kelly, including the BBC's reporting practices that led to the claim the Blair government had "sexed up" the dossier on Iraq's weapons of mass destruction prior to the Iraq War. The Hutton Report cleared the government of any wrong-doing but strongly criticized the BBC, leading to the resignation of both the governor of the board of directors, Gavyn Davies, and director general, Greg Dyke. Despite the saga provoking a hostile attitude toward the BBC by many leading figures in the Labour Party government, Paul Smith and Jeanette Steemers have noted that within the government there remained a significant residue of ideological support for the BBC and the principles of public service broadcasting, with prominent debates having positioned the BBC as a "quintessentially British institution," likened to the National Health Service.[9] Given the assumption that the BBC would have a key role to play in the government's plan for switchover from analog television to fully digital transmission (thereby freeing up lucrative spectrum space in the process), this then provided a pragmatic reason for a pro-BBC stance. Smith and Steemers go on to suggest that the BBC was only too keen to reinforce the impression of its crucial part in "building digital Britain" when it came to its own contribution to charter review, *Building Public Value: Renewing the BBC for a Digital World.*

Building Public Value represented the wholesale adoption by the BBC of "public value" as a notion for achieving efficient public management. As Richard Collins has discussed, the concept was formulated by U.S. scholar Mark Moore and translated for the U.K. market by Robert Hewison and John Holden, and later by Gavin Kelly and Stephen Muers's paper for the Cabinet Office, *Creating Public Value.*[10] Kelly and Muers's paper emphasized two practices: "co-production" (involvement of users in "partnership" with providers) and "contestation" (competition) as the means through which public value can be realized.[11] For Collins, the BBC's adoption of public value doctrine in the mid-2000s responded to the critique of the corporation's divergence from public service principles in its broadcasting practice and to the challenges of the contemporaneous review of the BBC's charter. Yet, he posits, the Moorean concepts of "co-production" and "contestation" are of limited applicability to the BBC: "[The BBC's] implementation of Public Value doctrine weakly meets the norms set out in Moore's and Kelly and Muers' canonical accounts. Conventional free to air 'push' broadcasting means that there are few contacts between provider and user. It is a mode of delivery that's intrinsically hostile to co-production. 'Pull' online broadcasting has the potential to be more dialogic and thus offer more possibilities for co-production but, for the foreseeable future, 'push' broadcasting is planned to remain the BBC's main line of business."[12]

While one might be persuaded of an incompatibility of co-production, in Moorean terms, with the "push" dynamic of traditional broadcasting, I question whether Collins's assessment of the BBC's application of public value takes adequate account of the shift from broadcasting as "main line of business" toward a networked multiplatform model of content production and distribution. Such a shift in emphasis might demand, as Karol Jakubowicz has argued, a change of name and conception from public service broadcasting to public service media, "encompassing a much wider range of platforms than just plain old radiodiffusion."[13] Collins recognizes the dialogic potential of new forms of online broadcasting as one of the proliferating contacts, or touch-points, that offer the increased potential for user/provider co-production. Yet by taking insufficient account of the increasing significance of such forms within the BBC's "line of business," he neglects to offer a nuanced reading of such dialogues and their negotiated and/or contested nature.

This chapter engages with the "bundled project," an emergent BBC production strategy between 2001 and 2006, as the corporation attempted to reposition itself as a multiplatform public service provider. In 2001, then–BBC director of new media and technology Ashley Highfield polemically announced that the "days of commissioning programmes are over—we are now only commissioning projects that have levels of interactivity." This movement from programs to "projects" signaled a shift to post-broadcast production strategies that dispersed both the "text," as an object of study and industrial construct, and its audience across multiple platforms. While I have explored different project configurations elsewhere,[14] in this chapter I concentrate on the "bundled project" and its relationship to debates about co-production and the role of the BBC in the digital age, particularly with respect to how these have shaped the BBC's adoption in March 2005 of a 360-degree approach to integrated production and commissioning under its more recent Creative Future strategy, with "mobile, online and interactive TV programming teams working directly in the planning, commissioning and creation of programmes."[15]

At a time when the meaning of public service broadcasting, let alone television, is undergoing profound and ongoing review, this chapter points to the need to closely study both the production practices and texts of digital TV in tandem with their economic and/or policy structures. Such an analysis suggests that not only is the BBC increasingly a multiplatform organization, but also that co-production does have a place, albeit problematically, in its "pull" strategies of the digital future. In so doing, it elucidates a tension between the BBC's drive toward building digital Britain and the need to ensure its relevance within that space once viewers/users have become accustomed to the freedom of choice and personalization offered in a digital, multiplatform mediascape. While Jowell's statement above suggests the BBC must negotiate a tension between colonization and positive growth for the BBC in terms of the market, the example of the "bundled project" discussed here suggests this extends to how the BBC's production practices frame the corporation's relationship to its audience as well.

This tension is perhaps best encapsulated by then–BBC chairman Michael Grade's opening speech to the Interactive TV Show in 2004: "One of the BBC's current slogans is: Information, education, entertainment, interaction, wherever, whenever, however you want it. We like to think of it as the 'You-can-run-but-you-can't-hide' strategy."[16] In appending interactivity, on-demand, mobility, and choice to the Reithian edict of "inform, educate, and entertain," Grade embraces the "producerly" role of viewer/user as active self-scheduler and/or participant, consuming content on the go, on his/her chosen platform. Yet with Grade's very next breath, the empowered and free-ranging viewer/user as co-producer becomes quarry in the BBC's quest for ubiquity and market dominance. How this tension—between trusted guide to, and omnipresent and overbearing guard of, the digital landscape—plays out in relation to the emergent multiplatform projects of the time carries important implications for how we understand the BBC's attempts to deliver and reframe notions of public service as "public value" in the digital age.

It is in relation to these expressed intentions to experiment with platform-specific but nonetheless linked content, which might well deliver on the "interaction, wherever, whenever, however you want it" promise but equally service the "You-can-run-but-you-can't-hide" quest for ubiquity, that one may place the multiplatform "bundled project."

Marketing terminology defines "bundling" as "offering several complementary products together or offering additional services in a single 'package deal.' Groups of services or products may be bundled in different combinations appealing differently to different segments."[17] Drawing on such notions, I characterize the bundled project as an offering consisting of content dispersed across a range of proprietary channels and platforms and beyond into third-party spaces (both physical and virtual) through the formation of strategic partnerships with other organizations, under an umbrella brand and/or campaign. The structuring logic here is that through offering up a broader range of linked content, one increases the possible viewing/using combinations and probability of appeal to a wider range of "segments" (or in this case viewers/users). These segments might then be aggregated as a "total audience" for the bundled package of content.

Packaging complementary services together achieves scale and impact, with bundled projects tending to be afforded "event" status. This comment, made by Peter Cowley (then–managing director of digital media for Endemol, the production company behind pioneering multiplatform format *Big Brother*), predicts that such events will have an ever more significant role to play in an on-demand world: "The big broadcast channels will become even more important, and will be packed with events, or 'big pillars of the schedule' from which programming will drip and feed onto the multitude of digital channels and platforms."[18] Cowley's definition of multiplatform events suggests that the potential for greater impact that these high concepts or "big pillars" possess— their "event-ness"—is by dint of their "super-sized" scale and sheer relative dominance of the schedule at particular times. As John Caldwell has identified in relation to U.S. television miniseries, sports events, and the like, "event-status programming" also involves an element of self-conscious presentation of itself as original, distinctive, and important[19]—that is, as distinct from the programming that surrounds it, not merely through size but also through other characteristics such as massive investments of budget and production resources and, thus, relatively high production values, as well as a tendency to be scheduled at prime time. For these reasons they represent significant corporate risk and function somewhat like retailing "loss leaders," which may lose money but nonetheless typically provide "marquee points of entry" that entice viewers to sample other products.

Though clearly Caldwell describes industrial strategies that operate within a particular U.S. commercial context, nonetheless his argument raises interesting questions in relation to the BBC's bundled project formation. These arguably work on two levels: first, at a macro level in relation to how projects as "event-status programming" might operate in a public service context; and second, at a micro level, in relation to how different elements *within* the bundle might interrelate.

"BUNDLING BRITISHNESS": *A PICTURE OF BRITAIN*

The industrial strategy of linking cultural forms is by no means a recent phenomenon. Indeed, as Bellamy et al. demonstrated in their work on the "spin-off" as television program form and strategy, spin-offs have a long history within television scheduling.[20] What is more recent, however—as Simone Murray's "content re-cycling" and "media convergence's third wave," P. David Marshall's "new intertextual commodity," and Henry Jenkins's "transmediality" all suggest—is a discernible shift toward greater simultaneity in the release of highly inter-referential content across a wide range of media platforms.[21] Different media/content might attract different niches within the audience, but the integrated transmedia approach offers a form of universality through appealing to multiple constituencies that may be aggregated and, ideally, crossed over. While others have focused on such industrial strategies within a (U.S.) commercial context, one sees the appeal of such an approach as a means to satisfy aspects of a public service remit couched in discourses of "the universal" and "the national" and as a means to measure that success (through crossover engagement in, for example, new technologies).

A format favored by the BBC's earliest examples of event campaigns mobilizing multiplatform interactivity, in particular its facility to enable large-scale public voting, was that of compiling "nation's favorites" lists around a particular theme. *Great Britons* (2002) aimed to discover who the nation considered to be the greatest Britons of all time through telephone, online, and interactive television public voting. *The Big Read* (2003), whose call to action was to nominate one's best-loved book, consisted of programming across a number of the BBC's terrestrial and digital television channels alongside radio broadcasts and a dedicated BBCi Web site. In tying in this content with a range of initiatives with schools, libraries, national literacy organizations, and charities, as well as with publishers and book retailers, the BBC sought to emphasize its successful role less as broadcaster than as orchestrator of a multipartnered, multiplatform campaign whose public service was in generating debates around, and reflections on, national identity and, also, personal "transformation."

Though no doubt building on its antecedents above, *A Picture of Britain*'s (2005) multiplatform textual formation was markedly more sophisticated, with user interaction moving beyond simple voting to generation and contribution of content. Alongside a "landmark" BBC1 six-part television series presented by David Dimbleby, *A Picture of Britain*, which explored the art inspired by British landscapes, ran a multitude of elements: *A Digital Picture of Britain*, a six-part series visiting the same six regions as *A Picture of Britain*, challenging well-known photographers to produce new, compelling images of Britain's rural and urban landscapes for BBC4; bbc.co.uk/apictureofbritain, a Web site featuring a competition for the best amateur photographs capturing the contemporary British landscape and a gallery of selected entries; red-button interactive TV applications, showcasing the most popular pictures submitted to the Web site and a digital photography master class providing practical tips and "on location" trade secrets from the professional photographers featured in *A Digital Picture of Britain*. In addition, BBC3 commissioned a series of regional films featuring the work of contemporary artists; Radio 3 *Nightwaves* commissioned a series from British writers about the influence of landscape on their work; BBC Blast (aimed at a youth demographic) launched a mobile phone photo competition; *Countryfile* and *Landward* commissioned related items; even the BBC Proms joined in with a first night featuring music themed around *A Picture of Britain*. All of these activities were complemented by a major exhibition at Tate Britain in the summer of 2005 (the BBC's strategic partner for the project), an exhibition of winning photographs submitted to the Web site by viewers/users at the National Museum of Photography, Film and Television (NMPFT) in Bradford, and a series of public talks exploring artistic perspectives given by the Open University, with the participants' own proprietary Web sites further promoting the project.

The BBC1 series, *A Picture of Britain*, was referred to within the surrounding institutional and industrial discourse as a "landmark." Following in a tradition of television arts programming characterized by presenter-led exegesis of cultural developments, arguably heralded by Kenneth Clarke's *Civilization* (BBC, 1969), *A Picture of Britain* followed venerable broadcaster David Dimbleby as he traveled across the country exploring how art has been inspired by the British landscapes and how artworks, in turn, have shaped our view of the landscapes around us and, it is implied, our view of "ourselves."

It is evident in the aerial shots of sweeping vistas, the sheer amount of location shooting as Dimbleby tours the length of the British Isles, and the sweeping specially commissioned orchestral score that *A Picture of Britain* was afforded the sizable budget befitting its landmark or "event" status. The fifth episode of the series, titled the "Home Front," illustrates the series' mobilization of signifiers of a certain Britain, opening with a montage of timeless rural landscapes of the southeast, accompanied by Dimbleby's narration celebrating the "sweet smelling hops, orchards and hidden villages of Kent." Dimbleby goes on to visit William Blake's cottage, as "Jerusalem" swells on the soundtrack, before interviewing Winston Churchill's daughter.

While this description would seemingly position *A Picture of Britain*'s register as one of nostalgia, in a vein akin to the "Heritage Industry" trenchantly described by Robert Hewison, the series does not offer a hermetically sealed past. Indeed its negotiations of the present's "intrusions" are telling.[22] The series's title sequence introduces the themes of identity, art, and the technologies of reproduction: Dimbleby atop an undulating hillside, seemingly unchanged and untouched, binoculars to eyes (even his sight of the landscape is mediated). Suddenly, the (filmed) landscape dissolves into a painterly rendition, itself generated by computer graphic software, as we observe Dimbleby observing this too (see figure 1). These moments of technical trickery are not the preserve of the titles. Most often they feature in segments around paintings, as if seeking to "bring them alive" by distorting their perspective and breaking into the picture plane to render them in three dimensions. One might view these aesthetic treatments as deployed in the service of the project's broader objectives to promote engagement with the digital, to "build digital Britain," through the linkage of the traditional with the new—arguably a linkage resonant with that between the marquee element within the bundle: the landmark broadcast show scheduled to appeal to a mainstream audience and the digital portfolio networked from it.

Another linkage among the various textual elements within the bundled formation is shared branding and motifs; for example, the digital manipulation of paintings that features in *A Picture of Britain* (BBC1) is carried through in the title sequence for *A Digital Picture of Britain* (BBC4). Figure 2 features a series of screenshots from the sequence, mapping how oil paintings and photographs are "exploded" through

FIGURE 1 *A Picture of Britain*'s title sequence introduces the theme of identity, art, and the technologies of reproduction: the (filmed) landscape dissolves into a painterly rendition, itself generated by computer graphics software.

pixilation—pixels that then come together to form other paintings and photos. However, this is not to say that the elements share an aesthetic register—in fact quite the reverse. In the *Masterclass* on the interactive television application, presenter Tom Ang and photographers from *A Digital Picture of Britain* offer tips to the viewer from within a pared-down studio. The production values of this element in the bundle are in stark contrast to the lavish spectacularity of *A Picture of Britain*'s terrestrial landmark program. They are thus indicative that as instructional-educational discourses have come to the fore within an element, so the spectacularity and the budget that affords it has receded. Whereas the aesthetics of the *Masterclass* are minimalistic, with a bare set and stark lighting, those of the *Viewers' Gallery* are reminiscent of a computer slide show of photographs (which in many ways it was), edited and packaged up with tricksy composites and dissolves between images that reprise the pixel motif discussed above.

In this brief survey of some of the key aesthetics of certain elements within the bundle, I have indicated that there is a range of differing

FIGURES 2.1–2.4 A mini-sequence from the titles for *A Digital Picture of Britain* shows paintings dissolving into other paintings or photographs via a motif of exploding pixels, emphasizing the bundled project's theme of the relationship among visual representation, technology, and identity.

production values and aesthetic registers (and budgets). I have also, however, begun to elucidate some of the threads that tie the elements together beyond the branding approach of closely related titling of each of the elements and their logos, such as the use of the pixel motif and the transitional graphics among paintings, photos, and actuality. However, the ways in which the elements within a bundled project might be "bound" in order to comprise a coherent "offering" warrant further investigation, particularly in an assessment of how cross promotion and the management of user flows seek to "build public value."

When viewing the closing credits from *A Picture of Britain*, one was greeted by a multitude of messages and calls to action, all of which were designed to promote other elements within the bundle. Along with production credits for the BBC1 series, a trailer in the left-hand corner of the screen ran for *A Digital Picture of Britain* on BBC4, and a digital onscreen graphic in the top right-hand corner incited one to "press the red button" in order to enter the interactive TV application and watch the *Viewers' Gallery*, here promoted as "Your Pictures." Just prior to this credit sequence ran a trailer for the following week's episode of the BBC1 series, accompanied by a narrator's incitement to "see more pictures featured in this series at Tate Britain." Turning to figure 3 and onto BBC4, one sees how, again, screen real estate was maximized through the use of windowing in order to run closing credits for the immediately preceding program (*A Digital Picture of Britain*) and an onscreen graphic, this time promoting the *Masterclass*, as well as the Web address to the project's microsite (bbc.co.uk/apictureofbritain). Had one "pressed red," one would have been able to view the *Viewers' Gallery* interactive television application and be invited to visit the associated Web site and, more than this, submit a picture in the hope that it might be rated as good enough to feature in the gallery. The Web site served as a nexus for all the various elements linking out to information on each aspect and also worked as a repository for photos submitted by viewers/users.

Such cross-promotion is also evident *within* the fabric of the elements; however, the conventions of the particular element dictate the degree to which the promotion is "permitted." Thus, whereas the interactive TV *Masterclass* enthusiastically drove home the point that there was an associated Web site by showing its address in extreme close-up and in *A Digital Picture of Britain* the *Masterclass* digital onscreen graphic was ever present, at the other end of the spectrum, the red-button call

FIGURE 3 The final credit sequence of *A Digital Picture of Britain* provides a "Chinese menu of options," with the screen real estate used to promote other project elements: the interactive *Masterclass* application and the Web site.

to action appears only in the final minutes (that is, as late as possible) in *A Picture of Britain*. Richard Williams, then interactive executive in the BBC's interactive factual and learning department, which made the series, spoke of the perceived sanctity of the landmark program among producers:

> Producers are reluctant to put calls to action in programs—they don't want them to impinge on their masterpieces! Instead of, for example, putting a call to action at a relevant place in the program (for example when mentioning a painting at the Tate, go on to say that there is an exhibition accompanying the Project) it will be part of a host of messages that hit the viewers at the end of the program. There's a fear among television producers that a call to action, for example, a reference to the web within a show itself, will mean people get up, switch off and go to the web, when it doesn't work like that.[23]

Williams went on to observe that "There's still a linear approach to television whereas we need to think more about hypertext and ways of linking out from the program. Rather than bombarding [viewer/users] with messages at the end of the show, a Chinese menu of options, we need to give them a couple of clear options that could work in either a networked or circular way."

Williams's comments are telling in a number of ways. First, multi-platform projects, and the strategies to ensure an interconnection of their constituent elements, require the development of new production practices and, more broadly, cultures that might be resisted by television producers more comfortable with existing conventions. Second, those new practices are heavily influenced by nonlinear models of content delivery. Third, such practices are highly experimental and in flux, and projects such as *A Picture of Britain* have served as test cases in working out how best to direct and channel viewers/users from one element within a bundle into another. Finally, in the development toward a networked or circular way of channeling, there are ideal user pathways inscribed within a project configuration that aim to elongate as far as possible the viewers/users' engagement within the project's experience, whether that be watching its television element, or viewing its gallery online or via the interactive TV application, or uploading an image one has taken to its Web site, or even going to view the associated exhibition at the Tate.

In an assessment of such structuring logics, it's useful to draw upon John Caldwell's notion of "second shift aesthetics and practices"—the shift from the serial flows of the pre-digital toward tangential and cyclical flows, as industrial strategies develop to master both textual dispersal and user navigations across brand boundaries.[24] This is not to say that terrestrial scheduling plays no part—at least not in the context of bundled projects such as *A Picture of Britain*. Linear terrestrial scheduling is still very much in evidence, with BBC1's *A Picture of Britain* series's Sunday prime-time slot typifying the normative positioning of a landmark series of its kind. Using the "linking" strategy to maximize crossover among the BBC's portfolio of channels, BBC4's *A Digital Picture of Britain* is scheduled to start immediately after the BBC1 series, providing, as Richard Williams described it, a "switchover moment." The viewer/user might now be outside of BBC1's flow but remains within the "flow" of the project.

Of course one might go against the user flow channeled in (that is, not switch over to BBC4, never press red, encounter the project via the

Web site, and thus enter it from a different "gateway" than the BBC1 linear series, and so on), but, nevertheless, user flows are manifest. Particular invitations are issued at certain times and are inscribed across the textual terrain in order to marshal movements and incite certain responses. Were one to answer the "call to action" and press red, one would find oneself faced with a menu offering a range of options—the interactive applications being to view either the *Masterclass* in order to improve one's own photography or the *Viewers' Gallery*, which might well inspire one to get out into one's land/urbanscape and perhaps even take a photo oneself, putting those *Masterclass* tips into practice. The structuring logic behind the "ideal" user flow is one in which educative discourses—and their instructional address—become progressively central, as do invitations for viewer/user participation.

The bundled project demonstrates an experimentation with textual form that must be contextualized by the BBC's move toward greater integration of commissioning of interactivity and programming in the period. As Emma Somerville, then the head of interactive TV programming, conveyed: "We are now commissioning interactive programmes alongside the programming commissioning process. That's been quite a fundamental move for us and it's working out incredibly well. We have developed a good understanding of our audiences, and we are now starting to understand the types of services that work really well. . . . Interactivity allows us to explode the linear schedule."[25] *A Picture of Britain* evidences that textual expansion, such as the "explosion of the linear schedule" described by Somerville, may not necessarily be the preserve of digital spaces. Its user flows potentially lead away from all types of screen and out into surrounding physical spaces. As interactive executive, Richard Williams commented about the overarching aim of the project: "There was an unspoken shared strap-line between the parties involved: be inspired to value your countryside and the landscape around you. It was about acting on this inspiration and getting into it, and even taking a photo of it."

In the spirit of its public service objectives, user flows here do not lead onto sites whose affiliation is based on commercial transactions but into the spaces of the wider world. Of course, in keeping with the cyclical movements of second-shift aesthetics, the "improved viewer" (skilled up after the *Masterclass*) might, after looking at one's surroundings with new appreciation, choose to photograph them and submit the said photograph(s) to the Web competition in the hope of seeing them displayed in the *Viewers' Gallery*, or again, back away from the screen, in the exhibition at the NMPFT. With strategic partnerships such as this, and with the Tate exhibition, the project thus takes the user into other public institutions and spaces, such as galleries and museums, with the "real world" institutions functioning as yet another platform to be subsumed within its expansionist, though largely benevolent, drive.[26]

As Richard Williams's comment suggests, there might have been an "unspoken strap-line between parties involved"—an aim to engender an appreciation of one's surroundings, of considering how they have been represented through painting and photography, and of contributing one's own representation of those surroundings to build a composite "nation's album." However there remains, with highly dispersed texts such as bundled projects, a question of how a "unified (and unifying) discourse" might be conveyed through a multitude of sites (each with their concomitant conventions and aesthetic registers) to a wide range of users/viewers. Furthermore, the new look window aesthetic of television, typified by the "Chinese menu of options" credit sequences evidences, according to Karen Orr Vered, a shift from a unified and direct address to a dispersed address to a differentiated and niched audience.[27]

There would appear to be a tension, then, to be negotiated when bundling projects in this way. On the one hand, there is the underlying "slice and dice" logic of the portfolio as niche; the range of access (and economic and cultural capital) of viewers/users to the tools, both technological and cultural, by which to answer a campaign's demands; the fragmentary effect of the aesthetics of navigation inherent with textual configurations of this sort; and the fractal, composite, and indeed partial view of Britain—and Britishness—that might emerge in the strictly delineated and "quality-controlled" plot within the textual terrain for the viewer/user's own creative response. On the other, there is the public service drive to pull together a range of disparate elements—and audiences—under a branded campaign in the hope of achieving impact and reach; to seek to connect the elements along an axis of individual transformation through increasing participation; and thus to service the public value aim of creating broader "social value" through a campaign to encourage the nation to "picture itself"—that is, for the viewers/users to act as co-producers in the building of "digital Britain."

For Michael Nutley, then editor of trade magazine *New Media Age*, the need for the BBC to actively counter "fragmentation" is paramount if it is to continue to serve a function: "The real job of a public service broadcaster in a future of media fragmentation lies in almost a reversal of its former role, in explaining what all the citizens of the UK have in common, rather than in offering them content based on their differences. . . . The challenge for the BBC is to take us out of our increasingly targeted media niches and introduce us to the rest of the UK."[28] Nutley's interpretation gives an indication of why the BBC's bundled multiplatform events tend toward subject matter based on "what we have in common," whether it be the books and/or figures that "represent" us; the commemoration of national events; or, in the case of *A Picture of Britain*, the landscape that surrounds us and its representation (and in that of its follow-up, *How We Built Britain*, 2007) of Britain's architectural past, present, and future. By "bundling Britishness" in this way, the BBC attempts a reconfiguration of public service broadcasting as public value, serviced through the content-led aggregation of niches. In turn digital take-up is, hopefully, supported and driven through linking the familiar to the new, encouraging the crossover of niches while a multiple address is, nonetheless, marshaled in the service of an overarching campaign to build individual and social capital for the nation.

As an experiment in bundled projects of this kind, *A Picture of Britain* was judged, in production terms, to be a format worth emulating in the *How We Built Britain* campaign, with the "landmark" television element again written and presented by David Dimbleby. As Mary Sackville-West, its executive producer, commented, "*A Picture of Britain* absolutely set the template on which we modeled ours. . . . We learnt huge lessons from *A Picture of Britain*. You need to make sure you have all those elements, and big country-wide projects such as these lend themselves to art and architecture. The buzz of being multiplatform is very important—not everything will be but at the BBC now it's a matter of course."[29]

Sackville-West's comment suggests that particular subject matters are deemed by BBC producers to lend themselves well to this type of national bundled campaign, and, as the templating of the model indicates, subjects such as art and architecture may well continue to be privileged with the bundled project "treatment," possibly to the detriment of other subjects that fit less easily into established codes of cultural value. Her comment also illustrates that multiplatform projects, with their buzz or ability to impact upon and indeed dominate through sheer scale and multisite presence, were by that time being viewed as "a matter of course" for a BBC seeking both to provide linked content in all the places one might want it and at the same time position itself as ubiquitous and omnipresent across a panoramic vista of "360 degrees." As I have traced, the emergence—and templating—of the bundled project clearly illustrate the movement toward the integrated creative approach signaled by the switch to 360-degree commissioning in 2006, and, indeed, its successes no doubt played a part as a "proof of concept" that such multiplatform approaches could bear fruit. I want to turn now to how the development of the BBC's 360-degree approach to commissioning positions the BBC in the context of a multiplatform digital television mediascape, impacting on both its position within the market and its relationship with viewers/audiences, now reimagined as "co-producers."

FROM BUNDLED TO 360-DEGREE COMMISSIONING: CO-PRODUCTION, PUBLIC VALUE, AND THE MARKET

The BBC's increasing reliance upon, and demand for, similar multiplatform concepts that potentially provided a multitude of touch-points with viewers/users would, in broader industrial terms, serve to power the further integration of linear and digital interactive production both in-house and in the independent sector. However, the 360-degree commissioning approach was not without its critics, who highlighted a number of potential issues. First, as the British Internet Publishers Alliance highlighted in its response to the government's Green Paper on the BBC's charter, the earlier Graf Report on the BBC's online activities had been critical of 360-degree commissioning, arguing that it can "create a culture and organisation that, at best, is confusing and, at worst, is a recipe for dodged responsibility when dealing with third parties."[30]

This fear of confusion, of the further muddying of what were already felt to be opaque BBC commissioning processes (and thus a fear that the independent sector would be unfairly disadvantaged), was similarly articulated by production trade magazine *Televisual*. In an article by Jon Creamer devoted to "360-degree commissioning" in September 2006, *Televisual* voiced concerns that commissioners didn't know how to commission or budget for 360-degree commissions; that production companies were not set up for them; and that the development of stand-alone new media forms could be arrested, suffocating discrete digital media ideas at birth.[31] At the same time, in the same issue of *Televisual*, Adam Kemp, then the BBC's commissioning editor for arts, music, performance, and religion, rallied the production community to "always think big and think about the 360 degree application. . . . We do far less little one-off discrete shows. I'm after big campaigning events."[32] Creamer's article replied by voicing producers' fears that one-offs or "little programmes" would lose out. Moreover, further justification for this last concern came with the lower than expected license fee settlement in January 2007—creating, in the BBC's estimation, a £2 billion shortfall and causing BBC director general Mark Thompson to steer toward a policy of "fewer," "bigger," and "better" commissions, while maintaining the intention to take "big creative risks."[33] In this scenario, bundling and multipartnering would become even more crucial as the means to achieve both impact and reach—two of the measurements within the BBC's renewed charter remit. The ramifications of the BBC's increasing emphasis on a multiplatform commissioning policy for an independent sector struggling to keep abreast of the concomitant changes to commissioning, production, and distribution practices would be doubly felt, as other broadcasters such as Sky and ITV followed suit in adopting the BBC-pioneered "360-degree approach."

In July 2006, the BBC announced the earliest, and most profound, reforms of the Creative Future strategy: a full-scale organizational restructuring to be in place by the summer of 2007, in order to "enable 360-degree commissioning and production and ensure creative coherence and editorial leadership across all platforms and media."[34] Figure 4 provides a diagrammatic representation of this restructured organization, with any reference to television completely absent (or any medium). Content has been "unshackled" from platform, with three giant divisions covering a raft of multiplatform activities and services encircled by the Future Media and Technology division. This division would be tasked with identifying and developing new ways for audiences to find and use content. The largest of the three content divisions and the one most pertinent to this inquiry, titled BBC Vision, was to be responsible for in-house multimedia production, commissioning, and audiovisual services, including the TV channel portfolio, and digital services like high-definition and interactive television.

The BBC's root and branch transformation (or at least performance of an intention toward transformation) into a public service "content pro-

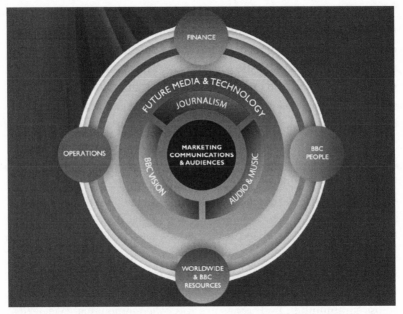

FIGURE 4 Diagram of the BBC's Creative Future institutional restructure to a 360-degree organization: "platform-agnostic content" encircles the audience.

vider" that so believes in 360-degree commissioning that, as figure 4 illustrates, it represents *itself* organizationally as a circle would seem to evidence its unquestionable commitment to the enabling of multi-platform concepts. However, Anthony Lilley, interactive producer and chair of the Producers Alliance of Cinema and Television's (PACT) Interactive Policy Group, greeted the restructure with a large degree of cynicism as to the potential for creating a genuinely interactive "creative future":

> The balance of the TV industry effort right now seems to be 90% on how to evolve from what they know—how to sort out the rights, the technology and the business models to create TV 2.0. In the rush for video-on-demand gold, they're missing the main event. The social changes we're now seeing from broadband, the impact of technology on the creativity of the "people formerly known as the audience" and of the mobility on the contexts in which we use media, need much more attention. Many TV folk have a habit of understanding every other medium only as it relates to TV.[35]

While no doubt polemical, Lilley's assessment of the evolution (and mutation) of industrial production practices and cultures provides a useful commentary on the negotiated, contested, and indeed deeply disruptive nature of processes of media convergence. His comment also touches upon the notion of audience as creative force in relation to such processes, implying that this changed status has been insufficiently attended to by many in the television industry.

That said, Mark Thompson's public recognition of the profoundly disruptive effects of the "second wave of digital," with their potential to sweep away the foundations upon which much of traditional media have been built, conveyed the corporation's engagement with the threat, and opportunities, of the "creative audience."[36] This "second wave in digital" Thompson characterized as all media—sound, picture, text—available on all devices, all the time; that media being searchable, movable, shareable; fully individualized scheduling of TV and radio; and radical interaction, content generation, and pooling/sharing of that content across communities. By Thompson's acknowledgement that "We need a new relationship with our audiences. They won't just be audiences any more, but participants and partners"[37] and the placement of the creative audience at the core of the BBC's vision for the five years up to the predicted completion of digital switchover in 2012, one may argue that the BBC is cleverly juggling with continuing to deliver on its role as "trusted guide" to the digital (retaining a more normative public service role) at the same time as maneuvering into a position as partner, but still ultimately "enabler," *within* the digital. Indeed, as in the case of the exemplar bundled project, *A Picture of Britain*, one sees how the multiplatform bundling of "landmark" terrestrial television with digital interactive and user-generated elements allows for the BBC's occupancy of these roles— trusted guide and enabling co-producer. While these two roles may call for contrasting modes of address, they are underpinned by the shared notion of an audience "transformed."

In terms of the second of these positions, that of enabling co-producer for the creative audience, wouldn't such a position suggest that the BBC is indeed attending to "the impact of technology on the creativity of the 'people formerly known as the audience,'"[38] and so perhaps isn't getting sufficient credit from commentators such as Lilley? The BBC's Creative Future strategy might, on the face of it, sit well with a public value conception of co-production described by Richard Collins thus: "a part-nership between users and providers . . . [that] potentially combines downward accountability to users, but to users as citizens rather than as subjects or consumers."[39] However, *A Picture of Britain* illustrates both that the BBC structures user flows to support public service objectives and that the "co-production" by viewers/users is subject to similar struc-turing logics and tactics. Additionally, it demonstrates that within the notions of public value and connecting communities delivered through the services (broadcast and otherwise) that the BBC provides for "audi-ences" and "co-partners" with users/viewers, there may remain a tradi-tional view of audiences as being in need of "transformation," in terms discussed by Sonia Livingstone et al. That is, in crucial ways, the audi-ences are perceived as "ignorant of or distanced from the world, requir-ing the BBC's bridging of the gap and transformation of the audience into an informed and engaged public."[40]

Hence, while the creative future envisaged by the BBC may well posi-tion the "creative audience" at the heart of the 360-degree vista, recogniz-ing that viewers/users have new ways to encounter—and traverse—that panoramic (digital) landscape, there is a risk that its ubiquitous presence, providing guidance across the terrain, signposting routes, and marshal-ing movements, will prove to short-circuit its discourses of, and visions for, user/viewer freedom, emancipation, power, creativity, and indeed genuine co-production. As James Bennett has argued, the BBC's digital strategies exhibit an inherent tension between, on the one hand, public service as personalization and consumer choice and, on the other, pub-lic service as provision of a balanced diet or, somewhat paternalistically, what's good for you that you might not choose for yourself.[41] Indeed, the quote from Michael Grade above captures this tension between the "pull" dynamic of on-demand by the creative viewer/user and the "push" dynamic of ubiquity and trusted guidance to the audience as quarry. I have traced how the evolution of such multiplatform textualities as the bundled project must be contextualized by the BBC's movement, dur-ing the period, toward a reconfigured notion of the (broadcast) delivery of public service to (beyond broadcast) "building public value." Within this conception, the BBC's pioneering of "360-degree commissioning" is not the means by which public service might be delivered—it is not a mechanism for delivery; it is seen as an essential part of the public value that is built for digital Britain. However, such notions of public value are complicated by the tension between such expansion and both market colonization and audience freedom—a tension that may prove difficult, but urgent, to resolve if the BBC is to continue to retain its role, and its license-fee funding, once digital Britain has been built.

NOTES

1. Ashley Highfield, quoted in David Teather, "Working with Dinosaurs: Interview with Ashley Highfield," *Media Guardian*, February 12, 2001. Available at http://www.guardian.co.uk/media/2001/feb/12/newmedia.mondaymedia section.

2. Quoted in Paul Smith and Jeanette Steemers, "BBC to the Rescue! Digital Switchover and the Reinvention of Public Service Broadcasting in Britain," *Javnost-The Public* 14 (2007): 43.

3. Transcript of Tessa Jowell's speech at the BBC's Public Purposes Seminar, July 20, 2004; available at http://tinyurl.com/242n67s, original at http://bbc charterreview.org.uk.

4. Jane Roscoe, "Multi-Platform Event Television: Re-conceptualizing our Relationship with Television," *Communication Review* 7, no. 4 (2004): 365.

5. For example, see Bobby Johnson, "Britain Turns Off—And Logs On," *Technology Guardian*, March 8, 2006, discussing the findings of Ofcom's 2006 Media Literacy report. It reported that television viewing had declined in recent years for the first time in history and that the "reach" of television—the number of people switching on for at least fifteen minutes—had declined by 2.5 percent among those aged between twenty-five and thirty-four. The shift was even more marked among younger users, with reach declining by 2.9 percent among the under-twenty-fives during the same period, especially as spending more time on time-intensive activities like Weblogging (blogging) and surfing social network sites like MySpace.com could continue reducing their consumption of other media. Johnson does rightly go on to acknowledge, however, that the TV and Internet are not mutually exclusive—for example, one might surf the Web with the television on in the same room.

6. Ofcom, *The International Communications Market Report: Key Points* (London: Ofcom, 2008).

7. Department of Culture, Media and Sport, *White Paper—A Public Service for All: The BBC in the Digital Age* (London: HMSO, 2006).

8. Most recently this was epitomized by the BBC Trust's decision to reject BBC proposals to develop local video services on its online site because of the potential impact on the local newspaper industry. The review involved not only a public value test by the trust, but also a simultaneous market impact assessment by media regulator Ofcom, http://news.bbc.co.uk/1/hi/business/7741244.stm.

9. Smith and Steemers, "BBC to the Rescue!"

10. Richard Collins, *The BBC and Public Value*, ESCRC Centre for Research on Socio-Cultural Change (CRESC), Working Paper 19 (CRESC, Open University/University of Manchester, 2006); http://www.cresc.ac.uk.

11. Ibid.; emphasis in original.

12. Ibid., 53.

13. Karol Jacubowicz, "The Beginning of the End or a New Beginning in the 21st Century," paper presented at the *RIPE@2006 Conference: Public Service Broadcasting in the Multimedia Environment: Programmes and Platforms*, Amsterdam, November 15–18, 2006; http://www.yle.fi/ripe/Keynotes/Jakubowicz_Keynote Paper.pdf.

14. See James Bennett and Niki Strange, "The BBC's Second-Shift Aesthetics: Interactive Television, Multi-Platform Projects and Public Service Content for a Digital Era." *Media International Australia* 126 (2008): 106–19.

15. Justin Pearse, "BBC Thinks Interactive from the Start," *New Media Age*, March 17, 2005, 1.

16. From Michael Grade's opening speech at the Interactive TV Show Europe 2004 in Barcelona, October 14, 2004. Available at http://www.bbc.co.uk/pressoffice.

17. American Marketing Association, "Marketing Directory," *Marketing Power .com*, n.d.

18. Poz Hulls, "Real New Media Deal: An Interview with Peter Cowley," *Televisual*, March 2006, 45–46.

19. John Thornton Caldwell, *Televisuality: Style, Crisis, and Authority in American Television* (New Brunswick, N.J.: Rutgers University Press, 1995), 163.

20. Robert V. Bellamy et al., "The Spin-off as Television Program Form and Strategy," *Journal of Broadcasting and Electronic Media* 34, no. 3 (1990): 283.

21. Simone Murray, "Media Convergence's Third Wave: Content Streaming," *Convergence* 9, no. 1 (2003): 8–18; P. David Marshall, "The New Intertextual Commodity," in *The New Media Book*, ed. Dan Harries (London: BFI Publishing, 2002), 69–81; Henry Jenkins, *Convergence Culture: Where Old and New Media Collide* (Cambridge, Mass.: MIT Press, 2006).

22. Robert Hewison, *The Heritage Industry* (London: Methuen, 1987).

23. Interview conducted by author, August 31, 2005. Unless noted otherwise, all quotations from Williams are taken from this interview. Karen Orr Vered has noted, in her discussion of the new look "windows aesthetic" on television, how cross-media references like the textual scroll of a URL serve as *suggestions* (emphasis in original) of interactivity. The viewer cannot "go to" the Web site via the television; she can only learn of its existence from television. Nevertheless, such references serve to acknowledge cross-media ownership and new economic (and, I would argue, cultural) configurations for the industry. For further details, see Karen Orr Vered, "Televisual Aesthetics in Y2K: From Windows on the World to a Windows Interface," *Convergence* 8, no. 3 (2002): 40–60.

24. John Thornton Caldwell, "Second Shift Media Aesthetics: Programming, Interactivity and User Flows," in *New Media: Theories and Practices of Digitextuality*, ed. Anna Everett and John Thornton Caldwell (New York: Routledge, 2003), 127–44.

25. Interview with Emma Somerville, head of Interactive TV Programming [*itvt: Interactive TV Today*], November 18, 2004.

26. It should be noted that the gallery partner for this project was Tate *Britain*—an institution (not as monolith but as dynamic formation) itself very much bound up in the circulation of discourses of Britishness.

27. Orr Vered, "Televisual Aesthetics in Y2K," 50.

28. Michael Nutley, "Is the BBC a Twentieth-Century Idea Whose Time Has Almost Passed?" *Wired Sussex/New Media Age*, December 2005; http://www.wiredsussex.com.

29. Interview with author, August 1, 2007.

30. Quoted in British Alliance of Internet Publishers, "Memorandum by BIPA," May 31, 2005.

31. Jon Creamer, "TV Turns Up the Heat to 360," *Televisual*, September 2006, 22–25.

32. Adam Kemp, quoted in ibid., 20.

33. Mark Thompson, "Delivering 'Creative Future': The BBC in 2012," speech given at QE2 Conference Centre, London, July 10, 2007; http://bbc.co.uk/pressoffice.

34. BBC Press Office, "BBC Re-Organises for an On-Demand Creative Future," *BBC Press Release*, July 19, 2006; http://www.bbc.co.uk/pressoffice.

35. Anthony Lilley, "TV Folk Need to Get with the Genetic Programme," *Media Guardian*, August 28, 2006, 6.

36. Mark Thompson, "Creative Future—The BBC Programmes and Content in an On-Demand World," *Royal Television Society Fleming Memorial Lecture*, April 25, 2006; http://www.bbc.co.uk/pressoffice.

37. Ibid.

38. Anthony Lilley, "TV Folk Need to Get with the Genetic Programme," *Media Guardian*, August 28, 2006, 6.

39. Collins, *The BBC and Public Value*, 6. See also Bennett and Strange, "The BBC's Second-Shift Aesthetics," for an analysis in support of such a view.

40. Sonia Livingstone et al., "Citizens and Consumers: Discursive Debates during and after the *Communications Act* 2003," *Media, Culture and Society* 29, no. 4 (2007): 632.

41. James Bennett, "The Public Service Value of Interactive TV," *New Review of Film and Television Studies* 4, no. 3 (2006): 263–85.

JEANETTE STEEMERS

LITTLE KIDS' TV

*Downloading, Sampling, and Multiplatforming
the Preschool TV Experiences of the Digital Era*

The preschool children's television industry, like all sectors
of the TV industry in North America and Europe, has faced
myriad challenges in recent years, such as channel proliferation, audience fragmentation, and declining budgets. Initially
these proved beneficial for content producers. There were
more channel outlets to promote programming and a boom
in international sales and merchandise licensing for globally
successful brands such as *Dora the Explorer*, *Bob the Builder*,
and *Teletubbies*; these helped to offset funding shortfalls from
broadcaster commissions. From the mid-1990s Nick Junior
(1994) and Noggin (1999) in the United States began to challenge PBS as the premier player in U.S. preschool television,
while in the United Kingdom the successful exploitation of
some preschool television properties across borders and platforms underpinned the stock market launches of several
companies, led by HIT Entertainment (1996), Entertainment
Rights (1999), and Chorion (2002).

However, by 2007 the preschool children's television market was saturated with content, and children's television production in general was facing a funding crisis. The crisis
proved particularly acute in the United Kingdom, where a
successful campaign to restrict food advertising for high fat,
sugar, and salt (HFSS) foods around children's programming,

accompanied by a decline in broadcaster commissioning and spending levels, has forced producers of all types of children's programs to think about new funding models and new approaches to content. This is all happening at a time when the industry is also facing the challenge of technological transformation, where even the very youngest children, according to CBeebies controller Michael Carrington, are supposedly "proactively recording, downloading and sampling content," requiring broadcasters to reach out to them in different ways "through online, mobile and TV experiences."[1]

Within the broader context of international developments, this chapter investigates how the British preschool television community is responding to the emergence of a multiplatform environment and the extent to which digital media may provide new opportunities, given that children are increasingly drawn to a wider range of media activities than just television.[2] It starts by charting the recent context of television for younger children aged up to six and then detailing how they came to be seen as a valuable target audience with the rise of multichannel and digital television during the mid-1990s before children's television experienced a more recent decline in commissioning levels. Outlining the increasing engagement of preschoolers with digital media activities, it considers how broadcasters and producers have responded to the opportunities and challenges that have arisen in attempting to engage with multiplatform content. Based on interviews and industry analysis, this chapter questions whether new platforms offer a viable and complementary alternative distribution outlet for preschool content producers, suggesting that traditional broadcast players are likely to remain dominant in the marketplace on the strength of their marketing expertise, greater brand awareness, and larger resources.[3] In so doing, it demonstrates the difficulties for independent producers working in the increasingly convergent digital landscape, whereby broadcasters not only demand content to be exploitable across multiple platforms, but simultaneously also often function to limit independent producers' opportunities — together with other risks associated with online distribution — for the exploitation of IP rights across these new platforms.

Of course the preschool media market represents only a very tiny part of the children's media market, let alone the general television marketplace. However, its evolving production practices and strategies in response to digital developments have implications for the wider television industry in the digital era, constituting a change in the culture of production. Arguably, the preschool sector serves as a microcosm for production and funding issues within the broader international and digital television industry. It shares many of the economic and production issues faced by the industry as a whole but is also distinctive because children's television has always been seen as a socially important programming area, central to any conceivable notion of public service broadcasting. More important still, the focus on children's television and preschool television in particular affords us some insight into the ways in which the industry is trying to capture the interest of children, who are growing up as "digital natives," capable of interacting with a variety of digital media platforms and content.

THE BROADER CONTEXT OF PRESCHOOL TELEVISION

Historically the preschool audience was not a major concern of the television industry, and the first significant preschool programs in the United States and United Kingdom were connected with wider issues around children's development and well-being rather than their potential as a market segment. In Britain during the 1950s, when television for preschool children first started, there was some tentativeness by the BBC (then a monopoly broadcaster) about whether television was appropriate for the three- to five-year age group and whether "mother" might simply use it as a babysitter. According to David Oswell, the BBC preschool audience was not "natural" but created in the 1950s to address these uncertainties. The production of programs like *Andy Pandy* in 1950 for the *Watch with Mother* slot for children aged two to five, represented "the *invention* of this small audience *for broadcasters* and within *the institution of broadcasting*" in order to facilitate the relationship between mother and child through joint viewing.[4] In the United States attempts to provide content for preschoolers were impeded by the revenue-driven orientation of commercial television, which did not view preschool children as a financially viable audience to attract advertisers.[5] Thus it was nonprofit public television that took on the mantle of quality programming for preschoolers, but always with an educational slant.[6] This was particularly so for *Sesame Street*, PBS's flagship preschool show (produced by the Children's Television Workshop), which launched in 1969 and was specifically designed and researched to appeal to disadvantaged children and to promote literacy and numeracy.[7] In both the

United States and the United Kingdom, therefore, early preschool provision was limited in quantity and scope but highly principled in terms of producer assumptions and knowledge about the audience and its needs.[8]

Notwithstanding a lack of commercial interest in this audience, provision for preschoolers was also limited by a lack of space in broadcasters' schedules because of the competing demands of other forms of programming. For example, in the United Kingdom provision by the generalist channels, BBC1 and 2, and commercially funded public service broadcaster (PSB), ITV1, peaked in the mid-1970s at about 1,500 minutes a year. However, by the 1990s this had shifted to minority channels (BBC2 and Channel 4) as BBC1 and ITV began to compete for daytime adult audiences.[9] In the United States too the scheduling of preschool programming had to be accommodated within the rest of PBS's daytime schedules.

However, this perception of preschool as a minority audience, guided by public service goals but with little commercial value, changed from the mid-1990s because of the interplay and confluence of two important factors. First, multichannel cable television (and later digital television) resulted in a massive expansion in airtime that permitted broadcasters to target children, including preschoolers, through dedicated channels or blocks. Second, the children's television community began to recognize the value of separating preschoolers from older children, not just in terms of audience needs, but also in terms of market segmentation and "distinct brand identities" that could be exploited across borders and markets in home entertainment and consumer products.[10]

Where America led, Britain and others would soon follow (KiKa and Super RTL in Germany; Tiji in France; Z@ppelin in the Netherlands). In 1994 U.S. children's cable specialist Nickelodeon revamped Nick Junior, a branded preschool block it had launched in 1989, and announced that it would be spending $30 million over three years to produce preschool programs in competition with PBS because it recognized the growing importance of preschoolers and their parents as consumers.[11] Disney followed with its own dedicated preschool block, Playhouse Disney, in 1997. These changes of strategy would have been influenced by substantial merchandising revenues accumulated in the early 1990s from *Barney and Friends, Shining Time Station* (featuring *Thomas the Tank Engine* from U.K. producer Britt Allcroft) and, of course, *Sesame Street*— revenues that were fueled by broadcast exposure on PBS.[12] U.S. expansion also benefited U.K. preschool producers who exploited what was then an undersupplied niche, although the market has since become saturated and dominated by cable networks' in-house productions.[13] During this period a small number of British producers, most notably HIT Entertainment, developed relationships with Nick Junior and PBS to ensure access to broadcast platforms, which could be used to create an ancillary business (consumer products, DVDS) for their programming in the lucrative U.S. market.[14]

While a small number of British producers were making headway internationally during the 1990s with culturally neutral programming that appealed to global audiences (stop-frame animation, costumed character shows), similar growth was experienced within the United Kingdom, with £22 million spent on original preschool programming by 2002. However, by 2006 expenditure by all broadcasters had halved to £11 million, with CBeebies and commercial PSBS accounting for the majority (£5.9 million and £1.8 million, respectively).[15] The number of original first-run preschool hours broadcast by PSBS had also fallen dramatically to 132 hours, with the BBC accounting for 92 hours.[16] The number of preschool hours broadcast in total was still impressive at over 15,428 in 2006, but it comprised mainly repeats, as broadcasters took advantage of recycling programming to an audience that changes every two to three years.[17] The domestic market in preschool programming had flowered briefly but had contracted suddenly when wider economic problems hit the children's sector in 2006. This was intimately related to the financial pressures felt by the United Kingdom's main commercial public service broadcaster, ITV.[18] Having reduced its financial commitment to children's television over many years, ITV stopped commissioning children's content in December 2005, removing about £25 million a year from the funding pot.[19] In January 2007 it ceased broadcasting children's programming altogether on weekday afternoons on its terrestrial service because it no longer generated adequate advertising revenues.[20] Advertising revenues had been vulnerable for years, but the situation worsened when regulatory authority Ofcom started to implement a ban on advertising for HFSS around programming aimed at the under-sixteens.[21] These events have left the BBC as the dominant force in British children's broadcasting, although it too is facing budget cuts from a lower than expected license fee increase in 2007.

Increasingly, therefore, children's television producers and broadcasters, like television producers and broadcasters more generally, are looking to exploit the opportunities of digital media platforms (Internet, gaming, mobile, video-on-demand) to bridge deficits in funding and promote their output. Indeed, for preschool production the outlook may be less bleak than for other forms of programming (drama, factual) in the digital era because preschool is deemed more attractive for international sales and ancillary exploitation. A small number of properties (*Teletubbies, Bob the Builder, Thomas the Tank Engine*) have been very successful, fueling expansion in the sector as producers plugged budget deficits with external funding from co-production, overseas presales, stock market money and predicted future profitability on consumer product and DVD revenues. Indeed animation and preschool are estimated to account for 90 percent of the £69 million generated by U.K. children's television producers from program sales (£35 million), home entertainment (£11 million), and consumer products (£23 million) in 2006, far exceeding the amounts actually spent by U.K. broadcasters on original production (£11 million in 2006).[22] Most important, many independent producers regard alternative methods of distribution as a way of reducing what they regard as the dominance of broadcasters and distributors in the value chain because "As a market it makes much more sense to go straight to the consumer, ideally without a broadcaster (if you can)." Lobby group Save Kids TV (SKTV) has argued that the future production of indigenous children's content rests on the Internet, user-generated services, and cross-platform services that are more innovative than broadcast television precisely because there are "no established conventions, regulations or business models to protect."[23]

However, multiplatform distribution demands different business models, and this is the puzzle that all participants are trying to unlock. Arguably it represents a particular challenge for producers, who must look for ways of exploiting multiplatform opportunities while negotiating their place within a production ecology in which players coexist, cooperate, and compete with each other.[24] In the United Kingdom this includes a dominant multiplatform broadcaster in the form of the BBC,[25] as well as other existing commercially funded broadcasters and international, mainly U.S., players, such as Nick Junior and Playhouse Disney, operating on digital satellite and cable platforms. This production ecology favors the broadcasters' dominant position, particular that of the BBC, limiting the opportunities for producers to exploit the potential opportunities of multiplatform developments that this chapter will now briefly set out.

THE POTENTIAL OF MULTIPLATFORM FOR PRESCHOOL CONTENT

Web-based content and video-on-demand services pose challenges and opportunities for all broadcasters and producers. At one level they are a potential source of competitive advantage, encouraging new ways of interaction with audiences/users, and they can be used to strengthen brands and generate additional revenues. Yet as alternative platforms to television they also constitute a threat because they compete with traditional media for consumer attention and resources. In the children's market, the situation is more complex still because of the specific characteristics that differentiate children from other sections of the audience. Chief among these is the perceived vulnerability of young audiences and the harsh realities of a commercial marketplace, which may run counter to the "well-being, needs, wishes, rights and wants of children" who are not yet consumers in their own right but "citizens in the making."[26] In practical terms of generating revenues this means there are limits in building a business because it is not possible to charge young children directly for content, and there are also restrictions (voluntary industry codes) on online advertising targeted at them.[27]

Older children, however, are proving adept early adopters of online, mobile, and interactive services.[28] Content providers claim that they are connecting with older children through video games and Web destinations that allow children to "upload content and edit stuff and write their own jokes [and] film stuff," thus driving revenues in other product areas. However, the industry's approach to the younger preschool and early years group aged two to six has been different, focusing on parents as well as children, because it is usually parents who help their children to download "stuff to color in" or play games together with their child in a "lap top" situation. Children up to the age of six are not regarded by the industry as a key market for downloads, mobile phones, or social networking sites. However, this age group does now actively engage in quite complex media activities and is "immersed" in media practices and new technologies almost from birth. In a U.K. survey in 2005 of 1,852 parents and caretakers by Marsh et al., 81 percent of families with children up to age six owned a computer, with parents reporting 53 percent of zero- to six-year-olds using a computer daily, compared with 42 per-

cent who never used one. The top Web sites were mostly TV channel–
or program-related, including (1) CBeebies; (2) CBBC; (3) Nick Junior;
(4) *Bob the Builder*; (5) *Barbie*; (6) *Tweenies*; (7) *Thomas the Tank Engine*;
(8/9) *Teletubbies* /Disney; and (10) *Balamory*. Parents reported that their
children demonstrated "impressive skills and knowledge" in relation to
new technologies. Favorite activities included games and printouts, but
most children required parental help. In Marsh's study only 5 percent of
children age six or younger reported having visited a Web site on their
own, but it was the children's interests that drove use—often stimulated
by seeing programs on television. Some preschoolers are then clearly
engaged in online activities, but television remains their most frequent
form of media engagement, accounting for about eighty-two minutes of
their day.[29]

Although the usage of the zero- to six-year-old group is modest by
comparison with older children, the spread of broadband Internet access with the bandwidth to accommodate video is stimulating growth
in Web-based TV and interactive platforms for children, including some
services for younger children. Children are already accessing social networking sites like Facebook, MySpace, and Bebo; video/file-sharing sites
like YouTube and Piczo; and online games like RuneScape. However,
these sites are usually targeted at older children and restricted to the
over-thirteens. Children's sites include virtual worlds like Club Penguin
(owned by Disney) and the BBC's Adventure Rock; virtual pet worlds such
as Webkinz and Neopets (owned by Viacom); games site Nicktropolis
(part of Nickelodeon); and personalized Web pages such as MYCBeebies
and MYCBBC. None of these are specifically targeted at preschoolers, although Club Penguin has the youngest age profile, with users as young
as six. With seven hundred thousand paying members, it was acquired
by Disney in 2007 for $350 million.[30] Virtual worlds like Club Penguin
and RuneScape have proved that there are ways of monetizing content
through subscription, but none of these are based on existing television
properties.

Alongside the branded preschool/young children's sites of U.K.-based
broadcasters CBeebies, Nick Junior, Cartoonito (Cartoon Network), Five,
and Playhouse Disney, which function primarily as online extensions of
their broadcast content (clicks-and-bricks), there are also TV character–
and program-based sites, run by rights owners, but no separate Web-
based U.K. destinations for preschoolers (pure plays). The situation is

rather different in the larger U.S. market, which also has a burgeoning video-on-demand industry on cable.[31] In the United States KOL Junior, an offshoot of Internet portal AOL, provides a preschool Web site with games, printables, music, stories, and full streamed episodes from a small range of preschool series, including U.K.-produced *Jim Jam and Sunny*. Other preschool sites in the United States providing streamed video are linked with digital cable (both as free video-on-demand services and linear channels). They include Kabillion Junior, PBS Kids Sprout, and Qubo, which are all joint ventures among U.S., U.K., and European companies. As free channels, these currently serve as an additional cross-promotion outlet for the programming of content owners, who might not otherwise be able to secure access for their programming on U.S. children's channels to drive their other business interests.[32]

For British-based preschool producers wishing to make their programming available online or via video-on-demand in the United Kingdom, third-party alternatives to broadcasters are largely restricted to general Web-based aggregator services like YouTube, Joost, Babelgum, Vuze, and Jalipo, where preschool does not have a high profile.[33] The arrival of the BBC's iPlayer at the end of 2007, an online free catch-up service that allows viewers to watch programs seven days after transmission as streamed or downloaded episodes, has also muddied the waters. Large amounts of preschool content from CBeebies schedules are available for free on the iPlayer, including a dedicated CBeebies iPlayer (http://www.bbc.co.uk/iplayer/cbeebies). As the chapter outlines below, this is indicative of the unevenness of relationships between established broadcasters and producers within the digital era.

UNEVEN PLATFORMS: BROADCASTERS AND PRODUCERS IN A MULTIPLATFORM ERA

All preschool broadcast channels in the United Kingdom operate Web sites as they seek to strengthen their brands and build relationships with children and their parents, but according to Save Kids TV, these are "little more than promotional extensions of their broadcast offerings."[34] Broadcasters have an advantage over producers, therefore, in their established brand equity, technical expertise, content, and existing relationships with viewers and (in the case of preschool channels) with parents. In Britain CBeebies has made the largest strides in developing an online and interactive presence. Framed as part of the BBC's public service commitment, the success of CBeebies underpins the corporation's continued existence in the digital era by promising to act as a safe destination for a vulnerable audience in a highly competitive marketplace. The CBeebies site was redesigned in 2007 and features pages devoted to individual programs, games, stories, printables, suggestions for "make and do," songs, Internet radio, short streamed video clips, and information and advice for parents. This commitment to digital media for young children and their parents is built into CBeebies' annual service license, which positions CBeebies as a leader in the "development of new media interactive content and applications for the target age group . . . enabling audiences to participate or to deepen their experience of a programme. Online and interactive sources should support the service, including enhanced text-based information for parents and carers as well as stimulating stories, games and puzzles for preschool children."[35]

As a multiplatform brand (television, radio, online), CBeebies has shifted from a "TV commissioning process" to a "content commissioning process,"[36] addressing BBC director general Mark Thompson's argument that the BBC should "no longer think of itself as a broadcaster of TV and radio with some new media on the side" but should aim "to deliver public service content to our audiences in whatever media and on whatever device makes sense to them whether they're at home or on the move."[37]

As part of this process in-house and independent producers are encouraged to think about the Web and enhanced TV as part of a more joined-up process that integrates online and interactive components, but not all programs are suitable for online exploitation. According to the head of BBC Children's, Richard Deverell, "Very few [shows] merit a website, mobile, fully interactive TV, radio and possibly a book or magazine."[38] CBeebies has an internal online team and budget to develop Web pages for specific properties with interactive potential, including acquisitions (*Gordon the Gnome*), commissions (*In the Night Garden*), and in-house productions (*Space Pirates*). Indeed *Tommy Zoom*, an in-house animated/live-action series about an environmentally motivated boy superhero, started off as a Web project designed to encourage boys aged four to six to read. Although some producers see this as a useful cross-promotional activity, as the chapter details below, external producers do not benefit financially from a presence on the Web site—which carries no advertising and has no links to e-commerce sites—raising questions as to how to monetize such multiplatform commitments.[39]

Outside of the BBC, Nick Junior's, Playhouse Disney's, and Five's

Milkshake Web sites replicate much of what is available on cbeebies (games, clips, downloads). Nick Junior has used its site to pre-launch full streamed episodes of key programming, notably u.k.-produced commission *Roary the Racing Car* (Chapman Entertainment) and U.S. import *Yo Gabba Gabba*. It regards the Internet as a complementary outlet that enhances television and builds excitement.[40] However, most sites show only streamed clips rather than downloads, possibly because of technical limitations, the costs, and the risk of undermining their core television offerings.[41]

A further challenge for the preschool production ecology revolves around how television content can be adapted for other platforms. While this can produce creative responses, arguably the adoption of multi-platform commissioning processes—particularly by the bbc—further strengthens the broadcasters' position. Most audiovisual online content produced for British children is derived from existing television material. While broadcasters have the resources to subsidize their online presence as part of their wider promotional activities, for smaller producers engagement with digital media constitutes more of a risk with little guarantee of financial return. Broadcasters are keen for producers to think beyond television, which cbeebies controller Michael Carrington suggests

> [is] a case of the pendulum having to swing in a big way to get producers to think about these things because traditionally they've all sat in their little box making a tv show in their cottage. And now it's time to get out of the cottage and think about all of the other aspects and elements that children are engaging with content. And so what we've done is thrown the pendulum the other way and said "think about 360 degree programming." That sounds a bit scary because it means that you've got to spend more money and where does that extra money come from?[42]

Among television executives and producers there is also wariness about digital media concerns taking priority over creative considerations. According to Nick Wilson, director of children's television at Channel Five, "I think that anybody who lets their content be dominated by what they're going to put on the web is going to come to a sticky end because I still think content is absolutely king."[43] This view is supported by producers, who emphasize the importance of starting with a strong linear narrative and distinctive characters before they start to think about on-line or interactive applications:

> I don't think you can start with the technology. I think you have to start with character or with a really great idea, like another idea that I've just pitched today is about a space dog, and he's an alien dog with really superior intelligence and he finds it really humiliating. So it really expresses what kids can feel about the indignities that their parents put them through. So, to me, that's a great concept. That's a really funny, original idea. Now that could have all sorts of applications. You could have a space dog game on the computer. You could have a space dog Tamagotchi. At this point that's not how I would be thinking. I would be thinking about who that character is, what the story is, developing the relationship between them.

However, for other producers digital media are changing what they do, as they try and shape their content in ways that reflect children's changing media consumption habits. This starts during development and means thinking beyond television: "The big change has been, it used to be television series that one produced, purely storytelling, and now it's about a concept, an idea that kids can follow wherever they're going. Whereas a TV series used to be the hub of the wheel, that's now just another spoke. You've got TV series for the games, for the toys, you've got the play patterns. . . . They're buying into an idea, and we're trying to create ideas that can move equally across all these different media, so they'll take more of the lead in the play pattern world."

The Internet is the preferred digital media platform above mobile and games for preschool content, but the development of an online presence for preschool television properties requires a more stripped-down approach than content aimed at older children. Sites are basic, with simple activities, and it is always assumed that children are accessing them together with their parents—much as it used to be assumed that young children watched television with their mothers. According to one producer who has used feedback from parents and educational consultants to fine-tune the Web presence of its properties,

> For preschool it is completely different. When we rebuilt the brand websites, some of the feedback suggested that some of the games, while incredibly simple, might be a bit difficult for tiny people to do.

So we are having to do things like introduce more games that are just spacebar motivated, so all they have to do is press the spacebar at the right time. . . . I think they get introduced to computers at a very early age now . . . but they have to sit there with their parents. So when we're thinking about what we're going to create for online we make the assumption that they're unlikely to be sitting there on their own. Certainly the three year olds will need the carer to be sitting with them saying "why don't we do this?" At the end of the day the most popular thing on a preschool website is the black and white printouts that they print out and color in.

This simplicity also needs to extend to the technology used to access online content so that parents can "be bothered to do it" with the child.

Despite such creative responses to producing multiplatform content, independent producers have struggled to exploit such opportunities. While broadcasters' approach to multiplatform, and online in particular, is largely complementary to their mainstream broadcasting activities, for many cash-starved British independent producers, money from new platforms remains a major hurdle. This is particularly true for producers in the children's market, with producer revenues from digital media and video-on-demand largely insignificant and online representing an additional cost rather than a means of revenue generation.[44] According to one commercially funded broadcaster, "The question mark is how we commercialize it, which we haven't come to a conclusion on yet, and obviously isn't an issue the BBC have to worry about, whereas we do. Whatever we do on our website has to pay for itself. So there have to be revenues from somewhere—from advertising or whatever."

Commercially funded broadcasters and producers with Web sites can generate revenues from multiple sources, including selling advertising/sponsorship space, site subscriptions, the sale of merchandise (e-commerce), and taking a percentage of all partner sales, which occur as a result of being directed from a partner site.[45] While the BBC's status as a public service broadcaster prevents the corporation from benefiting from direct transactional activities or advertising, this is not the case for its commercial subsidiary, BBC Worldwide, which does advertise online and allows BBC content to appear on advertiser-supported sites (for example, YouTube). For independent producers who license their content to third-party Web or video-on-demand services, revenues derive predominantly from revenue shares, based on subscriptions or advertising or a mixture of both. This is particularly problematic given that, as discussed above, mobile content remains unsuitable for the preschool market despite being easier to monetize, while preschool children and their parents constitute too small a niche market for advertising, and restrictions on HFSS food advertising on television are unlikely to be flouted online in the United Kingdom.[46] Nor can the preschool audience be construed as a viable pay-per-view market, with parents unlikely to pay for preschool content, which they can get free either online or on traditional broadcast outlets.[47] Low revenues also mean low production budgets for online content.[48]

The pressure to monetize content from a number of digital media platforms means that some larger producer-distributors "are certainly looking at download, web content, what can be downloaded to a PSP or a handheld" during development and are investing heavily in their own brand-based Web sites to drive sales in other areas. According to one head of international sales at a leading children's television distributor, "There is not a single production that we do that doesn't absolutely look at a 360 degree environment. . . . The web 2.0 experience is exactly where we're going." Many programs are now developed with an associated Web site in order to "give children more exposure to the brand," even if it is limited to simple games and printables. However, the Internet is a "cluttered medium," and existing television brands are still regarded as the quickest and most efficient way of creating awareness among a larger target audience. While multiplatform applications are seen as an important development that *may* offer producers some freedom from aggregators/distributors, all producers emphasize the importance of securing a broadcast television sale, preferably to CBeebies, Nick Junior, or Five, because these outlets provide "your first and greatest impact," driving other important revenue streams in DVD and licensed product.

While television is therefore a necessity, Internet revenues remain an uncertain and secondary source of income. Producers are unsure about how to make money from the Web and are anxious about losing control over their properties to third parties. According to one U.K. producer, "Our strategy as a company is probably the same as everybody else's in that we're all searching for new financial models. And we're searching for financial models that don't effectively leave us simply as a service provider at the end of the day." Among smaller players this uncertainty is compounded by their own perceived lack of expertise in the online arena, particularly in marketing and customer service.

For the time being, online or mobile platforms are seen more as promotional space than as revenue generators, as a means of getting program brands into the public domain or as precursors to discussions with potential funders and licensees. For example, Entertainment Rights launched its live-action costumed character series *Jim Jam and Sunny* on KOL Junior in the United States because it would not necessarily have had a massive broadcast audience in the highly competitive U.S. marketplace. The show's format further lends itself to online distribution because it is highly segmented and can be broken down into stand-alone clips, games, and songs. Similarly, the live-action costumed character music show *Yo Gabba Gabba* started off as an online pilot in 2006 on sites like YouTube and MySpace before attracting the attention of Nick Junior in the United States.[49] This is an approach that works well for short-form animated content, which some producers are now developing online first in the hope that it may transfer to television later if there is sufficient audience feedback. The Net is therefore seen as a "way of testing ideas," allowing producers to get reactions from "the biggest focus group around," for a small amount of outlay, using low-cost technologies like Flash animation.

Rights issues and revenue shares are another area that has proved a sticking point because processes and procedures are not yet settled in a fast-evolving market, as the 2007–2008 Writers Guild of America (WGA) strike in Hollywood illustrated. There is an inherent tension between broadcasters wishing to use content they have funded in online situations and producers who wish to use that content elsewhere. For broadcasters the conflict centers around exclusivity, licensing terms, and revenue shares. In the United Kingdom the terms of trade agreed in the aftermath of the 2003 Communications Act allow producers to exploit their programs in secondary markets that were previously the preserve of free-to-air broadcasters, but the allocation of digital media rights has not always been straightforward.[50]

Producers would argue that they are not unwilling to get involved in new platforms that bring their content to a larger audience—particularly if the broadcaster grows the brand and this benefits DVD and licensed product sales. Rather, they are unwilling to let broadcasters take additional rights that are not part of the traditional broadcast bundle—

particularly if the broadcaster has not fully funded the production and the producer has had to secure deficit finance. In some territories, but less in the United Kingdom, broadcasters seek to acquire exclusive rights across the board; such rights diminish producers' ability to secure a financial return on their productions. In the view of one producer-distributor,

> We are very happy for any of our licensees, irrespective of the size of the broadcaster, the country, where their background is, whatever, to pick up as many rights as they want. But there has to be some kind of commercial reward to the rights owners, particularly when that show is not fully funded, because traditionally if it's not fully funded by the broadcaster, you have to go elsewhere to make up the difference. If the broadcaster is picking up all those rights, we're not getting any revenues back from it even if . . . they're using it commercially, whether it's ad supported or subscription based. And if we're not getting anything back from that, how do we make up that difference? . . . For me, the perfect position on all these new rights is that everyone takes a non-exclusive position: the broadcaster gets rights non-exclusively, we still get some rights non-exclusively, so we still get some rights on commercial platforms. And then everybody's win-win. That's not always the broadcasters' position.

For producers the best way to exploit digital rights is to keep license terms short (eighteen months to three years) and non-exclusive to take account of any new developments in a fast-moving market. However, this sometimes puts them into conflict with broadcasters who want extensive and exclusive rights, which can undermine a producer's revenue opportunities in other areas—notably DVD:

> The big challenge is having to sign off on something where someone will take all platform rights and any media hereafter invented and doesn't actually tell you what they're going to be doing with it because they haven't got that far. . . . And we do have to think about things like "how is this going to impact upon our home entertainment partners?" because they're an important part of what we do, certainly in the UK and in other territories, so it's about getting the balance right between how much content we make available on various online platforms or VOD platforms and how do we keep DVD special and keep driving people to go and buy DVDs?

Another area under pressure from the Internet in particular is sales by territory. Traditionally broadcast sales have taken place on a territory-by-territory basis to maximize revenues. However, Web sites are not limited to one country. Geo-filtering allows online content such as program clips to be restricted to a certain territory, protecting pay and broadcast free-to-air licensees in neighboring or same-language markets, but these deals are increasingly under pressure from outlets that want to be available in multiple territories. With further concerns raised by some producers over the insecurity of digital rights management systems on new platforms such as YouTube, independent producers are left stuck between a desire to try new platforms but also maintain and protect the commercial value of their rights in other areas.

Digital technology has turned out to be something of a mixed blessing for preschool producers. In the first wave of multichannel and digital expansion the preschool market was recognized as commercially valuable, and a number of preschool blocks and channels emerged on both sides of the Atlantic. These in turn raised awareness of programming, which benefited other revenue-generating areas in home entertainment (DVD) and licensed merchandise. For a brief period, broadcasters in the United Kingdom—foremost the BBC—increased their commissioning levels and spent to fill their new schedules. While broadcasters did not always pay enough to fully fund the most ambitious shows, producers were buoyed by a vibrant international marketplace and secondary revenues. However, this brief flowering has proved rather illusory. British broadcasters pay little for programming—no more than 25 percent of the budget for animation or costumed character shows with licensing or international potential—but producers are finding it more difficult to fund budget deficits.

Digital media platforms have provided little of an alternative to producers. While older children promise to be a market for gaming products and mobile downloads, the prospects for the preschool market are limited by the unsophisticated nature of the audience and the many competing sources of content that are free and widely available. The second wave of digital multiplatform media therefore offers rather fewer opportunities for preschool content as a business. Current developments suggest that television will continue to be an important factor in the commercial exploitation of preschool television and that big-name trusted brands and traditional content associated with television—the BBC, Nickelodeon, Disney—will continue as dominant players.[51] In spite of the radical newness of digital media and online spaces for this age group, they are still largely colonized by existing television companies, offering little financial comfort to those smaller producers with ambitions to produce high-quality multiplatform content for young children, who, after all, promise to be the next generation of digital natives. The existing networks cater for the preschool market as a niche, but there is little institutional plurality or plurality of supply as dominant broadcasters constantly repurpose content for a variety of platforms, including content that they own, commissioning surprisingly little new material from external suppliers and undermining the overall plurality of the sector. While some of the challenges and opportunities detailed here may be distinctive to the preschool production ecology, the ability of existing broadcasters to establish strong bonds with tomorrow's "digital natives" suggests that digital, multiplatform television may continue to be dominated by the existing players for a long while yet to come.

NOTES

The research undertaken for this chapter was funded by a grant from the Arts and Humanities Research Council (AHRC) (119149).

1. Michael Carrington, "BBC Children's Webchat for Independent Producers," May 24, 2006; http://www.bbc.co.uk.
2. Jackie Marsh et al., *Digital Beginnings: Young Children's Use of Popular Culture, Media and New Technologies* (Sheffield: Literacy Research Centre, University of Sheffield, 2005); Victoria Rideout, Elizabeth Vandewater, and Ellen Wartella, *Zero to Six: Electronic Media in the Lives of Infants, Toddlers and Preschoolers* (Menlo Park, Calif.: Kaiser Family Foundation, 2003).
3. All quotations, unless otherwise indicated, are taken from personal interviews. With the exception of particular channel controllers, these have been anonymized.
4. David Oswell, "Watching with Mother in the Early 1950s," in *In Front of the Children: Screen Entertainment and Young Audiences*, ed. Cary Bazalgette and David Buckingham (London: British Film Institute, 1995), 37–38.
5. Norma Pecora, *The Business of Children's Television* (New York: Guilford Press, 1998), 99; Karen Raugust, *Merchandise Licensing in the Television Industry* (Boston: Focal Press, 1996), 30.

6. Linda Simensky. "Programming Children's Television: The PBS Model," in *The Children's Television Community*, ed. J. Alison Bryant (Mahwah, N.J.: Lawrence Erlbaum, 2007), 132.

7. See Edward Palmer and Shalom Fisch, "The Beginnings of *Sesame Street* Research," in *"G" Is for Growing: Thirty Years of Research on Children and Sesame Street*, ed. Shalom Fisch and Rosemarie Truglio, 3–25 (Mahwah, N.J.: Lawrence Erlbaum, 2001).

8. Maire Messenger-Davies, "Babes 'n' the Hood: Pre-School Television and Its Audiences in the United States and Britain," in Bazalgette and Buckingham, *In Front of the Children*, 16.

9. David Buckingham, Hannah Davies, Ken Jones, and Peter Kelley, *Children's Television in Britain* (London: BFI, 1999), 98.

10. See Lyn Eryl-Jones, "Playtime All the Time: CBeebies, A Case Study," *Advertising and Marketing to Children*, July–September 2003, 3.

11. Bill Carter, "Cable Challenger for PBS as King of the Preschool Hill," *New York Times*, March 21, 1994, 1.

12. Pecora, *The Business of Children's Television*, 108.

13. Jeanette Steemers, *Selling Television: British Television in the Global Marketplace* (London: BFI, 2004), 134.

14. Ibid., 134–35.

15. Ofcom, *The Future of Children's Television Programming* (London: Ofcom, 2007), 62; Oliver and Ohlbaum Associates, *The UK Children's Market* (London: Oliver and Ohlbaum, 2007), 26.

16. Ofcom, *The Future of Children's Television Programming*, 30.

17. Ibid., 30.

18. See Karen Lury's chapter in this volume.

19. Stephen Andrews, ITV Digital Channels program director, comments during the BAFTA Children's Committee Public Debate, September 13, 2006. At the end of 2007 ITV started commissioning a small amount of material for its digital children's channel, CITV.

20. See Oliver and Ohlbaum, *The UK Children's Market*, 15; Ofcom, *The Future of Children's Television Programming*, 55.

21. Ofcom, *Childhood Obesity: Food Advertising in Context* (London: Ofcom, July 22, 2004); Ofcom, *Television Advertising of Food and Drink Products to Children: Options for New Restrictions* (London: Ofcom, March 28, 2006).

22. Oliver and Ohlbaum, *The UK Children's Market*, 32. The £69 million figure is almost certainly an underestimate as it does not include "international license sales," which might add another £70 million.

23. Save Kids TV (SKTV), *Response to Ofcom Consultation: "The Future of Children's Television Programming,"* December 17, 2007, 2.

24. Simon Cottle, "Producing Nature(s): The Changing Production Ecology of

Natural History TV," in *Media Organization and Production*, ed. Simon Cottle, 170–71 (London: Sage, 2003).

25. See Niki Strange's entry in this volume.

26. Maire Messenger-Davies, BBC *Digital Review: CBEEBIES and CBBC* (London: DCMS, September 2004), 10.

27. Ofcom, *The Future of Children's Television Programming*, 193.

28. Sonia Livingstone and Magdalena Bober, UK *Children Go Online: Final Report of Key Project Findings* (London: London School of Economics and Political Science, 2005).

29. Marsh et al., *Digital Beginnings*, 27–39.

30. Jonathan Webdale, "Virtual Goldrush," *C21Media.net*, November 21, 2007; http://www.c21media.net/common/print_detail.asp?article=38734.

31. Ed Waller, "A Demanding Business," *C21Media.net*, March 4, 2008; http://www.c21media.net/common/print_detail.asp?area=2.

32. Ed Waller, "Kabillion-Dollar Business," *C21Media.net*, October 16, 2007; http://www.c21media.net/common/print_detail.asp?article=38114.

33. Poz Watson, "Welcome to the Age of Internet TV," *Televisual*, August 2007, 25–28.

34. Save Kids TV (SKTV), *Response to Ofcom Consultation: "The Future of Children's Television Programming,"* December 17, 2007, 5.

35. BBC Trust, *CBeebies Service Licence*, April 30, 2007, 2.

36. Richard Deverell, Controller of BBC Children's cited in Jules Grant, "Joined-Up Thinking—Part One," *C21Media.net*, February 1, 2007. http://www.c21media.net/common/print_detail.asp?article=34315.

37. Mark Thompson, "Royal Television Society Fleming Memorial Lecture 2006: Creative Future—The BBC Programs and Content in an On-Demand World," April 25, 2006; http://www.bbc.co.uk/pressoffice.

38. Cited in Jules Grant, "Joined-Up Thinking—Part One," *C21Media.net*, February 1, 2007; http://www.c21media.net/common/print_detail.asp?article=34315.

39. Interviews with independent producers.

40. Debbie MacDonald, senior vice president of programming, Nickelodeon UK, Showcomotion Conference, Sheffield, July 6, 2007.

41. Ofcom, *The Future of Children's Television Programming*, 194.

42. Interview March 6, 2007.

43. Interview with Nick Wilson, director of children's programs, Channel Five, November 28, 2006.

44. Oliver and Ohlbaum, *The UK Children's Market*, 33.

45. Sylvia Chan-Olmsted and Louisa Ha, "Internet Business Models for Broadcasters: How Television Stations Perceive and Integrate the Internet," *Broadcasting and Electronic Media* 47 (2003): 601–2.

46. See Louisa Ha and Richard Ganahl, "Webcasting Business Models of Clicks-

and-Bricks and Pure-Play Media: A Comparative Study of Leading Webcasters in South Korea and the United States," *International Journal of Media Management* 6, nos. 1–2 (2004): 84.

47. See ibid., 75; Jim Curtis, "Get Shorty," *C21Media.net*, June 30, 2006; http://www.c21media.net/common/print_detail.asp?article=31096.

48. See Malcolm Bird, "When's It Going on TV," *C21Media.net*, April 10, 2006; http://www.c21media.net/common/print_detail.asp?article=29914.

49. Christian Jacobs, Magic Productions, co-creator of *Yo Gabba Gabba*, Showco-motion Conference, Sheffield, July 6, 2007.

50. See Richard Haynes, *Media Rights and Intellectual Property* (Edinburgh: Edinburgh University Press, 2005), 95. Under terms of trade agreed with producers' association PACT, the BBC is allowed free video-on-demand rights for seven days before and after the first television transmission for use on the iPlayer. C4, Five, and ITV have negotiated a thirty-day free window for video-on-demand and pay-per-view. Download-to-own rights in all cases are exclusive to the producer with an 85/15 revenue share in favor of the producer. There are no such agreements with cable and satellite channels, and each deal is subject to negotiation. In November 2007 the BBC concluded a new rights framework with producers for stand-alone new media content, recognizing that interactive producers also own the rights of the content they create, just as television producers do. See Leigh Holmwood, "BBC Agrees New Rights Framework," *The Guardian*, November 26, 2007; http://www.guardian.co.uk.

51. See David Hesmondhalgh and Sarah Baker, "Creative Work in the Cultural Industries," *International Symposium: Transformations in the Cultural and Media Industries* (September 2006), 3–4; http://observatoire-omic.org.

KAREN LURY

"THE BASIS FOR MUTUAL CONTEMPT"

The Loss of the Contingent in Digital Television

In the face of the abstraction of time, its transformation into
the discrete, the measurable, the locus of value, chance and the
contingent are assigned an important ideological role—they
become the highly cathected sites of both pleasure and anxiety.

Mary Ann Doane, *The Emergence of Cinematic Time*

By the time one has passed a given step, put it behind one, the
next one is already there. By the time one knows everything, one
has already understood it all. . . . Were it not for that sequencing in
time, and were the entire knowledge to crash in upon a person on
the spot, at one fell swoop, it might well be that neither one's brain
nor one's heart would cope with it.

Imre Kertesz, *Fateless*

In her groundbreaking article, "Information, Crisis and Catastrophe," Mary Ann Doane used an economic model—drawing on catastrophe theory—to identify the "deep structure"
of commercial television as time.[1] She argued that television
does not just simply use and regulate time for the viewer but
persistently refers, via its mode of address and in its representations, to time and temporality. It does so, she suggested, to
legitimate the importance of television and to justify its invasive presence in our lives. She argued: "The major category of
television is time. Time is television's basis, its principle of
structuration, as well as its persistent reference."[2]

My chapter is a response to, and a development of, Doane's argument in this article, drawing on her later work on time and the image from her book *The Emergence of Cinematic Time: Modernity, Contingency and the Archive*. As the epigraph above suggests, it is her later focus on the contingent—the captured accident, the "something else," or the extraneous detail captured by the mechanical reproduction of the analog image—that underpins my argument. I will suggest that while certain aspects of digital television now rely and emphasize the performance of contingency, they do so in order to actively repress the contingent itself. What follows is therefore a description of the rigidity and hollowness of time as it is manifest in some aspects of digital television. For me, this represents the way in which broadcast television's previous operations—such as the creation of shared intimacy, empathy, and social cohesion—are called into question. In effect, it becomes evident that broadcasters no longer seek to entertain or serve their audiences but to control them.

Control is achieved, primarily, through performance and modes of address and secondarily, but increasingly, through the manipulation of the image itself. Across a variety of television genres the performance of television actors and presenters in the digital era comes closer and closer to existing corporate models of customer service, in which employees are trained to act spontaneously within carefully rehearsed roles, or as Heather Hopfl suggests, to reproduce "the professionalization of performed hypocrisy."[3] Professionalized hypocrisy is manifest in television by the appearance of naturalness and spontaneity, openness, and self-reflexivity, which actually represent, as Hopfl suggests, "the predictable and consistent performance of a well-regulated machine" and are thus "spontaneous in the sense of mechanical automatisms."[4] Corpsing—as an aspect of performance in which the "mask slips" and the potential for the shared revelation of a concealed ambivalence (of the actors and the audience)—is now apparently legitimated within this form of presentation. So rather than the corpsing of the performer exposing a breakdown of the system, or an "instance of the unpredictable," such moments are actively promoted as part of the "reality" of the interaction between audience and presenter. Thus the potentially disruptive qualities of the "corpse" are now contained by a system in which other aspects of contingency are similarly controlled. In fact, televised performance in the digital era could be said to be defined by the "regulation of the corpse."[5] I will suggest that this regulation applies not only to living performers

but also, increasingly, to the representation of people and material artifacts from the past.

In the first part of this chapter I investigate ITV's short-lived attempt
to animate—literally bring to life or bring "live"—what had previously
been "dead time" within the schedule via a series of related interactive
quiz shows collectively known as "ITV Play." In a discussion focusing
on the organization of time and the performance of the presenters in
these programs I will demonstrate that the repression or regulation of
contingency (in the form of chance) and corpsing (aspects of performance such as verbal fluffs, laughter, and a personalized and interactive
relationship between performer and audience) generates a context in
which the presenters (always) and the audience (increasingly) are aware
that their apparent intimacy, and the truly alarming or utopian potential of contingency, is an illusion. Following Hopfl's arguments in relation to the training and production of a corporate personality, I suggest
that this has, not surprisingly, generated the basis for a relationship of
"mutual contempt" among broadcasters, their employees, and the television audience.

In the second part of the essay, I want to further my examination of
the loss of contingency and its consequences for television and move
from thinking about how television regulates live performance and the
present and, instead, explore time on television in relation to its representation and (re)creation. That is, I will investigate how the digital *production* of images (CGI, or computer-generated imaging) seemingly compels television producers to illustrate stories about the future and the
past in a manner that refuses history and abuses science. I suggest that
the digital production of images has allowed for an even greater manifestation of what Doane originally called "simulated visibility." As she suggests, this simulation is driven by television's compulsion to manufacture images that are spectacular and that ignore or supersede the claims
of (visually inadequate) indexical evidence or scientific speculation. This
tendency is determined by television's desire to illustrate information,
argument, and recollection with images that Doane described as functioning in a manner that "If it could be seen this is what it might look
like."[6] That is, digital television has exaggerated television's tendency
to privilege visibility over the limitations of the indexical "trace," despite the fact that it is this "trace" that awards authority and sentiment
to the television image. In a discussion of two recent history programs

(*Virtual History: The Plot to Kill Hitler and Auschwitz*) and one "natural history" series about an anticipated future (*Life without People*) I argue that the seductive potential of digital imaging creates a spurious sense of omnipotence for the viewer. The irony of such images is that as digital (that is, as wholly determined) images, they still refer to or depend upon the authority awarded by the previously contingent aspects of the analog image. Although digital images may be dressed or distressed to appear "as if" they were indexical images, the audience is increasingly aware of these strategies and recognizes them for what they are. Indeed, one could see such images as immobile "death masks" that obscure and regulate the unpredictable qualities of the corpse to which they refer. Since there is no possibility that the contingent will "accidentally appear" in the digital image, it cannot provoke either the pleasures or anxieties that Doane describes. Digital images are controlling, safe images in which the more terrifying aspects of the contingent—described in the epigraph from Kertesz—cannot threaten, as there is no point in which the totality of knowledge (or what Doane calls an "excess of designation") will "crash in" on the viewer. Instead everything has already been understood, as Kertesz says, "step by step," and to do otherwise would be, precisely, unimaginable.[7] Digital images effectively function as a protective carapace—a glittering, hard shell—protecting the viewer from the fleshy mess and mortality of the history and reality that lies beneath. The loss of the contingent means that these images cannot "touch" or move us as analog photographs once had the potential to do. As Bernard Stiegler explains in relation to his encounter with Nadar's photograph of Baudelaire:

> I know that I'm not going to be able to touch Baudelaire by putting my finger on his photographed face: he is dead and gone. And yet the luminances that emanated from Baudelaire's face at the moment Nadar's camera captured and froze it forever *still touch me, beyond the shadow of a doubt*. This moving [émouvant] (it arouses, in me, a dull movement): the ghostly effect is, in this instance, the sentiment of an absolute *irreversibility*. And this is what is so singular about this "touch": it touches me, I'm touched, but I'm not able to touch. I'm not able to be "touched" and "toucher" [*touché* and *touchant*].[8]

It is the very completeness and increasing sophistication of digitally generated images on television that necessarily eradicates the potential for the audience to be touched or to feel "moved." The sentiment and singularity of the analog image is being replaced by the slick momentum of what Stiegler has called the "calculated" image. In the era of CGI we are propelled by digital image sequences into encounters with simulated actors and a simulated past in which the irreversibility of time has no purchase.

ITV PLAY

ITV Play was an interactive quiz game launched simultaneously on ITV1 (terrestrial) and ITV2 (digital) on April 1, 2006. Originating from a successful German format, the program was initially shown between midnight and 4 a.m. This proved successful, and an entire digital channel—called ITV Play—was launched shortly after as a stand-alone part of ITV's digital provision, transmitting twenty-four hours a day, seven days a week. The format of the show was simple: a quiz was presented live by one or more presenters in the studio, and viewers were encouraged to call in and win a varying amount of money for each correct answer. While each quiz was broadly similar, different programming blocks (each usually four hours long) were themed and given titles, such as "The Mint," "Quizmania," and "Glitterball." "Glitterball" looked like a cross between the long-established game show *Wheel of Fortune* and the BBC's lottery program. While the studio itself is relatively bare, the lights are bright, and the host stands before a large screen onto which the questions and answers are projected (figure 1). While "cheap and cheerful," the show conforms to basic light entertainment conventions in terms of its televisual presentation and mode of address. As a slight variation, "The Mint" had a more detailed set and was dressed to appear like an "opulent" domestic interior with a "cash vault" placed center stage. In all of the programs the background music was a muted "rave" mix—unsurprisingly much like the music that is played on the telephone during a call center wait. Otherwise, aside from the presenter's constant chatter and the occasional voices of viewers who had gotten through to the studio, the sound mix included faint cheers or roars of encouragement, which were apparently emanating from a nonexistent studio audience. The likable, attractive, and persuasive hosts (a variety of young men and women working alone or in pairs) encouraged the viewer to call in and provide answers to a range of different questions. Many of the quizzes were in the form of a word poser—for instance, "What words begin with

FIGURE 1 ITV Play game shows, such as "Glitterball," address the viewers through familiar television performance tropes but, in animating the previously "dead time" of late-night TV, constantly promise "This is next!" and that "this" is what they have been waiting to see.

the preposition 'UP'?" Other quizzes were loosely tied to general knowledge questions or plausible sounding "guessing games," familiar from shows such as *Family Fortunes*—for example, "What items might you expect to find in a woman's handbag?"

Over the four hours of a program block the amount of money to be won rose and fell for certain periods, meaning that the prize for a correct answer might be as much as £1,000 or as little as £200. Tension and excitement were established, first, through the hosts' performances: speaking directly into the camera, they connected to the audience by moving closer to the camera when talking to callers, occasionally pausing when answers were given, but otherwise maintaining an almost constant flow of "improvised" chatter. Such performances required stamina more than skill, and the hosts also maintained an unnerving degree of unblinking eye contact as they encouraged viewers to call in "to win"—the recurring catchphrase being, "You have to be in it to win it." Second, suspense and the hard-sell atmosphere were accelerated via temporal condensation—in one recurring stunt, a two-minute time period would be shown counting down on the in-studio screen, apparently guarantee-ing that "someone" would get through in this time frame. The quizzes were deemed not to be gambling (since you could compete for free via the Web site) and were initially categorized as "games of skill" by Ofcom (the United Kingdom's broadcasting regulator). However, it became in-creasingly evident that to win anything would take some ingenuity: first, there was the initial problem of getting through; second, one would have to somehow intuit the right answer, which was not as easy as it seemed—notoriously, two of the winning answers for "What might you find in a woman's handbag?" were a "balaclava" and "rawlplugs" (wall plugs). The program therefore echoed a variety of existing programming formats. As a quiz show, it was closely associated with familiar games of chance originally transmitted on broadcast television, such as *Wheel of Fortune* and *Play Your Cards Right*, but in its use of "magical thinking" (that is, a mix of compulsion and self-delusion) it seemed to rely on the same kind of gullibility made evident in the recent phenomenon of *Deal or No Deal*. In this show, contestants must try to guess—or apparently work out a "system" that allows them to identify—how much money has been randomly assigned to a number of boxes and that they must eliminate in the right order to secure the biggest cash prize. Like ITV Play, *Deal or No Deal* persuades contestants that they have control over entirely random events. This coincides entirely with Doane's characterization of the way in which the contingent is both a goal and a threat to the visual systems of modernity. For modernity, she argues, is informed by an "epistemology of contingency" in which visual narratives (among other discourses) function "to acknowledge and pay homage to the power of contingency and at the same time to subject it to a system."[9] In its use of onscreen chatter and grinding persuasion, ITV Play's programming sub-jected the contingent (luck, gesture, smiles, and players) to a system that was apparently, but not really, the same as previous games of chance on British television. Rather than basing its system on an assumed, local-ized, and general knowledge (what *might* be in a woman's handbag), ITV Play deferred to the absurdist logic of sophisticated word games (what *could* be in a woman's handbag). In this sense, ITV Play only simulated the utopian qualities of the contingent, expressed however superficially, by earlier light entertainment television quiz shows. In fact, ITV Play was a lottery, *masquerading* as a game show, in which the rules had been changed without telling the players/audience.[10]

In its first year of operation, ITV Play earned £20 million in profits—perhaps not a huge amount of money considering that ITV's annual program budget is estimated at £1 billion, yet in terms of the digital advertising revenue for ITV (targeted at £150 million in that year) it was clearly an important and lucrative source of revenue for a company losing money elsewhere. And it is not the only program—digital or otherwise—that charged its viewers since this is now a routine practice within many contemporary programs—in other quiz formats, talent shows, and reality programs. Indeed, these seemingly different types of program are identified generically by the industry as "Premium Rate Service (PRS) programming" and are increasingly important for other commercial broadcasters such as Sky, as well as being adopted and adapted by public service broadcasters such as the BBC.

Yet the success of ITV Play was short-lived. Coming to a head in March 2007, both the police and British politicians began to investigate this and other "interactive quizzes" and television phone-ins in general. Some interesting statistics began to emerge about the program. In particular, the revelation as to the number of callers per minute came as a shock to many commentators and viewers. While numbers ultimately settled down to around 300 to 400 callers per minute, in the early days of ITV Play, and at peak times, this could go up to 1,000 callers. Callers were, of course, charged 75p per call whether they got through or not. An individual who called more than 150 times in one session was advised that he or she would automatically be withdrawn from selection, thus indicating that he or she should stop playing; however, the person was still charged for that call. With only 50 calls or so actually going on air in any four-hour period, the chances of getting through were estimated at between 1 in 400 and 1 in 8,500.

Was it simply scandalous or the future of television? To the show's producers it seemed, at first, to represent the possibilities of a digital interactive future. Eckoh—the company in control of the program's calling system, VISTA—promoted the program and its console, arguing that VISTA "gives ITV Play's production teams a comprehensive real-time snapshot of all calls to the show, allowing producers to make changes and modify the progress of a programme on-the-fly, depending on the level of viewer reaction. Thus, the production teams and programme presenters are able to recognise and acknowledge regular callers, referencing personalised information about their previous involvement in the show."[11] Tanya Carus, a former commissioning editor of ITV Play, suggested that it created a direct, immediate, and intimate relationship between broadcaster and viewer: "TV has never had a direct relationship with the viewer or consumer. The customers were always the advertisers—they're the clients who TV companies need to please. They are whom they deal with on a one to one basis. ITV, for the first time, is creating a very strong relationship between ITV and the viewer. It is a direct, transactional relationship."[12]

For television broadcasters, this kind of programming manipulates, exploits, and fills time in a way that secures some easy profit. For the television audience, it provokes a kind of "riveted boredom" familiar to the late-night viewer: you know that the television is dull, you should go to bed, but you just want to see what happens next, so you wait, and somehow it is three o'clock in the morning. In many ways, it is similar to the experience of watching rolling news channels on a poor news day or blearily staring at advertising reels in airports or, in the United States, watching the video loops in medical waiting rooms. Anna McCarthy describes the experience of "waiting room" television in this way: "When considered as televisual affect, waiting seems to be the opposite of the liveness so often ascribed to television—and in fact is closer to deadness."[13]

In relation to ITV Play I think it would be more appropriate to claim that what the programming produced was not quite deadness but television that was artificially lively because the format was designed to ensure that almost nothing happened. Unsurprisingly, this creates a context in which the concept of "liveness" is obsessively rehearsed. Indeed, presenters frequently indulged in rather desperate chatter about how they were "live, the program's live, and you are live," thus overstating their position to an extraordinary degree and ironically suggesting that perhaps they were not really convinced about how "live" or alive they really were. To refer to Hopfl once more: "The training of organizational staff to perfect dramaturgical roles to be played out in specific performance areas and for a defined audience leads to a level of exchange where actors who are devoid of personalities play to audiences who are deprived of theirs."[14]

In other words, ITV Play created programming in which dead-eyed performers pleaded with half-dead audiences to play meaningless games in which neither skill nor chance had any real currency and which served simply to expose the new economy of contempt on British digital television. In the second part of the chapter I will move from the present tense of television and suggest that there are now also a series of apparently serious programs that act as an inverted mirror image of this graveyard of light entertainment. I now therefore want to turn my attention to representations of the past and future in documentaries in which the dead also, apparently, "come to life."

LIFE AFTER PEOPLE

In History's documentary *Life after People* it is a speculative "future time" that is created.[15] Using contemporary analog footage of towns that have been deserted—such as Chernobyl—and extensive CGI animation of how key landmarks (the Brooklyn Bridge, the Eiffel Tower, and Buckingham Palace) might be after years of neglect, the program aims to take the viewer on an amazing "visual journey." As is common in many contemporary documentaries, this spatial metaphor (a journey) is framed, or actually superseded, by temporal progression. Rather than a journey taking place across the globe (from one landmark to the next), the journey is anchored in temporal terms—"hours," "days," "weeks," "months," and "years" after "people have disappeared." At one level— in terms of the direction given by the voiceover and inter-titles—the narrative presents an entirely speculative hypothesis with an illusory historical inevitability. Yet the constraints of contemporary documentary formatting and the budgetary imperatives in relation to the cost of images actually results in a peculiar temporal instability. For example, the program begins—as many documentaries now do—with a form of integrated trailer. By this I mean a short introductory sequence in which the producers are imploring their audience: "Don't switch channels! Coming up soon—the *really* exciting bits." Here the most exciting or dramatic images of the documentary (in this instance the ultimate collapse of those familiar landmarks) are glimpsed or "promised" to the viewer at the beginning of the program. Yet since it is ultimately revealed that these landmarks may fall only after centuries (150 years), the fact that the viewer has "already seen" a future (that may not happen anyway) creates a rather odd sense of déjà vu by the time the images are actually seen in context. Thus one imperative of digital television (don't lose your fickle audience) necessitates an ultimately illogical slippage in terms of the temporal narrative of the program upon which, otherwise, it is at great pains to insist. Equally, in the program's constant repetition of key sequences (necessitated to some extent by their expense and the need to use them as much as possible) it risks boring the viewer. While rolling news coverage often employs similar "loops" of footage so as to cover an event as it is unfolding, the associated loss of "sensationalism" in news is mitigated—to an extent—by the remaining indexical qualities of these images.[16] Here, the CGI is plausible but never convincing. As the producers actively promote the program in relation to its technological innovativeness, the audience is completely aware that these are not real images. This is despite the fact that their authority—and specifically their effect on the audience—will be dependent on their (illicit) reference to the "this is was" of photography (even if, in this instance, this is a confusing "this really will be"). As Stiegler explains in relation to the way in which the photographic, analog image is superseded by the digital map, "Photons become pixels that are in turn reduced to zeros and ones on which discrete calculations can be performed. Essentially *indubitable* when it is analog (whatever its accidental manipulability), the *this is was* has become essentially *doubtful* when it is digital (it is non-manipulation that becomes accidental)."[17]

There is no "this is was" in the digital image, and therefore the related speculation of the "this will be" dwindles and is fatally undermined. The authority, indiscreet potential, and sentimental frisson of the contingent has evaporated. One reviewer, for example, complained: "I'm not even that impressed with the computer-generated imagery, which is at the heart of this show, if indeed it has a heart. I don't know how many monkeys with Macs it took, but it still doesn't look real, especially when it starts moving. Someone's pleased with it though, so much so that everything needs multiple showings. Tower Bridge—down it comes, again and again. And the Seattle Space Needle—crash, crash, crash (from a slightly different angle). Stop it!"[18]

The reviewer's complaint is that the images do not seem "real" (enough); instead, I would suggest that the problem is that the events are, on the one hand, framed as inevitable (catastrophic consequences that are modeled using the apparently scientific but actually superficial gloss of CGI) but, on the other hand, are also presented—temporally speaking—as elastic (they continually "bounce back" to happen "again and again"). As such, these images therefore lack Stiegler's key quality of "irreversibility." While analog images can be replayed or reversed, we know that the events they record have only happened once. Here the flexibility of the digital images and the demands of the budget and the impetus toward spectacle determine that the program presents opportunities for these events to happen again and again (and again). More pertinent, since what is being watched is a CGI animation of a fabricated event (not an indexical record of the event itself), it is not just that we are *seeing* the event again and thus confirming "what happened" in all its dramatic certainty; rather, the event *is* happening again, and this undermines its impact on the viewer since it confirms that it never happened (because of course it hasn't!). In the current context of television, viewers are no longer impressed enough by either the technologically uncanny ("It looks so real, it's unnerving") or by the technologically marvelous ("Wow! How do they do that?"). In other words, expectations as to what looks "real" enough for television have increased, and everyone now knows that it is made by "monkeys with Macs." The reviewer here also insinuates that the program doesn't have a heart. I would argue that it does but that it is, intentionally or not, repressed by the impact of the CGI. For me, the real touch of disaster—the certainty of catastrophe—in the program is related to the analog footage of present-day Chernobyl. The conventional documentary images of the city of Chernobyl, which is now abandoned after the nuclear disaster in 1986, are affecting—a skeleton of a dog curled up on a bed, the dust and the mundane, pathetic qualities of the abandoned buildings that resonate or speak in a way the CGI images rarely manage. It is precisely the banality of these images that confirms their potential to express the contingent. Yet within the context of the documentary this sequence's power is undercut by the way in which it is exploited. A historical event that took place in the past is being revisited in the present to illustrate a story about the future— and the story of Chernobyl is thereby reduced to information or illustration. The program's use of the footage is therefore similar to the way in which Doane understands our contemporary response to the famous Lumière film of workers leaving their factory: "Although it proffers to the spectator a wealth of detail and contingency—the different types of clothing of various workers, the use of bicycles, the direction of gazes, et cetera—its significance is ultimately constrained by its association with the 'birth of cinema.'"[19]

Used to illustrate a fabricated future, the footage of Chernobyl serves a purpose that is not its own. The potential of the contingent (the overwhelming, myriad details that demonstrate our uncertain grasp of history) in the analog sequences is restricted, "ring fenced," by a narrative context that privileges the CGI sequences offering a simulation of the future, supposedly terrifying, but in which everything has already been calculated, in which everything has already been seen, and in which every pixel has a predetermined function. This results in a version of the future that is without history—there is no "trace" of the past to be located in the CGI sequences, and there is no argument or evidence present in the program as to why "people have disappeared" in the first place.

VIRTUAL HISTORY

It is sometimes important to treat history without looking back . . . bringing the viewer a sense of the immediacy of historical events.

The above justification for the use of CGI and animation is made by Dunja Noack, the director of the Tiger Aspect/Discovery program *Virtual History: The Plot to Kill Hitler*, and it gives some indication of the temporal confusion engendered (and presumably intended) by a range of different historical documentaries currently being produced for both American and British television.[20] *Virtual History* is best known for its controversial use of a mix of digital compositing and CGI, which was employed to "morph" archive footage of Hitler and other war leaders' faces onto present-day actors (figure 2.1). This animation was used to (re)create intimate scenes featuring war leaders as they conducted their business on July 20, 1944, the day of the failed attempt to assassinate Hitler. These short sequences include Hitler receiving his daily "vitamin" injection; Churchill in his dressing gown reading bombing reports over his breakfast in bed; Stalin waking on his sofa and being greeted by his housemaid/mistress; and Roosevelt being painfully lifted from his bed to his wheelchair. Aside from the complex animated technique utilized, the quality of the image in these sequences has also been carefully "degraded" and colored to simulate the appearance of actual archive material. Elsewhere in the program, CGI is deployed to build and rebuild key locations (such as Hitler's bunker in Poland, known as the "Wolf's lair," or Roosevelt's personal train). Different techniques are also used to evoke a forensic, or faux "*CSI* feel," to the narrative mode of address (see figure 2.2). These techniques include the simulation of image

FIGURES 2.1 AND 2.2 The use of CGI and a *CSI* aesthetic in *Virtual History: The Plot to Kill Hitler* creates a peculiar temporal confusion, dictated by the economics of digital television production and distribution.

enhancing (moving closer in to the map in a manner akin to surveillance or "spy" cameras), the frequent manipulation of images to expose a "blueprint" architecture underneath, and the incorporation of multiple or split screens, particularly when using actual archive material. In addition, there is a generally edgy or mobile quality to the camera work (which simulates a handheld feel), and this is most noticeable in relation to the presentation of contemporary experts speaking from a variety of locations. Responses to the program varied, with most reviews and articles concerned about the potential of the techniques being used to create "false" history. My interest here, however, is not in the possible exploitation of the technique itself but how it dominates within a rigid and controlling narrative context in which contingency is once more "performed" and contained.

One of the peculiar aspects of the documentary (and something that is increasingly common in documentaries that follow the Discovery model) is the amount of repetition, not just in terms of what is said, but also in relation to the image. The expensively recreated scenes of the various war leaders, for example, are repeated throughout the program, even though, as the inter-titles insist, "time" (which is connected to the actual temporal progress of the historical day in question) is moving on. As in *Life after People*, the program is dominated by temporal rather than spatial concerns. The four leaders are brought together temporally even though geographically (and therefore in reality, temporally speaking) they were far apart. The progress of each leader's day seemingly happens at the same time (implied by the use of inter-titles that tell the time in the manner of the American drama series *24*) when in reality they would have been in different time zones (Stalin in Moscow would be eleven hours behind Roosevelt in San Diego, while Churchill in London would have been only an hour behind Hitler in Poland). This temporal elision might have been largely irrelevant in a more conventional historical documentary. Yet in its explicit ambition to generate tension (the sense of time ticking away, the dramatic "countdown" to the time at which the bomb explodes) the program destabilizes any sense of temporal veracity and therefore its own authority. Once more, the assumption of a potentially distracted audience requires the manufacture of an "exciting" narrative—a compulsive and excessive "What will happen next?" dynamic to events. While many historical documentaries have used degrees of temporal elision or foreshortening, in this instance, the argument and the storytelling power of the program are fatally undercut because the authority usually guaranteed by the archival footage and photographs is weakened by the fact that some of it is faked. The process of masking actual and contemporary performers by a CGI composite of different dead statesman is an uncanny example of the "regulated corpse." "Performed contingency," as manifested by the apparently intimate encounters with world leaders in their "back stage" moments, in addition to the distressed quality of the images (which are, variously, bleached, spotted, and "shuttery"), is a key aspect of the program and foregrounded by the related promotional material. However, the performance of contingency simply reveals that the potentially disturbing and distracting qualities of the contingent—in the form of the live actor's performance or in the accidental inclusion of unnecessary details—are entirely controlled or repressed. In addition, the dislocation of actual archives (the original analog images of the leaders' faces used in the digital reconstructions) destroys the indexical authority of these images. When Stiegler touches the face of Baudelaire in the photograph, he knows that he is not actually "touching" Baudelaire, but the singularity of the image means that he still feels touched *"beyond the shadow of a doubt."* The digital composite that is used to construct Hitler's "likeness," however, has been touched and retouched so often that there can be no sense of an "absolute *irreversiblilty*"; instead singularity has been replaced by a spurious sense of control through which the "ghostly effect" of the index is repressed.

While *Virtual History* is perhaps an extreme example, CGI is now used routinely on a range of history programs. For instance, in the BBC's 2005 six-part series *Auschwitz*, written and produced by Laurence Rees, one of its most publicized virtues was the offering of the "first major reconstruction" of the camp. CGI, dramatic reconstruction, and eyewitness interviews with surviving personnel were used throughout the series; however, I want to focus on one particular sequence, from episode 5, "Frenzied Killing." This particular episode concerned the intensification and the actual mechanics of the mass murder at the Auschwitz camp toward the end of the Second World War. One typical sequence offers a mix of contemporary images and other archival material (film and photographs) as well as CGI. It begins with a present-day aerial view of the camp, circling over the ruins of the huts and the crematoria. From this perspective, the viewer is presented a sense of "the past" in the present and images that, as the camera and therefore the viewer circles closer and closer to the ground, begin to offer a tactile brush with material evidence since these are, evidently, analog images. Here the images and the ruins they picture act as a concrete document of the past, admittedly imperfect (one can't really see much), but they are nonetheless clearly indexical evidence of the past itself (something was there once) and, simultaneously, of time having passed. Intercut into these images, short sequences of archive film and photographs are also incorporated. Unlike the ruins of the camp, these images *represent* the past, but since they are

FIGURE 3 *Auschwitz* provides a CGI "walk-through" of the gas chambers and crematorium, bringing the past "alive" in a manner akin to a videogame "ego-shooter" perspective.

recognizably recorded images and bear traces of their authenticity (they are not perfect images; we cannot see everything as clearly as we feel we ought to) and of their passage through time (they are faded, grainy, incomplete), in this sense, they too offer an indexical trace or frisson for the viewer. Once we have "landed" at ground level, the sequence makes a transition to CGI. In effect, we are taken underground to a CGI "walk-through" of the gas chambers and crematorium (figure 3).

The effect is certainly spectacular and (for this viewer at least) unnerving. Tobias Ebbrecht—more convinced than I am by this particular sequence—provides a useful description: "The first-person perspective known from ego-shooter computer games is adopted: through the three-dimensional space the impression of consistency is generated, which is important for the cognitive and emotional immersion of the user into the artificial world of the game."[21] In terms of the effect on the viewer, Ebbrecht goes on to suggest the following:

In the empty rooms the wandering camera evokes shots from historical documentaries such as Alain Resnais' *Nuit et Bruillard* (*Night and Fog*, 1955) or Claude Lanzmann's *Shoah* (1985). These digital regenerations of the past are deserted locations and could function as allegories for the dehumanization of the victims by their German perpetrators. It is the audience which has to put together the experiences of the victims and the recreated locations of the annihilation in their minds. Digital regeneration does not replace the power of the imagination. Together with a factual perspective on the history of the Holocaust, the audience is given room to imagine the unimaginable.[22]

I think that Ebbrecht is mistaken. In *Shoah*, the contemporary footage of the camps is powerful precisely because it is not intertwined (segued) with archival material. Lanzmann's intent—surely—was to insist that the horrific events did actually happen ("Here is the evidence") and that they should not happen again (it happened *then*). In contrast, the trajectory provided by the "ego-shooter" perspective, which takes the viewer through the CGI representation of the camps, is intended or designed to bring the past "alive" in precisely the way Lanzmann would find abhorrent. This CGI animation and its clear association with computer games (and particularly Second World War–themed games such as *Wolfenstein: Enemy Territory*) is a narrative of anticipation, not of reflection. As the "camera" moves cautiously through the space, it feels as if we are waiting for "something" around the next corner. In terms of temporality the gas chambers as presented in these sequences are not about the past (what happened here) but about the future (is there something about to jump out at us?). As regards *Night and Fog*, while it is true that this CGI animation is eerily similar to the famous sequence that shows the gas chambers within Resnais's film,[23] unlike Ebbrecht, for me, the smoothness and completeness of the CGI does not provide a suitable "space for the imagination" or for reflection but a too easy (if admittedly suspenseful) journey. I think this is because the images are frictionless and climate-free and, like many digitally animated sequences, curiously weightless. In contrast, this is the sequence from *Night and Fog* as described by Emma Wilson:

> A voice-over narrates: "The only traces now, if you know what they are, are on the ceiling. Scrabbling nails scoring even concrete." There is an explicit relation between the voice-over and the shots. The voice-over here serves an explanatory function. Yet, as the camera moves over this scarred concrete, in a single shot tracking this palpable record, the relation between the human markings and the atrocity to which they bear witness, and of which they offer material proof, challenges rationality and sense-making. In his move between animate and inert matter, Resnais offers evidence in the form of grotesquely malleable concrete.[24]

There is no sense of the "grotesquely malleable concrete" in the CGI of the chambers: the images are inert, complete, since they are not evidence but illustration; despite the creation of narrative suspense, there will be no shock, no unanticipated detail in this sequence that could, potentially, overwhelm the viewer. This is the threat posed by contingency. As Doane argues, "The threat is that of an excess of designation, an excess of sensation that excludes meaning and control."[25] In Resnais's film, the viewer encounters the past, not without explanation (there is a voiceover), yet here the images are not just illustration (in service to the voice) but simultaneously tug at the viewer in a manner that can't quite be put into words. The archive of the gas chambers compels viewers to imagine touching (the rough surface of the concrete, scored by fingernails), but what it pictures cannot be touched. To refer again to Stiegler, we can see that it is once more the limitations and the singularity of the indexical image that are essential if we are to *feel* anything and if we are to *know* something about the history of Auschwitz. Thus I would argue that in the context of a major documentary series, when images of the gas chambers are required as evidence, they should remain, precisely, *untouched*. In contrast, in their nonaccidental, nontraumatic completeness, the CGI images of the camps will have been repeatedly "touched up" and tweaked. CGI cannot provide us with a witness to events but only a facsimile of events; as such, the gas chambers they picture are a simulation. They are enslaved images that cannot provoke any emotion that has not already been anticipated by the animators and that have no authority; indeed, their presence may undermine our faith in the evidence presented elsewhere in the program.

In the episode "Knowledge or Certainty" from the classic BBC documentary *The Ascent of Man* (1973), Jacob Bronowski examines the arrogance of science and relates this directly to the desire or compulsion to "see" more. Bronowski offers an exploration of the different ways in which science has increasingly attempted to "see" and thus apparently to "know" the world (through photography, X-rays, infrared imaging, and electron microscopes). Throughout the program he champions the ambition and achievements of science but laments the fallibility of humankind in the application of scientific knowledge. In the closing scenes of the episode, Bronowski is in the grounds of the Auschwitz camp; in a surprising move, this dapper professor walks forward into a dark pool and crouches down to sift the water and murky residue between his fin-

FIGURE 4 Jacob Bronowski's gesture, toward the conclusion of *The Ascent of Man*, reminds the audience of the limitations of the image, suggesting that seeing is not the same as knowing.

gers (figure 4). He then speaks: "I owe it as a scientist to my friend Leo Szilard, I owe it as a human being to the many members of my family who died at Auschwitz, to stand here by the pond as a survivor and a witness. We have to cure ourselves of the itch for absolute knowledge and power. We have to close the distance between the push-button and the human act. We have to touch people."[26]

For me this sequence articulates precisely my discomfort at the use of CGI; I may be drawn in by animated sequences, I may have a sense of space and suspense, but ultimately I am offered only a spurious sense of control, and it is the creative industry of the unseen animators that controls what can and cannot be seen. Thus, I may be excited by these sequences, which simulate movement, but I remain unmoved and "untouched." In contrast, in the absurdity of his gesture and performance Bronowski touches me; as he ruins his suit, as he interrogates the gloopy mess of the pond, his touch animates me, upsets me. His gestures are, in themselves, not accidental, but I know that he is there, "was there." What he says is important, but it is his willingness to cede control to his environment that provokes an empathetic lurch of understanding. As the film is deliberately slowed, each image of this sequence becomes a material object. By reminding the audience of the limitations of the image (its fragility, its constructed nature) and its materiality (as a film image, it has tangibility and an indexical quality), these stilled images expose their potential for contingency. In this sequence Bronowski is performing, but he does not "perform contingency." While his actions and words will have been scripted and are intentional, the motivation for the performance is to make us aware of the "background" for his speech (the grounds of Auschwitz). This is the contingent—the incidental details of the bog, earth and mud, the unseemly and barely legible human remains—that might have been overlooked because our attention has been focused on him "as the figure who speaks." By forcing us to reconsider, to look again, and to look differently, Bronowski and his production team generate a context in which the "crashing in" of the whole is entirely possible. Furthermore, as each frame is stilled, the audience is deliberately exposed to the breaking down of the program's narrative and visual system, thus asking us to consider the utopian, resistant qualities that are also inherent to contingency. For as Doane herself concludes, "Contingency is a witness against technology as inexorability, a witness that it could have been otherwise."[27]

It is the inexorable qualities of digital technology as it has emerged in some forms of digital television that have made this television viewer despair. Primarily, I mourn the loss of contingency on television and its related utopian and terrorizing potentiality, and I am dismayed by what I see as the revelation of television's digital "death's head" in the United Kingdom, whether this takes the form of zombie-like hosts mumbling banalities in the darkest hours of the night or documentaries creating reanimated corpses that undermine our ability to care about or believe in visual evidence. If I am so disdainful now, it is only because I think television matters, for the sense of a shared intimacy it can provoke and for the imperfect, but common, culture of empathy (rather than contempt) to which it once aspired.

NOTES

I would like to thank Philip Schlesinger for suggesting that I read *Fateless*.

Epigraphs. Mary Ann Doane, *The Emergence of Cinematic Time: Modernity, Contingency and the Archive* (Cambridge, Mass.: Harvard University Press, 2002), 30; Imre Kertesz, *Fateless*, trans. Tim Wilkinson (London: Vintage, 2006), 249.

1. Mary Ann Doane, "Information, Crisis, Catastrophe," in *Logics of Television:*

Essays in Cultural Criticism, ed. Patricia Mellencamp (Bloomington: Indiana University Press, 1990), 222–40.

2. Ibid., 237.

3. Heather Hopfl, "Performance and Customer Service: The Cultivation of Contempt," *Studies in Culture, Organization and Society* 1 (1995): 48.

4. Ibid., 53.

5. The regulation of the corpse and corpsing is now inherent to the era of "reality television" (which in the United Kingdom began to dominate television production in the mid- to late 1990s—the first *Big Brother* was transmitted on British television by Channel 4 in 2000). To witness a performer apparently "corpsing" is no longer disruptive in the way that I once, perhaps naïvely, assumed it to be. The cumulative effect of reality television and its blurring of private and public behavior has, I believe, changed the performance styles and the meaning of performance of not just "ordinary people" on television but also professional television actors and presenters. For an earlier discussion of "corpsing," see Karen Lury, "Television Performance: Being, Acting and 'Corpsing,'" *New Formations* 27 (1996): 114–27.

6. Doane, "Information, Crisis, Catastrophe," 237.

7. Kertesz, *Fateless*, 249.

8. Jacques Derrida and Bernard Stiegler, *Echographies of Television*, trans. Jennifer Bajorek (Cambridge: Polity Press, 2002), 152; emphasis in original.

9. Doane, *The Emergence of Cinematic Time*, 30.

10. ITV Play obviously has a close relationship to other digitally transmitted television narrative forms that are more explicit in their exploitative function, specifically "texting" channels (such as Gaydate or the soft-core Babe TV) and shopping channels (particularly the auction-based shopping channels, which use similar kinds of temporal acceleration). For more on the address and pacing of shopping channels and other "text-based" digital channels, see Stephanie Marriott, *Live Television: Time, Space and the Broadcast Event* (London: Sage, 2007), and Yngvil Beyer et al., "Small Talk Makes a Big Difference: Recent Developments in Interactive, SMS-Based Television," *Television and New Media* 8, no. 3 (2007): 213–34.

11. "Launch of the UK's First Mass Participation Telephone Game." Eckoh is now defunct since they have lost their contract, probably because of the ensuing scandal. More information about Eckoh and ITV, see "Eckoh Technologies Renew Interactive Telephony Contract with ITV," available at: http://tinyurl .com/3afz6tn. The original source material, at http://www.eckoh.com, was accessed August 17, 2009.

12. Quote from unpublished telephone interview with Tanya Carus conducted by James Farrell on November 22, 2006. This was part of a presentation on ITV Play by Farrell and his fellow students—Roya Kopff, Katherine Marshall, Laura Rennie, and Daniel Fricker—at the University of Glasgow for an under-

graduate course on television analysis. I would like to thank them for inspiring me and providing some of the research material.

13. Anna McCarthy, "The Rhythm of the Reception Area: Crisis, Capitalism, and the Waiting Room TV," in *Television after TV: Essays on a Medium in Transition*, ed. Lynn Spigel and Jan Olsson (Durham, N.C.: Duke University Press, 2004), 194.

14. Hopfl, "Performance and Customer Service," 59.

15. "History," known formerly as the "History Channel," was launched on January 1, 1995; the channel is owned by an A&E joint venture (Hearst, Disney, NBC) and Sky News Corporation. It operates, in various forms, in the United States, the United Kingdom, Australia, New Zealand, Portugal, Israel, Spain, Italy, and Latin America.

16. For an important discussion on the relation of looping news footage to understanding and empathy and "witnessing," see John Ellis, *Seeing Things: Television in the Age of Uncertainty* (London: I. B. Tauris, 2000).

17. Derrida and Stiegler, *Echographies of Television*, 153; emphasis in original.

18. Sam Wollaston, "What Would the World Look Like without Us? *Life after People* Showed Us—Again and Again," *The Guardian*, May 26, 2008; http://www.guardian.co.uk/media/2008/may/26/television1.

19. Doane, *The Emergence of Cinematic Time*, 23.

20. Dunja Noack, quoted in Charlotte Crow, "Box Populi," *History Today*, January 2007, 5.

21. Tobias Ebbrecht, "Docudramatizing History on TV: German and British Docudrama and Historical Event Television in the Memorial Year 2005," *European Journal of Cultural Studies* 10, no. 1 (2007): 48.

22. Ibid., 49.

23. Indeed it seems likely that they were reproduced to do so—and perhaps the original film itself was too expensive.

24. Emma Wilson, "Material Remains: *Night and Fog*," *October* 112 (spring 2005): 109.

25. Doane, *The Emergence of Cinematic Time*, 32.

26. The text can be found in the publication produced to support the series: Jacob Bronowski, *The Ascent of Man* (London: BBC, 1973), 374.

27. Doane, *The Emergence of Cinematic Time*, 232.

MAX DAWSON

TELEVISION'S AESTHETIC OF EFFICIENCY

Convergence Television and the Digital Short

The two-minute webisode is a very strange beast. Two minutes
to a cliffhanger. I don't know if webisodes are going to be around
long-term.

Ronald D. Moore, executive producer, *Battlestar Galactica*

Our goal is to take the content and use it any way we can.
How do we do a two-minute version of *csi* and get paid for it?

Les Moonves, president and chief executive officer, CBS Corporation

Following an extended period during which the research priorities of the discipline of television studies were oriented
around audiences and reception practices, since the 1990s
television scholars have "returned" to the television text.[1] In
conjunction with this aesthetic (re)turn, scholars have undertaken to map the shifting horizons of the television text, re-
visiting and revising foundational models of television's textuality in ways that account for dispersals, extensions, and
expansions of the medium's narratives and storyworlds across
media. For instance, Will Brooker has documented how the
diegesis of the series *Dawson's Creek* "overflows" television's
boundaries, spilling out into immersive Web sites that merge
television "with the vast diversity of the Internet."[2] Along similar lines, Jamie Sexton writes of the "leakiness" of television's
texts, and Matt Hills of the "hyperdiegeses," or "vast and de-

tailed narrative space[s]," constructed by cult television series.[3] In dialogue with these projects of diegetic cartography, critics have plotted out the contours of the narratives that unfold within these expansive spaces. Hence Jason Mittell details the "narrative complexity," and Jeffrey Sconce the narrational metareflexivity, of series such as *The X-Files* and *The Simpsons*.[4] Taken together, these studies make a compelling and nuanced argument for the connection between developments in television narration and visual form and contemporary processes of technological and industrial convergence, an argument that in turn has illuminated historical links among technology, political economy, and aesthetics.

Though it is less often noted, the same processes of convergence that have facilitated the dilation of television's intricate narratives and their dispersal across vast "transmedia" storyworlds also give rise to short-form Web and mobile video formats that aggressively *contract* the scale of television and the stories that it tells.[5] Shorts of no more than a few minutes in length have assumed prominent places within U.S. television networks' and studios' multiplatform programming strategies and moreover have come to factor prominently in many television industry workers' understandings of television's future. According to one industry journalist, digital shorts—the short-form ancillary texts produced by television networks, studios, or independent producers as digital extensions of present or past television series for commercial and/or promotional purposes—represent "the future of television—or at least, one of the futures of television: freestanding, not time-sensitive, short enough to engage and enjoy comfortably."[6] "Over the long-long-long-term, generationally long," explained the head of Lionsgate, the studio responsible for such prestige dramas as *Mad Men* and *Breaking Bad*, "it's very likely that the genre—which I'll call short-form, truly short-form of five minutes—may be the way in which people consume a lot of entertainment media, putting movies aside."[7]

Not content to watch this "generational" shift from the sidelines, television networks and studios have adapted their programs for viewing on digital platforms. To bring television programs to PCs and mobile devices, networks and studios clip, condense, and distill thirty- and sixty-minute-long episodes until they fit into containers of between one and five minutes in duration. These digital shorts comprise a significant portion of the content available on networks' and studios' Web sites, on video aggregation Web sites like YouTube, and on portable devices such as iPods and mobile phones. At Apple's iTunes store, for instance, viewers may download free video "starter kits" for the ABC series *Grey's Anatomy*, which promise to fill us in on "everything [we] need to know" about the happenings at Seattle Grace Hospital in a matter of minutes. For a monthly fee of $15, the Verizon VCast service delivers to subscribers' handsets two-minute *Lost* "mobisodes," recaps of the CBS daytime stalwart *The Young and the Restless*, and standalone clips from Comedy Central's fake-news shows. At the commercial content aggregation Web site Hulu, excerpts from *Saturday Night Live* and *The Family Guy* consistently rank among the most watched videos, in many cases outperforming full-length episodes of the same programs.

Despite the pronounced emphasis Web sites and mobile video services place on recycled and adapted materials, television's digital shorts have developed their own native aesthetic, an *aesthetic of efficiency*, characterized by streamlined exposition, discontinuous montage and ellipsis, and decontextualized narrative or visual spectacle.[8] This aesthetic tracks across the diverse collection of narrative and non-narrative shorts that television networks and studios present on digital platforms. Many shorts start *in media res*, with no indications of their spatial or temporal context, and end abruptly, prior to the resolution of their dramatic tension. Some perform virtuosic feats of synopsis, reducing entire seasons or series to rapid-fire montages, as is the case of "*Lost* in 8:15," a promotional video recapping the first three seasons of the labyrinthine *Lost*. Many are synecdochial and distill vast and complex source texts to their most recognizable elements. And like "*Lost* in 8:15," which announced its duration in its title, many make it a priority to brandish their economy, using onscreen clocks, progress bars, diegetic references to duration or deadlines, or other conspicuous temporal cues to assure viewers that despite all indications to the contrary, a four-minute Webisode is not a waste of time but rather a marvel of efficiency.[9] This fetish for brevity carries over to the streamlined *portmanteaus* and trademarked brand names that media conglomerates' marketing divisions have coined to identify their digital shorts—names like "minisodes" (Sony Pictures Television), "mobisodes" (News Corporation), and "Two-Minute Replays" (NBC Universal).

This chapter examines the terms of the digital short's aesthetic of efficiency; the presumptions that shaped it during its formative moment; and how creative professionals, industry executives, and cultural intermediaries have subsequently applied it within increasingly de-differentiated spheres of production and consumption. In the process, it endeavors to contribute new perspectives to a growing body of television scholarship situated at the intersection of political economic, formalist, and aesthetic traditions. Television studies' (re)turn to the television text has produced an abundance of valuable scholarship on television's most ambitious serial dramas, including numerous studies of *Lost*, *The Sopranos*, *Battlestar Galactica*, and *Buffy the Vampire Slayer*. But for all the attention television studies scholars devote to these and other similarly ambitious series, we have allowed the opposite end of television's narrative scale to slip through the cracks.[10] As a result, we know surprisingly little about the digital short, a form of television that has played an instrumental role in television's merger with digital media, and that looms large in the industry's projections of its own future.

What follows is an attempt to submit television's digital shorts to a "critical pressure" every bit as firm as that which television critics have recently applied to the medium's most complex narratives.[11] I propose that despite their obvious derivativeness and the larger commercial instrumentalities that they so baldly serve, digital shorts are every bit as worthy of—and capable of rewarding—these pressures as are the television programs that are their sources. To begin, I locate the emergence of the digital short during the late 1990s and trace its metamorphosis from ad hoc response to the properties of first-generation digital hardware and infrastructure to archetype for a new aesthetic. Next, I examine some of the ways in which television networks and studios have promoted and strategically appropriated the digital short's aesthetic of efficiency in the context of their dealings with their partners and contractors. I conclude the chapter by relating the digital short to television studies' own recent aesthetic (re)turn. Behind this renewed interest in television form lie unaddressed questions of value and judgment, specifically questions about which kinds of texts we believe warrant serious evaluation in the first place. My final section closes in on these questions and outlines criteria against which we might evaluate television's digital shorts.

FROM HARDWARE AESTHETIC TO AESTHETIC OF EFFICIENCY

The digital short's aesthetic of efficiency has been shaped by technological, institutional, and cultural forces that have grown thoroughly convoluted over the course of the last two decades. One way we might begin to untangle this complicated weave is by tracing out the history of the U.S. television networks' forays into Web and mobile distribution and exhibition, paying special attention to the ways in which digital shorts have factored in the industrial predicaments that have arisen along the way. From videotape to cable to digital downloads, the advent of new technologies of distribution and exhibition has repeatedly necessitated the renegotiation of formal and tacit agreements governing transactions of capital and intellectual property among television networks, studios, syndicators, and industry workers. The struggles that flare up at these moments have implications not only for the balance of power among the numerous factions that make up the U.S. television industry, but also for the content and form of programming as it moves among television's proliferating sites and screens.

The first experiments with exhibiting films, videos, and television programs on the Web occurred in the late 1990s, at a time when the limited capacities of computer hardware and restrictions on Internet bandwidth required would-be exhibitors to keep the sizes of digital video files to an absolute minimum. Shorter videos meant smaller files, which in turn meant faster load times, better image and sound quality, and (potentially) more pleasurable experiences for viewers. As Barbara Klinger has explained, these requirements were instrumental to the coalescence of a "hardware aesthetic," or a set of evaluative criteria organized around popular understandings of the Web's properties as a venue for motion picture exhibition. This hardware aesthetic made a virtue of technological necessity, elevating the compromises required by hardware and infrastructure to the status of a medium-specific formal language.[12] As audiences grew more accustomed to watching shorts on the Web, they came to recognize brevity as a desirable quality of Web video, to the degree that, as Daniel Chamberlain has noted, duration has emerged as one of the primary criteria on which viewers evaluate the merits of Web videos.[13]

In the 1990s, U.S. television networks and studios moved quickly to establish Web presences and were early investors in a number of the dotcom video ventures.[14] But before they could fully exploit the commercial opportunities presented by digital platforms, networks and studios were required to revisit the terms under which they conducted business with each other and with their respective partners and contractors. For decades, the business of television had been organized temporally, in accordance with conventionalized sequences of development, production, promotion, exhibition, and distribution, so that the initial broadcast presentation of a program was followed by between two and three network reruns, off-network syndication, overseas distribution, and, in some rare instances, the collection of programs onto physical media for distribution to viewers via rental and/or retail channels. By introducing new distribution and exhibition opportunities into this established schema, digital platforms threatened to unsettle many of the arrangements, relationships, and practices that it structured, including networks' licensing deals with studios; network-affiliate exclusivity arrangements; agreements governing the distribution of profits generated through syndication, rental, and sell-through markets; and networks' and studios' relations with the industry's workforce.

It was in this context that television networks and studios discovered in digital shorts short-term aesthetic solutions to industrial predicaments with long-term repercussions. The digital short's hardware aesthetic allowed television companies to simultaneously confront and avoid convergence's consequences, to convey to viewers, shareholders, advertisers, and the trade press that they were adapting to new technologies and evolving audience tastes and a shifting competitive landscape while scrambling behind the scenes to do everything possible to avoid altering the terms of their relationships with their partners and contractors. By withholding full-length programming from the Web in favor of brief clips, trailers, recaps, behind-the-scenes footage, and other repurposed materials, networks established Web presences without incurring substantial startup costs and without making their programming vulnerable to digital piracy. Shorts likewise bought networks time to negotiate new arrangements with affiliates, syndicators, distributors, and studios over distribution and exhibition windows and the disbursement of future revenues generated by digital sales, rental, syndication, and advertising. Similar delay tactics enabled networks and studios to put off inevitable arbitration with Hollywood unions, as loopholes in guild contracts allowed networks to repurpose brief excerpts of programs for promotional purposes.

Television networks' strategic embrace of short-form video's hardware aesthetic occurred against the backdrop of technological developments that removed many of the hurdles that had initially restricted the durations of Web videos. Thanks to the increased penetration of broadband Internet access and the introduction of high-speed mobile data networks, by 2005 it was possible to distribute full-length television programs via digital networks. With Apple's introduction of a video iPod in October of that year, U.S. television networks and studios made their first forays into distributing their programming via the Web, offering $1.99 downloads of episodes of their prime-time series via Apple's iTunes storefront. Soon after, networks began offering advertiser-supported streams of select prime-time series on their home pages, and later via video aggregators like Google Video and the joint NBC Universal–News Corporation venture Hulu. Though rights disputes with studios occasionally prevented networks from releasing some of their programs to digital platforms, by 2007 it had become standard for U.S. television networks to offer digital downloads or streams of recent episodes of most of their prime-time programs.

With the elimination of the technical barriers that had initially kept the durations of Web and mobile videos to a few minutes or less, digital video's hardware aesthetic mutated into an aesthetic of efficiency oriented around conspicuous displays of temporal economy. Digital shorts were no longer short because technology dictated they must be. Rather, this brevity was transformed into an aesthetic signature that cemented their place alongside the 140-character Twitter tweet, the Flash micro-game, and the viral video in what *Wired* in 2007 called the "new world of one-minute media."[15] Ironically, the digital short's aesthetic of efficiency emerged as an emblem of Web and mobile video's novelty and distinctiveness from the "old" medium of television precisely as U.S. media companies were using shorts created from recycled broadcast content to put off making changes to their programming strategies and business models. The sheen of novelty associated with this emergent aesthetic thus masked the reactionary tendencies of the media companies that were promoting the digital short as television reborn for the digital age.

The conditions under which this transition from hardware aesthetic to aesthetic of efficiency took place illustrate the magnitude of networks' and studios' ongoing investments in short-form video. These investments were and remain at once economic and ideological in nature. Even with the widespread availability of full-length television episodes on digital platforms, the economic value of digital shorts remains undiminished: relative to full-length television programming, shorts are cheaper to produce and distribute and generate multiple opportunities for sponsorship, synergy, and brand extension. As a result, networks and studios continue to rely on shorts as low-cost, low-risk solutions to the challenges associated with programming a proliferating array of digital platforms.

Shorts likewise fit snugly within television industry *doxa*, in particular within media companies' preferred models of the differences between television and new media and their respective audiences. As I have noted elsewhere, television networks and studios have since the 1990s approached the task of programming digital platforms via an axiomatic theory of medium specificity, which dictates a rather rigid schema for assigning content to specific media platforms.[16] Lisa Gersh, the president of the Oxygen cable network, summarized this theory in an interview with the trade journal *Multichannel News*: "Every platform is made to do different things—radio did one thing before television came along, which did another thing. . . . The broadband platform is the place for short-form programming, while most long-form content lives on television."[17] Similar attitudes are shared by networks' and studios' partners in the telecommunications and consumer electronics industries. According to one telecommunications analyst, "Diminutive screens make long-term, non-stop viewing unappealing, not a wonderful user experience. . . . The most likely mobile TV applications will . . . need to fit in about a 3-to-20-minute time frame . . . Most people won't watch TV on a cell phone for much longer than that, except for some special, out-of-the-mainstream reasons."[18]

The theory of medium specificity disseminated by the major stakeholders in Web and mobile television complement an equally axiomatic set of assumptions about the tastes and tolerances of digital media audiences. For instance, many industry professionals and professional industry watchers marshal consumer research on "millennials" or "digital natives" (those born since 1982), along with decades-old arguments about the impact of electronic media upon young people's cognitive capacities, to portray Web viewers as serial multitaskers capable of focusing their attention for only short periods of time.[19] As one cable executive explained, "We're serving the YouTube generation . . . so even if the economics are not aligned yet, you still want to be trafficking in the culture and content of your audience."[20] Along similar lines, a Sony Pictures Television executive described its minisodes as an effort to "take classic shows and, rather than try to jam them into the digital world, look at what the consumer wants."[21]

The notion that the digital short's aesthetic of efficiency reflects (for better or for worse) nothing more nor less than the television industry's desire to give Web viewers what they want (or what programming executives surmise they are cognitively equipped to handle after years of exposure to MTV, cable news crawls, video games, and viral videos) exercises powerful influence on both the industrial and the popular understandings of TV–digital media convergence.[22] This doxa is strategically incomplete and conceals the significant sway industrial imperatives—namely, the imperative of preserving established arrangements between networks and studios and their various partners and contractors—exert on digital television narration and form. To be sure, in programming digital platforms, television networks and studios take cues from their audiences, or at the very least from their audience research departments. Yet we may be equally certain that media companies would not continue to make digital shorts such prominent components of their multiplatform programming strategies if doing so did not make economic sense. Television networks program their digital outposts with shorts because, to paraphrase the cable executive quoted above, they remain an effective means of bringing culture, content, and commerce into alignment. The prominent place digital shorts occupy within television networks' and studios' multiplatform initiatives is first and foremost a testament to the efficiencies shorts afford to television networks and studios as they attempt to address—or delay addressing—the industrial predicaments wrought by convergence.

RENEGOTIATING THE BOUNDARY BETWEEN CONTENT AND PROMOTION

The nature and extent of the U.S. television networks' and studios' reliance upon digital shorts was underscored by the 2007–2008 Writers Guild of America (WGA) strike. A central point of contention between the WGA and the Alliance of Motion Picture and Television Producers (AMPTP) was the compensation of guild members for programming delivered on digital platforms. At the commencement of the strike in November 2007, writers' compensation rates for digital media were based on a formula set at the dawn of the home video era that made generous allowances to cover the high costs of manufacturing and distributing videocassettes. With the advent of DVD, these costs plummeted, and studio profit margins skyrocketed. But writers' residual rates remained the same, meaning that writers continued to receive only a small fraction of wholesale revenues of DVD sales, "or about 4 to 6 cents for every DVD sold."[23] Even this rate was better than what writers received for digital downloads and streams. Many networks balked at compensating writers for programs distributed via digital networks, reasoning that as they were not required to compensate writers for the use of their intellectual property for promotional purposes, they were under no obligation to share with writers the revenues generated by digital downloads and streams, provided they designated these presentations as promotions.

The clash over new media compensation came to a head in *The Accountants*, a short-form Web serial spun off of the NBC sitcom *The Office*. One of the first Web shorts to be scripted by a prime-time series's writing staff, *The Accountants* appeared in ten advertiser-supported installments over the course of the summer of 2006 at NBC.com and was later packaged as a special feature on the DVD release of *The Office*'s second season. The series was deemed a commercial success by the network and won its writers an Emmy in the new category of outstanding broadband comedy. Yet it also provoked an acrimonious dispute over the location of the boundary separating digital content from television promotion. This dispute illustrated the degree to which questions about digital television narration and form have become embedded within labor politics, as both NBC and the Web series's writers attempted to use digital shorts to achieve favorable bargaining positions in negotiations over the television industry's divisions of profits generated by digital shorts. In these negotiations, digital shorts took on a double significance, at once factoring as points of contention in struggles between capital and labor and as important weapons in these struggles.

The dispute over *The Accountants* stemmed from NBC's equivocation on the question of whether the Webisodes were Web promos for *The Office* or an original series in their own right. Publicly, to audiences and sponsors, the network promoted *The Accountants* as "original, exclusive," and advertiser-supported content. To launch the Webisodes, NBC mounted a public relations push that highlighted the participation of Greg Daniels, the series's head writer and executive producer, and described *The Accountants* as a "serialized," "edge-of-your-ergonomically-

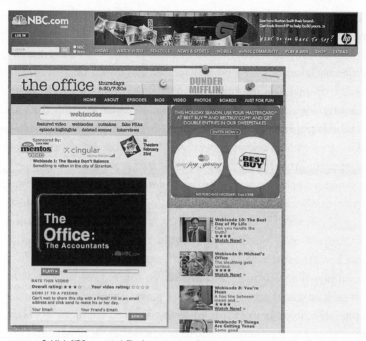

FIGURE 1 Publicly NBC presented *The Accountants* as "original, exclusive," and advertiser-supported content, while in its dealings with its creators, it categorized *The Accountants* as a promo, thereby indemnifying itself against the writers' demands for compensation. (Screen capture from NBC.com.)

designed-seat whodunit" that extended the broadcast series's storylines while the program was on summer hiatus.[24] As is typical of original Web programming, NBC presented *The Accountants* in streaming format with advertiser support. Viewers accessed the Webisodes via a video player surrounded by banner advertisements and a graphic reminding viewers of *The Office*'s time slot. Each installment was preceded by a brief "pre-roll" commercial for Toyota (see figure 1).

The participation of *The Office*'s cast and writers and the presence of these ads suggested that *The Accountants* was indeed an original short-form Web series. NBC took a contradictory stance in its dealings with the Webisodes' writers and actors and the Hollywood guilds representing them and categorized *The Accountants* as a promotion for *The Office*. "NBC Universal has a contract in place with its TV series producers to create promotional, made-for-Internet content, which include Webisodes," explained a spokesperson for the network's parent conglomerate. "We're asking our producers to fulfill their obligations in creating these materials."[25] This was not the first time that writers had challenged

NBC Universal over the placement of the boundary between content and promotion; during the summer of 2006, the NBC Universal subsidiary Sci Fi Network went through difficult negotiations with the producers of *Battlestar Galactica* over a similar matter. Following this earlier incident, the WGA asked its members to not participate in the production of Web and mobile content for NBC Universal subsidiaries until the guild had reached an agreement with the AMPTP over compensation. NBC Universal responded by filing a grievance with the National Labor Relations Board, charging that the WGA's actions violated labor laws.[26]

The dispute between the guild and NBC Universal carried over into the 2007–2008 WGA strike. During the strike, NBC stocked its Web site and digital outposts with deleted scenes, alternative takes, cast interviews, making-of documentaries, behind-the-scenes footage, clips, trailers, and recaps. Explained one NBC executive, "We're trying to do lots of online videos, just not ones written by a writer on the show." NBC had offered similar shorts on its Web site prior to the strike. But with all production on hold, the network turned to recycled materials to sustain its multiplatform programming initiatives and to consolidate its bargaining power. Further muddying the distinctions between television promos and digital video content, NBC and its affiliated cable networks packaged deleted scenes and cast interviews as "unscripted Webisodes," clips as "episode highlights," and recaps as "Two-Minute Replays." In an article in the trade publication *Television Week* titled "NBC Finds Webisode Workaround," network executives boasted they would program digital platforms with or without the WGA's cooperation.[27]

On the other side of the picket line, striking writers turned to digital shorts as well, using short-form Web videos to explain and publicize the WGA's platform. Prior to the strike, many guild members had made public their disdain for digital shorts and the restrictions short-form programming placed on their craft.[28] In one noteworthy instance, the writers of the comedy *30 Rock* used their scripts to take shots at NBC Universal's digital ambitions, making the nemesis of protagonist and fictional NBC president Jack Donaghy a vapid West Coast network executive responsible for green-lighting an inane "ten-second Internet sitcom." But many of these reservations seemed to evaporate over the course of the hundred-day strike. At the start of the strike the WGA launched its own dedicated YouTube channel, which became a repository for more than one hundred short videos featuring WGA members and their supporters. Meanwhile, writers left without work by the strike workshopped original concepts for short-form series at the Web site Strike.tv.

In the WGA's YouTube uploads, questions of value were never far from the surface. In one of these shorts, titled "*The Office* Is Closed," picketing members of the cast and writing staff of *The Office* discuss the Emmy they were awarded for their work on *The Accountants* and express their frustrations at NBC's refusal to acknowledge the economic and aesthetic value of the Webisodes. In the video, cast and crew members engage in an impromptu comedy routine in which they push NBC's reasoning to its illogical fruition, describing *all* television programming as promotion. "You know what my favorite promotion is?" writer-actor Mike Schur asks. "*Lost!*" "That's such a good promotion," agrees writer-actress Mindy Kaling, before launching into a discussion of some of her other favorite television "promos." The video concludes with Greg Daniels issuing NBC management a challenge: "I encourage the company to send the lawyers in to write the episodes, because the lawyers are very creative. Terming a full-length airing of an episode with paid-for commercials online a promo is a really good example of creativity and imagination" (see figure 2).[29]

The videos appearing on the WGA's YouTube channel offer an alternative perspective to the hackneyed democratic rhetoric, pseudoscientific cognitivism, and specious medium theory industry executives and trade journalists disseminate as they attempt to rationalize television networks' and studios' digital programming strategies. In videos like "*The Office* Is Closed," striking writers cast the networks' and studios' deployments of digital shorts in an altogether different light. Instead of portraying shorts as the outcome of television companies' attempts to discover the aesthetic possibilities of a new medium or as components of producers' efforts to cater their content to the Web audience's degenerative attention span, writers identified digital shorts as cynical gambits on the part of greedy media conglomerates to extract additional productivity from the labors of creative professionals. As an example of what John Caldwell has termed "ground-up worker ephemera," "*The Office* Is Closed" provides an indication of the strategic importance shorts assumed on both sides of the picket line. If for networks and studios shorts represented a way of avoiding change, to striking guild members they offered a means of inciting it by forcing closed-door labor disputes into the public eye.[30] Digital shorts enabled writers to

FIGURE 2 Picketing members of the cast and writing staff of *The Office* discuss the Emmy awarded for their work on *The Accountants* and express their frustrations at NBC's refusal to acknowledge the economic and aesthetic value of the Webisodes.

make visible an unglamorous but nonetheless crucial aspect of creative labor that remains absent from behind-the-scenes documentaries, self-reflexive scripted dramas and comedies, and other "insider" accounts of television's production processes—that is, the negotiations that establish the terms under which creativity is commodified within the U.S. television industry.[31]

At the conclusion of the strike, the WGA and AMPTP reached a compromise over where networks, studios, and creative professionals would draw the boundary between television promotion and digital content. But the notion that promotion and programming might be designated absolute categories, and that promos and content (and the individuals who create them) might be segregated from one another, seems disconnected from, if not antithetical to, the conditions created by the forms of industrial, technological, and cultural convergence that provoked the strike in the first place. The Webisodes produced since the conclusion of the strike attest to the impossibility of keeping these categories distinct. Nearly all of the digital shorts found on television networks' and studios' Web sites and mobile portals promote something, be it the products of a sponsor who has underwritten a mobisode's production, an upcoming season premiere or DVD box set release, a high-concept prime-time brand, or all of the above.

The compound promotional functions carried out by digital shorts are well illustrated by *The Rookie*, a short-form serialized spin-off of the espionage drama *24* that debuted on the Web in 2007. *The Rookie* was produced by a division of the multinational consumer products conglomerate Unilever in cooperation with Twentieth Century Fox Television, the studio that produces *24* for Fox, and promoted Unilever's Degree for Men deodorant. To recreate *24*'s distinctive style, Unilever licensed the series' digital countdown graphics, score, and sound effects and hired *24*'s director of photography to direct. Each of its three- to five-minute-long Webisodes served triple duty, functioning as an installment in a serialized drama about a rookie Counter Terrorist Unit agent, a deodorant commercial, and a promo for the sixth season of *24*. Degree commercials aired during prime-time episodes of *24*, and in-store *24*-themed Degree promotions alerted audience members to the existence of the Web serial, which was simultaneously aired as a series of episodic thirty-second commercials on News Corporation's networks.[32]

Not every digital short features brand integrations as comprehensive as *The Rookie*'s. That said, all digital shorts are branded entertainment, so to speak, in that they function as advertisements for the brands of the television series on which they are based.[33] Thus while an unambiguous contractual distinction between promotion and content may be desirable from the standpoint of WGA members, it can become an impediment to a critical engagement with the forms and functions of television's digital shorts. In making this argument, my intention is not to endorse the AMPTP's pre-strike platform. Quite the contrary, the divide erected under the concessions won by the WGA serves a necessary purpose within the context of the U.S. television industry's volatile labor market. That said, the designation is ultimately limiting, as it obscures what is perhaps the major accomplishment of a short like *The Accountants* or *The Rookie*: to blend promotion and content in a way that narrative television itself seldom does.

ASPIRATIONS AND AESTHETICS

At the start of this chapter I proposed that digital shorts are every bit as capable of withstanding "critical pressure" as are the programs that are their sources. In fact, they would appear to confirm James Walters's contention that digital media invite and reward the form of "interpretative or 'text'-led" aesthetic analysis that has gained traction within television studies since the 1990s.[34] Digital shorts readily submit themselves to a "forensic" mode of television spectatorship: their Web and mobile interfaces allow us to view and review them, to step through them one frame at a time, and to freeze or reverse the flow of their diegetic time.[35] Moreover, shorts may highlight and intensify fleeting moments, isolating clips as short as a few shots and as long as an entire scene from the narratives in which they appear and from television's broader textual flows. Shorts nominate particular moments or sequences of moments of television as important and worthy of analysis and provide critics and viewers with the technical means of carrying out close readings. In this respect, they carry out a task that is an essential prerequisite of aesthetic criticism: the identification of bounded textual elements that are at once exemplary and representative of a greater whole for which they can be asked to stand.[36]

Granted, the acts of nomination that shorts carry out are inseparable from the commercial objectives of the media companies that commission, produce, or distribute them. Shorts are often called upon to fulfill multiple commercial functions, to at once promote programs, networks, stars, and ancillary products and to garner advertiser support or retail revenues. Thus a single Webisode may hype the appearance of a sweeps period guest star, the release of a DVD box set, and a new deodorant spray, while a network-produced recap may play up storylines involving one cast member in coordination with an actor's appearance in a feature film being released by an affiliated movie studio. But recognition of these promotional functions need not discount the insights that close analysis of television's digital shorts may yield. Quite the contrary, it is the brazen fashion in which shorts carry out their commercial obligations that make them so revealing. As highly concentrated versions of television programs designed to compel viewers toward full-length, advertiser-supported or pay-per-view presentations or retail opportunities, digital shorts disclose a great deal about the U.S. television industry's conceptions of its programs and audiences. Shorts' inclusions and omissions reveal those aspects of a program's storyworld that a short's producers and/or distributors believe are and are not important, as well as what they believe is and is not important to that program's "ideal" viewer. Along similar lines, as digital adaptations of texts originating in what was until recently an analog medium, shorts are revealing of television companies' conceptions of what digital media are, the kinds of stories they are equipped to tell, and the audiences they address. Digital shorts thus offer a privileged vantage point through which we may apprehend specific television programs, as well as the industry that produces, promotes, and presents them.

Thus far, however, television studies has yet to capitalize on these insights. What little attention television's digital shorts have received has come mainly from an unsympathetic popular press that is far more at ease with questions of value and judgment than the field of television studies. The same entertainment beat reporters, media bloggers, and newspaper television critics who have marveled at the immediacy and authenticity of the Webcam serial *lonelygirl15* or the ingenuity of the latest "Chocolate Rain" remix have been merciless in their assessments of television's digital shorts.[37] For example, a review of the *Heroes* Web spin-off *Nowhere Man* in 2009 on AOL's TV Squad blog began with this diatribe: "Need a laugh? Watch the new *Heroes* web series. And yes, you'll be laughing at it, not with it. Mostly because it's awfully unoriginal, unfunny, and it revolves around two of the most useless characters in the *Heroes* universe. . . . The five-and-a-half minute opener, which premiered Monday, is mostly laughably bad, forgettable and uninspired."[38] Popular critics have dismissed television's digital shorts as crass and misguided attempts to cash in on the short-form Web video craze. In many respects, they are not wrong: many digital shorts *are* horribly "unoriginal, unfunny, and . . . uninspired." Many shamelessly shill for sponsors, cramming their flimsy narratives with excruciatingly long close-ups of cell phones, hood ornaments, or soft drink cans. Many appear to have been carelessly edited and confusingly fade in or out in the middle of dialogue. And many sacrifice ambiguity and complexity for painful obviousness and redundancy, addressing audiences as if they were too distracted to follow anything but the simplest of stories.

In light of the suspect quality of many digital shorts, it would be easy to write off television's digital shorts as television for those who, as one reporter put it, "find thirty-minute sitcoms too deep and drawn out."[39] But to do so would mean to forgo the considerable insights that the digital short's aesthetic of efficiency yields into the connections between new media form and old media political economy. In this concluding section, I want to outline an alternative set of criteria for evaluating television's digital shorts that might enable us not simply to learn to live with digital shorts, but also to appreciate the quite considerable aesthetic accomplishments of which I believe they are capable.

In an important article on television and aesthetic criticism, Jason Jacobs argues that in order for aesthetic criticism to be effective and relevant television critics must ask questions "about the different aspirations of different kinds of television, which ultimately requires thinking less about 'television' and more about particular genres and programmes."[40] While Jacobs originally made this point in reference to the challenges of evaluating examples of different generic traditions, his argument is equally relevant to television's digital shorts. That is, if ancillary digital shorts like *The Accountants* or *The Rookie* are in fact a form of television— and this is certainly a matter we must debate further—then the basis of our evaluations of them should be their successes and failures at realizing their own aspirations, as opposed to their adherence to standards devised for the evaluation of broadcast television or other media forms.

What are the aspirations of television's digital shorts? Clearly, they are multiple. Much in the same way as different television genres and programs aspire to different goals, so too must individual digital shorts possess their own individual purposes. For instance, the aspirations of freestanding "unbundled" clips, which offer themselves to viewers as synecdochial figures for the much larger texts from which they have been drawn, would certainly be different from those of synoptic two-minute replays, which must contend with the challenge of managing the memories of audience members with varying levels of knowledge of a series's past.[41] But while the aspirations of television's digital shorts may be diverse, all digital shorts contend with the same core problematic: that of encompassing and reconciling the tension between television's artistic and commercial functions.

On television, this tension is dispersed across the timetable and across the dial, where it plays out between the medium's texts, paratexts, advertisements, and interstitials. With digital shorts, by contrast, television's fundamental contradictions are concentrated and intensified. Expected to carry out the functions of promos, content, and commercials all at once, shorts visibly strain under the pressure of containing these antagonistic demands within themselves. This strain surfaces on the screen in identity crises of the type outlined above. Is *The Rookie* a deodorant commercial or a minor chapter in the narrative of *24*? Is

The Accountants a promo for *The Office* or an original Web series? Is the *Heroes* spin-off *Going Postal* a transmedia extension of the superhero drama or a product placement showcase (see figure 3)?

As these examples suggest, digital shorts rarely realize their aspiration of reconciling this tension. Far more often they implode under the pressures of balancing their promotional and commercial obligations with any narrative ambitions their creators might harbor. However, when digital shorts do manage to bring their creators', distributors', and audiences' demands into alignment, the effect can be quite powerful. In the lead-up to the debut of the seventh and final season of the series *The Shield*, the cable channel FX posted at Hulu short clips from upcoming episodes. Included among these clips was "Vic versus Shane," an excerpt from the season premiere. Of the many varieties of digital shorts, unbundled clips like "Vic versus Shane" would appear to be the least ambitious. The clip makes no attempt to overflow *The Shield*'s narratives or diegesis. It does not introduce new characters, initiate new storylines, fill in gaps in past plotlines, or deepen viewers' connections with peripheral characters. Put bluntly, it does not claim to be anything other than a promo. That said, "Vic versus Shane" succeeds where many original Web and mobile series fail. In seventy seconds, the clip draws its audience into the convoluted story of *The Shield*'s crooked cops, ensnaring viewers in a moment of disorienting yet breathtaking drama. Then, as quickly as it drew them in, the clip ends, directing viewers to FX for the resolution and context it has denied them (see figure 4).

"Vic versus Shane" opens with chaos, a black screen cutting to a jumpy, handheld shot of Detective Shane Vendrell as he attempts to pacify a bound and gagged woman. This shot—and the loud and disorienting music that accompanies it—is almost immediately interrupted by a jarring cut to a reverse shot of the butt of a pistol smashing down on Shane's head. The next shot reveals that Shane's assailant is Vic Mackey, the chief protagonist of *The Shield* and Shane's former partner. Vic and a fellow cop drag Shane into another room, pummeling him with kicks and punches as he frantically struggles to explain that the Armenian gangsters that the trio had robbed during the series' second season had put a hit on Vic's wife and daughter and that to protect them Shane has played warring mob factions against one another. Following Shane's confession, a horrified Vic backs off. Looking up at his former partner from the ground, Shane moans, "I'm paying off your debt in favors." The clip

FIGURE 3 With digital shorts television's fundamental contradictions are concentrated and intensified: Is the *Heroes* spin-off, *Going Postal*, a transmedia extension of the superhero drama or a product placement showcase? (Screen capture from YouTube.)

FIGURE 4 Clips of *The Shield* on Hulu, such as "Vic versus Shane," mimic and extend the ambiguity that many contemporary serials carefully cultivate; such an aesthetic is amplified in this clip by the rough edits that mark its beginning and end. (Screen capture from Hulu.)

ends abruptly, fading to a silent title card advertising the date of the episode's debut on FX.

In a matter of seconds, Shane's confession races through six seasons and more than seventy hours' worth of the series' history, rattling off a barrage of names, alliances, and double crosses, all without the benefit of explanation or context. As is the case with many contemporary prestige television dramas, *The Shield* carefully cultivates viewer loyalty by reducing to a bare minimum the expositive redundancies television writers have long relied on to bring new or lapsed viewers up to speed on serial narratives. Viewers are thus required to watch each of the series' episodes in order to keep track and make sense of its multiple, multiseason story arcs. "Vic versus Shane" foregrounds and amplifies this ambiguity via the rough, jarring edits that mark the clip's beginning and ending. The two edits made to excise "Vic versus Shane" from this episode's narrative come at particularly inopportune moments, denying viewers cues that might help them place the events it depicts within the larger narrative to which it belongs. The full scene as aired on FX opens with a series of shots following Shane from his car to the interior of his apartment, where he finds his wife bound and gagged. In the clip, however, this sequence has been eliminated. The scene's dramatic climax has been omitted as well: in the uncut version aired on television, Shane apologizes to Vic once again, assuring him that "I would never do anything to hurt your family." Vic's reply—"Lem was family"—penetrates to the origin of the animosity between the former partners, alluding to Shane's murder of a fellow member of their unit.

Absent these critical cues, "Vic versus Shane" lacks context and closure. It is incomplete and can be disorienting to a viewer who is unfamiliar with the series's history. The only background information for the clip comes from Shane's confession and from the terse (and decidedly vague) synopsis that accompanies it on Hulu. The viewer is told that this clip is from the first episode of the series's seventh season but is given no cue as to where in the episode this scene falls or how much time has elapsed between this scene and the events depicted in the prior season's finale. Likewise, there is no establishing shot to anchor the clip in space; from the frantic sequence of shots that precede Vic's appearance, it is unclear where Shane is and who is the bound and gagged woman on the couch. With only two edits, "Vic versus Shane" translates the opening scene of *The Shield*'s final season into a powerfully enigmatic fragment that can be reconciled only by tuning in to the episode's premiere on FX. The elliptical editing of the stand-alone clip becomes a means of inducing viewers to enter into and move through the circuit that links the various wings of the News Corporation empire to which both Hulu and FX belong. "Vic versus Shane" is thus a promo for *The Shield* and an incitement to consume across media platforms.

By traditional measures, the accomplishments of "Vic versus Shane" pale when held against those of *The Shield*. However, when we take a clip such as this one on its own terms, as I have attempted to do here, we stand to appreciate that "Vic versus Shane" is every bit as worthy an object of analysis as is *The Shield*. Recognizing the accomplishments of this or any other digital short requires that we move beyond the simple dualism of the distinction between promo and content. But perhaps even more crucial, it requires that we look beyond television studies' traditional standards of excellence or quality — in other words, standards that recognize and reward, for instance, cinematic visuals, literate dialogue, rounded characters, generic hybridity, narrative complexity, or social realism. This need not mean lowering our standards by lightening up on the "pressure" that we place on these texts; rather, I suggest that we would be better served by adjusting our evaluative criteria to reflect the political economic conditions under which digital shorts are produced and the interlocking narrative, commercial, and promotional imperatives they are expected to carry out. As television's convergence with digital media approaches critical mass, making digital shorts a more commonplace component of audiences' media diets, an aesthetic is required that is as open to the artistry of the seventy-second promo as it is to that of the seventy-hour serial.

NOTES

Epigraphs. Moore is quoted in James Hibberd, "NBC Finds Webisode Workaround," *Television Week*, March 26, 2007, 1; Moonves is quoted in John M. Higgins, "TV to Go," *Broadcasting and Cable*, September 26, 2005, 12.

1. James Corner, "Television Studies and the Idea of Criticism." *Screen* 48, no. 3 (2007): 366. For additional remarks on television studies's recent return to questions of aesthetics, see Jason Jacobs, "Television Aesthetics: An Infantile Disorder," *Journal of British Cinema and Television* 3, no. 1 (2006): 18–33.
2. Will Brooker, "Living on *Dawson's Creek*: Teen Viewers, Cultural Convergence, and Textual Overflow," *International Journal of Cultural Studies* 4, no. 4 (2001): 457.

3. Jamie Sexton, "Case Study: Television and Convergence," in *Tele-Visions: An Introduction to Television Studies*, ed. Glen Creeber (London: BFI, 2006), 160–68. London: BFI, 2006; Matt Hills, *Fan Cultures* (London: Routledge, 2002), 137. See also John Thornton Caldwell, "Convergence Television: Aggregating Form and Repurposing Content in the Culture of Conglomeration," in *Television after TV: Essays on a Medium in Transition*, ed. Lynn Spigel and Jan Olsson (Durham, N.C.: Duke University Press, 2004), 53; Janet Murray, *Hamlet on the Holodeck: The Future of Narrative in Cyberspace* (New York: Free Press, 1997), 255; Kristin Thompson, *Storytelling in Film and Television: Understanding Classical Narrative Technique* (Cambridge, Mass.: Harvard University Press, 2003).

4. Jason Mittell, "Narrative Complexity in Contemporary American Television," *Velvet Light Trap* 58 (2004): 29–40; Jeffrey Sconce, "What If? Charting Television's New Textual Boundaries," in Spigel and Olsson, *Television after TV*, 93–112.

5. Henry Jenkins, "Transmedia Storytelling"; http://www.technologyreview.com (accessed May 4, 2006).

6. Robert Keating, "The Future of Media: Television"; http://www.mediapost.com (accessed October 13, 2008).

7. Kevin Beggs, quoted in ibid.

8. In some respects, this aesthetic is not unlike that of motion picture trailers. However, contrary to trailers, which trumpet their status as advertisements via the use of direct address, most digital shorts go to great lengths to obscure their purpose or provenance. In addition, unlike trailers, Web shorts are presented to the audience as "authored" texts. For more on the unique aesthetic of motion picture trailers, see Lisa Kernan, *Coming Attractions: Reading American Movie Trailers* (Austin: University of Texas Press, 2004).

9. Daniel Chamberlain terms this phenomenon "temporal conspicuity." See Daniel Chamberlain, "Watching Time on Television"; http://flowtv.org/?p=615 (accessed August 9, 2008).

10. This is despite the fact that there is a large body of scholarship on fan-created digital ephemera and user-generated video.

11. Jason Jacobs, "Issues of Judgement and Value in Television Studies." *International Journal of Cultural Studies* 4, no. 4 (2001), 443.

12. Barbara Klinger, *Beyond the Multiplex: Cinema, New Technologies, and the Home* (Berkeley: University of California Press, 2006), 75, 196.

13. Daniel Chamberlain, "Watching Time on Television"; http://flowtv.org/?p=615 (accessed August 9, 2008).

14. Ellen Seiter, "Television and the Internet," in *Electronic Media and Technoculture*, ed. John T. Caldwell, 227–45 (New Brunswick, N.J.: Rutgers University Press, 2000).

15. "Snack Attack!" *Wired* 15 (March 2007): 125.

16. Max Dawson, "Little Players, Big Shows: Format, Narration, and Style on Tele-

vision's New Smaller Screens," *Convergence: The International Journal of Research into New Media Technologies* 13, no. 3 (2007): 234–35.

17. Quoted in R. Thomas Umstead, "Broadband Channels: Ready for Primetime"; http://www.multichannel.com/article/CA6340644.html (accessed November 1, 2008).

18. Roman Polz, "Ten Predictions about the Cell Phone Industry in 2007"; http://www.convergedigest.com/bp-bbw/bp1.asp?id=444&ctgy=home (accessed December 17, 2008).

19. See, for instance, David E. Mumford, "Make a Connection with Tech-Savvy Millennials," *Television Week*, November 13, 2006, 11. For more on the history of these tropes, see Michael Z. Newman, "From *Sesame Street* to Snack Culture: The 'Short Attention Span' in American Media History," *Media, Culture, and Society*, forthcoming.

20. Brian Graden, quoted in James Hibberd, "Shorter Shows for New Media," *Television Week*, October 9, 2006, 18.

21. Steve Mosko, quoted in Bill Carter, "Coming Online Soon: The Five-Minute *Charlie's Angels*," *New York Times*, April 30, 2007.

22. So axiomatic is the notion that the online and mobile audiences are willing to watch or capable of watching only in increments of a few minutes (or seconds) that in 2007 one industry trade magazine instructed aspiring multimedia producers to regard ninety seconds as the upper limit for the duration of Web videos, as "Web viewers have much shorter attention spans" than television audiences. Daisy Whitney, "Top Five Tips for Would-Be Web Video Producers," *Television Week*, October 8, 2007, 12.

23. Richard Verrier and Meg James, "What's Making Writers and Studios So Nervous?"; http://www.latimes.com (accessed April 12, 2009).

24. "No Summer Vacation for NBC's *The Office*"; http://www.nbcumv.com (accessed March 12, 2008).

25. Dave McNary, "NBC Brings Feds into Fight"; http://www.variety.com/article/VR1117948657.html?categoryid=14&cs=1 (accessed September 5, 2006).

26. James Hibberd, "NBCU Files Labor Complaint against WGA"; http://www.tvweek.com/news/2006/08/nbcu_files_labor_complaint_aga.php (accessed November 13, 2008).

27. Vivi Zigler, NBC executive vice president of digital entertainment and new media, quoted in James Hibberd, "NBC Finds Webisode Workaround," *Television Week*, March 26, 2007.

28. One notable exception in this regard is writer-producer Joss Whedon, who during the strike self-financed and produced the three-part Web "Internet miniseries event" *Dr. Horrible's Singalong Blog*. Contrary to many other show runners, Whedon rhapsodized about the freedoms that the digital short afforded to him as a creator. See, for instance, Matt Rousch, "Exclusive: First Look at Joss Whedon's '*Dr. Horrible*'"; http://community.tvguide.com/blog-

entry/TVGuide-Editors-Blog/Roush-Dispatch/Joss-Whedon-Dr/800042425 (accessed November 7, 2008).

29. "*The Office* Is Closed"; http://www.youtube.com/watch?v=b6hqPoco_gw (accessed May 13, 2008).

30. John Caldwell, "The Insider's Promotional Surround: Rationing Production Knowledge, Managing Unruly Machines, and Worker Buy-In," paper presented at the Promotional Surround Workshop, Nottingham, July 20, 2009.

31. Lest this account of the strike appear to romanticize the WGA's noble fight against the evil AMPTP, it bears noting that the strike was also about policing professional boundaries, especially those separating guild members from amateur video bloggers, advertising copywriters, new media hyphenates, reality TV segment producers, and any other individuals who write for television and/or digital media platforms without credit (and often without compensation). The new minimum basic agreement (MBA) put in place at the resolution of the strike in February 2008 established the terms under which these individuals could be denied compensation and credit at the same time as it put in place protections to safeguard the interests of guild members. The agreement established that writing for new media platforms, including the Web and mobile devices, would be covered by the guild's contract if "(1) it is written by a 'professional writer' or (2) the program is derivative of an MBA-covered program or (3) if the budget is above any of three thresholds: $15,000 per minute; $300,000 per program; or $500,000 per series order." These qualifications essentially amount to an attempt to codify the designation of authorship in the face of technological, cultural, and institutional developments that have collapsed long-standing distinctions between producers and consumers—in other words, to designate what is and is not an authored text and, by extension, who is and is not an author. From the perspective of writers, then, the digital short was an important weapon in a battle waged on two fronts: on one hand, against the networks and studios, and on the other, against an encroaching horde of amateur or non-union producers. See http://www.wga.org/contract_07/mba_summary.pdf (accessed July 28, 2009).

32. "*24* Spinoff Deal Is No Sweat for Fox," *Hollywood Reporter*, January 19, 2007, 42.

33. This is clearly the case with regard to *24: Conspiracy*, another short-form spinoff of *24*. Each minute-long *24: Conspiracy* mobisode concentrates the basic arc of a typical hour-long episode of *24* to a recap; one or two high-intensity narrative clinches; an instance of threatened, implied, or actual torture; and a cliffhanger ending before concluding with a sneak preview of the following installment. It would appear that all that is missing is a commercial until one realizes that the serial itself consists of twenty-four minute-long commercials for the *24* franchise.

34. James Walters, "Repeat Viewings: Television Analysis in the DVD Age," in *Film*

and Television after DVD, ed. James Bennett and Tom Brown (London: Routledge, 2008), 65.

35. Here I am adapting Jason Mittell's notion of forensic fandom, a mode of fannish engagement "that encourages viewers to dig deeper, probing beneath the surface to understand the complexity of a story and its telling," to describe the viewing style that shorts encourage. See Jason Mitell, "To Spread or to Drill?"; http://justtv.wordpress.com/2009/02/25/to-spread-or-to-drill (accessed July 18, 2009).

36. Jonathan Bignell, "Exemplarity, Pedagogy, and Television Studies," *New Review of Film and Television Studies* 3 (May 2005): 15–32.

37. *Lonelygirl15*; http://www.youtube.com/user/lonelygirl15?blend=1&ob=4 (accessed May 22, 2009); "Chocolate Rain"; http://www.youtube.com/watch?v=EWTz2xpQwpA (accessed May 22, 2009).

38. Mike Moody, "Need a Laugh? Watch the New *Heroes* Web Series"; http://www.tvsquad.com (accessed July 30, 2009).

39. Mick Farren, "Attention Span Threatened by Advancing Minisodes!"; http://www.lacitybeat.com (accessed August 7, 2007); see also Josh Wolf, "Minisodes: For Those Who Find 30-Minute Sitcoms Too Deep and Drawn Out"; http://www.cnet.com/8301-13508_1-9748620-19.html (accessed August 3, 2007).

40. Jacobs, "Issues of Judgement and Value in Television Studies," 430.

41. Unbundled clips are short excerpts produced by dismantling integral television texts into fragmentary, yet self-contained, segments. See Max Dawson, "Little Players, Big Shows: Format, Narration, and Style on Television's New Smaller Screens." *Convergence: The International Journal of Research into New Media Technologies* 13, no. 3 (2007): 233–34.

DANIEL CHAMBERLAIN

SCRIPTED SPACES

*Television Interfaces and the Non-Places
of Asynchronous Entertainment*

As older media systems come under the influence of the
digital and as new media technologies emerge, screen-based
interfaces have become essential aspects of the entertainment
media ecology. The images in figure 1 represent examples of
these intermediaries between individuals and media content.
As the front line of our interactive media experiences, emergent media interfaces consist of screens and the means to
interact with them—often a remote control, touch screen, ac-
celerometer, or computer mouse. Media interfaces are everyday experiences, inherent in the most advanced smart phones
and digital media recorders, as well as in now prosaic digital television converters and basic automobile audio systems.
At their least obtrusive, these interfaces provide annotations
on media engagements, regularly displaying details on media
titles, creators, ratings, and viewing status. More essentially,
they often provide the means to find content in the first place
and generally give users a sense of control over the vast media
landscape. The emerging importance of media interfaces certainly has to do with their function as both discrete visual
spaces and layers on top of media content but is guaranteed
by the role they play as the locus of technological interactivity
with entertainment media. As the virtual spaces in which
users navigate menus, follow links, register preferences, and

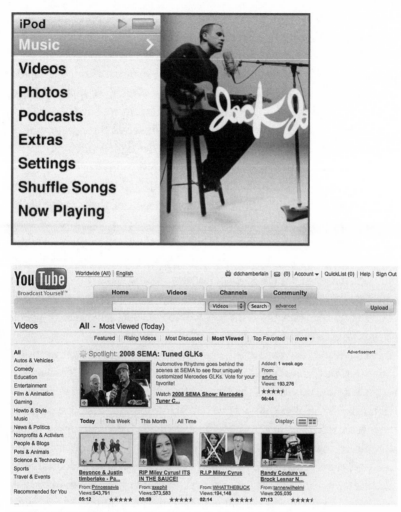

FIGURES 1.1 AND 1.2 Interfaces act as visual intermediaries between individuals and media content. (iPod screen capture from Apple.com and YouTube.)

program searches and subscriptions, media interfaces are the visible tip of a software layer that increasingly structures our engagements with text, audio, and video. Whether choosing to listen to music, watch feature-length films, catch up on television programming, or consume short-form entertainment, we must often first engage an interface before experiencing media.

While media interfaces are convergent artifacts often designed to organize multiple media types, the rise of the media interface is most apparent in the delivery of television programming. The presence of such interfaces is inherent in explicitly Web-based means of delivering television or television-like content. Services such as NBC.com or Hulu are essentially new interfaces for the delivery of material previously made available through other channels. It is not a stretch to appreciate the function of a television interface in this context, as we have become accustomed to interacting with computers themselves through graphical user interfaces. Similarly, microprocessors drive digital video recorders, digital cable and satellite boxes, the digital television converters necessary to receive over-the-air broadcasts in the United States, and, increasingly, digital television sets themselves. In each of these cases, from computer screens to wide screens to the most basic digital converter, television interfaces have accompanied the remediation of television. While a similar remediation has pushed interfaces to become paramount in our everyday engagement with audio, newspapers, and books, television interfaces stand out because we are accustomed to looking at screens for content and now also find ourselves looking at code-generated graphical images layered on top or in place of moving images.

Because they are so present and immediate, it is tempting to get caught up in the surface layers of television and media interfaces. We might ask how intuitive is the layout of a set of interface screens? How responsive is the physical input system? How pleasing are the designs of the interface screens or a device's form factor? Is the interface as a whole friendly or cold, complicated or straightforward? The general tenor of instruction and criticism in the field of interface design is dedicated to addressing questions such as these. The answers are almost invariably predicated on an ideological foundation of usability and simplicity, with the oft-stated goal of having the interface recede into the background so that content can be enjoyed.[1] It is on such terms that most companies have conducted their market research and the few critics that actively consider media interfaces have structured their analyses.[2] Such functionalist considerations, centered on the visible and interactive elements of media interfaces, are helpfully attentive to the spatial dimensions of media interfaces yet allow the surface layer of interfaces to screen out a more complicated set of technological, industrial, and cultural forces that serve to structure and take advantage of the easy ubiquity of media interfaces.

This chapter argues for a more culturally engaged understanding of media interfaces. The essence of the argument is that media interfaces present themselves as simply functional non-places but are in fact the experiential moment of more complex interactive scripted spaces that reveal much about the status of television and television studies in the digital era. "Non-places" and "scripted spaces" are critical terms deliberately appropriated because they have been designed to read cultural formations through spatial discourses, an approach that is useful here because it helps to situate the very real spatial and functional aspects of media interfaces within a broader consideration of the ecology of media interfaces. Extending the analysis of media interfaces in this manner reveals that the new functionalist aesthetics of media interfaces are situated within complex industrial flows of a twenty-first-century media industry that is increasingly bound up with digital processes that structure most every experience of television. Ultimately, a critical analysis of media interfaces suggests that a fully realized analytic for digital television must account for the broader cultural function of software as well as the hardware and content so often the objects of critical study.

NON-PLACES: THE INTERFACE AESTHETICS OF METADATA

Perhaps the most important, if not the most obvious, point to make about television interfaces is that the experience of watching television is dramatically impacted by their presence and function. Most apparent is the simple fact that these interfaces take up screen space—or indeed introduce screens—when they are actively being used, adding new elements into the aesthetics of television. In the least invasive situations, this might be as simple as a time indicator showing at what point a television program was paused—helpful information layered on top of television programming (see figure 2). At other times a media interface can take over an entire screen, requiring a viewer to navigate a maze of menus or scroll through options prior to accessing the desired programming. While the majority of the marketing and journalistic rhetorics surrounding new television technologies focus on choice and control, the immediate viewer experience is one of looking at and responding to a new type of image on the screen. These images, the media interfaces, seem to have become the non-places of television; they are transient, functional, crucial screens that connect us to the content we supposedly desire.

This usage repurposes the term "non-places" as developed by Mark

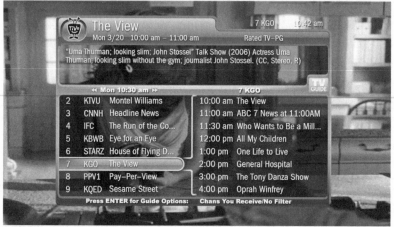

FIGURES 2.1 AND 2.2 Interfaces introduce new aesthetic elements into television. (TiVo screen captures from PVRcompare.com.)

Auge in *Non-Places: Introduction to an Anthropology of Supermodernity*. "Non-places" has two distinct meanings for Auge. On the one hand, the term refers to spaces of transport/transit/commerce/leisure that are in-between places; on the other, it refers to the relations, primarily anonymous, that people have in these spaces. Auge sums up his neologism: "As anthropological places create the organically social, so non-places create solitary contractuality."[3] Media interfaces perform a similar interstitial function for individuals interested in media content, serving as functional environments that offer up their own characteristics yet are not in themselves destinations. However, just as airports, malls, and retail transit establishments may be ephemeral and rootless from some perspectives while for others they are sites of work, play, politics, and historical development, media interfaces also reveal tensions among individuals, corporations, freedom, and control.

Moreover, media interfaces have an aesthetic of their own—an aesthetic of metadata—that threatens to change the manner in which we find, select, and appreciate television. Rather than just attending to temporally organized broadcasts, individuals using enhanced television technologies also navigate metadata-described interfaces, foregrounding genre, popularity, alphabetical order, featured actors, duration, or any number of other metadata tags. As suggested above, these screens are generally critiqued on their usability or simplicity or, in other words, how cleanly they organize the metadata that describes all of the programming options.[4] But interfaces are actively screening metadata, deploying them as key aesthetic features, as navigational elements leading to related screens, and as actionable criteria upon which media experiences are customized. Highlighting the name of an upcoming program on a TiVo grid or similar interactive programming guide, for example, can reveal the genre, year of production, rating, viewer rating, actors, summary, and other bits of descriptive information; the same data are used by the YouTube interface to suggest related videos and guide viewer behavior. In most programming guides, the main element used to initially organize viewing choices is still the channel of distribution, yet many systems allow, and some systems emphasize, other criteria, such as genre or rating; still other, more advanced, services are viewer-configurable along any number of metadata-driven criteria. Snap-Stream's Beyond TV, for example, foregrounds a category browsing feature in its interface as well as a search service that will automatically record programming that matches user-entered terms in metadata categories such as episode title, description, rating, or station call sign. With the rise of television interfaces, the act of screening metadata becomes a seamless part of the television viewing experience: the primary channel grid is often visited immediately upon turning on the television; supplementary information is presented with each channel change or use of time-shifting controls; informative and affirming time bars appear and recede with each touch of the controls; experienced users learn to perform their televisual maintenance—programming future recordings, deleting unwanted material to make room on a hard drive, searching for interesting upcoming options—while low-attention programming continues in the background or as a small image in one corner of the screen. On the surface, media interfaces create a framework of simple menus, translucent screens, friendly icons, and cheery sounds. These frames are filled not simply with content, but often with layers of metadata that take on a look of their own. Moreover, both the frames and the metadata explicitly invite user interaction. The form of media interfaces is therefore also function: the process of screening metadata simultaneously filling the screen with stylized data and precipitating the personalization and control promised by the interface.

The impact of applying and foregrounding metadata can also be seen quite powerfully at work on Google's YouTube service. Like the related Google Video, YouTube uses genre and popularity for filtered views of stored content and offers open-ended searches to parse the sheer number and diversity of hosted videos. In addition to the ability to search titles, descriptions, and genres, YouTube foregrounds user-generated tags, discussion groups, and other forms of social organization. The importance of metadata to the YouTube viewing experience is such that the functional aspects of the video player—play/pause button, time bar, volume controls—are forced to compete for attention with dozens of metadata-defined hyperlinks. Arguably part of YouTube's early success is due to the manner in which the prominent placement of related, featured, and popular videos encourages visitors to the YouTube site to keep clicking from one video to the next.

Ultimately, screening metadata is even more potent when media interfaces work with agents and *adaptive* agents to collect programming based on preselected tags. Metadata is crucial for sifting through the open-ended stream of media content and in some ways is now determinative of which programming is viewed. Even as metadata work to drive new televisual aesthetics, they also form the basis around which emergent television systems begin to offer advanced features. As William Uricchio notes, the application and processing of metadata allow emergent television technologies—like the DVR, YouTube, or video podcasts—to disrupt and reorganize televisual flow. Most important, Uricchio argues that metadata protocols and filters (such as search engines or adaptive agents) are not neutral but "determine what texts we will be able to locate": "Consequently, there is a great deal at stake for both producers and viewers in terms of precisely what will be labeled and how, and thus what will be seen."[5]

The implications of such developments can be seen in the efforts of digital cable and satellite television providers, who initially sought to ease the challenge of findability by upgrading from the simple scrolling guide channels of analog cable to more complex electronic or interactive programming guides. These guides were capable of providing detailed information about both current programming and that occurring weeks in the future and were in limited ways sortable via certain metadata categories; the latest versions of such guides are also compatible with newer offerings such as video-on-demand, high-definition channels, and DVRs. Going further still, TiVo has set itself apart through its deliberate integration and celebration of metadata-driven agents. Aside from the ease of time shifting, TiVo is probably best known for its "Season Pass" and "WishList" features, through which subscribers can set agents to automatically record programs described by certain categories of metadata—like series title, actor, director, genre, or keyword. Beyond this, TiVo offers a "Suggestions" service that recommends and automatically records programs based on users' preferences; this adaptive agent works through a collaborative filtering system based on millions of subscribers rating individual programs.[6] In the case of "TiVo Suggestions," an adaptive agent relies on both metadata and the networked nature of the TiVo system. YouTube offers similar features, allowing viewers to subscribe to channels of content organized by creator or keyword, and offering related videos featuring metadata similar to the video currently selected.

The process of screening metadata is crucial in three regards. First, it organizes users' relations to content by foregrounding descriptive information that distinguishes an individual video or television program from the mass of entertainment and information on offer. Content without metadata has become the proverbial tree in the forest, unknown if not unfindable. Interfaces assume their importance in direct proportion to their ability to package and present metadata in forms that both inform users about content and flatter their mastery and control over a world of audio and video that has become unimaginably large. Second, metadata are the actionable data that allow the service to function behind the scenes. Third, screening metadata is also the process of filtering out information deemed unhelpful, undesirable, or, in some cases, unprofitable. If the great benefit of television interfaces is that they allow users and their agents to locate content on the basis of metadata, the downside is that the selection of which metadata to create, store, index, and display is left primarily to the companies providing these interfaces and to the content producers and distributors who work within these systems. Users are not given the entire database of information describing content to filter on their own, nor may they create new categories of information to be captured. While the set of metadata provided by services like TiVo or iTunes is explicitly limited by their corporate providers, the user experience of the more expansive keyword and tag-based organization of YouTube is increasingly influenced by the categories, favored videos, and promotional efforts that dominate the screens of their purveyors. The screening of metadata sometimes allows users to find content they want and sometimes to find the content others want them to see.

More ominously, therefore, we can also think about the aesthetics of interfaces by considering what they screen out. By providing functional screens and overlays, television interfaces emphasize their status as non-places, encouraging viewers to interact and engage at a surface level while allowing more complex operations to continue beneath the surface. When looking at colorful wish lists, suggestions, and favorites, we are considering our own customized view of the vast array of content available; because we could not possibly know about—let alone view—every television show or video available, we must settle for some means of sorting and selecting. Television interfaces allow us to screen out possibilities, in many cases by flattering our stated and inferred preferences, but often reflecting the priorities of the entities behind the interface. Recognizing that the sheer blizzard of digital information available is too great to fathom directly, Steven Johnson has argued that interfaces allow us to ignore complexity:

> It is undeniable that the world has never seen so many zeros and ones, so many bits and bytes of information—but by the same token, it has never been so easy to ignore them altogether, to deal only with their enormously condensed representatives on the screen. Which is why we should think of the interface, finally, as a synthetic form, in both senses of the word. It is a forgery of sorts, a fake landscape that passes for the real thing, and—perhaps most important—it is a form

that works in the interest of synthesis, bringing disparate elements together into a cohesive whole.[7]

Although Johnson was more concerned with the graphical user interface of the computer screen, his argument applies equally to the extension of the computer's graphical user interface across the spectrum of convergent media technologies. Johnson's account is compelling, but we must add to it a political accounting. Television interfaces are designed to perform certain functions and limit others. They are designed by individuals and companies that have their own interests and agendas. As a result, television interfaces are screening out more than content, more even than shifts in the media ecology; they deploy their ideological simplicity to hide the complex functioning of code and networks that ultimately control what shows up on the screen, as well as those entities that influence the code and networks.

INTERACTIVE SCRIPTED SPACES

If media interfaces are performing cultural work that goes well beyond that suggested by their typical take-up as non-places, how might we best conceptualize their cultural function? Moving from one spatial metaphor to another, it seems that we might instead consider a model that explains the spatial proclivities of media interfaces in relation to the broader technological, political, and cultural constructions that make them possible. While the term "scripted space" has been used to describe exceptionally planned physical environments, the argument below abstracts this concept from its primarily spatial meaning and repurposes it as *interactive scripted space* to frame the contemporary cultural and economic implications of emergent media technologies. The most developed use of the term "scripted space" to date can be found in Norman Klein's *The Vatican to Vegas*, where Klein deploys it to describe the "special effects" that architects, designers, planners, and entertainers have for centuries used to deceive, direct, and delight visitors to exceptional places.[8] As his project is pointedly a "history of special effects," he presents examples that range from the baroque architectural efforts of the sixteenth century to world's fairs of the nineteenth and twentieth, arguing that a scripted space is one in which planners have gone to great lengths to design an environment that generates an expected reaction from visitors to the space. Building on these early examples, Klein proceeds to connect the designed experiences of the twentieth century—the cinema, Disneyland—and the twenty-first—Las Vegas, video games, computer-generated video effects—to a broader history of designed spaces.[9] Across these varied eras and environments Klein sees similarities in the attempt of designers to chart a path that visitors to a space will follow, as in the way the painted ceiling domes of Renaissance Italy attract the eyes up-ward or the panoramas of the Victorian era immerse visitors in a bodily experience. Scripted spaces are designed to entice and enthrall visitors, flooding their mental and corporeal faculties with carefully calibrated sensory inputs. And yet the very power of scripted spaces is that they are intended to hide their design, to place the emphasis on the experience of the visitor rather than the genius of the system. As Klein argues, scripted spaces quite carefully work to give individuals a powerful sense of agency within an environment that has been exquisitely calibrated: "The scripted space is a form of predestination, where the consumer 'acts out' the illusion of free will."[10] This construction is quite important to Klein, as he largely understands consumers of scripted spaces as actors playing out a narrative that has been plotted in advance. It is important that this primary experience is merely the visible realm of a much larger cultural project:

> We cannot ever rely simply on our personal relationship to a movie or a scripted space. That is only a third element within the whole: program; design; reception. We must take each step on its own, and see the problem as ideological (program); epistemological (script); and ontological (reception). In other words, at the level of the program, the political use of ideology is fundamental, and must be studied that way (how political interest is manifested within the codes generated to protect those at the top, or condemn their perceived enemies). At the level of the script, there is a code of how knowledge is supposed to be set up, how the branches and winding paths reveal a knowledge. And on the level of reception, the virtual is always relative; there is always a crisis about real/unreal, a suture between the two that makes the story exciting. . . . At the heart of these philosophical issues is a sense of codes themselves, how they are hidden, how they are turned into real space, how they are hinted at cautiously, and whether there is ever a codified version that applies as the ideal form of reception (there isn't).[11]

As Klein sees it, scripted spaces are not just about the script, but also about a more complex relationship that brings together the programmers, the script that is programmed, and the consumers who engage with the script. This model is supple enough to foreground questions of power without reducing such forces to a one-way flow. Klein does, however, privilege the agency exercised by those interests involved in establishing the program and sees little political power for consumers. He acknowledges consumer pleasure in experiencing scripted spaces and rightly suggests that the success of any scripted space is its ability to charm with both the "gimmick" and the "machinery."[12] By allowing individuals with disparate critical competencies (or interests) to revel in the ontological experience ("Wow, this is amazing!") or the ideological competency that brought it to them ("How did they do that?"), well-executed scripted spaces disarm consumers not simply through the power of spectacle, but also by empowering them with the feeling that they are in on the trick, are part of the system. But Klein argues that even these insightful engagements are largely preprogrammed, another trick to get participants in a scripted space to ignore the actual scripting process. As special effects impress consumers in the ontological realm and raise questions about the ideology behind the system, Klein suggests that "we accept the epistemology as a truth," as the script itself takes on the quality of an arrangement that simply exists in the world. Our full participation in the scripted space blunts our critique of the space itself, and thus scripted spaces become an accepted aspect of our everyday experience. We can tell each other that Disneyland is a carefully "Imagineered" construction, even point to the Disney Corporation and its many subsidiaries as the forces behind its facade, yet Disneyland persists as a feature of the built environment and a lure to millions of visitors. Everyone knows that Las Vegas is clearly a fantasy space that has effectively prescripted the actions of its visitors, yet millions gleefully play their part with the full knowledge that the house always wins. The power of scripted spaces is not in their special effects but in their ability to incorporate experience and critique as forms of interactivity that can be sold back to consumers.

And so it is with media interfaces. This concept of the scripted space can be quite usefully amended to provide specific insight into the interactive underpinning of contemporary emergent media. Klein himself connects the special effects of the cinema to those of physical environments and makes passing references to the scripted nature of computer games. Extending the concept of the scripted space to emergent media means first thinking through the ontological registers of emergent media technologies and systems. As suggested above, the phenomenological experience of media interfaces rests upon both the carefully designed nature of the experience and the implicitly interactive character of the design elements. Beyond even the aesthetics of metadata, the most sophisticated media interfaces emphasize the user's relation to the interface by foregrounding elements and displays like playlists and queues that reflect interactivity and customization. As Tara McPherson suggests in her study of Web browser navigation, the key factor at work in the modalities of experience generated by interacting with interfaces is that users are provided a set of "related sensations" as they feel the impact of their clicks and interactions through the interface.[13] These are explicitly volitional phenomena, as the distinguishing characteristic of each of these modalities is that users feel a sense of choice and feedback. McPherson also insists on tying her phenomenology back into a broader cultural and economic system in which interfaces entice consumers to participate in circuits of exchange: "Choice, personalization, and transformation are heightened as experiential lures, accelerated by feelings of mobility and searching, engaging the user's desire along different registers which nonetheless still underwrite neo-Fordist feedback loops."[14] This medium-specific analysis emphasizes the valuable position occupied by the interface—in this case the Web browser and its navigational conceits. While graphical user interfaces as we generally think about them have a history that is situated alongside the development of the personal computer and the Internet, we might think more broadly about media interfaces as the graphical intermediaries that now structure our interactions with all emergent media devices and media experiences. Like Web browsers, media interfaces introduce new modalities of experience that both elide the complexities of the systems they represent and commodify user interactions. If we use the rubric of the scripted space, media interfaces can be considered the equivalent of the spatial environment in that they constitute the ontological realm of reception. The experience of emergent media technologies is built less upon the special effects of the spectacle, however, than around the effect of interactivity at the interface. In essence the experiential modality of the media interface is about choice and personalization, expressed through interaction with the interface itself. We can see this at work in the popular celebrations of TiVo's friendly interface, the iPhone's touch-screen haptics, and Hulu's streamlined presentation and personalized queue. The media interface is effectively a scripted space, impressing consumers with an engaging experience that largely obscures the complex script that makes it possible.

If media interfaces can be thought of as the realm of reception for an interactive scripted space, the script that frames the function of emergent media technologies is essentially comprised of distributed network infrastructures and the protocological code that manages the flow of data through these networks. The function of this script is split, as it is responsible both for creating an aesthetically pleasing spatial environment and for facilitating the interactive processes that constitute the special effects of the scripted spaces of emergent media. Whereas most of the examples of scripted spaces provided by Klein are planned by a single, often identifiable, entity, a distributed assemblage of interests analogously scripts the emergent media ecology. Although the mechanism may be different, the effect is quite similar, as the visible and compelling interactive scripted space of the media interface draws attention away from the relatively unscrutinized aspects of the networks and code that make the interfaces function. Network infrastructures and code essentially provide the epistemological structure that supports the legible scripted spaces found in media interfaces. Because these systems are designed to function by incorporating user desire into the script itself, the emergent media script produces knowledge for and of its users.

Continuing the example of contemporary television interfaces, we can see that significant industrial struggles have developed over which corporate entity will assume the dominant role in providing the script that drives the interactive scripted spaces of television interfaces. Established Hollywood distribution entities, production companies, advertisers, hardware manufactures, and relative upstarts like TiVo and Apple each offer models for whom and how television interfaces will restructure dominant televisual experiences. TiVo, for example, represents both the most fundamental challenge to the televisual status quo and a model for its maintenance. For even as TiVo's time- and place-shifting capabilities severely undermine the outmoded Nielsen system of audience measurement based on sampling, TiVo has found a way to position itself as an entity directly serving viewers, advertisers, and distributors. TiVo explicitly connects the circuits of televisual exchange by consciously offering a superior software-controlled user experience that simultaneously commodifies the interactivity it allows; viewers are invited to interact, and the data generated by these interactions are sold by TiVo to the rest of the television industry. If TiVo can be thought of as the catalyst for televisual interface dissemination and industrial destabilization, and YouTube as a site that placed user-generated content side-by-side with corporate offerings, the most significant recent development in the advance of televisual interfaces is the response by the Hollywood content producers/broadcasters. With their business models challenged by both time-shifted viewing and unregulated online redistribution of programming, each of the major U.S. broadcasters has established an online presence. Each of the U.S. broadcast networks began to experiment with online video streaming in 2006, generally inserting single-ad breaks at various points in the programming. In addition to the challenge of balancing the promotional functions of their Web sites against the demand for online viewing, broadcasters have also dealt with the problem of online streaming rights. Even in an era favoring networked-owned programming, broadcasters cannot simply offer everything online that they do over the air without extensive negotiations with multiple production companies.

NBC is the most interesting example to explore because it has taken the unusual step of providing content for streaming and downloading at the NBC.com site and also partnering with News Corporation to create a high-profile destination for Hollywood-produced television programming, Hulu.com (see figure 3). On the NBC site itself, which has changed a number of times between 2006 and 2009, each streamed series has both its own mini Web site—where clips, information, and activities can be found—and a separate space featuring a Flash-based video player designed for streaming ad-supported content. The video-player interface forms a frame around the content itself, with the standard controls for play/pause, volume control, and time bar perpetually present. Like video streaming options from ABC and CBS, the time bar is broken into sections, with each section of content viewable only after the streaming of a new advertisement; half-hour programs tend to be divided into four sections, hour-long shows into six. Like offerings from the other major broadcasters, the NBC streaming service and interface are basic and occasionally frustrating, with broken videos, repetitious advertise-

FIGURES 3.1 AND 3.2 Metadata and adaptive agents organize users' relations to content, screening what can and can't be seen. U.S. networks began to experiment with online video streaming in 2006. (Screen captures from NBC.com and Hulu.)

ments, and difficult navigation. NBC, like its broadcast competitors, described its effort as promotional and experimental. The tension between NBC's interest in serving its own promotion and research needs and its interest in meeting the demand for content from site visitors is evident in the cluttered layout of each show's sub-site, the separation of promotional content like Webisodes from broadcast content, and the multiple means of navigating to the video player. Such clumsy navigation is evidence of a half-hearted attempt to compete with file-sharing technologies and upstart services, such as YouTube, Joost, and Apple, while still grappling with the imperatives of corporate branding and promotion. As suggested by James Bennett in the context of the BBC's use of interactive television, a clear organizational mandate can result in interface navigation that is simple and familiar for users.[15]

In order to establish a more fully featured broadband video-on-demand service NBC partnered with News Corporation in 2007 to develop the stand-alone site Hulu, which publicly launched in March 2008. This service, which offers television and feature film programming, both current and back catalog, was explicitly designed with video-sharing and social-networking principles so that it seemed up-to-date with its competitors. Like YouTube, Hulu is a dedicated video distribution site that allows for the streaming, sharing, and embedding of centrally stored content. Unlike YouTube, Hulu offers only content owned by its owners and affiliates, so visitors can expect to choose from a wide, yet incomplete, array of programming owned by NBC, Fox, ABC, and the producers and distributors that have struck deals with Hulu. Hulu streams both short clips and entire episodes of television programs, organizing its content by popularity, title, or network. To earn revenue and defend the advertiser-supported model of television distribution, advertisements are delivered before and at intervals throughout the programming. Beyond its Web-savvy name—which reportedly means both "holder of precious things" and "interactive recording"—Hulu is clearly a well-funded conglomerate response to the perceived threat of emergent television distribution systems.[16] Recognizing the imperatives of the post-network era, NBC is hedging its bets. Much as Catherine Johnson has argued that an individual television program may contribute to the brand identity of multiple television networks, NBC-owned programming plays a major role in the continued success of many emergent television ventures.[17] At the same time, NBC maintains an ownership or partnership role in many of these efforts, even as it struggles to determine what role the NBC brand should play. It maintains the flagship brand associated with the broadcast network, owns or has ownership stakes in a number of cable/satellite networks, was an early investor in TIVO, sometimes sells programming through Apple's iTunes store, streams some programming from its own site, and has partnered with News Corporation to develop Hulu.

Hulu sets itself apart from NBC's original online video distribution system in three key ways. First, unlike the parochial, partial, and chaotic collection of programming streaming at NBC.com, Hulu claims to deliver content from more than fifty sources, including properties owned by News Corporation and other erstwhile competitors. While this choice to un-brand network-owned programming might seem surprising given the tremendous resources broadcasters typically invest in packaging and promoting their content, it is in keeping with broader conglomerate strategies of tiering and targeting.[18] By pointedly emphasizing the viewer's ability to customize his or her own content flow, viewing environment, and video sharing strategies, Hulu marks a move away from the promotion-heavy approach long favored by broadcasters toward a social networking model in which viewers do the sequencing and promotional work themselves, creating video queues and sharing videos with other viewers in their personal social networks. Second, Hulu is a video-centric site and bears few obvious traces of its corporate ownership. Whereas NBC.com is torn between promoting programming and brand—with an array of transmedia efforts like fan groups, chat forums, downloadable promotional items, and special events—Hulu is focused on providing video. As a result, it is much easier to find and view content on the Hulu site. In this manner, as when Apple approached the music business and TIVO released its early equipment, a streamlined corporate mission has translated into an intuitive user experience on the Hulu site. Last, Hulu organizes and delivers its content through simple and feature-rich interfaces. Like the YouTube example considered above, Hulu uses metadata categories to organize content. The home page and most subsidiary pages feature a range of related and most popular options, and clearly marked tags allow searching by title, genre, and network or studio. Although options for user-generated tagging are absent, Hulu has developed a metadata-centric interface designed to ease and encourage extended viewing sessions. Beyond the standard set of video playing controls—which pleasingly fade out after a few seconds of viewing—Hulu has also included in its player interface a series of options to enhance the manipulation and viewing of content. Prominent icons encourage viewers to share videos via e-mail, embed videos on their own Web sites and blogs, and even select portions of content for sharing. In addition to allowing playback at multiple scales—small, large, full screen—Hulu includes interface controls that allow for the dimming of the computer that surrounds Hulu's video and a pop-out feature that causes a scalable video window to open and play without any surrounding Web browser content. Such attention to the details of the video interface makes for a more pleasurable viewing experience and, in line with Hulu's broader efforts, helps to position Hulu as a contemporary to upstart video streaming services. Of course, a smooth interface and contemporary styling help to distract from the fact that Hulu is simultaneously configured to track and commodify viewing behavior.

While NBC may be competing against upstarts like YouTube by developing multiple distribution channels, its biggest challenge might come from companies not traditionally associated with television or video. Microsoft, for example, continues to tweak its Media Center version of the Vista operating system, launched in January 2007, even as it is simultaneously marketing Interactive Program Guide software to cable operators. Microsoft's Media Center and the competing efforts from Apple are designed to provide a common media interface across computer, television, and portable screens so that a user's content can be accessed from any of these devices in the same manner. Of course with this standardization come the limitations and influences of their corporate providers. In this manner, digital rights management software is often included as part of the ultimate product, which is sold to consumers on the basis of its flexibility and user empowerment. Just as these two companies have spent the past two decades developing and introducing competing, yet similar, graphical user interfaces, they are set to repeat the process with media interfaces. In the process they are becoming significant players in the media distribution business, as evidenced by the individual and collective deals they have negotiated with the traditional distributors of music, television, and film. The crucial position of media interfaces in these industrial struggles is underscored by the series of copyright and patent lawsuits that have been filed against TiVo and Apple's iTunes by erstwhile competitors, just as an earlier generation of lawsuits was filed (and settled) over Apple's and Microsoft's use of various windows interfaces in their operating systems.

PROGRAMMING THE SCRIPTED SPACE

The full power of the scripted space analytic rests in its insistence upon situating these distributed efforts as part of a broader techno-cultural formation. Sketching out a sense of the program behind the interactive scripted space of emergent media interfaces involves updating the concept of the scripted space itself to include not only hierarchical notions of ideology and power, but also the more contemporary modulations of control that work through the decentralized processes of mass customization and user feedback. Asking questions about the ideological dimensions of the scripted spaces of emergent media means determining whose interests are served by a script that demands user interaction. To answer this question we can look toward those entities that specifically traffic in the collection and use of the data produced through user interactions, like TiVo, Hulu, NBC, or even mobile phone service providers, cable operators, data aggregation firms, and, in some cases, government agencies. In order to provide interactive experiences and moments of customization for their users, companies providing emergent media services through the scripted spaces of interactive media interfaces must collect information on user interest and desire and then tailor the user experience based on this information. Critics like Siva Vaidhyanathan and Mark Andrejevic have argued that the companies that provide services based on user interaction data should have their practices scrutinized. Andrejevic in particular has suggested that the problem is of transparency and asymmetry, as these corporations have the ability to amass vast amounts of information about their users' habits but rarely, if ever, make this information available for users to review and question.[19] Such critiques are appropriate if our primary concern is, like Siva Vaidhyanathan's, in the centralization of power, or in the new role of surveillance, and in particular the role of dataveillance, in the course of our everyday engagements with technology.[20]

We must also ask, however, how these surveillant practices fit within a broader shift in forms of social power. The disciplinary societies described by Michel Foucault have in many ways morphed into societies of control, and this transition is accelerated specifically by the broad deployment of media networks and interfaces that work to respatialize power away from the monumental forms associated with Foucault's bureaucracies. Gilles Deleuze anticipates such a shift in social power, arguing for consideration of a control society that reworks Foucault's discipline to the point that societies "no longer operate by confining people but through continuous control and instant communication."[21] Media interfaces are quite pointed examples of how control operates in a networked age. They are delivered up as experiences that offer a promise of empowerment, of consumer sovereignty over technology, information, and consumption. Through the interface consumers are invited to "take control" over their television experiences. As William Boddy has noted, TiVo's initial marketing efforts went so far as to emphasize how their service shifted some aspects of control over television programming to TiVo-enabled viewers.[22] And yet it is precisely through these interactions at the interface that individuals subject themselves to broader exchanges of social power. Although each specific exchange might be understood as an individual exerting a moment of control while also yielding data to be commodified by a particular corporate interest, the collective action of billions of individuals making such exchanges through media interfaces represents a tangible shift in the modulations of power. Though these rhetorical constructions of "control" are not quite homonymic, neither are they equivalent; while each describes an enabling of power, the flow of power is asymmetrical: control exercised by users is generally accounted for (and literally counted) by the companies that provide the services, but viewers generally have no visibility into the control exercised by these providers.[23]

The program behind the interactive scripted spaces of emergent media is not simply that of the media conglomerates discussed above, nor of Silicon Valley upstarts, but an entire post-Fordist economic system that works through decentralized spatial practices and the incorporation of individual desire more directly into systems of production. Rather than just pointing out which entities currently manage such scripted spaces, we might instead consider how the broad pattern of economic and cultural changes has created a techno-spatio-political system in which various entities—corporate, entrepreneurial, political, and governmental—can advance their own interests through the eager participation of individuals willing to exchange valuable data for specific media experiences.

As the practice of engaging interfaces occupies an ever-greater portion of our time spent with entertainment media, they introduce functions and aesthetics that impact the very experience and meaning of the media themselves. A part of the assemblage of every new entertainment media technology, media interfaces are relatively indifferent to the source and type of content, equally organizing programming previously thought of as music, television, photography, Web video, or feature film, and equally applicable on a television screen, a laptop computer, a Web site, or a portable media player. As a result of their broad distribution, convergent possibilities, and seductive functionality, media interfaces have offered personalization and control as a challenge to liveness and flow as the dominant ontologies and ideologies of contemporary entertainment media. And these changes are not confined to the living room. Televisual interfaces, and indeed television itself, move both within and outside of the home, across laptops and portable media players, repurposing offices, commutes, and hotel rooms.[24] While these devices deploy different form factors and offer varying degrees of functionality and engagement, their interface screens act as consistent and often customized means of organizing and accessing content.

Taking media interfaces seriously has two consequences for the critical study of television. On one hand, even as we turn our attention to new modes of engagement with entertainment media and metadata, we should remain attentive to the cultural focus that defines so much of the study of television. This means considering how emergent media interfaces refract and redefine our understanding of the gendered, raced, and classed nature of television viewing. William Boddy, Lynn Spigel, and others have convincingly documented the gendered dimensions of the introduction of radio and television.[25] David Morley, Ann Gray, Ellen Seiter, and others have rigorously demonstrated that the social and cultural contexts in which technologies such as the VCR and the Internet enter the domestic environment have a great deal to do with the gendered and classed nature of their use.[26] We should be alert to similar tendencies in the continued convergence of entertainment and computer-based media. Approaching these changes to the televisual ecology systemically, John Caldwell has noted media conglomerates' tendencies to develop multichannel niches along the axes of race and gender, and Lisa Parks has argued that the convergent media system is best understood as one of flexible microcasting "organized around social distinctions (whether gender, age, race, class, sexuality, or lifestyle) that are arranged to maximize profit for media producers, networks, and advertisers."[27] Building on these considerations of programming strategy and audience hyper-commodification, media interfaces and metadata systems further the personalization of media experiences and thus participate in a system geared toward commodifying "layers of individual identity, desire, taste, and preference."[28] Although the language of space and power lends itself to the abstraction of individuals into users, we must continue to recognize that cultural processes as complex as the televisual remain scripted as much by social difference as by computer code and flows of power.

On the other hand, we might also consider how the move toward interface-mediated experiences with television and entertainment media represents an opportunity to broaden the suite of critical and conceptual tools available for the study of television and media in the digital age. As suggested in the preceding analysis, we might move in this direction by pushing further in our consideration of television as a cultural form now imbricated with software and code. Questions of television and the digital are often aimed at looking for ruptures—in distribution models, in image capture and processing, in regulatory regimes, or in extrinsic challengers to the television's cultural function. The critical consideration of television and media interfaces demonstrates that we should also be looking for affinities. Interfaces are now part of the dominant television experience in the United States and will certainly be part of every effort to deliver television over the Web or other IP systems. Televisual experiences are now scripted, now coded, and engaging both software studies and cultural studies will be essential to understanding what television has become.

NOTES

1. Jenifer Tidwell, *Designing Interfaces* (Sebastapol, Calif.: O'Reilly Media, 2005); Peter Moville, *Ambient Findability* (Sebastapol, Calif.: O'Reilly Media, 2005).
2. For example: *Engadget* references "the intuitiveness, ease, and power of the original DVR"; in Dave Zatz, "Hands on with the TiVo Series 3!," Engadget, posted September 12, 2006; http://www.engadget.com/2006/09/12/hands-on-with-the-tivo-series3; "As Apple demonstrated with the iPod, a simple, intu-

itive interface scheme makes all the difference in the mass consumer market"; in Leander Kahney, "New UI Showdown: Apple vs. TIVO," *Wired*, posted September 13, 2006; http://www.wired.com; "From the very beginning ease-of-use was a goal of the team"; in Matt Haughey, "The PVRBlog Interview: Ten Questions with TIVO's Director of User Experience, Margret Schmidt," PVRblog, posted December 8, 2004; http://www.pvrblog.com.

3. Mark Auge, *Non-Places: Introduction to an Anthropology of Supermodernity* (London: Verso, 1995), 94.

4. For example, *Wired*'s discussion of Apple iTunes and TIVO interfaces: "TIVO more than any other company so far in digital TV has proved the value of a great interface. It's the main reason the company's fans are such die-hards—much like Apple fans, in fact"; Leander Kahney, "New UI Showdown: Apple vs. TIVO," *Wired.com*, posted September 13, 2006; http://www.wired.com.

5. William Uricchio, "Television's Next Generation: Technology/Interface Culture/Flow," in *Television after TV: Essays on a Medium in Transition*, ed. Lynn Spigel and Jan Olsson (Durham, N.C.: Duke University Press, 2004), 176–77.

6. A detailed guide to how the TIVO Suggestions service works can be found in Ali Kamal and Wijnand van Stam, "TIVO: Making Show Recommendations Using a Distributed Collaborative Filtering Architecture," paper part of the Proceedings of the Tenth ACM SIGKDD International Conference on Knowledge Discovery and Data Mining, Seattle, 2004; http://portal.acm.org/citation.cfm?id=1014097.

7. Steven Johnson, *Interface Culture: How New Technology Transforms the Way We Create and Communicate* (San Francisco: Harper, 1997), 237.

8. Norman M. Klein, *The Vatican to Vegas: A History of Special Effects* (New York: New Press, 2004).

9. It should be noted that Klein dates the end of the twentieth century to the fall of the Berlin Wall, and thus his chronology is slightly different from that which is commonly accepted.

10. Norman M. Klein, "The Electronic Baroque: Jerde Cities," in *You Are Here: The Jerde Partnership International*, ed. Frances Anderton and Ray Bradbury (London: Phaidon Press, 1999).

11. Klein, *The Vatican to Vegas*, 328.

12. Ibid., 329.

13. Tara McPherson, "Reload: Liveness, Mobility, and the Web," in *New Media, Old Media: A History and Theory Reader*, ed. Wendy Hui Kyong Chun and Thomas W. Keenan (London: Routledge, 2005), 201.

14. Ibid., 206.

15. James Bennett, "Interfacing the Nation: Remediating Public Service Broadcasting in the Digital Television Age," *Convergence* 14, no. 3 (2007): 286.

16. Jason Kilar, "What's in a Name?" Hulu Blog, posted on May 13, 2008; http://blog.hulu.com/2008/05/13/meaning-of-hulu/.

17. Catherine Johnson, "Tele-Branding in TVIII: The Network as Brand and Programme as Brand," *New Review of Film and Television Studies* 5, no. 1 (2007): 5–24.

18. John Thornton Caldwell, "Convergence Television: Aggregating Form and Repurposing Content in the Culture of Conglomeration," in Spigel and Olsson, *Television after TV*, 68–69.

19. Mark Andrejevic, *iSpy: Surveillance and Power in the Interactive Era* (Lawrence: University of Kansas Press, 2008).

20. For a discussion of the term "dataveillance," see Greg Elmer, *Profiling Machines: Mapping the Personal Information Economy* (Cambridge, Mass.: MIT Press, 2004). For a detailed look at the perils of concentration, see Siva Vaidhyanathan, *The Googlization of Everything* (Berkeley: University of California Press, 2010).

21. Gilles Deleuze, *Negotiations, 1972–1990* (New York: Columbia University Press, 1995), 174. For a more engaged critique of the relationship of Deleuze's control societies and emergent media, see Elmer, *Profiling Machines*.

22. William Boddy, "Old Media as New Media: Television," in *The New Media Book*, ed. Dan Harries (London: BFI Publishing, 2002), 242–53.

23. For more on the asymmetries of surveillance through emergent media technologies, see Mark Andrejevic, *Reality TV: The Work of Being Watched* (Lanham, Md.: Rowman and Littlefield, 2004); see also Andrejevic, *iSpy*.

24. See Max Dawson, "Little Players, Big Shows: Format, Narration, and Style on Television's New Smaller Screens." *Convergence: The International Journal of Research into New Media Technologies* 13, no. 3 (2007): 231–50.

25. William Boddy, *New Media and Popular Imagination: Launching Radio, Television, and Digital Media in the United States* (Oxford: Oxford University Press, 2004); Lynn Spigel, *Make Room for TV: Television and the Family Ideal in Postwar America* (Chicago: University of Chicago Press, 1992).

26. David Morley, *The Nationwide Audience* (London: Routledge, 1992); Ellen Seiter, *Television and New Media Audiences* (Oxford: Clarendon Press, 1999); Ann Gray, *Video Playtime: The Gendering of a Leisure Technology* (London: Routledge, 1992).

27. Caldwell, "Convergence Television," 68–69; Lisa Parks, "Flexible Microcasting: Gender, Generation, and Television-Internet Convergence," in *Television after TV: Essays on a Medium in Transition*, ed. Lynn Spigel and Jan Olsson (Durham, N.C.: Duke University Press, 2004), 135.

28. Parks, "Flexible Microcasting," 135.

TELEVISION, INTERRUPTED

Pollution or Aesthetic?

Vestiges of the aesthetic claim to be something autonomous,
a world unto itself, remain even within the most trivial product
of mass culture. In fact, the present rigid division of art into
autonomous and commercial aspects is itself largely a function
of commercialization.

Theodor Adorno, "How to Look at Television"

In aesthetics, as in other provinces of inquiry, radical novelties
frequently turn out to be migrant ideas which, in their native
intellectual habitat, were commonplaces.

M. H. Abrams, *The Mirror and the Lamp*

D: anyone who wants to chat? :)
S: what about
D: anything
D: Im bored
S: Im going to see the hulk movie
D: Nice :)

General Chat Channel, *World of Warcraft*

There is a crucial scene in *The Counterfeiters* where the Nazi
leader, Herzog (Devid Striesow), who is running the operation to produce counterfeit currency in Sachsenhausen, con-
fronts the Jewish forgers with the judgment on their efforts.
If the fake notes have been detected, then the Jews, who have

until now experienced relative comfort and protection, will be relegated to the status of ordinary prisoners. This is a point in the film where the moral complexity of the forgers' situation is prominent: on the one hand, at stake is not only survival but also their professional pride as criminals in producing the perfect forgery; on the other, their success will contribute to the war effort of a regime that has brutally incarcerated and murdered millions of Jews like them. The scene is shot in a large room with the prisoners assembled facing Herzog and his guards as he tells them about the Nazi agent who recently visited a Swiss bank and deposited a stack of their counterfeit British bills. The film then becomes a flashback accompanying Herzog's narration of events. Even though the bank's own experts believe the notes to be genuine, the agent insists on their being sent to the Bank of England for verification. At this point we cut back to the present; Herzog is holding an envelope in his hands, and we and the prisoners realize the decision of the bank and the fate of the forgers is about to be revealed in a grotesque echo of an awards ceremony. He pulls the note from the envelope and reads it out.

At this moment my screen went blank except for a gray onscreen graphic bar across its top and the red letters "PA," and in my headset the chief cabin steward announced that since we were beginning our descent, they would be turning off the in-flight entertainment system. On some flights there is often five or so minutes of grace, depending where one happens to be seated, when viewers can disentangle themselves from the narrative worlds they've been consuming, but on this occasion the cabin crew was rushed, and I realized that I'd probably have to wait for my return journey in two weeks in order to discover the fate of the forgers. This I did, pulling up the film from the menu and scrolling forward to the point where I'd been interrupted.

To some extent watching in-flight entertainment is analogous to watching digital television. I could control what material to select and the order and pace at which to watch it; interruptions happened either at my own volition or because of interference from beyond the digital system: the chronology of the flight path and its associated patterns of refreshments, meals, announcements, and encouragements to sleep that structure any long-haul flight. This mesh between individual subjective mood and the global organization of choices—even where they are quite flexible, allowing reviewing, pausing, etc.—is similar to the ways in which contemporary broadcast, cable, and digital television is experienced. However much control this allowed, I obviously could not influence the broader structuring aspects of the flight that meant the plane had to descend at a certain time and place. Similarly, in digital television there is the industrial management by networks and other providers over access and patterns of transmission and delivery (for example, the pacing of the publication/release of seasons/series/episodes) that the viewer cannot control. Digital television, with its potential to be molded to the currents of individual mood and desire, makes prominent the question of the ways in which television's means of delivery—traditionally the broadcast schedule, but now a complex web of entry points and ownership—shapes our experience of television aesthetics. Can we continue to think about the specificity of a medium that seems so dispersed and unstable as an object of study? To what extent does our augmented ability to control our consumption of television affect our evaluation of it? Is my experience of watching *The Counterfeiters* (a film watched on a personal television screen) at all relevant in my evaluation of it as a text? To put it another way: would an evaluation of *The Counterfeiters* as I first watched it demand an account of the medium that delivered it? Was the television screen more like a portal to a film experience, and if so, does the distribution of content matter in our evaluation, enjoyment, and assessment of it?

For television studies it was always the case that such a demand would at least be felt because it was hard to ignore the structural embeddedness of material in the broadcast schedule, in television's global, national, and local flow. But digital television is promoted and to an increasing extent consumed, at least in part, in terms of its ability to purify the connective tissue of the schedule, to remove the adverts, promotional material, and other pollution that gets in the way of the "pure" text. The prominence of "the medium" as a touchstone in our evaluation of works comes about to a large extent because those works can demand that this is an aspect to which we pay attention in order to experience their full creative force; some shows demand that we take into account medium specificity.

In order to explore these matters more concretely I turn to the work of John Caughie and Stanley Cavell, both of whom, in very different ways, attempt to grasp television's specificity in relationship to the live currents of the everyday. This leads me to a discussion of the nature of attention and concentration, where I want to point to the duality of our consumption of television: we can view it live (at the moment of its first broadcast/publication/release), where it is freighted with the present-tense-ness of the first experience of a new cultural product, and we can view the same material later, as a recorded, controllable, repeated, and perhaps more obviously packaged commodity form. Such a duality raises important questions regarding digital television's medium specificity, asking us to think about how this is different from thinking about our first encounters and then subsequent encounters with other kinds of cultural production and art. Finally, I offer some examples of digital media that incorporate many similar aspects of television and point to the ways in which digital television might alert us to a broader sense of the ways in which we might grasp and evaluate cultural production and expression.

TELEVISION: INTERRUPTION AS MEDIUM SPECIFICITY?

I want to begin by addressing the issue of interruption, not least because many of the promises of digital technology are about tailoring one's viewing so as to minimize interruption and intrusion of material that one does not want to see. To recap what is by now a familiar narrative: new distribution technologies (DVRs, online services, and portable devices), together with the involvement of wider media and telecommunications industries in the production and distribution of products (many of which are indistinguishable in quality, presentation, and generic coding from radio or television's broadcast forms), as well as the continuing presence of broadcast, cable, and satellite scheduling, produce a complex environment where some of the traditional assumptions about the television medium are in a state of uncertainty and flux. In the past, television studies had to acknowledge the importance of the delivery of television within a national broadcast schedule, and it was the nature of this schedule that stimulated various theorizations of the medium as a whole. The technological process of distribution, which was traditionally free, immediate, and synchronized across large populations, seemed to be an uncomplicated matter. Most theories of television tended to stress its immediate connections to the fabric and rhythms of everyday life in terms of time, modes of address, and ideological content.

Of course, digital television does not remove everyday life—indeed, it seems attuned to a particularly privatized and individualized everyday—but its online, onscreen variations allow users to mitigate or entirely remove the unwanted or surplus marks of the traditional schedule. Those traces, where they remain, inhere in the individual programs or other material that digital users have mined. This means that the idea of interruption as a feature of the medium is transformed into one of textual pollution that can be removed, rather than an aspect of the medium that has to be endured, tolerated, or (in some cases) enjoyed. To what extent is this "pollution," which digital technology allows us to avoid (if we choose), actually a crucial aspect of the medium? If we take that pollution away, is there anything distinctive left? Does the prominence of a medium's distinctive or specific aspects necessarily mean they are important or significant?

Television's profoundly interrupted nature has been a prominent feature of scholarly engagement with the medium. Some have seen this interruption (commercial breaks, promotional material, and other segmented textuality) as part of an overall flow, part of the primary and distinctive nature of the televisual;[1] others have drawn attention to the way in which television programs themselves seek to establish their distinction from this flow as textually discrete and aesthetically coherent units.[2] Outside scholarship there is also the understanding of television interruption as a bothersome impurity that might be avoided or otherwise tolerated through various social, technical, or contemplative strategies (making tea, TiVo, appreciation).

There are several kinds of interruption that are relevant to television. The first, as on my flight, is the global structuring kind over which the viewer has no control. This is likely to be manifested in two ways: textually, so that what we want to continue watching is stopped while something else is shown (say, a commercial); or non-textually where the social world intrudes or otherwise interrupts. Traditionally there have been various ways to mitigate the second kind while watching television—turning off the phone, making sure nutrition and toilet needs are taken care of well in advance, or otherwise sealing our viewing time and space as best we can against the rest of the world. The difference between the VCR—the earliest domestic weapon against the interruption and chronological authority of the broadcast schedule—and digital television technology seems to be that the various ways to own, time-shift, and otherwise mine texts are promoted as the obvious and routinized ways to interact with the medium rather than viewing the schedule in real time.

"Who *wants* to watch adverts, promos, and the rest of the connective tissue of the television flow?" seems to be the compelling appeal to common sense that digital television marketers deploy most frequently.

There is another kind of interruption that is non-textual and much more intimately involved with another sense of time, the subjectively felt sense. In this sense we interrupt ourselves or discover some aspect of us that is antagonistic to the continuation of our attention. This can be characterized as our availability or susceptibility to interruption or as our potential for or disposition toward distraction. It is this aspect to which, according to John Caughie, traditional television's scheduling and forms respond—an acknowledgement that it is in competition with the everyday distractions of modernity: "The time and space of television always seem to pull its texts back into the everyday [where] . . . the time of everyday living is always liable to interrupt the time of viewing. Even when the phone does not ring or when commercials do not break into the flow, the *possibility* of interruption seems significant for the forms of attention we bring to television and the kinds of pleasures we expect."[3]

Caughie is careful to acknowledge both the diversity of kinds of interruption and the variability in the prominence and intensity of interruption across different programming types, channels, and points in the schedule, and he is careful not to overstress interruption as a unique vulnerability of television (compare reading a novel or the organization of time in the theater). For Caughie, television's relationship to the everyday determines in various ways its textual behavior so that it is both structured and experienced quite differently from film; in many genres this means "organizing expectation and attention into segments and a multiplicity of plot lines as a way of compensating for interruptability."[4] For example, in his monograph, *Edge of Darkness*, he argues that the significance of seriality in the structuring of fictional television narratives is intimately connected to television's awareness of interruption as a possibility: "The centrality of serialization seems to me to have a lot to do with what I take to be one of the defining characteristics of television as a domestic technology: its interruptability. Though it may often get the undivided attention of its audience—or of viewers equipped with video recorders or DVD players—television cannot assume it."[5]

For Caughie this distinguishes television from the way cinema is "structured to ensure unbroken attention and absorption." The result of this distinction is that television's interruptability leads to a narrative form organized around segments rather than toward a causality in which "missing a causal link—through inattention or interruption—can be fatal to the coherence of the narrative."[6] Already we can see problems with the widening of one sense of the medium across its various mediums. This account of interruptability just won't work in the same way across all genres. We need only think of the difference between a live news or sports broadcast and a drama to realize how vast the differences might be. Our sense of the difference may or may not be important—it is precisely the fact that it is hard to specify in advance the importance that makes general accounts of a medium so varied as television inevitably wanting. As a way around this problem Caughie insists on the everyday—another vast and varied thing—as the constant that is addressed by television. So in the kind of television that Caughie deems "serious"—mostly fictional genres—the trace of the everyday "seems to lie in forms of attention and subjectivity which do not depend on fantasmatic identification, on losing oneself in identification with the narrative space, but offer instead a relaxed detachment."[7]

"Relaxed detachment" is one kind of involvement among a range of responses, all of which have to acknowledge the demands of the everyday, both as they are internalized in television's address and in their potential to intrude in the lives of the viewers.[8] Television is awkwardly positioned in this account since it must continually solicit the attention of the potentially distracted viewer and effectively aggravate that potential by deploying programming breaks to incorporate commercials and promotional or other connective material. It is little wonder that a major appeal of the digital distribution and consumption of television programs is precisely in the avoidance of that aspect that threatens an already precarious maintenance of attention.

Caughie's work is important in reminding us of the significance of television as a major agent in the cultural history of attention. Attention is the primary thing that risks being interrupted both by television's textual behavior and by the intrusions of the everyday in the world of the viewer. The nature and quality of our attention, especially the means by which it is recruited, stimulated, and maintained, is surely an important aspect to our understanding and appreciation of the products of cultural expression, and the location of our encounters with them is not inconsequential. For example, Charles Rosen notes the peculiar experiential deficits of musical recordings in the following way:

> Listening to records is a less gripping experience than hearing a concert or playing oneself. . . . With records, there is always the possibility of interrupting one's listening by leaving the room for a moment or by conversation. . . . The concert coerces attention: the performance, with lowered lights and the demand of silence, cannot be interrupted or repeated, and must be seized at one hearing; the work has to be perceived as a whole, and we cannot go over some of the details again. This focuses attention in a way that is more difficult to achieve by listening to records, which tends to dilute and disperse the attention necessary for difficult music, in the same way that watching a video in a room at least partly lighted is less intense than seeing a film in a darkened theater.[9]

Even as he acknowledges the irritations of the social setting ("rattling programs," "coughs"), for Rosen it doesn't matter how much one concentrates on a recording since one cannot replicate that "coercion" of attention at a live concert performance. That sense of cultural production that must be seized at the moment it occurs can be related to the experience of watching the live broadcast of television within a schedule, as opposed to the "dead" version of television as a recording. Caughie's work implies that television's distinction inheres in its close acknowledgement of the socialized everyday world from which it is viewed and whose attention it must recruit. Before digital media we could say that television exhibited its bid for attention in distinctive ways but that this has become more muted since digital forms of television make it appear closer to other kinds of commodity. I will return to this point below.

Rosen's point about the coercion of our attention is also important because it reminds us of the vitality of television sound and its importance in the recruiting of our attention. In the live broadcast schedule, title sequences, commercials, and promotional material all use distinctive sounds and music as part of their bid to maintain, recruit, or restore our attention, but that attention, once held, can be purely aural. Radio always allowed listeners to go about other business as they listened, and many programs were explicitly designed as accompaniments to other work or play, delivering music and talk in various genres. That aspect of radio is utilized, of course, as well by television so that it retains a sense of being on, and even attended to, when it is not in fact being watched.[10] Combine this with the fact that increasingly our everyday is one where the viewing object is not necessarily bound to a schedule, then the kinds of attention that are solicited and available become quite extensive. Viewers might set aside time for the concentrated watching or rewatching of a DVD or download, a trend seemingly acknowledged in the genre of contemporary television drama, with its foregrounding of incremental characterization, backstory rationing, and enigma webbing, which precisely reward frequent attentive viewing and reviewing. Or our viewing might be collective and celebratory, relaxed, casual, expectant, listening but not viewing—in other words, the entire range of behavior, the diversity of which is celebrated and theorized by over three decades of television studies audience scholarship, which explicitly engaged with the relationship between television and everyday life.[11]

To a great extent theorizations of television's relationship to the everyday constitute the most significant examination of non-textual aspects of television aesthetics in the field. It is important to remember that it was primarily feminist television scholarship that first examined the relationship between the formal qualities of the medium and the ways in which these intersected with, shaped, or responded to the lived gendered experience. In particular Tania Modleski's work represents a crucial and emblematic stage in bringing to our attention the relationship between the forms of attention shaped by (domestic) routine and interruption and their relationship to the textual and narrative aesthetic of television genre (soaps).[12]

Caughie's work is clearly indebted to these formulations but is more concerned with the medium's relationship to other media than to gender. In contrast to cinema he argues that "'good' television asks for our perceptual intelligence rather than our anxious love [associated with cinephilia] and that, in both its location in everyday space and its formal rhetoric, it may offer an exteriority to be appraised rather than an interiority in which to lose ourselves."[13] This sense of the medium and viewers' distance from immersion and intense emotional involvement is redolent of Kantian aesthetics. It means that we cannot lose ourselves in television since we are anchored or tethered to the everyday, either as formal rhetoric or location. But insofar as we wish to utilize its abilities of selection and control, digital television demands our attention:

it is we, rather than the network scheduler or broadcast executive, who have to select, program, download, rip, or otherwise instruct our digital media. This raises a slightly different (Kantian) issue: the question of will.[14] Digital television foregrounds more strongly than other kinds of television the issue of human agency and will since interactivity and exhortations to "join in" are two of its prominent features. When television's mode of address gravitates toward the "for me" rather than "for the nation" or communal, when it is part of a personalized menu attuned to my narcissistic interests, then perhaps the tethers of the everyday are less secure. If the issue really is one of attention, the fact that digital television permits us to select, to choose, and to order our viewing experience implies that our will is being called upon—that we have to, through selection and choice, intend to watch what we are watching in a way that aligns us differently from either the relaxed detachment or dispersed glancing traditionally associated with accounts of television viewing. The effort of will, the calling forward of our attention and concentration, is of course not guaranteed just because it is possible to select and control television. Indeed, we may actively choose something precisely as a suitable background combination of sound and image. Choosing to concentrate depends at least partly on our willingness to invest time in viewing something we hope will reward that effort and, perhaps in the hope that we will be lost in the text, make us forget that it is effort at all. As with Rosen's description of the attention coerced by the nature of live performance, we could argue that if its content is easier to own and control, our attention is less secure in relation to digital television. Knowing that we can simply pause, rewind and repeat, or download another time might easily promote a casual, inattentive kind of viewing, one that samples content knowing that our attention can be activated more fully, if needed, another time.

What is made uncertain by digital television is not only the forms of attention we might bring to the medium but also its relationship to the organization of time. On my flight, for example, the timetable for descent was beyond my control, but the fact that I missed the end of the film was really my own fault: I simply neglected to estimate my remaining time in the air against the running time of the movie I selected, and my (in)attention to time seemed, until the interruption, intensely insulated from other demands. Interruption alerts us to the fact that we are still connected to the continuing flow, or present tense, of the outside world.

One attempt to theorize the aesthetics of the medium in relation to time is Stanley Cavell's "The Fact of Television."[15] Cavell tries to clarify what he calls "television's way of revealing its medium," which is crucial to understanding the "aesthetic interest of television." He acknowledges that the increasing distribution of video and cable "will make problematic whether television will continue to exist primarily as a medium of broadcasting" and claims that he is interested in "making conceptual room for understanding the aesthetic possibilities of such developments." That conceptual room leads him to "characterize the material basis of television as *a current of simultaneous event reception.*" This current has a feature whereby the nature of the medium *forces* its formats to participate in this continuous current, and part of what is internalized both in television's continuities and interruptions is what Cavell describes as "signs of life." For Cavell, it is television's monitoring of these signs that is central to its aesthetic, and the successful formats of television "are to be understood as revelations (acknowledgements) of the conditions of monitoring."[16]

This points to the feature of the current (suggesting both the contemporary and indicating the continuous) in my articulation of this aesthetic medium's physical basis. It is internal to television formats to be made so as to participate in this continuity, which means they are formed to admit discontinuities both within themselves and between one another and between these and commercials, station breaks, news breaks, emergency signal tests, color charts, program announcements, and so on, which means they are formed to allow these breaks, hence these recurrences, to be legible.[17]

The idea of a monitor seems to capture a very contemporary way in which television can be watched on a variety of screens beyond the traditional single-purpose television set—devices such as computer laptops, media players, and phones that connect to various currents of information and material. But Cavell's idiosyncratic account is also suggestive in relation to Caughie's view of interruptability: to what extent is "monitoring for signs of life" so distant from Caughie's claim that television internalizes and responds to the rhythms of the everyday? Both Caughie and Cavell understand television's nature as a medium as one that cleaves

to an essential quality marked through its relationship to the present—
the acknowledgement of the everyday through the internalization of the
possibility of interruption for Caughie, and the monitoring of signs of
life for Cavell.[18] Both are grounded in a sense of the television's proximity to the present and the social, although Cavell characterizes the
insistent banality of the everyday more pessimistically. However, as I've
suggested, digital television allows us to experience programming away
from this everyday—to own it, review it, and watch in our own time—
and it is to this status of television as a commodity, extrapolated from
the everyday, that I want to turn my attention now.

DIGITAL TELEVISION: INTERRUPTION AS POLLUTION?

The intimate way that television calibrates itself in relation to a range
of time—local, national, global, individual—perhaps accounts for
its "stickiness" as a medium, in the sense that the social and cultural
present tense strongly adheres to its output. As John Ellis argues, "Television is immediate and contemporaneous, belonging to the specific day
of its broadcast. It is never general, always specific."[19] This may explain
the fact that when we look at old television, it doesn't just look different;
it looks different in different ways. And while everything by necessity is
a product of its time, television's adhesion to the everyday and its render-
ing as a current of transmission attach it to the present in an intense and
variously distinctive way throughout its history. Television always has a
"now"—its moment of first transmission—that present-tenseness that
is also bound to a national broadcast schedule. In the past, that might
have been a strongly defining aspect of the experience of a given show
or broadcast. However, it would be a mistake to insist on the primacy
of this "first-time" principle in our assessment of television. Television,
once outside of its first-time, live-broadcast-being, does not become dead
and inert in syndication or DVD box sets. It is important to avoid erect-
ing an opposition between "good" television that is live, addressed to the
national and all about augmenting social cohesion, and a "bad" globalized marketplace for "dead" television as commodities: the digital download and DVD box set. The cultural products we wish to interpret and
appreciate live on and evolve (like ruins) in relation to the demands of
interpretation, critical pressure, and forms of appreciation to which we
submit them. Because digital television makes more obvious and visible
television's commodity forms this in no way should make us bemoan

their industrial provenance; similarly our understanding of the industrial origins of particular television shows and their embeddedness in webs of commercial exchange need not determine our eventual appreciation and use of the products themselves. Understanding that *Now, Voyager* was produced within the classical Hollywood system gives us little insight into its achievements as a work of art; of course the production and marketing of HBO series such as *The Sopranos* and *Deadwood* is determined in part by the needs and appetites of capitalist rhetoric and expansion. But acknowledging or exploring such facts hardly exhausts our interest in the shows.

It is true, however, that digital television threatens the universal experience of television's social function. Digital television's promises of control imply disconnection and separateness from the usual nationally socialized presence of television.[20] Television maintains its interruptability and currents of reception, but we do not have to participate in them in order to watch it. Are we still watching television when we watch an entire season of *The Wire* on DVD in a row? Is this no longer "television as television"? Mark Lawson, *The Guardian*'s television critic, thinks it is not: "Television should be considered, for better or worse, as television. . . . I am suspicious of those who avoid these landmark series on TV, waiting until the complete season is released as a box of DVDs, then consuming them through a weekend. While this approach can be allowed with *24* (adding a time game of our own to the ones the series plays), it must generally be wrong. The point about television programmes is that—unlike theatre or cinema—they live within a flow of other images: sports, commercials, wars. Television should be watched—and written about—as television."[21]

I take this as a serious objection, and one to which both Caughie's and Cavell's accounts of the medium seems to lend support. That said, perhaps the insistence on this kind of television is a product of the relative masking of television's commodity form until recently, a form that is made most prominent by the promises and promotion of digital technology not just for increased access to content but increased control and ownership over it. Milly Buonanno designates the way in which personal video recorders detach content from the time constraints of television flow as "disembedding" and argues that this creates the conditions "of an elective encounter, potentially unique at the moment it happens, between a programme 'taken out' of its proper context and a viewer who is 'isolated' in his or her own viewing."[22] As Buonanno points out, while this might diminish television's potential for "social integration," it is, in itself, hardly different from the consumption of other cultural products such as books or newspapers. More to the point, this has been an aspect of the medium, if not an always visible one, since television was able to be recorded.

Almost from the beginning television in its commodity form has been designed, packaged, delivered, and sold as individual units. Until quite recently the only people who had access to individual television programs—that is, before they became recordable at home and buy-able in shops—were the program makers, buyers, and reviewers—in other words, people who were closely associated with the industry. Programs were historically bought and sold at events hosted by networks and broadcasters exhibiting pilots and other examples of their wares to one another. It is notable that during such programming fairs the exhibitors did not think it necessary to include advertisements or other kinds of interruption in order to authenticate the television they were exhibiting as "television." For example, the publicity pack for program buyers attending the BBC Enterprises Showcase held in Brighton in 1978 describes the following facilities: "An increased total of eight large viewing rooms have been equipped with top quality sound insulation and air conditioning to screen about 150 of the best and most recent BBCTV programmes. In addition there will be a large video cassette library of programmes for screening 'as requested' in seven purpose built viewing rooms, also with first rate acoustics and air conditioning."[23]

Access to an on-demand library and quality screening facilities where *Ripping Yarns* and *Horizon* could be watched in comfort would rightly be considered a luxury in the late 1970s. Here the assumption is that what is of interest to program buyers are the programs themselves, and every expense is made so that they can watch these shows in comfort in order to evaluate them. This process is part of the buying and selling of television as a commodity.[24] One of the problems in thinking, even at this very tentative and general level about television as a commodity (which, of course, industrial analyses have been doing so unremarkably and comfortably for decades), is that cultural criticism has frequently understood commodification as a problematic aspect of modernity. But to what extent is our relationship to commodities best expressed as necessarily one of distance or detachment, as thinkers such as Walter Benjamin and George Simmel claim? Cavell argues that Walter Benjamin "tracks the impoverishment of (Western, late capitalist) experience, and relates it to a distance from objects that have become commodified, hence mystified in their measurement not for use but for the signs of exchange."[25] But this kind of distance from television as a commodity seems at odds with our intimacy with many kinds of television, even those in the most obvious of commodity forms, the DVD. James Walters argues that "television purchased on DVD is divergent to these modes of viewing [those facilitated by digital video recording] as it constitutes a specialized item which is obtained away from the flow of broadcast television entirely: an artifact in its own right."[26] Acknowledging the history of the television as a commodity form may allow us to begin to think through the distance between the two and throw into question the extent to which DVD television is "away . . . entirely" to quite the extent Walters claims. It would also mean that histories of digital television might come to avoid the idea that it is primarily a history of the commercialization of television. It may not even be the case that television is more commercialized, but merely that the visibility of its commercial dimension is now more prominent. This in no way negates the potential of television in its social and communal aspirations, but it may make it rather more obvious that television has been—and now is, emphatically—an industrial system of commodity production and consumption. For those who champion public service broadcasting principles this dualism has long been evident, with state-funded public service broadcasters forced to pretend that programs were not what they had to be: objects of value for industrial exchange. In the United States television has always been more readily accepted as a commodity because its sponsorship and advertising aspects were so clearly integrated into the textual and scheduling fabric of the medium, a fact made gleefully prominent in the title of Les Brown's groundbreaking industrial ethnography, *Television: The Business behind the Box*.[27] But there is more, I suspect, to the ontology of television as a commodity than the sheer fact of its industrial underpinnings, however they may have been masked or occluded—often quite appropriately—by other things that grasp our attention.

The diminishment of the prominence of interruption and the possibility of disconnection from the live current of the everyday suggest that television's specificity as a medium is no longer sustainable. One way to alleviate the friction between the desire for medium specificity and the pressure of concrete usage that undermines it is to abandon the rigidity that specificity tends to imply. Milly Buonanno does just this by developing a wonderfully sensible claim that television is an "open medium" capable of accommodating a wide range of viewer orientation: "It is precisely because television allows us to switch between looking and listening, between involvement and detachment, and because it offers us both demanding and relaxing forms of cultural entertainment and social participation, that it can claim to possess the true and authentically distinctive qualities of an open medium. It is flexible; and it is resistant both to theoretical imposition and to the empirical experience of fixed, essential and unchanging characteristics."[28]

Buonanno does have a persuasive point that seems particularly relevant to television in its digital manifestations, but the problem with an "open medium" is that one begins to wonder whether it is so open as to qualify as a medium at all. Philip Auslander has argued that "Television has transcended its identity as a particular medium and is suffused through the culture as 'the televisual,'"[29] while Noël Carroll claims that we should forget medium-specific accounts of moving images altogether: "What is and what will be the principle that makes our enterprise coherent will not be that it concerns a distinctive medium, but that the various media under examination are all examples of the moving image. . . . Forget the medium; watch the movement—the movement of history and the movement of the image."[30]

Carroll's dislike of theorizations of media that fetishize their distinction from others is certainly appealing as a way to avoid the kind of evaluation of films, television shows, and other "moving image" media that relies on criteria that are exclusively derived from how the text reveals aspects of the medium in which it was produced. There is a lot more to *The Sopranos* than the fact it is a television program, and whatever the show reveals about the significance or nature of its medium is unlikely to be exhaustive of its aesthetic or artistic achievements. Nonetheless, what seems wrong about Auslander's and Carroll's confident dismissals of medium specificity is precisely that there is something distinctive about television (and film) that generalizing them loses. Buonnano's claims about openness and flexibility of television manages to hold onto a sense of television as something at least minimally different, which prevents it from disappearing altogether as an object of study. It is hard to "forget the medium" of television precisely because its various instantiations can insist on our taking its value and achievements as a medium into account. What we need to decide in "our examinations" is the relative importance and significance of this prominence; it is the generativity of our theorization of the medium, the way that it illuminates rather than fixes or specifies, that counts.[31]

It is fair to say that television has a certain peculiarity in relation to its commodity form, although it is not unique. On the one hand, there is the television that is published or broadcast live—now, in the present—that we can view for the first time as part of a wider audience. On the other, there is the television that is recorded, retrievable, and re-viewable either as repeats, home recordings, DVD, or other media purchases. Textually they may well be identical things, and some forms—most obviously news, sporting, and current affairs forms—may be better experienced as present-tense live. Television's instant textualization of the present can be subsequently reviewed and interpreted and appreciated in a range of ways. It is certainly the case that where we believe we have a once-only chance of encountering a film or television program, our attention may be more heightened. As commodities, say as DVDs, we possess television shows, we own them, and our ownership and therefore our access is continuous. As live broadcast our control is not so secure, but is it any more "authentic," "real," or "connected" than its textually identical recorded version?

One thing that digital television and media convergence makes increasingly clear is the fact that television as a medium was always an ever-shifting, and nationally specific, as well as internationally responsive, blend of cultural expression and information, that it innovated aesthetically and stylistically but also adapted narrative, visual, and presentational rhetorics from a variety of other media and art practices. "Convergence" implies movement toward the same point, but the history of television and the current digital environment suggests instead the dispersal of television aesthetics, intermingling with other media and screen aesthetics, in a promiscuous, migratory, fast-breeding fashion. It is precisely this dispersal that makes the identification and examination of particular and (perhaps only briefly) "distinctive" aspects of a medium valuable since it enables us to grasp how they function under different demands and pressures as they are adopted and adapted by other media.

The qualities of interruption, the current of the present, and the sense of monitoring "signs of life" are aspects of television but not confined to that medium any more than narrative or performance is. Other digital media have their own forms of interruption, delay, and distraction, as well as their claims to be connected in various ways to the present. But like digital television and *unlike* television, interruption tends to originate in relation to the volition, circumstances, and currents of attention of user/player/viewer rather than textually. There is that stronger sense that we interrupt our involvement or that our subjectivity comes to feel wanting even where it is engaged with the textual and seeking further stimulation ("Anyone want to chat. . . . I'm bored"). Nonetheless, there are striking similarities. For example, some accounts of blogging as a medium draw on aesthetics that are akin to early television's promotion of intimacy and immediacy as central experiential values. Andrew Sullivan, for example, has written persuasively of blogging as a medium that combines the immediate responsiveness of live conversation, the intimacy of friendship, and the utility of a record in a context that amplifies them on a massive scale of connection and retrieval: "On my blog, my readers and I experienced 9/11 together, in real time. I can look back and see not just how I responded to the event, but how I responded to it at 3.47 that afternoon. And at 9.46 that night. There is a vividness to this immediacy that cannot be rivaled by print."[32]

Like many concerned with delineating the distinctiveness and force of the medium that they champion, Sullivan describes the distinctive way in which blogging connects people more authentically, strongly, and viscerally than any other media: "This is writing with emotion not just under but always breaking through the surface. It renders reader and writer . . . linked in a visceral personal way."[33] This promotion of emotional proximity is part of a wider discursive framework that promotes digital technologies in terms of "unmediated connection." In a milder form, such discourses of liberation from the constraints of earlier forms of communication and mediation might simply point to the absence of industrial paraphernalia, the rules and discourses of professional media life that have, in their baroque hyperadministration, vitiated the freshness of interpersonal encounter. For example, Clive James's Webcast interviews with celebrity writers, published in partnership with the

Times Online (London), were developed from his own amateur efforts conducted in the library of his home and published on his Web page. James claims that since these interviews take place outside the paraphernalia and routines of industrial production, his Webcast interviewees tend to be more at ease, relaxed, and "authentic."[34]

In some ways, then, such claims for new digital technologies resemble those made for television itself in its earliest years—claims that promised intimate, close proximity to authentic personalities and real events as they happened. But instead of a window onto a public world the connection takes place in more individuated and privatized communities. Online multiplayer videogames seem at first glance to demand more of our time and attention and concentration. But as the epigraph at the beginning of this chapter signals, they also contain space for the expression of torpor and boredom. Being connected to other players in a videogame certainly carries with it the sense of live performance, one that compares favorably with Rosen's account of a live concert. Yet even when we are connected to such games, there are ranges to our participation and involvement that depend on a complex interaction among our time, that of the game, and that of other players. To talk about being connected online covers a range of access to a diverse set of things with mixed levels of responsiveness.

Let's look at one case: *World of Warcraft*—an online multiplayer fantasy game—is always "live" and continuous in the sense that whenever one logs into the game, the world is always there, fastened to the real time of the server that hosts it so that, for example, the changes between night and day in the fantasy world happen at the same time as in the real one.[35] Although this world is immediate and continuous and one can chat/play/quest/fight with other players, this does not mean it avoids either interruption or other forms of pollution. The interface displays a text-based chat screen where players can "talk" in written form (players can also talk in speech if they wish), but their talk is completely unrestricted and may range far away from the concerns of the game itself. Unlike broadcast television with its visible, frequent desire to recruit attention, the game world of *World of Warcraft* can become extremely dull, depending on a player's level of participation. The usual patterns of boredom, unhappiness, and torpor can come to the fore in the player's experience in ways that would be masked by the industrial mediation of television. Instead of pollution and interruption—which are negli-

FIGURE 1 "Chat channels" in *World of Warcraft* exemplify the way in which players' will, intentionality, and commitment are demanded in the bargain that might secure enjoyment. (Screen capture from *World of Warcraft*; European server accessed October 30, 2008.)

gible[36]—the player's own interruptions, moments of boredom or distraction, are much more prominent (see figure 1). It is *the player's* will, intentionality, and commitment that are demanded in the bargain that might secure enjoyment. Typically players will mention that they will be "AFK" (away from keyboard) for a while in order to complete the everyday tasks that television studies in its audience study mode would find familiar (answer the door, make tea, go shopping, etc.). The world and the game (and the player's character in the world) continue without the presence of the player. The commodity form here is both obvious and obscure—on the one hand, the purchase of the game and the monthly subscription fees that permit continued participation in the world seem similar to, say, a viewer's continued subscription to television services. But participation in the game world is also represented quite concretely in the development and augmentation of the fictional "characters" that one "inhabits" ("operates" is perhaps a more accurate word) while in that world. In fact it is these characters that are often traded on online auction sites since they represent a considerable investment of time, which is, in turn, rewarded within the game by its amelioration of time-consuming activities (particularly movement speed) at higher character levels. Like television, the success of *World of Warcraft* must lie in part on its highly socialized nature, but our understanding of it as a commodity needs to go beyond its industrial organization and provenance and more toward its creation of a means to reproduce private labor and social exchange as a means for producing the game's fantasy universe.

Other online games that seem to require continuous active involvement can also allow relaxed spectatorship or non-attendance. *Call of Duty 4* is an online shooting game that renders modern warfare environments in photorealistic detail; and yet it is still possible to nip out for a cup of tea or sit back and watch the battle before a player decides to get involved in the next round. The discourses of relaxed detachment and rapt immersion and engagement cannot account for the second-by-second changes in subjectivity, attention, and engagement that such games reward, solicit, and permit. As in the case of digital television, such games seem to highlight the diversity of engagement that is in fact common to our encounters with the full range of cultural commodities.[37] What is distinct about games is that their forms of interruption are highly patterned, controlled, and not at all commercial: loading screens interrupt play as the teams migrate from one map to another; there is the delay in waiting for other players to join a battle or simply waiting for a server to become active enough to join (a matter of watching numbers aggregate on a screen; as figure 2 suggests, this is not visually stimulating at first glance but may indeed be so if one wishes to play urgently). The ranges of intimacy and proximity that a medium makes available may well not be immediately apparent from our initial textual encounter with it, which is why concentrated repeated encounters with it are necessary for reliable appreciation. Nevertheless, these games—anchored in time and space—pose a very difficult problem for issues of evaluation and interpretation. They are live and real at the moment of play, but how can we grasp their aesthetic beyond this sense of immediate involvement? Again, these newer forms of digital media pose problems that are similar to the ones I have identified in relation to television. A feature they share with television in its more prominent commodity form (apart from matters of screen aesthetics or the design of soundscapes and mise-en-scène) is that their spaces can be repeatedly engaged by players, even where the particular collection of players varies from game to game. This spatial familiarity and repetition, while it can lead to the boredom and frustration hinted at above, also allows a thicker sense of evaluation since familiarity breeds informed expertise even where it might stimulate contempt. As with television we have the

FIGURE 2 Video games produce distinctive forms of interruption, which are generally highly patterned, controlled, and not at all commercial—often involving simply waiting for screens to load or other players to join a server.

dualism of the live, once-only encounter and the lasting, repeatable experience of spatiality that one can assess and evaluate at leisure.

Web pages may change by the second or remain inert for years; online services promise instant news, chat, comment, and response, but there is rarely a continuous "current" of information in the same way as a television- or radio-transmitted schedule. Online newspapers produce pod- and vodcasts, as well as streaming items that sound and look like radio and television programs. As stylistic and visual rhetorics bleed among online, television, movie, and other screen media (as well as the intermingling of narrative, genre, and character we find across all cultural expression and production), we find both interruption and the "monitoring of signs of life" that Caughie and Cavell identify as distinctive about television.[38] Loading bars—the horizontal measures that fill or glow according to the extent of download or installation completed—have taken shape as iconic signs of activity, connection, and vitality.[39] Windows Vista incorporates glowing bars in some of its software, even where the computer is not online; the scrolling lines of information and text at the bottom of the screen on the Fox News network emulate—in a functionally pointless but stylistically resonant gesture—a computer's loading bar as if to stress its connections to the current of life exemplified not by television but by the Net. Other online video players deploy circular, pulsing animations that indicate activity (the transmission or loading of material) that effectively mask the extent or rate of completion but remain emblematic of a living, moving connection between user and source. It is not that television becomes devalued once we recognize its stronger visibility as a commodity, but that it has the potential to inflect how we consider other more obvious commodities.

There are also things that remain frustratingly beyond our control in the digital world. For those whose primary access to that world is the computer rather than the television, such distractions, delays, and interruptions can accumulate or become nested in a range of ways that impact on our attention and concentration. The experiencing of modernity as a distancing force is nothing new.[40] Television's full membership in the world of commodities is made palpable and unavoidable through its transformation into digital television; this opens new ways of thinking about its history and its present without needing to abandon the theoretical insights of the past. Not every medium needs to remain distinct and unique in order to produce works we find valuable. There are certainly costs to the loss of television's socialized and communal address, but there are also benefits in acknowledging that our experience of the medium is (and was) not so distant or distinct from our consumption and appreciation of other commodities. We should avoid seeing television outside its live present-tense-ness as a counterfeit version of the real, socialized, and nationalized medium. Indeed it is television's very existence as a commodity that allows us to appreciate its achievements at all.[41] What this means for our estimation of its value is a question that demands our attention.

NOTES

I would like to thank Stephen Crofts for his comments and advice.

Epigraphs. Theodor W. Adorno, "How to Look at Television," *Quarterly of Film, Radio and Television* 8, no. 3 (spring 1954): 214; M. H. Abrams, *The Mirror and the Lamp: Romantic Theory and the Critical Tradition* (Oxford: Oxford University Press, 1953), n.p.; The General Chat Channel (a European server), accessed June 11, 2008. A chat channel allows online players in the world of a game to communicate in text boxes that appear on the game's interface as they are playing or, in this case, waiting for something to do.

1. See Raymond Williams, *Television: Technology and Cultural Form* (London: Routledge, 1992 [1975]); John Caughie, *Television Drama: Realism, Modernism, and British Culture* (Oxford: Oxford University Press, 2000).

2. See John Thornton Caldwell, *Televisuality: Style, Crisis, and Authority in American Television* (New Brunswick, N.J.: Rutgers University Press, 1995).

3. Caughie, *Television Drama*, 136.

4. Ibid., 139.

5. John Caughie, *Edge of Darkness* (London: BFI, 2007), 51.

6. Ibid., 51–52.

7. Caughie, *Television Drama*, 139.

8. There are a number of obvious problems with this, such as the fact that television is used to watch a vast number of films and the fact that "relaxed detachment," like interruptability, is so general a term it can be used to describe encounters with or responses to a vast range of cultural objects.

9. Charles Rosen, "Who's Afraid of the Avant Garde?" *New York Review of Books* 45, no. 8 (May 14, 1998).

10. A scholar who is a senior consultant in the field of television ratings recently told me of a situation that happened when he was taking part in a television diary survey. He discovered himself listening to the television in the kitchen area, where he could hear it but not see it. He phoned the ratings company to ask what he should put in the diary—"Am I watching television or not?"—and was told to describe the activity as "whatever it means to you."

11. Indicative landmark scholarship in this area would be Charlotte Brunsdon and David Morley, *Everyday Television: "Nationwide"* (London: BFI, 1978); Roger Silverstone, *Television and Everyday Life* (London: Routledge, 2006 [1994]); David Gauntlett and Annette Hill, *TV Living: Television Culture and Everyday Life* (London: Routledge with British Film Institute, 1999); and Shaun Moores, *Media and Everyday Life in Modern Society* (Edinburgh: Edinburgh University Press, 2000).

12. Tania Modleski, "The Search for Tomorrow in Today's Soap Opera," *Film Quarterly* 33, no. 1 (1979): 12–21. For a detailed account of the development of Modleski's argument, see Charlotte Brunsdon, *The Feminist, the Housewife and the Soap Opera* (Oxford: Oxford University Press, 2000), 60–65.

13. John Caughie, "Telephilia and Distraction: Terms of Engagement," *Journal of British Cinema and Television* 3, no. 1 (2006): 15.

14. I am grateful to Tony Bennett for his presentation, "On Not Watching Television: Character, the Will and Social Class" (Centre for Critical and Cultural Studies, University of Queensland, September 29, 2008), for alerting me to this aspect of viewing.

15. Stanley Cavell, "The Fact of Television," in Cavell, *Themes out of School: Effects and Causes* (Chicago: University of Chicago Press, 1984).

16. Ibid., 241–53; emphasis in original.

17. Ibid.

18. It is significant that both scholars discuss the medium in relation to their conceptions of film. Cavell contrasts film and television's different articulations of genre and seriality, while Caughie claims that film's narrative and forms of address are much more entangling to subjectivity than television.

19. John Ellis, "Television and History," *History Workshop Journal* 56, no. 1 (2003): 281.

20. See, for example, Helen Wood and Lisa Taylor, "Feeling Sentimental about Television Audiences," *Cinema Journal* 47, no. 3 (2008): 145.

21. Mark Lawson, "Foreword: Reading *Six Feet Under*," in *Reading* Six Feet Under: TV to Die For, ed. Kim Akass and Janet McCabe, xxi–xxii (London: I. B. Tauris, 2005).

22. Milly Buonanno, *The Age of Television: Experiences and Theories*, trans. Jennifer Radice (Bristol: Intellect, 2008), 69.

23. BBC Written Archives T66/110/1 BBC Enterprises TV Press Office File.

24. Derek Kompare, "Publishing Flow: DVD Box Sets and the Reconception of Television," *Television and New Media* 7, no. 4 (2006): 335–60, and Milly Buonanno both explore the nature of the emergence of television as a form of library or archive.

25. Stanley Cavell, *Philosophy the Day after Tomorrow* (Cambridge, Mass.: Belknap Press of Harvard University Press, 2005), 245.

26. James Walters, "Repeat Viewings: Television Analysis in the DVD Age," in *Film and Television after DVD*, ed. James Bennett and Tom Brown (London: Routledge, 2008), 70.

27. Les Brown, *Television: The Business behind the Box* (New York: Harcourt Brace Jovanovich, 1971).

28. Buonanno, *The Age of Television*, 41.

29. Philip Auslander, *Liveness: Performance in a Mediatized Culture* (London: Routledge, 1999), 2.

30. Noël Carroll, *Engaging the Moving Image* (New Haven, Conn.: Yale University Press, 2003), 9.

31. As Janet Harbord argues in relation to Siegfried Kracauer's development of the concept of contingency for the medium of film, "The failure of *Theory of Film* to properly designate the specificity of the medium . . . is arguably more generative in its production of concepts than a decisive taxonomy could ever be" ("Contingency's Work: Kracauer's *Theory of Film* and the Trope of the Accidental," *New Formations* 61 [2007]: 99).

32. Andrew Sullivan, "Why I Blog," *Atlantic Online*, November 2008; http://www .theatlantic.com/doc/print/200811/andrew-sullivan-why-i-blog.

33. Ibid.

34. Clive James, "Clive James' Interviewing Secrets," *Times* (London), October 3, 2008.

35. Always, that is, except when the world is stopped for a few hours for "weekly maintenance."

36. Occasionally companies will spam the chat screen, selling various things; pollution is as much likely to be the result of players adding elements to their game interface and cluttering it as it is a function of the game itself.

37. A fact that Donald Sassoon's *The Culture of the Europeans: From 1800 to the Present* (Hammersmith, U.K.: Harper Collins, 2006) demonstrates has been the case for the past two centuries.

38. Karen Lury's essay in this volume points to the way some television shows continue to include (indeed intensify) the kinds of narrative redundancy that one might expect of a medium that has internalized the shifting attention of distracted viewing; conversely, shows such as *Fringe* acknowledge and attempt to mimic the purifying abilities of personal video recorders and DVD television experience by reducing narrative breaks in what the Fox network has called "remote-free TV."

39. See Daniel Chamberlain, "Watching Time on Television," *Flow TV* 6, no. 4 (July 2007); http://flowtv.org/?p=615.

40. The insistence on a medium's ability to distance its viewers is important to a number of scholars (Caughie, as noted above), but see also Patrice Petro, *Aftershocks of the New: Feminism and Film History* (New Brunswick, N.J.: Rutgers University Press, 2002); George Simmel, *The Philosophy of Money* (London: Routledge, 2004).

41. Brunsdon identifies the expense of new forms of television as something not as yet sufficiently acknowledged: "There is expensive television that is 'not television,' 'cable, satellite, or DVD'; and . . . much cheaper television understood within more functionalist paradigms in terms of how it perpetuates the social order" ("Is Television Studies History?" Cinema Journal 47, no. 3 [2008]: 131).

PART 4

USER-GENERATED CONTENT

Producing Digital Audiences

JOHN T. CALDWELL

WORKER BLOWBACK

*User-Generated, Worker-Generated
and Producer-Generated Content within
Collapsing Production Workflows*

The television industry talks out of both sides of its mouth. Especially about user-generated content (UGC), which it habitually conflates with piracy. The production trade *Television Week* shamelessly offered the following antithetical statements in the same issue. One article sounded the alarm: "Sending a cease-and-desist order (to an illegal downloader) is like sending a letter to a Colombian drug lord," and, "Who will step up to disband TV's pirates?"[1] At the same time, an accompanying column solicited the very same industry readers to the trade's tvweek.com Web site by boasting, "*Television Week* is trawling video web-sites to find the hottest clips spreading on the Internet,"[2] even as it bragged and marveled that "This [CNBC] clip is everywhere. It has appeared on YouTube, Metacafe, Break, and various blogs. . . . By August 8 the video had been viewed more than 973,002 times on YouTube."[3] Shocked that many of the network TV pilots previewed at the recent spring up-fronts had already spread uncontrollably across the Internet long before their fall broadcast premieres, the trade's obviously conflicted editorial posture failed to confirm a more likely scenario. As I argue in this chapter, this kind of unauthorized "piracy" is precisely the kind of activity that studios and networks now intentionally generate if buzz-needy new shows are to have any chance of being "found" and circulated by viewers in the vast multichannel, multiplatform clutter. Studio and network lawyers now obsessively guard proprietary screen content through threats and lawsuits, while their very own marketing departments down the hall bulk-load and hand out their proprietary screen content as promotional fodder and fan bait across the Internet. Official stance: control. Unofficial practice: a sanctioned but disavowed content-fragment free-for-all.[4]

As industry ostensibly loses control of its proprietary content in a world producers optimistically hype as providing viewers with access to any content, any time, any place, it has also had to adopt, hijack, mimic, ape, or internalize the very unruly behaviors of its audiences as a model not merely for consumers, but for its own workforce in production as well. Scholars tend to focus far more on the new volatilities of digital media consumption rather than on the no less volatile convulsions unfolding now in digital media production spaces. I would argue that these warring volatilities are in fact two complementary sides of the same coin. This chapter addresses some of the odd reversals and contradictions that now characterize the television industry as it tangles with and obsesses upon UGC in its attempt to discipline and monetize each rapidly appearing digital media platform. Among other things, such a study suggests that ostensible media piracy is actually a very lucrative form of commercial viral marketing; that UGC regularly transforms the unruly crowd into producer-generated users (PGU); and that the do-it-yourself (DIY) outsider ethos now serves not as alternative media but as a valuable form of mainstream workforce "bootstrapping" and outsourcing.

Why think about digital television through the lens of production labor's complex interactions with audiences? Prominent new media theories tend to follow a binary model of media and culture. These frameworks are alternately tech-centric (Negroponte), fan- and user-centric (Jenkins), interface- and software-centric (Manovich), or industry- and economy-centric (Schiller).[5] All provide convincing and influential accounts of digital media phenomena, yet they also tend to downplay or look beyond one essential category in the new media equation: production labor. Spending any time with contemporary television production workers quickly shows how inadequate the old categories are that cleanly separate producers and media workers from audiences and consumers. Various accounts examine how fans and digital media users appropriate the means of production and so function as producers. But fewer have discussed how production workers themselves are aware of their simultaneous roles as audience members and online users. In fact, in interviews and ethnographic research, practitioners regularly invoke their experiences (or those of family members) as audiences and fans in explaining how and why new television forms, genres, and technologies function as they do. And these audience functions and competencies constantly inform decisions and practices on production soundstages and post-production suites. Audiences and fans may increasingly act as producers, but producers are always audiences and fans as well. Shifting focus to digital workers makes some sense since they now function as an emblematic nexus point between industry, consumers, and technologies. As such, they facilitate, enable, implement, and broker emerging digital cultures.

In this chapter I would like to think through four related phenomena: first, the very recent ways that media corporations have worked to import, mimic, rationalize, and commercialize ostensibly unruly UGC; second, the ways that online pre- or proto-UGC practices in the early 2000s (that is, before YouTube/MySpace) disrupted top-down "producer/studio tracking" and long-standing public relations "control" schemes; third, the ways that new digital technologies have disrupted carefully maintained labor relations by collapsing workflow hierarchies on the production side; and finally, the ways that production workers have embraced the supposedly unruly practices of viral video and social networking to negotiate rapid changes in production technology, industry economics, and underemployment. Considering the digitization of television through these four perspectives makes it clear that a range of "unauthorized" activities, or what I would term online worker-generated content (WGC), plays as formative a role in how producers and executives negotiate digitization as does the UGC that garners the lion's share of the headlines.

AMATEURIZED/PROFESSIONALIZED/COMMERCIALIZED UGC: WORKFORCE CHANGES

UGC has not simply disrupted television's onscreen content. It has also profoundly impacted production labor. Among other things, UGC has pushed media companies to master crowdsourcing in attempts to harness new online users to collectively generate marketing or productions proper for film and video companies. Crowdsourcing updates and displaces the far darker term outsourcing, a practice that helped U.S. film and television companies to weather difficult economic conditions in the 1980s and 1990s by laying off "inside" employees and sending production work outside of the studios and networks where it could be produced much more cheaply. A benign and utopian term, crowdsourcing represents in some ways the ultimate form of outsourcing since the new crowds that collectively make media content today (1) regularly "work" for free; (2) have no employee entitlements or benefits; and (3) are disorganized and so incapable of invoking labor law protections.

Broadcasters and production studios were quick to latch onto and exploit UGC. The trades and show-biz reports marveled at the speed with which mega-conglomerate News Corporation took over MySpace and Google took over YouTube in 2006, even as all scratched their heads trying to figure out how these massive "amateur" sites would make their corporate masters money.[6] Harnessing the uncontrollable hive of vast online user bases proved difficult, and many cynics argued that these top-down partnerships were less about interacting with the people than about stealthy consumer surveillance and data mining. Yet a range of more public initiatives showed that some affirmation of online production would probably always accompany the corporate viral marketing opportunities that UGC sites afforded. The 24/7 cable news channels, like MSNBC, made coverage of the online blogosphere a regular part of their programming in 2006. Advertisers solicited the best in amateur online videos in contests that guaranteed to broadcast the winners during television's high holiday, the Super Bowl, in 2006 and 2007. Reality cable networks like the Discovery Channel actively solicited viewer-produced videos and parodies and featured them as mock Discovery Channel programming in 2007. Many network programming departments harvested and aggregated UGC videos to create prime-time series like ABC's *i-Caught* in 2007 (see figure 1).

A full list of ways that conventional networks have used UGC is extensive and beyond the scope of this chapter. I am less interested in a comprehensive description of such direct acquisitions of UGC by dominant media than in how UGC practices have transformed the corporate and labor practices of dominant media's production cultures. Hollywood and network television's traditional standby defense mechanism, used to reestablish cultural or programming superiority when faced with alternative modes of production, has always been to simply buy out whatever alternative or "resistant" programming emerges outside of their bound-

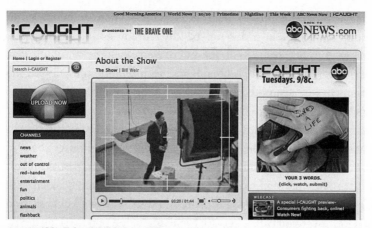

FIGURE 1 ABC's "i-Caught" Web page solicits and showcases UGC as the series' primary onscreen broadcast content in prime time in 2007–2008.

aries.[7] Yet merely and unimaginatively sticking YouTube videos into part of a programming day proved to be less lucrative with broadcasters or popular with audiences than the networks may have hoped. I would argue that a far more fundamental shift was unfolding in the ways that production companies and production workers themselves generated content in the shadow of pop culture's new fascination with UGC.

Many networks, including NBC and ABC, created online sites that solicited and featured YouTube-like uploaded videos from amateur fans of the networks. Yet these showcases represented little more than lip service on the part of the networks. In the fall of the 2006–2007 programming season, both NBC and ABC began to allow online users to download current prime-time programming immediately after series like *Heroes*, *30 Rock*, *Ugly Betty*, and *Desperate Housewives* aired. This created shockwaves in the production community since many of the labor sectors were owed "residuals" from ancillary distribution of shows on which they'd worked and were not being paid as the networks "gave their shows away" for "free." NBC and ABC eventually negotiated with the guilds on the issue of residuals, but their bigger accomplishment was to figure out ways to format prime-time shows in downloadable form with advertising inserted. If pages for uploading UGC did little to promote existing network brands, then chopping up and reformatting branded series to UGC scale proved somewhat more effective.

The unpretentious air and populism of "amateurism" was part of the original draw of UGC, but amateurism turned out to be a difficult beast to tame and monetize. Increasingly, the vast, horizontal, democratic cultural soup of Web-based video proved unwieldy, and media companies slowly began to professionalize the UGC enterprise. The net effect was to bring more control of UGC inside of the conglomerate. Yahoo, the number two Web search company, launched Yahoo Video to compete head on with YouTube by primarily featuring user-generated video in 2006. Yet by August 2007, Yahoo Video was ranked only the fourth most visited video site on the Internet by Nielsen NetRatings (behind YouTube, Google Video, and AOL Video). This less-than-impressive result led to the replacement of CEO Terry Semel with Yahoo co-founder Jerry Yang.[8] After the executive coup, Yahoo hyped its revamped approach to the press online as the creation of a "one-stop video portal." This newly visible and more user-friendly status would be achieved by no longer "silo-ing" videos into discrete, controlled categories. Yahoo thus eliminated preexisting categories that the corporation had originally imposed under the Semel regime. This was done not solely in order to allow users to more easily search for videos across borders but, more important, to allow "marketers . . . to buy access to a demographic across Yahoo and all its video content."[9] As this important example suggests, advertisers and market research—not online user-generated activity alone—drive dominant media's current push to access and open up the Web to free-wheeling video-centric usage.

The chief casualty in all of this is the amateur UGC that gave Yahoo Video at least some buzz in the first place. The company's new centralized approach may spur increased video viewing, but now only of videos made by higher-quality amateurs or "prosumers" or aspiring professional video makers. In place of the relative anarchy of amateur uploading, therefore, Yahoo now culls and discards the video dregs and semi-professionalizes UGC by putting online, as Yahoo's general manager for video states, "community elements (for UGC producers) like email and JumpCut," Yahoo's online editing software.[10] Advertisers are now wary of UGC's unruliness because, as Yahoo's director of video strategy Rebecca Paoletti asserts, UGC "content can be risqué and uneven in quality." Paoletti's more disciplined approach to sponsoring UGC is a contest inviting users to produce trailers for the summer movie blockbuster *Transformers* and a competition for user-generated Doritos commercials for the Super Bowl. "Advertisers are more comfortable sponsoring that type of content," explained Paoletti, underscoring the gradual but ostensibly necessary industrial "disciplining" of UGC.[11] Is your company unable to control the growing online chaos? Solution: provide semi-professional editing software and economic incentives to glean only the "quality" UGC (only new media that look like old media) since Madison Avenue knows well how to tolerate and monetize old media content.

If Yahoo now corrals and semi-professionalizes only "quality" UGC makers, Sony Pictures Entertainment movie and television studio goes further by explicitly professionalizing and industrializing UGC producers. Like Yahoo, News Corporation, and Google, Sony's knee-jerk corporate reaction to UGC in 2006 was mostly to buy a hot bit of UGC real estate named Grouper and to incorporate it into the conglomerate. A year later, however, Sony, like Yahoo, unceremoniously dumped its populist concept of an open video-sharing site and the amateurs that came with it. Putting the best spin possible on the final stage of the corporate sellout and the reinvention of Grouper as Crackle.com, Grouper founder and now Sony executive Josh Felser triumphantly announced to the industry, "We're out of the user-generated video business and in the emerging-talent business." Van Baker, research vice president at technology research company Gartner, justified Sony's housecleaning and what he termed its new "studio-centric" approach (providing funding, promotion, and syndication to outsiders) by saying, "There is so much video on the Internet now that it's *crying out* for a step up in quality. That's just media companies doing what they do best, which is finding and distributing good content."[12] Critics might instead call this benign pose a traditional hostile takeover of UGC camouflaged in the trade press by corporate doublespeak.

Sony now makes cash payments and disingenuous promises to those it woos—UGC makers and desperate outsiders—that a Sony partnership brings potential for Oscar consideration(!). These corporate gambits by Sony overshadow Yahoo's largely symbolic professionalizing incentives. Crackle.com's quarterly UGC competitions in three broad categories—animation, short form, and comedy—involve cash prizes, trips to Los Angeles, and meetings and pitch sessions with studio executives at Sony Pictures Animation, Sony Pictures Television, or Sony/Crackle's Improv Comedy Lab. Clearly, what started as the ad hoc, ground-up populist media making of UGC has been transformed into something Hollywood has mechanically mastered for a century: talent scouting and central casting. But Sony is far from alone in this transformation of UGC into

commercial demo reels, spec concept treatments, and studio talent pipe-
lines. Viacom solicited UGC short-form videos for its Test Pilots category
on the Atom Films Web site (which MTV acquired in 2006), and the
top submissions were then culled for airing on MTV's Comedy Central
cable series *Web Shows*. In its pursuit of the lucrative male 18–34 demographic, Lions Gate Entertainment studio also systematically scouts for
"edgy talent" to hire in the massive pool of amateur and gross-out videos
online. Following this move, the studio bought a share in online video
company Break.com in July 2007 to better compete with the UGC giant
YouTube.

The UGC syndication overhauls described above—where Sony, MTV,
and Lions Gate have mastered and mainstreamed outsider practices—
are based on long-standing studio hubris about media's minor leagues,
that "We know better than anyone else how to distribute." Such a stance
completely ignores the true lessons of YouTube: that nonlinear, networked sharing, through a vast "rhizomatic" network of online users
(a cybernetic metaphor) can generate popularity on par with any linear,
locked-down studio content pipeline (an odd, rigid, nineteenth-century
industrial metaphor). Yet the studio's new pipeline (distribution) metaphor for UGC increasingly rules in Los Angeles media companies. This
is because the Hollywood mode of production/distribution is deemed a
less risky, long-trusted, and known quantity, something far easier to in-
dustrially rationalize than the amorphous, unpredictable user-sharing
networks of YouTube. DreamWorks's reality series *On the Lot*, broadcast
on Fox in the summer of 2007, is a good example of how the UGC ethos
has been gleaned and wrested from the digital hinterlands in largely
symbolic rather than actual terms. Chosen from twelve thousand online submissions, eighteen young, untrained wannabes were flown to
Los Angeles to make films and fight out over who is the best filmmaker.
After many weeks of competition and elimination, on the culminating
night of the series, August 21, 2007, a single finalist was chosen as a winner in the competition and given a "one million dollar development deal
with DreamWorks." The final shot of the series showed the once UGC
amateur—now anointed "winner"—walking side by side with his Medi-
ci-like patron and mogul Steven Spielberg through the pearly gates and
into DreamWorks Studio.[13] As the camera craned, music swelled, and
end credits rolled up, the Darwinian lesson to America was clear—that
meritocracy and distinction drive industry's calculated method of natu-

ral selection. Only the best and luckiest, a statistical rarity, arise from the UGC dregs to begin a "real career" in film. What was lost in all of Fox's and DreamWorks's televisual celebratory showcase of bootstrap film-making populism was the fact that absolutely none of the production resources used for the scores of short films produced throughout the *On the Lot* summer were either amateur- or user-generated. In effect, like alien lottery winners, the show's earnest and awestruck aspirants were airlifted to Hollywood and given fully professional crews, onscreen talent, and production technologies to work on their amateur films. Television's how-to-make-it showcases like these, therefore, are DIY and UGC in pretense only. The newly discovered finalists here turned out to be largely replaceable cogs in a very well-oiled production machine—a machine that could make "quality" films regardless of the lucky monkeys the studio put at their typewriters to generate content.

The examples thus far paint a fairly dark, totalizing picture of the managerial powers of old media and producer-generated content (PGC) to discipline and channel normally unruly UGC into long-standing production, marketing, and syndication models. Yet the unsettling of workflow and production hierarchies, due to digitization, has also opened up room for more agency by professional workers. Pixel Corps, for example, self-identifies as a collective "guild for online creators around the world." Says the guild founder, "People . . . say, 'Can you produce the content?' We are just hired guns. We show up. We shoot. We are like a coalition of producers for hire."[14] The term guild evokes high-level craft associations (like the Directors Guild of America [DGA] and WGA) with medieval roots. Pixel Corps promotes commerce for its membership but constantly slides back and forth between its nonprofit charter and its for-profit productions. In doing so, the group voluntarily participates (as workers) in the same wave of user professionalization described above that studios and networks pursue from the corporate side. The online guild's publicity demands that its members—once only unpaid aspirants—now be addressed and respected as commercialized professionals. This organizing push by UGC makers to professionalize has been triggered in part because online creators have increasingly realized that many other media entities have made a financial killing off of their efforts. Stated one miffed blogger advocating for an official labor union for UGC-ers, "It would raise the professionalism. Maybe we could get more jobs, bona fide jobs."[15] The fact that online makers need to self-justify by arguing for distinctions between work-for-free and work-for-pay underscores the sorry state of labor relations and economic conditions in convergent media. The amateurish charms of grassroots DIY, therefore, have clearly begun to pale as UGC is commodified and commercialized by major media companies.

If aspiring online workers are instrumental participants in the desperation to professionalize UGC, as described above, then their corporate clients and allies are architects bent on commercializing UGC. Sony provides Crackle.com, for example, a "mid-seven-figure production budget, allowing it to produce exclusive Web-only content in the $2,000 to $28,000 per episode range. These amounts are based on anticipated payback and revenue sharing from multipurposing and syndicat[ing] content to third party IPTV, social-networking and viral Web distribution sites, including MySpace, Facebook and AOL as well as various Sony [handheld] devices."[16] While these payment schemes upgrade the financial resources of amateur UGC producers significantly and make the "no royalty" business plans of pre-dot-com-crash predecessors like Pop.com and DEN seem callous, such relatively low-budget levels horrify seasoned TV producers, who see in these minuscule, budget-collapsing expectations a threat to their onscreen livelihoods. In their own publicity, Sony and Crackle.com seem oblivious to the fundamental contradiction that their commercialization of UGC has raised. Their business plans boldly, if illogically, state that the studio "will largely draw on professional-quality amateur video submitted by outsiders and filtered through an experienced 15-person staff." Welcome to the brave new doublespeak world of professionalized amateurism.

COLLAPSED WORKFLOWS AND LABOR HIERARCHIES

> Tales From the Bottom of the Film Business. . . . Life Below the Line. . . . I'm a filmmaker and writer, but most of the time, for money, I listen to stuff. (And I write this anonymously because you can't afford to piss people off when you need to eat).
>
> http://lifebelowtheline.blogspot.com

UGC's commercialization, and the growing confusion between professionalization and amateurism just described, can be productively understood alongside interrelated institutional changes in production (see figure 2). Specifically, digitization has facilitated a collapse and con-

FIGURE 2 The "indie" do-it-yourself approach to bootstrapping labor was seen as a union killer by Hollywood camera operators, who discussed the topic on a Web site in the late 1990s (left). By 2007 the same camera organization (SOC) tries to promote itself and its ideals in the clutter of DIY-UGC with its own MySpace page (right).

fusion of production workflow and upended traditional labor hierarchies. Workflow refers to the route that screen content travels through a production organization and its technologies as it moves from the beginning (origination, imaging, recording) to the end (post-production, mastering, duplication, exhibition) of the production/distribution process. What the film/video trades now optimistically term hybrid workflows might more accurately be termed an unruly workflow free-for-all. This is because current workflows no longer follow self-evident linear stages that lead unproblematically to next stages according to decades-old convention. For example, the recent shift from 35mm duplicate negatives (DN) or film interpositives (IP) as a mastering format to the new digital intermediates (DI) format has broken down all kinds of heretofore sacrosanct job distinctions on the set and in post-production suites. In fact, the once linear sequence through which filmed material went before being printed and broadcast has fallen apart. Because of these recent shifts to digital, visualization and effects functions once reserved for post-production now dominate production, and skills once limited to production now percolate through post-production. Even as digital UGC has confused distinctions between the ostensible front end (professional producers) and back end (amateur users) of media creation and circulation, DI processes have confused the front end (cinematography, produc-

tion design, directing) and back end (digital and visual effects, coloriz-
ing, and directing) of both worker relations and the production workflow
sequence. These forms of collapse and confusion are not unrelated.

Five examples dramatize these workflow reversals. First, visual
effects supervisors (once relegated to post-production) now compete at
the earliest stages during pre-production against two older crafts that
traditionally controlled the "look" of a film/show for a director: the director of photography (DP) and the production designer (or art director). All
three crafts—the DP, production designer, and visual effects (VFX) super-
visor—now argue that they are entitled and responsible for the overall
look of a film/video production. Second, the shift to the DI (as the new
non-film mastering format) has caused the invention of wholly new jobs
like the data wrangler. This worker must now manage the footage metadata (technical information about how to recreate the desired image in
any format in the future) on the set during shooting and throughout the
entire process. In the old days—before 2002—cinematographers and
their assistants traditionally managed image metadata (basic color, exposure, processing, and printing information) throughout production.
Today, however, the camera departments are ceding these functions
since the images they film are stored on computer hard drives instead
of film magazines. Third, the function of lab timing and color grading
in post-production has shifted from one labor sector, with its own craft
conventions (film lab timers), to another, with different craft conventions (broadcast video colorists), cultivating the sense of disenfranchise-
ment in workers from the film-origination world. Fourth, increasing
cost economies, miniaturization, and technical capabilities have moved
some back-end post-production tools directly into the front end of the
production chain (see figure 3). For example, Final Cut Pro editing systems are now commonly used by directors and their assistants during
shoots for rough-cut and rough-color correction, while sophisticated
digital previsualization tools developed to create the illusion of tracking shots in post-production (like Previzion HD) are now being brought
out of computer-generated imagery (CGI) and post-production and onto
the set during filming to allow directors to "previsualize" their mechanical shoots (rather than just digital effects). Fifth, front-end production
tools and practices are increasingly dragged into the back end of post-
production. For example, many DPs now demand and struggle with producers to gain the right to grade DVD masters to maintain the intended

FIGURE 3 After digital UGC, even pros push the limits of digital downsizing. Here a one-person crew bolts its post-production laptop editing "suite" to its camera, completely collapsing normal distinctions in the production to post-production "workflow."

look of a film for its home video distribution window (traditionally an afterthought in the workflow). The old sense of easily identifiable, successive stages (production work's beginning, middle, and end) no longer holds. As a result, job descriptions are up for grabs, not just for the prosumers described above, but for many seasoned professionals as well.

Said one vindicated self-serving new digital technology proponent, Mark Patel, in light of these unruly reversals in workflow, "In the traditional filmmaking model, the post process used to be a slave to production—in the hybrid model, the physical production process becomes slave to the digital realm."[17] The slavery metaphor suggests the real-world stakes involved in the collapse of workflows. Workers from traditional set-based filming modes (DPS, ACS [assistant camera operators], video-assist operators, production designers, and timers) face increasing underemployment from the collapse, while new digital workers (data wranglers, colorists, visual effects supervisors, and CGI artists) encroach on the once stable and regulated production space of the set. Digital proponents like Patel explain and justify the process in utopian and benign terms, arguing that "much like children, technology eventually needs to find its own way in the world." Such platitudes mask the real implications of the shift: decades-old, union-regulated, technically standardized, mentor-managed workflow assignments are crumbling in favor of untested, non-union, nonstandardized, manufacturer-managed work-flow assignments.

Evangelists for collapsing digital workflows hype the aesthetic shift in seductive, simplistic, economic terms: "As with any production . . . the biggest cost will always be time and manpower. Where there are a lot of people working for a long time, the cost of technology is generally secondary. . . . Reducing the time to produce movies is [the] goal."[18] This advocate obscures, however, that digitization doesn't really save costs. It merely shifts most of the production budget away from human on-the-set workers into expensive digital technologies. The proponent here sharing his personal theory with other editors in the trade *Post* turns out, not illogically, to be the marketing director for a high-end proprietary CGI manufacturer selling the new digital pipeline.[19] Whether these remarks can be called earnest video craft talk or stealthy trade marketing, the lesson is clear: digital technologies confuse both workflows and job hierarchies and promise savings by eliminating low-level jobs in order to centralize production at costly, high-level CGI studios. In this way, therefore, this "earnest" trade talk is really just part of a highly partisan smoke-and-mirrors high-tech economy promoted during a time of in-dustry instability.

Workflow was once conventionalized and managed by a long-standing coalition of labor groups, guilds, technologists, and studios. Now the advent of wide-ranging nonstandardized digital cameras in production and digital work stations in post-production means that the "rules" of the new digital realm are being rewritten, not by unionized crafts workers but by individual corporations intent on selling their proprietary equipment (and thus the proprietary workflows that go with it). From 2004 to 2007 a supposed industry-wide coalition called High Def Expo made the following claims to anxious practitioners contemplating the shift to digital: "Liberate your creative process! Discover the true freedom of a non-linear image workflow! . . . The tapeless revolution has spread . . . from post houses to cinematographers. This . . . workshop illuminates the process of becoming completely tapeless, illustrates the entire workflow from image acquisition to data archive, and shows you how you can join the non-linear, tapeless revolution."[20] Closer inspection of this industry-wide, high-def boot camp shows that it was primarily sponsored not by any craft association (like the American Society of Cinematographers [ASC] or American Cinema Editors [ACE]) or by neutral standards organizations (like the Society of Motion Picture and Television Engineers [SMPTE]) but by something far less collective, consensual, or ecumenical: Panasonic and its lens provider, Fujinon. The problem is that Panasonic's new "P2" workflow is different from Sony's new workflow, which is different from Technicolor's new workflow, which is different from Panavision's or Hitachi's or Phillips's workflows.[21]

WGC AS INDUSTRIAL RESPONSE: UNAUTHORIZED WEB SITES AND LEAKY STORYWORLDS

> It makes me crazy when I hear some producer who's making $7 million say they have to take a movie out of the country because labor here is too expensive. I'm making the lowest (hourly wage) on the set, but it's electricians and construction guys who are doing the hardest work with the biggest risks.
>
> Crew member complaining online about the lies and cruelty of producers

The mainstream workflow and technology changes just described do indeed matter to questions about UGC because all of the factors considered thus far work to stress and displace the oversupply of film/video professionals into online activities and worlds that are already well traveled by lay users and fans. Sometimes this online worker activity aims to argue for, justify, and reestablish long-standing forms of industrial legitimacy. Sometimes it betrays severe intercraft contention via the snarking churning within what feels increasingly like the industry's sinking old-media ship. At other times, WGC functions merely as social networking or as a means to find new clients and commercial work.[22]

Now more than ever, because of new and unruly online activities by workers, the industry is enmeshed in a messy dance to control information and gossip that pass from a studio or network to the trade press. Almost every film/TV company takes the position that all company information or news is proprietary. Confidentiality and nondisclosure agreements are obligatory, even for unpaid interns and production assistants (PAS). Unauthorized storytelling by workers is a threat that must be monitored and managed. Even if the film/video trades can be easily and regularly "bought off," individual workers are far more difficult to control. In essence, film/video institutions today are leaky. Online worker gossip can easily wash away the best-laid plans of a network's or studio's development and marketing schemes.

What started as an unruly online threat, however, was quickly hijacked as a mainstream corporate business strategy (see figure 4). Studio

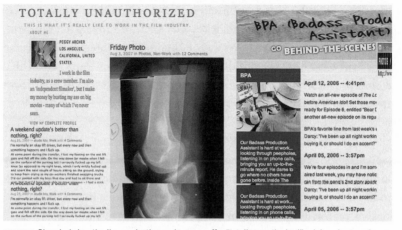

FIGURE 4 Blogs by below-the-line production workers now offer "totally unauthorized" griping about producers and X-rays of job-related injuries (left), while production assistants post lame diaries of star sightings on the set (right).

marketing bosses, that is, soon saw this supposedly uncontrolled narrative cyber-insurgency as an opportunity for profitable countermeasures—specifically the creation of fake buzz. Fake online gossip and fan buzz by studios looks and sounds like authentic fan or practitioner buzz, and companies will go to great lengths to have their Web authors dumb down and de-style their stealth-gossip messages to make them look authentic. Far from being apologetic about this stealth practice, longtime studio bosses liken this practice to the ways that antibodies are used to fight infection in the body: "It's a viral marketing technique. . . . Those message boards have what we call 'seeding'—like you seed a lawn. They seed the board with [propaganda]."[23] TV executives show no remorse or even ambivalence when caught and accused of stealth espionage against fans, claiming that chat is no different than advertising. The practice is widespread: corporate employees—operating as stealthy lurkers and identity poseurs—actively masquerade among online fandoms and audiences. While this viral seeding started in chat rooms and fan sites, it now takes the form of UGC-esque videos systematically planted on YouTube and various sharing sites as well.

The ongoing battle between information leaking by workers and pre-emptive disinformation planting by corporations is only one example of a wide range of online digital activities that pit film and video workers against their corporate bosses. Another sobering example of film's and television's use of digital media to manage information comes in the pre-YouTube form of online tracking boards.[24] Traditionally, gossip and buzz about screenplays and potential new projects in film and television circulated informally around Los Angeles through telephone conversations and casual meetings among those with enough clout to acquire or green-light a film or television series. The off-the-record and unobservable nature of these discussions reinforced and perpetuated the critical claims by outsiders, new writers, and producers that the industry was an old boys' network—in effect, a coalition comprised of those with similar interests even if they ostensibly worked for competitors. Shared gossip about scripts making the rounds could sink a project even before a screenwriter or producer went from studio A to studio B. A narrative grapevine ruled the development pipeline, controlled by executive and agency storytellers with privileged inside looks. Agency and studio tracking continues to take place through exclusive communication back channels—much to the consternation of writers and producers who would rather get a fair and unbiased reading of a script after they pitch it to a studio or network. Web-based FilmTracker spends considerable effort hyping and ensuring exclusivity and privacy for each of its tracking groups. It also describes the mission and purpose of its back-channel networks as a form of community building among (competing) executives, and it promises secrecy, privacy, and exclusivity. BaselineFT's Film-Tracker service is only the most recent way that those in charge of film and television content control what gets developed. FilmTracker works by controlling how and which scripts get gossiped about and—more important—who gets to participate in generating the buzz that results. While stealth marketing, Internet lurking, and fake buzz work well in the gossipy world of viewers on the back end of distribution, as discussed above, rigidly controlled access to agency and studio tracking boards on the front end of development constrains practitioner gossip as well.

Although industry has found ways to rationalize and discipline online gossip as a business practice, gossip is by nature unofficial and unruly, never being completely controlled from the top. By September 2004 several groups mounted countermeasures to the heavy-handed control and exclusion typifying producers' tracking boards like FilmTracker. The WGA counterattacked on its Web site with a link to a screenwriters' Web board that tracked the reputations—good and bad—of producers across town. Once word spread, this online rebuttal board created howls of self-righteous protest from producers and studios who claimed that it was "unfair" for screenwriters to take cheap shots at producers, especially from the cover of anonymity. Many producers found their reputations besmirched when screenwriters told tales of how they were exploited and abused. Although some producers earned high marks, many got hit hard. Screenwriters seemed perplexed at the negative response and double standard. Other online monitoring sites, like Totally Unauthorized and Defamer, have taken up the WGA's counter-studio-tracking-board ethos by posting damning behind-the-scenes stories about producers anonymously.

For a town built on maintaining the illusion of exclusivity for both its A-list talent and screen content, tiffs regularly spin out of control in the viral world of tracking and countertracking boards. Consider the following cease-and-desist order circulated widely online as a warning to those trained in the fine art of industrial gossip:

> We are counsel for Peter Jackson, Fran Walsh and Philippa Boyens. It has come to our attention that a copy of our clients' screenplay "The Lovely Bones" has unlawfully been placed on this tracking board without the consent of our clients, whose copyrighted works are being illegally exploited. A secret ID word has been imbedded [sic] in each copy of the screenplay and we are presently investigating the source of the leak and appropriate action will be taken. . . . We hereby demand that the webmaster of this tracking board immediately remove the screenplay from the site and that all individuals immediately cease and desist from any further dissemination of the screenplay.[25]

Defamer quickly mocked the ridiculous and illogical pretense of producer and director lawyers: "The Jackson camp should probably take pains not to throw too big a scare into the assistants; if the entire script-covering underclass finds itself too paranoid to touch *Bones* for fear they're holding a copy with the 'secret ID word' embedded within (we're guessing it's something like 'fucknewline'), negotiations for the sale might stall indefinitely as annoyed studio execs are forced to actually read the screenplay themselves."[26] This sorry, but symptomatic, interchange exposes the complete illogic of the industry trying to regulate and control screen information that the industry has first deliberately placed into a commercial viral environment defined by wild forwarding and excessive downloading.

> Upcoming [WGA strike] picket events which may be of interest: . . . Thursday will be the first in a series of "Teaching Thursdays" at Gate 2 at Warner Brothers from 9–12. This is a great idea, where writer/producers will gather to answer questions and discuss the craft with anyone who wants to ask. This week's genre is Medical Dramas. . . . I was at Paramount this morning, participating in the . . . picket. I'll always have a special place in my heart for Paramount, since it's where I had my first job.
>
> Screenwriter using WGA strike and What It's Like Web site to build solidarity
> and teach aspirants and outsiders how to write screenplays

All of the recent headlines about social networking and online video activities ignore the fairly basic point that social networking has always been the way that American film and television production has functioned. Online resources have dramatically increased the ways by which social networking is accomplished and advantage is leveraged by film and video workers in production cultures. I'd like to start this section by discussing three cases, the first a rather benign and optimistic one; the next, rather sobering and alarming ones; and the last showing how several parts of production culture have themselves been "YouTubed."[27]

Recent books, like *Convergence Culture*, celebrate the emergence of fan groups as productive resources for media companies.[28] What fewer acknowledge is that media workers themselves have been given additional productive tasks through professional social networking sites — as de facto research and development departments — for production equipment manufacturers, not just for the production companies and studios that officially employ them. Says Michael Horton, editor and founder of the four thousand–member Los Angeles Final Cut Pro User Group, "Most if not all of the changes and additions to FCP were the direct result of vocal users. . . . We knew that Apple was listening as they sent two representatives down to our first meeting. On three occasions we asked the world to give us their top 10 FCP requests. The majority of the top 10 results always found their way into new versions of FCP."[29] Under studio- and network-era Fordism, union workers regulated and relayed technical knowledge to younger assistants on the job. In the post-Fordist, post-network era outsourced contract workers create socio-professional networks to survive and master constantly changing hardware and software. Since the mid-1990s, major equipment manufacturers (Avid,

Apple, Media 100) have had direct access to these social networks via user-group message boards on the Web. Online access to worker social networks flattens the knowledge economy in the digital crafts by cutting out the managerial middlemen in the traditional union-based labor chains. This flattening of technical hierarchies makes the free flow of information and feedback two way.

Pre-YouTube-era Web sites, hosted by professional labor organizations—like the Society of Operating Cameramen (soc)—regularly included overt social networking strategies intended to build solidarity among a widely dispersed set of workers. Sobering indications of the human stakes involved are found posted online by below-the-line workers like cinematographer Michael Negrin. He earnestly appeals to colleagues to resist indie newcomers on the set in a posting titled "Protecting the Role of the Camera Operator," where the threat to union worker livelihoods is described as coming from aspirants and outsiders—whom producers "discover," hire, and bring to the set.[30] They do not come up through the ranks but learn their craft in independent and low-budget sectors, like music video and indie festival film production. Even before UGC, the DIY ethos preached in many art and film schools and celebrated at Sundance-wannabe festivals worldwide produces edgy "artists" who mock and disregard long-protected union camera department assignments—much to the alarm of journeyman crew members. The current battle between UGC and WGC, therefore, has a long prehistory marked by tensions when just-discovered, multitasking outsiders get to cross over and become professionals. The era of YouTube and UGC has merely exacerbated this long-standing professional distrust of indies and outsiders.

One industrial response to YouTube has been the creation of professional film and video social networking sites that function as a combination job board, demo-reel showcase, gossip center, and trade news clearinghouse. ReelExchange is one of the most prominent of these professional video-sharing Web sites. Whereas FilmTracker, described above, is most heavily used by corporate types (producers, executives, and agents), ReelExchange is made for below-the-line film and video craft workers. The site directly mimics YouTube in design, iconography, and features. It promises potential video uploaders that the sharing/networking site will allow smaller-market film and video professionals to market themselves by uploading their demo reels, pitches, and bios for interested producers and production companies nationwide who would not otherwise have access to them. As ReelExchange developed and grew, several factors made it increasingly apparent that the site would never have the kind of free-form, rhizomatically expanding user base that YouTube has achieved. For starters, some threshold of professionalism must be demonstrated or asserted to gain entry to the uploading imperative of these pros. The copying, hijacking, and editing mash-ups of others' video content that has made YouTube popular, for example, has not taken over ReelExchange. This restraint (and constraint) is for good reason, given the need to maintain at least some vestige of perceived protection for the copyright holders that submit their comp reels, excerpts, and demos for the site. It's not just Viacom and Warner Bros., therefore, that rail against video sharing. Those looking for work and commercial clients do so as well. Finally, the commercial ownership and sponsorship of ReelExchange says much about why the sharing site will never achieve the ubiquity of YouTube. This people's and professionals' sharing site was actually launched by two technical trade publications: *Millimeter* and *Digital Content*. Far more than an example of enabling social networking and video sharing, therefore, the site in fact serves as a lucrative marketing "sponge" that sucks up an incredible level of detail about professionals (site members who want crew assignments and contract productions) for sale to those that drive the production trades (equipment manufacturers, media corporations, and advertisers). The ever-thinner printed production trades are clearly on their way out. In ReelExchange, *Millimeter* and *Digital Content* dramatically show what the future of film/video industry journalism is: a massive, nonlinear, video sharing site that clearly has as much to do with client research, corporate sales, and stealth marketing as it does with the faux-populism of video uploading.

Similarly, a look at prodblogs shows how rich the terrain of WGC can be for media studies scholars. Prodblogs don't just leak behind-the-scenes info as described above (which fuels the celebrity news industry), they also offer wide-ranging, provocative online self-disclosures and critiques from film and video workers. Some prodblogs share the blogosphere's snarky cynicism but direct it against their film and TV bosses. The site Burbanked complains: "I spent nearly a decade toiling in semi-obscurity in the development trenches of the Hollywood studio system, most of that time at Warner Bros. where I read roughly 14,238 screenplays and enjoyed about 20 of them. I played a small but critical—*critical!*—part in the development and production of about three movies."[31] The site's motto is "At *Burbanked*, screenwriting is king, no celebrity is safe and much of the marketing of studio movies is crap." Prodblogs by below-the-line workers tend to mix hard-edged corporate critiques with affirmations of the fortitude, commitment, and physical suffering required by the craft. The Blood, Sweat, and Tedium site makes worker suffering surreal by mocking TV producers obsessed with shooting in downtown Los Angeles because of its "gritty look," ignoring worker downsides: "cable runs fully submerged beneath six inches of shit and piss in those alleys [from homeless residents], where a lungful of the foul, choking stench is enough to make you vomit."[32] This is about as far from the executive-focused, utopian, buzz-driven studio tracking boards described above as one could get.

Yet what is remarkable about these sites and many others is their earnest, extensive pedagogical tendency to teach and mentor. Even the snarkiest sites regularly settle down to deliver incredibly detailed and valuable lessons about how specific crafts, technologies, labor arrangements, modes of production, auteurs, and genres work. In fact, I've found the prodblogosphere to offer more detailed and up-to-date primers on new film and video technologies and methods than the production textbooks in university classrooms and film schools. Where does this urge to teach—and to teach seriously and regularly—come from? More than just an opportunity to network, Seriocity, a blog by TV writer Kay Reindl, provides a detailed, knowing critique of the widespread practice of executive note-giving.[33] Such a practice doesn't just "crush the soul" of the creative cadre. It also destroys things that matter to the corporations as well: ratings, box office, and financial prospects. Script Goddess provides regular postings that lay out the details and nuances of one of the most underappreciated but important crafts on a set: script supervision. Unlike production textbooks or the trades (which disregard script supervision), this site provides prescient critiques of arrogant but naïve indie filmmakers and other ego-flawed "artists" (like DPs and directors) on the set:

> The first-time director was so enamored with the actors that he let our leading actor have free rein, which is great if you've got miles of film to burn and lots of time to let the actor "explore his character." Not so

good if you're the one trying to edit this crap together. I told him again and again that the actor can't be loud and arms flailing in the wide, and then soft spoken and demure in the close up. Not to mention not repeating his actions. The arrogant newbie director ignored my pleas, but fortunately for me while watching the dailies the editor freaked out and sat Cecil B. down and said, "I can't cut this crap together if you continue down this road." Thankfully, Cecil saw the light.[34]

One of the very best prodblogs that does for grips and electricians what Script Goddess does for continuity workers is Totally Unauthorized. Written by a lighting technician who calls herself Peggy Archer, this site provides regular critiques of the gender politics on sets alongside very useful tips about how to prevent electrocution, tie off electrical cable, and recuperate from lower back and knee injuries.[35] Unsolicited, Archer discloses insights on the peculiarities of working methods for which a scholar would have to work considerably to access. She explains, for example, the union logic of safe-and-slow gaffing: "We also don't want to look like we're in a hurry on set. If we're scrambling around like rats trying to find the only route off a sinking ship, the powers-that-be assume we're not in control of the situation and should perhaps be replaced by a more competent crew first thing Monday morning."[36]

While WGC, social networking sites, prodblogging, and self-disclosure share some traits with UGC, they provide stark contrasts to the self-reflexivity and online self-disclosure that issue steadily from contemporary film/TV corporations. Understanding digitization means acknowledging the significant gaps that exist between the corporate world—driven by viral marketing—and crew and worker worlds, where unauthorized self-disclosures provide a far more complex picture of digital television than DVD bonus tracks, producer Q&As, behind-the-scenes featurettes, tightly organized trade press junkets, and making-of documentaries. WGC should be seen as a necessary antidote and corrective to both the viral spin of corporate PGU and the populist-resistant assumptions of UGC.

THE LOGIC OF UGC/PGU/WGC

While media corporations may deem online trade narratives by their own workers as unruly threats, unauthorized WGCs serve several more basic functions in film and television production cultures—as rationalizations, solidarity making, guarantors of career mobility, forms of social pedagogy, and self-serving legitimation. Through these worker-generated practices, production personnel close ranks to weather change and mark their professional boundaries. These intense forms of communicative and narrative interaction fit ethnographer Andreas Wittel's model of networked sociality, in which technology-based cultural activities substitute for actual community for independent professionals in the new creative industries.[37] By circulating highly reflexive forms among themselves, practitioners do not simply learn new things. They also work to convince themselves that their distinctive value to the industry lies in some unique specialty of their guild, craft, or trade association. These narratives of self-affirmation, then, fulfill a broader need that labor sociologist Harry Braverman finds across the newer, flexible industries. That is, trade narratives verify that a storyteller has a specialized expertise that goes beyond the obligations of simple labor and proves that he or she can do the one thing required of any professional in film and TV: successfully, and repeatedly, negotiate one's own value.[38]

The examples considered here indicate that practitioners snark, expose, blog, and tell online trade stories as part of industrial habit and that the intensity of trade storytelling is extreme because professionals must work far harder to restrict access to industries where labor is as open as it is in Hollywood than in industries where it is closed.[39] In this way, production workers are less like those who tell trade stories in closed professions that restrict access through strict credentialing (like lawyers) than they are like those in professions marked by openness and calculated self-reliance (like salesmen or entrepreneurs). In the case of film and video production, workers tell trade stories to themselves and snark as forms of turf marking and exclusion, as ways to will into being professional affinities, and as navigational tactics their professional communities need in order to face technological change and economic uncertainty.

Many of the PGC activities described in this chapter make sense in the context of the following three basic goals, while WGC constantly shoots up unauthorized online flak to cloud the corporations' intent on making these same principles a reality:

(1) Everyone will work for free, or as close to it as possible. (*UGC as a gold mine for the overproduction of cost-effective screen content.*)

(2) Media corporations will gain advantage by creating experience-based work worlds that correspond to the new "experience economy" of consumers. (*Social networking as professional capital in lieu of wages.*)

(3) Industrial advantage will mean increasingly transforming the outsourced television production workspace into a nonhierarchical "ad-hocracy." (*Independent contractor crews and teams modeled on informal families and crowdsourcing.*)

The result is not that executives will continue to pursue viral methods only as a consumer phenomenon.[40] Rather, the industry's professional production mode for film and video workers will itself become increasingly viral and nonlinear. The online practices examined here suggest that industrial viral production practices are currently among the most cost-effective models for professional production in the hypercompetitive multichannel multimedia marketplace.

The amazing thing about this new unruly, collapsed, and volatile world of digital television production culture and prodblogging is that information and access to it—far from being restricted and controlled—leak irretrievably and excessively from it. Georgina Born, whose recent pioneering book on the BBC was made possible because of an unusual degree of access granted to the author by the corporation—sets up her entire book with a prologue titled "An Anthropologist among the White City Natives."[41] What Born and other scholars should also consider is that thousands of film and video production workers are themselves self-consciously banging out self-ethnographies on a weekly basis on behind-the-scenes blogs—like http://angryanthropologist.blogspot.com. Workers on these sites post insider knowledge—and analysis—in part because industry observers, scholars, and writers frequently err in describing even basic industrial practices. Television studies would benefit by taking this intense, sometimes agitated, and almost always jaded and cynical world of WGC—labor's explicit behind-the-scenes self-ethnographies—seriously. Examining UGC provides only half the story of how television is being digitized since both media corporations and their workers have been posing, posting, lurking, lying, flaming, fabricating, spinning, snarking, and defaming for some time. The professional, vocational, and commercial reasons for this kind of worker/user content generation are worth acknowledging with more care and detail.

One below-the-line electricians' Web site showed just how willing crew members are to share accurate information about production, even to writers and analysts who are after bigger intellectual and cultural fish: "If you're writing something and aren't sure about what any particular crew person does, please don't guess—just email me and ask. . . . I'll be more than happy to help. Unless you want me to go insane—in that case, just keep up 'with all the gaffers.' I'll eventually snap. I promise."[42]

NOTES

My thanks to Bryan Hartzheim for his research assistance on UGC and WGC issues and to Miranda Banks and Vicki Mayer for their many insights in the area of production cultures.

1. James Hibbard, "TV Industry Battles Piracy Hydra," *Television Week*, August 13, 2007, 1, 27.
2. See the trade's alarmed editorial, "Who Will Step Up to Disband TV's Pirates," *Television Week*, August 13, 2007, 9.
3. Stephanie Robbins, "Viral Video Pick of the Week," *Television Week*, August 13, 2007, 3.
4. While such duplicity is of course far from new in Hollywood or network television, the explosion of digital applications and uses outside of the heretofore regulated and rationalized industry has made doublespeak an obligatory and sometimes manic part of trade talk today.
5. For these characterizations and differences, see Nicholas Negroponte, *Being Digital* (New York: Alfred A. Knopf, 1995); Henry Jenkins, *Convergence Culture: Where Old and New Media Collide* (Cambridge, Mass.: MIT Press, 2006); Lev Manovich, *The Language of New Media* (Cambridge, Mass.: MIT Press, 2001); and Daniel Schiller, *Digital Capitalism* (Cambridge, Mass.: MIT Press, 1999).
6. While Google struggled to "monetize" its new partner YouTube, by 2007 other corporations took a more hostile approach, as when Viacom sued YouTube, legally pressuring the sharing site to mine and disclose its own data on purportedly stolen Viacom properties churning throughout the site.
7. Other examples of Hollywood's and U.S. prime-time television's buying out of outsider alternatives include Italian neorealism in the 1940s, cinema verité documentary in the 1970s, music videos in the 1980s, and home video in the 1990s.
8. The ratings comparisons from Nielsen NetRatings are quoted in Daisy Whitney, "Yahoo Revamps Video: One-Stop Site Designed to Draw Ads," *Television Week*, August 6, 2007, 1, 40.
9. Ibid.
10. Mike Folgner quoted in Daisy Whitney, "Yahoo Revamps Video: One-Stop Site Designed to Draw Ads," *Television Week*, August 6, 2007, 1, 40.

11. Paoletti quoted in ibid.

12. Baker quoted in Dawn C. Chmielewski, "Taking Amateur Video Up a Notch: Sony's Remade Crackle Will Award Talent with a Shot at Funding and Promotion," *Los Angeles Times*, July 16, 2007, C1, C3; emphasis added.

13. Spielberg's support seems unlike a marketplace tactic, and instead evokes the kind of patronage of artists that the wealthy Medici family and bank popularized in Florence and Tuscany during the Renaissance.

14. Alex Lindsay, quoted in Daisy Whitney, "Digital Dealmakers," *Television Week*, August 16, 2007, 8.

15. Leslie Robinson, a blog writer at ColoradoConfidential.com, quoted in Associated Press, "Bloggers Seeking to Form a Labor Union," *Los Angeles Times*, August 6, 2007, C2.

16. This quote and the one that follows are from Jim Benson, "Grouper Drops User-Generated Video," *Broadcasting and Cable*, July 16, 2007; http://www .broadcastingcable.com/article.

17. Maurice Patel, "Shifting Paradigms in Film Post Workflows," *Post*, July 2007, 56.

18. Ibid., 56.

19. *Post*, a film and video editors' trade journal, acknowledges that Maurice Patel is the "director of product marketing for Autodesk Media and Entertainment."

20. http://www.hdexpo.net/education/varicamp/vari_registration.html.

21. As if digitization were not confusing or disruptive enough, professional workers now must also pay premium amounts at enabling workshops (sponsored by Panasonic) to retool their skill sets, even though those educating the professional attendees channel them into narrow, soon-to-be obsolete proprietary technologies. What frequently happens, however, is that lower-budgeted workers regularly resist this corporate herding by hacking and cracking open proprietary processes in order to produce digital work-arounds that independents (not manufacturers) can control on a more cost-effective basis. Digital hacking, therefore, is also a valued production worker skill. See Nick Dager, "A Refreshing Look at Digital Workflow," *Post*, July 2007, 16.

22. The epigraph above is quoted in Mary McNamara, "A Voice for the Techies," *Los Angeles Times*, December 4, 2005, E1, E8.

23. Terry Semel, former chairman and CEO of Warner Bros. studios, quoted in Dana Calvo, "Fake Fans, Fake Buzz, Real Bucks," *Los Angeles Times*, March 20, 2001, A1.

24. This paragraph and the next one on studio tracking boards are adapted from chapter 2, "Trade Stories and Career Capital," in Caldwell, *Production Culture: Industrial Reflexivity and Critical Practice in Film and Television* (Durham, N.C.: Duke University Press, 2008), 69–109.

25. This cease and desist warning was quoted in Defamer, "Peter Jackson's Lawyers Don't Want Unapproved Assistants Reading 'The Lovely Bones.'" http://

defamer.gawker.com/257257/peter-jacksons-lawyers-dont-want-unapproved-assistants-reading--the-lovely-bones. Accessed April 18, 2010.

26. Ibid.

27. Source for epigraph above: "What It's Like," *lisaklink blog*, posted January 22, 2008; http://www.lisaklink.com.

28. Henry Jenkins's important and influential book, *Convergence Culture*.

29. Horton interviewed in David E. Williams, "Post Modern: Michael Horton, President of the Los Angeles Final Cut Pro User Group, Muses on the Future of NLES," *DV*, September 2007, 30.

30. Negrin's statement was posted on the SOC's *Camera Operators Magazine* Web site, a reprint from the spring–summer 1996 issue of the *Operating Camera-man*, accessed July 21, 2003, 1 (no longer posted). Available online at: http://faculty.uncsa.edu/film/elkins/380/soc%20articles/protecting_camera_opera-tor.pdf (accessed April 18, 2010).

31. Alan Lopuszynski, "About," http://burbanked.com/about.

32. This descent-into-hell allegory for below-the-line production is from http://hollywoodjuicer.blogspot.com (accessed April 19, 2008).

33. Comment posted March 19, 2008; http://seriocity.blogspot.com.

34. Available on the blog Script Goddess, at http://scriptsupervisorforum.blog-spot.com.

35. Peggy Archer is a pseudonym used to protect the identity of one of the most popular below-the-line bloggers/complainers on the Totally Unauthorized Web site, http://filmhacks.wordpress.com.

36. Totally Unauthorized, available at http://filmhacks.wordpress.com.

37. This theory is based on ethnographic work in the new media sector in England. See Andreas Wittel, "Toward a Network Sociality," *Theory, Culture, and Society* 18, no. 6 (2001): 51–77.

38. See Harry Braverman, *Labor and Monopoly Capitalism: The Degradation of Work in the Twentieth Century* (New York: Review Press, 1998), 82. I thank Vicki Mayer for suggesting this connection.

39. This concept of the varying value of self-selling in both open and closed labor systems is developed more broadly by Keith M. MacDonald, *The Sociology of Professions* (London: Sage, 1995), 184–85.

40. Viral marketing will continue to rein in marketing, even as it spurs new production approaches.

41. See Georgina Born, *Uncertain Vision: Birt, Dyke and the Reinvention of the BBC* (London: Vintage, 2005).

42. Peggy Archer, posted November 14, 2006; Totally Unauthorized, available at http://filmhacks.wordpress.com.

JEAN BURGESS

USER-CREATED CONTENT AND EVERYDAY CULTURAL PRACTICE

Lessons from YouTube

The first decade of the twenty-first century has seen a steady increase in the prevalence, visibility, and perceived significance of user-created (or user-generated) content on the Web. One of the ideas attached to these developments has been that the proliferation of user-created content—that is, media content produced by amateurs, outside of the traditional creative industries, as represented by blogs, Wikipedia, citizen journalism, and user-created video—promises to disrupt the modern relations of cultural production that have structured the broadcast era and to unsettle the expertise of established media and knowledge professions. Creativity is now seen by many policymakers and educators as normatively part of everyday life for ordinary citizens (especially young people) in contemporary capitalist societies, and in reality user-created content is a significant source of our shared cultural experience.[1] The implications extend beyond self-expression: user-led content creation and collaboration are increasingly understood as engines of economic and social value creation and, at the same time, sources of profound economic disruption in the commercial industries, while public service broadcasters, cultural institutions, and government departments are embracing user-created content and co-creation as part of their service missions.[2]

The media hype around the revolutionary potential of the

growth in user-created content reached fever pitch between 2004 and 2007. Early on it focused on blogging and later on photo sharing and "folksonomies," with Flickr as the poster child for Web 2.0, moving onto the battles over the legitimacy of knowledge in Wikipedia, before focusing obsessively for a time on YouTube following its unprecedented growth and acquisition by Google in 2006. By the end of 2006 *Time* magazine was announcing that its Person of the Year was "You," and the magazine ran a large number of articles celebrating the entrepreneurs, DIY celebrities, and "ordinary" content creators associated with Web 2.0, calling the phenomenon of collective production on the Web a "revolution," a view countered by cultural pessimists such as Andrew Keen, who called the whole thing a morally and intellectually dangerous "cult."[3]

However, these early dominant discourses around the democratization of media technologies (whether celebratory or alarmist) did nothing to disturb the existing roles and relationships of the cultural industries but merely reassigned the roles—consumers were transformed into DIY producers, and audiences had apparently activated themselves as citizen journalists or publishers. It has been television's mass audience in particular that has been reimagined in such radical terms, a view starkly illustrated by Clay Shirky's characterization of the "passive" inactivity of television viewing as a waste of "cognitive surplus," which in a post-broadcast age can be put to productive use in knowledge work, such as the creation or editing of Wikipedia entries.[4]

The crude inversion of industrial roles in the discourses surrounding ideas of a participatory media "revolution" emanating from the media and technology industries themselves should not come as a surprise; more significant is the fact that the technological determinism that underpins it is common to both the most celebratory and the most alarmist accounts of the implications of user-created content. Especially in the early stages of a new media form's emergence, when the media as a whole are attempting to pin down what it is "for" and what its social implications might be, as Steve Woolgar has argued, "even the hype about the hype is part of the hype."[5] That is, the countering arguments to the celebration of a participatory turn in digital media culture (often played out in exactly the same media sites) usually operate within the same frame of debate as the original arguments that they mean to question. For example, if the hype suggests that news blogs represent a new and more democratic form of journalism, then the counterhype will argue that blogs are untrustworthy or biased information sources. But in the early days of academic research and media commentary on blogging, it was less common to find a critique of the shared assumptions underlying these debates. Such a critique might have pointed out that the majority of blogging activities never had anything much to do with journalism in the first place—in fact, the main reasons for keeping a blog given by bloggers surveyed in 2006 were "creative expression and sharing personal experiences."[6] Following such logic, it is unlikely that the reality of how online video is used and experienced, via YouTube, for example, will match the rhetoric that imagines the masses of formerly passive television audiences transforming themselves into full-blown producers of online video.

Because of the publicness of the debates around the implications of user-created content and digital culture, the role of the humanities and social sciences in this context requires a double mastery of discourse—it is not enough to go around "debunking" the hype because, for one thing, hyperbole is a constitutive force in the field of study. In questioning the hyperbole around the earlier idea of virtuality, Woolgar begins from twin realities: first, the growth of Information Communication Technologies (ICT); second, the *discourse* around ICT, resulting in a widespread assumption that the growth of ICT should be understood "as the impetus for radical changes."[7] These realities mean that it is impossible for scholars and critics to disregard the preexisting terms of public debates while still hoping to participate in the public discussion. In Woolgar's case, the existing frames concerned the social impacts of ICT in the late 1990s; in the case of YouTube, they concern the implications of amateur creativity and user-created content. In the case of user-created content, online video, and television, an updated vocabulary is required, one that is capable of dealing with the altered roles of audiences and producers, derived from the evidence, without falling into the trap of endlessly creating buzzwords and thus simply mirroring the dominant celebratory discourse around Web 2.0.

This chapter argues that cultural and media studies' heritage in understanding the activity and productivity of audiences—particularly television audiences—makes the field peculiarly able to offer important insights into these questions around the cultural implications of user-created content. A return to the key ideas of cultural consumption as a set of everyday cultural practices asks us to view the cultural implications of YouTube not only in terms of the democratization of cultural production, but also in terms of the visibility and connectedness of everyday cultural practice, including the practices of television audiences. This new visibility and publicness also invite renewed engagements with the audience on behalf of media and cultural studies scholarship and, in particular, hold potential for evidence-based models of audience practices, cultural citizenship, and media literacy. In the discussion that follows I set out the debates about the changing role of audiences in relation to user-created content as they appear in new media and cultural studies. The discussion moves beyond the simple dichotomies drawn between active producers and passive audiences and instead calls on empirical evidence in order to examine the practices that are most ordinary and widespread. Building on the knowledge of television's role in facilitating public life and the everyday, affective practices through which it is experienced and used, I focus on the way in which YouTube operates as a site of community, creativity, cultural citizenship, and an archive of popular cultural memory.

THE VIEW FROM MEDIA AND CULTURAL STUDIES

The premise of the "passive" audience at the mercy of a dominant broadcast media industry is fundamental to some of the most influential discussions of how user-created content represents broader social and cultural transformations. In his acclaimed book *The Wealth of Networks*, Yochai Benkler examines the widespread shift from an industrialized manufacturing economy to a decentralized information economy, constituted via the Internet, within which amateur and volunteer contributions are of primary importance. When it comes to the media, however, Benkler's enthusiasm about the political possibilities of these new networks of social production relies—to some extent—on an imagined opposition between a preindustrial folk culture and the alienation of twentieth-century mass popular culture, which, largely thanks to TV, displaced folk culture and transformed individuals and communities from "coproducers and replicators to passive consumers."[8] Benkler discusses the emergence of user-led content production networks as a new folk culture that can contribute to the cultural element of liberal democracy, which he calls "cultural freedom," in comparison to the enslavement of the broadcast era: "By comparison to the highly choreographed cultural production system of the industrial information economy, the emergence of a new folk culture and of a wider practice of active personal engagement in the telling and retelling of basic cultural themes and emerging concerns and attachments offers new avenues for freedom. It makes culture more participatory, and renders it more legible to all its inhabitants."[9] In an essay in the technophilic magazine *Wired*, science fiction author and cultural commentator William Gibson went so far as to proclaim the death of the audience: "Today's audience isn't listening at all. It's participating. Indeed, 'audience' is as antique a term as 'record,' the one archaically passive, the other archaically physical. The record, not the remix, is the anomaly today. The remix is the very nature of the digital."[10] The key concepts of media and cultural studies work on television and its audiences could provide an alternative viewpoint to this disdain for audiencehood, one able to avoid the active-passive binary and its inversion in the post-broadcast era of Benkler's, Gibson's, and others' perspectives.

Indeed, even in technologists' own explanations of what Web 2.0 is and how it works, the idea of a linear chain connecting those who produce and those who consume content is profoundly disrupted. The term Web 2.0 was coined by Tim O'Reilly to describe a design agenda for the future of the World Wide Web, but it now functions discursively as both an imprecise buzzword and a description of the actual features of some of the most talked about social media platforms built around user-created or -contributed content, including Flickr and YouTube.[11] From the point of view of software development, it refers to the evolution of the World Wide Web from a network of static Web sites serving content to audiences toward an integrated computing platform serving interoperable, dynamic Web applications to productive users. So far, this sounds very familiar. But the term also implies some quite complex shifts in the way producers and users are understood.

There are several key areas in which the Web 2.0 model implies the need to reimagine the relations of cultural production in regard to digital media. The first of these is the shift from separate domains of content production, distribution, and consumption to a convergence of all three, resulting in the hybrid mode of engagement that Axel Bruns calls "produsage," defined as "the collaborative and continuous building and extending of existing content in pursuit of further improvement."[12] In this model, the users of a given Web service take on leadership roles, and are reimagined as a source, and not an end point, for both content and the ongoing improvement of the platform or service; designers and developers to some extent work with the understanding that emergent communities of practice will significantly shape the culture of the network—and even determine what the Web service or online community is "for." This convergence of the formerly discrete points along a linear value chain is most clearly exemplified by Wikipedia, whose users, at least in theory, are simultaneously the producers, users, editors, and consumers of the content. What was previously somewhat dismissively called user-generated content is now as essential to the success of any social media platform as its design, and the activities it encompasses include not only content creation, but also editing, annotation, commenting, repurposing, and redistribution. But perhaps the most culturally significant layer of the Web 2.0 model is most clearly represented by social media platforms like Flickr: the convergence of user-created content and social software to produce hybrid spaces where everyday creativity, intimacy, and friendship meet public visibility and connectivity. It is this characteristic of the new networks of cultural production that has the most profound implications for cultural participation, at least in potential, because this shift opens up new and diverse spaces for individuals to engage with a variety of aesthetic experiences at the same time as their participation contributes to the creation of those spaces, their communities, and even publics.

YouTube, perhaps more dramatically and visibly than any other platform to emerge so far, is produced by these convergences between market and nonmarket, personal and public cultural activity. Further, much of the user-created content that generates YouTube's value is utterly mundane in its origins and in its modes of circulation and linked via processes of remediation to a continuous history of everyday cultural practice that I have discussed elsewhere as "vernacular creativity."[13] User-created content, I argue, is often very ordinary indeed, and "the ordinary" is core business for cultural studies.

The British cultural studies concern with taking ordinary people's lived experiences and cultural practices seriously is particularly marked in work on television audiences.[14] The strand of audience and reception studies known as the active audience tradition in particular was reflected in an interest in fans as visible proof of such activity in the 1980s and 1990s.[15] The areas of contemporary humanities scholarship that have been most engaged in attempting to understand how the growth of user-created content and its attendant decentralization of distribution and evaluation are affecting the media and television industries often operate with fandom as a core concept, with both productive and problematic results. Approaching the reconfiguration of producer-consumer relationships through the lens of the productive media consumer, Henry Jenkins's work on "convergence culture" exposes fan and game cultures as neither entirely autonomous of the mass media and cultural industries nor passively dependent on or absorbed into them.[16] Jenkins demonstrates that these fields of cultural practice reconfigure the relations between production and consumption, industries and audiences, as well as old and new media. While for the most part the copyright holders still fiercely protect their intellectual property, in convergence culture there is also an increased awareness within industry of the benefits of dialogue and intercreativity between the producers of popular culture and their audiences.

Work that seeks to understand the changing power relationships between the formally constituted media industries (like television) and the fans who co-create the value of media properties is extremely important. However, these discussions tend to skew our view of user-created video toward fan videos and look suspiciously like the favoritism of which cultural studies has long been accused—that is, repeatedly focusing on the most spectacular or potentially revolutionary examples of popular culture rather than the most ordinary and widely experienced.[17] While the semiotic creativity and textual productivity of fans were arguably ordinary because of their embeddedness in the everyday lives of the fans themselves, they were nevertheless positioned as extraordinary by the interpretive lens of cultural and media studies, and in any case, fans were, and remain today, a minority of television audiences. Despite the popular hyperbole surrounding democratization and the extraordinary revolutionary potential of everyday content creation, textual productivity is not so extraordinary these days, even if it is not universally shared. While the vanguard status of fan communities continues to be recognized, the productiveness of consumer-citizens is now an ordinary part of the mainstream cultural public sphere. If not a radical and creative transformation from passive audience to active producer, then what does the nature of ordinary participation in social media platforms like YouTube look like?

YOUTUBE'S COMMON CULTURE

YouTube is a platform for video sharing that is used by many different participants, often with competing ideas of how online video should be used, including mainstream media companies, independent producers, vloggers, and musicians, as well as fans. For the purposes of this chapter, I am going to concentrate on the insights of a recent study, which I conducted with Joshua Green, of YouTube's most popular content for rethinking the active-passive and market-nonmarket divides in much of the dominant discourses on participatory culture.[18] The study aimed to develop an understanding of the forms and practices associated with the dominant or most popular uses of YouTube, which we refer to as YouTube's "common culture." It relied in the first instance on a large-scale content survey, drawing on a sample of 4,320 videos from four of YouTube's categories of popularity—Most Viewed, Most "Favorited," Most Responded, Most Discussed—gathered in the second half of 2007.[19] The coding scheme involved two primary categories: the apparent industrial origin of the video (whether it was user-created or the product of a traditional media company) and the apparent identity of the uploader (whether a traditional media company, a small-to-medium enterprise or independent producer, a government organization, cultural institution or the like, or an amateur user). We concentrated on the four categories of popularity noted above because we hypothesized—correctly, as it turns out—that comparing across them would give us a sense of the way different kinds of video content were made popular by audiences in different ways. The results of the study show that the activities associated with everyday audience practice and vernacular creativity, now remediated via online social networks—personal vlogging, quoting from television, or bedroom lip-synching—can be read through theories of personal media use as much as through the transformation of passive consumers into active producers.

Approximately half of the content in the sample was coded as "traditional media content," and approximately half as "user-created content." However, around two-thirds of the total number of videos in the sample was contributed by uploaders coded as "users"—uploaders represented as individuals not associated with media companies, production companies, or organizations of any kind. The videos coded as user-created content in the sample are diverse and exhibit what Henry Jenkins has identified as a "vaudeville aesthetic"—featuring short clips characterized by trickery and humor, an explicit awareness of an audience of peers, and a fascination with the technologies of digital video.[20] However, by far the largest genre category in the sample was that of the videoblog or "vlog" entry—videos based around a talking head, straight-to-camera presentation, and a quotidian setting. The dominance of the vlog entry as a particularly YouTube-centric form emphasizes the everyday located-ness and investment in interpersonal communication, rather than pro-ducerliness, that we identify as part of the "YouTubeness" of YouTube. And even some of the most spectacularly popular viral videos share the vlog entry's genealogy in the privatized spaces of everyday personal media use.

For example, one of the most popular user-created videos of all time is a bedroom lip-synch video—a form with a very long history in the tra-dition of bedroom cultures but now publicized via the online networks of participatory media. In the video, titled simply as the "Hey" clip, Lital Mizel and her friend Adi Frimerman lip-synch, dance, play air guitar, and generally goof around to The Pixies' song "Hey."[21] It had had sev-eral million views by mid-2006, remains one of the most popular videos on the Web site, and had received more than 24 million views by Octo-ber 2008. Demonstrating a sophisticated understanding of the rules of the vernacular genre on which she was drawing—the bedroom dance video—as well as a self-deprecating awareness of its status as a vernacu-lar form, Mizel explained the motivation and meaning behind the video: "We just turned on the camera and danced funny, . . . I keep asking people why do you like it, and they say, 'Because it's reality.' You see it's homemade, that we're so spontaneous and natural—dancing, having fun. It makes people remember when they were young and danced in front of the mirror."[22]

The "Hey" clip, along with the thousands of others like it, is both an example and a witty and self-aware celebration of the long traditions of the bedroom cultures of young people, particularly girls. Public media production and performance add new dimensions to these circuits of "privatized media use."[23] The unexpected fame that came with the popu-larity of the clip is a result of its recognizability as everyday cultural prac-tice and the sheer exuberance of the performances depicted within it; the precision of the editing of multiple versions of the lip-synch perfor-mance; and, arguably, its status as one of the first such uses of YouTube.

The genre of the bedroom musical performance or dance is now deeply embedded in YouTube's popular culture.[24]

The video "Guitar" is an equally ordinary example.[25] The video depicts a technically demanding neoclassical metal cover of Pachelbel's *Canon in D*, performed on electric guitar in a bedroom. The performer in the video—seated on his bed, backlit by the sunlight streaming in from the window, his face obscured by a baseball cap—is a South Korean guitarist named Jeong-Hyun Lim.[26] With over 40 million views to date, his video is among the most popular YouTube videos of all time and continues to attract new viewers, comments, and video responses.

Most of the response videos are either direct emulations (in which other bedroom guitarists test and prove their skills) or variations on the genre that the original "Guitar" video distilled if not originated. In addition to the approximately nine hundred direct video responses to the "Guitar" video, a keyword search for "canon rock" in YouTube returns more than thirteen thousand videos, the majority of which appear to be versions of the original "Canon Rock" track, performed not only on guitars but also on pianos, violins, and even a toy keyboard.[27] These video responses frequently emulate the original mise-en-scène—with the performer seated on a bed, backlit by light from a window, and looking down rather than at the camera. Perhaps the most interesting example is the montage video "Ultimate Canon Rock," a remix of forty versions of the rock guitar arrangement, all performed by bedroom guitarists and painstakingly edited together by YouTube user "impeto" to make a complete new version of the performance.[28] This video has received views in excess of 5 million as of November 2008, a level of popularity that amplifies and is amplified by the original "Guitar" version. In itself, "Ultimate Canon Rock" is an act of iterative vernacular creativity that has emerged as much out of the conversational dynamics of YouTube as a social network as it has out of any desire for self-expression. The video captures the ways in which small contributions from a large number of participants collectively add up to much more than the sum of their parts; the value of the video as an element in participatory culture cannot be attributed back to an original producer (because, for one thing, there isn't one). The video is also a particularly good example of an existing performance genre and one that is arguably paradigmatic of user-created content on YouTube—the virtuosic bedroom musical performance, straight to camera, vlog style.

The practices of media use that sit behind user-contributed television content can likewise be situated within long traditions of personal media use and audience practice. YouTube is used for sharing and repurposing television content, but these sharing and repurposing practices are disarticulated from both the hypercreative practices of fandom and from peer-to-peer file sharing (or, in industry discourse, "piracy"). They are mostly very mundane, rather than featuring the spectacularly creative "remix" aesthetic that is often assumed in celebratory accounts to characterize user-created video; and because of the technical constraints of YouTube at the time the study was conducted (the short maximum duration of videos and the low resolution), the use of YouTube to illegally distribute whole television episodes or films is not a dominant one in YouTube's common culture. Far more prevalent in our sample were short clips—effectively, quotations from television, uploaded and circulating in similar ways to user-created content. These clips were drawn primarily from television news—documenting and preserving shared moments in public life, like the 2007–2008 U.S. presidential campaign, natural events such as earthquakes, or "gotcha" moments featuring celebrities and politicians. There were a large number of very short clips from televised sports, capturing magical moments like winning soccer goals, along with montages or single clips from favorite sitcoms or serials, and an equally large number of music videos, often added to users' profiles as markers of cultural taste and identity. What these uses point us to is the extent to which participation in YouTube is often a logical and newly visible extension of ordinary television audience practices— akin to saying "Wow, did you see that?" or "I love this show/video/joke."

The prevalence of these clips and quotes points us toward thinking about how media content is used, rather than how it is received. Indeed, because of YouTube's flat architecture and one-size-fits-all approach to the re-presentation of content within the Web site, it makes little sense to separate the ways in which YouTube participants contribute self-created video from the ways in which they contribute and engage with video that originally came from television.

It is a lack of recognition of this convergence of everyday audience practice with user-led content creation in newly visible and connected public networks that creates so much confusion around the political economy of digital media production. The stubborn misrecognition of audiences as the end of a value chain, rather than co-creators of value, is clearly illustrated by the still ongoing legal action taken by media conglomerate Viacom against Google, in which Viacom accused YouTube of unduly profiting from the television giant's labor by allowing unauthorized copies of its content to be uploaded and viewed on the services.[29] "YouTube and Google retain all of the revenue generated from [users uploading videos]," the company claimed, "without extending fair compensation to the people who have expended all of the effort and cost to create it."[30] Because it is rooted in the idea of YouTube as a distribution platform that delivers content produced elsewhere to consumers, whose viewing practices expose them to advertising, the action has almost nothing to do with how people actually use media content, either before or after it has been uploaded to YouTube.

But unless it can be clearly demonstrated that there is a high level of originality and creativity applied to mainstream media content, thereby making available the fair-use argument (at least in the United States), the ordinary uploading of favorite clips or music videos to public networks seems indefensible. The fair-use argument is often based on either an assessment of originality and transformation in the work itself or of explicitly civic and educational purposes for its use. So an unintended consequence of moves against the corporate lockdown of YouTube, by or on behalf of copyright owners, is that critiques of copyright end up fetishizing forms of user-created content with a strong authorial or creative orientation—like fanvids, political parody, and anime music videos—implying that the value of user-created content is measured by the extent of its creativity.[31] Indeed the assumptions underlying the Viacom suit are that nontransformative uses of copyrighted material simply constitute illegal file sharing—mere piracy.

I would argue instead that it is important to understand the uploading of clips and quotes from television or music videos as an ordinary audience practice which, because of its new visibility (via publication to the YouTube network), produces new forms of social and cultural value that cannot simply be attributed back to the original producer. Disassociating the ordinary practices that result in user-created content from logics of production altogether takes us into different territory. Centering the discussion on how ordinary people use online media platforms and media content—whatever its original source—to connect with one another invites us to reframe the politics of participatory culture around issues of access, representation, participation, and citizenship rather than the more industry-oriented issues of authorship, intellectual property, and labor.

YOUTUBE, CULTURAL CITIZENSHIP, AND PUBLIC VALUE

An orientation toward use rather than production asks us to see the uploading, commenting, redistribution, and repurposing of online video as constituting the communicative practices of cultural citizenship, following the work of Joke Hermes, who suggests notions of citizenship "can also be used in relation to less formal everyday practices of identity construction, representation, and ideology, and implicit moral obligations and rights." For Hermes, cultural citizenship is defined as "the process of bonding and community building, and reflection on that bonding, that is implied in partaking of the text-related practices of reading, consuming, celebrating, and criticizing offered in the realm of (popular) culture."[32] Popular cultural texts and practices, she writes, are important because "they provide much of the wool from which the social tapestry is knit," and elsewhere Hermes argues that Internet communication, because it increases the visibility of what would formerly have been considered to be private or hidden practices of cultural citizenship, opens up space for researchers to develop revived models of the relationships between popular culture and publics[33]—an argument mirrored in William Uricchio's work on participation in peer-to-peer networks.[34] This model of cultural citizenship could just as easily apply to the creation, showcasing, and discussion of video content in YouTube, and particularly in relation to the mundane forms of contribution embedded in everyday life and existing media consumption discussed above.

If we look for everyday cultural citizenship rather than for spectacular creativity, we can see many examples even in the sample of most popular videos, most obviously in the huge number of videoblog entries that articulate personal experience to matters of shared public concern. Drawing on her ethnographic interviews with (mainly women) videobloggers, Patricia Lange argues that "public access to intimate moments and the discourse surrounding the video artifacts on the Web allow social boundaries and pre-existing assumptions to be questioned and refashioned," therefore converting the interpersonal and intimate identity work of everyday life to articulate to more public debates around social identities, ethics, and cultural politics. In these quiet moments Lange sees hope for an enrichment of public discourse: "By being vulnerable and sharing intimate moments and choices, it is possible to promote increased public discourse about formerly uncomfortable, distasteful, or difficult topics in ways that other media and other methods have not."[35]

The sharing of short television clips and quotes, identified in the sample of traditional media content in our study, also constitutes a mode of participation in the kinds of publics Lange identifies. Such practices illustrate what Hartley calls "redaction"[36]—practices of editing and republishing through which individual consumer-citizens engage with the world as members of particular communities. Sporting moments, like soccer goals, provide particularly vibrant examples. While at first glance these clips might represent a fannish relationship to a particular sport or sporting team, the discussions that take place in the comments sections of these videos frequently spill over into discussions of other matters of shared concern, most obviously nationality. So too the uploading of Filipino or Turkish soap opera episodes for the enjoyment of audiences located in various countries can be seen as acts of cultural citizenship akin to the media-sharing practices of diasporic communities identified by Cunningham and Sinclair.[37] The collective activities of amateur and pro-am archivists and curators also produce significant public value out of YouTube's basic affordances, supporting what is for many people the primary use of YouTube: to seek out vintage music videos, children's television shows, advertisements, and even weather forecasts[38]—the kinds of television that are least likely to be collected and canonized by the commercial television industry itself but that are most representative of the affective relationships audiences have with television as everyday experience.

YouTube is generating public and civic value as an unintended and often unsupported consequence of the collective practices of its users. But it is questionable to what extent the unintentionally produced cultural, civic, and social value of YouTube is truly being valued or safeguarded, especially by the company itself. Of course, even though YouTube is experienced as a public space, it isn't really public at all, but a private enterprise generating public value as a side effect of the active participation of consumer-citizens. YouTube highlights the ascendancy in digital culture of market-led platforms that enable civic participation and engagement to flourish while at the same time deriving (or attempting to derive) commercial value from them.

The political questions that arise from this reality can too easily be sidelined into neo-Marxist debates around "free labor"—an argument that if value is being created, then someone's labor must be being exploited.[39] There are important political problems with the corporatization of amateur and audience media use, but they look different with cultural participation, rather than exploitation, in the frame. For example, copyright—widely considered to be a barrier to creativity—looks different when we think of YouTube as a shared cultural resource and a popular archive than it does when we think of it as a platform for individual creativity or political commentary (although it is that too, of course). The need to answer to advertisers and a large number of national governments likewise is beginning to influence the extent to which YouTube is available as a truly shared resource to citizens of different countries, as localized filtering measures are introduced and at least appear to be being used to block content according to licensing restrictions.

Despite these constraints, if YouTube remains in existence for long enough, the result will be not only a repository of vintage television content, but also something even more significant: a record of contemporary global popular culture (including vernacular and everyday culture) in video form, produced and evaluated according to the logics of cultural value that emerge from the collective choices of the distributed YouTube user community.[40] Indeed, YouTube is arguably a more effective vehicle for the popular memorialization of television than are either broadcasters or cultural institutions because these latter institutions tend to memorialize television-as-industry and not television-as-experience.[41]

Cultural institutions (including public service broadcasters) are actively considering how such developments will impact on their own missions and practices,[42] but less consideration is usually given to the implications of commercial spaces taking on some of the work of cultural institutions without being tied to the same public and state-based responsibilities. Archivist Rick Prelinger argues that those who have provided the infrastructure that has unexpectedly produced these accidental archives, as in the case of YouTube, are mostly "blithely unconcerned by [the] questions of persistence, ownership, standards, sustainability, or accountability" that occupy professional archivists and their parent institutions.[43] Because YouTube offers its service based on commercial interests rather than public ones, there is no obligation to store these data beyond the commercial viability of the company that provides the storage service. Nor is there any straightforward way cultural institutions can re-archive material that shows up on YouTube because of legal barriers such as copyright law and YouTube's terms of use.

These questions of public value and the archive highlight some of the cultural implications of YouTube and its difference from broadcast media like television. While YouTube is in the reach business, with an economic model fundamentally based on delivering attention to advertisers, unlike television networks, YouTube does not program, collect, or (other than minimally) curate content; it provides a flat and accessible platform for an extremely wide range of contributors and interferes with their activities only to the extent that intervention is perceived as necessary in order to stay on the right side of the law. At the same time, this underdetermination can also be understood as underregulation—which is what gets the company so regularly into trouble with both big media competitors and censorious national governments. Because of its openness and underdetermination, YouTube is producing significant public value as an accidental cultural archive, and yet the questions of how or whether this enormous repository of cultural memory should be preserved and shared have yet to be properly asked, let alone answered. In this regard YouTube is of course very far removed from television broadcasting, particularly public service broadcasting, where these issues of archives and access have been a priority area of digital policy for quite some time.[44]

This chapter departed from the dominant discourses of individual consumers becoming producers to consider user-created content as a medium of everyday cultural practice, including the practices of audiencehood and cultural citizenship. To make sense of a site like YouTube, a media industry framework that considers user-created content as cultural production or distribution is most unhelpful; considering the range of practices engaged in by YouTube users (uploading, viewing, commenting, rating, favoriting, emulating, and copying) as a continuum of cultural participation situated in everyday life is more productive.

As Buckingham et al. argue in relation to the historical emergence of amateur filmmaking, while revolutionary rhetoric and a focus on the spectacular are long habituated frames for thinking about the diffusion of media technologies into the broader public, the realities of use are far more mundane and embedded within existing practices of media consumption and use.[45] The everyday practices of YouTube's participants and audiences—viewing, sharing, or commenting on both user-created and commercial content—are not always obviously producerly or creative, and in their ordinariness they mirror the cultural and social practices of television audiences. A key difference is that these previously invisible audience practices leave material traces on the YouTube network, and this evidence of an attentive audience is essential to demonstrating the value of YouTube to advertisers.

Still persistent is the idea that it is the freedom to turn from passive consumer to active producer (or even "produser") that defines the democratizing qualities of digital media technologies. Participation is defined as production; the everyday cultural practices of audiencehood are discounted as not only passive but also a thing of the past, epitomized by an understanding of television as old media. Lurking beneath the celebration of the creative consumer is the unreconstructed vision of the passive spectator for broadcast television, willfully marooned in a "suburban wasteland."[46] It is a sad reminder of how little impact cultural studies' work on the television audience has had on either the high-popular divide (and the gender stereotypes that go with it) or the media effects paradigm—both of which traditions underpin the "media panics" around the mass amateurization of video production in YouTube.[47] But it is this view of the consumption of popular culture as passive that cultural studies has been arguing against since the 1980s, and it is in this area that cultural studies has the most insights to offer to mainstream debates. Furthermore, because of the new visibility of television use afforded by the publicness of user-created content communities like YouTube, we have a renewed opportunity to develop an evidence-based model of audience practices, informed by the insights into the experiences and uses of television in everyday life that have been built up through ethnographic work over the past several decades.

In 2004, before the explosion of user-created content most visibly represented in YouTube, Sonia Livingstone raised the question of what implications the Internet might have for audience theory and audience research.[48] Several years later, the question of how audience practice figures as a constitutive element of the continuum of cultural participation that produces the content and value of Web 2.0 is still not well understood. If we are to make meaningful interventions into contemporary attempts to account for the significance and implications of participatory culture, then perhaps the proper next step for media, television, and cultural studies is to return to the core idea that audiencehood must be understood as a set of cultural and social practices made newly visible and public via the Web. While much popular and scholarly discourse imagines casual viewing of content as the lowest level of engagement, with creation as the highest level, perhaps it is time we took more seriously once again the question of the audience—asking what is involved in being an audience for user-created and user-distributed content, in media ecologies that also include television content, as in YouTube. This is especially important if user-created content has social value beyond the individualistic pleasures of production or self-expression and if its remediation as part of the networked cultural public sphere does indeed open up spaces for the practice of cultural citizenship.

NOTES

1. OECD, "Participative Web: User-Created Content," *Working Party on the Information Economy*, 2007; available at http://www.oecd.org/dataoecd/57/14/38393115 .pdf.

2. Department of Culture, Media and Sport, *White Paper—A Public Service for All: The BBC in the Digital Age* (London: HMSO, 2006); see also Niki Strange's chapter in this volume.

3. Lev Grossman, "*Time*'s Person of the Year: You," *Time*, 2006; Andrew Keen, *The Cult of the Amateur: How Today's Internet Is Killing Our Culture* (New York: Random House, 2007).

4. Clay Shirky, "Gin, Television and Cognitive Surplus: A Talk by Clay Shirky," *Edge: The Third Culture*; http://www.edge.org/3rd_culture/shirky08/shirky08_ index.html.

5. Steve Woolgar, "Five Rules of Virtuality," in *Virtual Society? Technology, Cyberbole, Reality*, ed. Steve Woolgar (Oxford: Oxford University Press, 2002), 1.

6. Amanda Lenhart and Susannah Fox, "Bloggers: A Portrait of the Internet's New Storytellers," *Pew Internet and American Life Project*; http://www.pew internet.org/PPF/r/186/report_display.asp.

7. Woolgar, "Five Rules of Virtuality," 1.

8. Yochai Benkler, *The Wealth of Networks: How Social Production Transforms Markets and Freedom* (New Haven, Conn.: Yale University Press, 2006), 296.

9. Ibid., 299–300.

10. William Gibson, "God's Little Toys," *Wired*, 2005.

11. Tim O'Reilly, "What Is Web 2.0? Design Patterns and Business Models for the Next Generation of Software," *O'Reilly Network*, 2005.

12. Axel Bruns, *Blogs, Wikipedia, Second Life, and Beyond: From Production to Produsage* (New York: Peter Lang, 2008). The succinct definition of the term quoted here is provided at http://produsage.org/produsage.

13. Jean Burgess, "Hearing Ordinary Voices: Cultural Studies, Vernacular Creativity and Digital Storytelling," *Continuum: Journal of Media and Cultural Studies* 2, no. 20 (2006): 201–14.

14. Ien Ang, *Living Room Wars: Rethinking Media Audiences for a Postmodern World* (London, New York: Routledge, 1996).

15. Henry Jenkins, *Textual Poachers: Television Fans and Participatory Culture* (New York: Routledge, 1992).

16. Henry Jenkins, *Convergence Culture: Where Old and New Media Collide* (Cambridge, Mass.: MIT Press, 2006); Henry Jenkins, *Fans, Bloggers and Gamers: Exploring Participatory Culture* (New York: New York University Press, 2006).

17. For further discussion of this issue, see Nick Couldry, *Inside Culture: Re-Imagining the Method of Cultural Studies* (London: Sage, 2000), 58–60.

18. The study was a collaboration between the ARC Centre of Excellence for Creative Industries and Innovation, Queensland University of Technology, and the Comparative Media Studies Program and Convergence Culture Consortium, MIT, and appears as Jean Burgess and Joshua Green, *YouTube: Online Video and Participatory Culture* (Cambridge: Polity Press, 2009).

19. The 4,320 videos were gathered by sampling from six days across two weeks in each of three months of 2007 (August, October, and November).

20. Henry Jenkins, "YouTube and the Vaudeville Aesthetic," *Confessions of an Aca/Fan*, November 26, 2006; http://www.henryjenkins.org.

21. Available at http://www.youtube.com/watch?v=-_cs01god48.

22. Quoted in Janet Kornblum, "Now Playing on YouTube," *USA Today*, July 17, 2006; http://www.usatoday.com.

23. Moira Bovill and Sonia Livingstone, "Bedroom Culture and the Privatization of Media Use," in *Children and Their Changing Media Environment: A European Comparative Study*, Lea's Communication Series (Mahwah, N.J.: Lawrence Erlbaum, 2001).

24. It is interesting to note that the list of "related videos" for the "Hey" clip, which is generated automatically based on user-assigned tags and keywords, features a large number of sexy performances-to-camera, including "booty dances," articulating the trademark YouTube raunch aesthetic to the basic formal "rules" of the lip-synch or dance video.

25. Available at http://www.youtube.com/watch?v=QjA5fazF1A8.

26. After several impostors came forward, Lim was revealed to be the "real" performer in the "Guitar" video in a *New York Times* article: Virginia Heffernand,

"Web Guitar Wizard Revealed at Last," *New York Times*, August 27, 2006; available at http://www.nytimes.com.

27. Available at http://www.youtube.com/watch?v=6xvd_620ec8.

28. Available at http://youtube-impeto.blogspot.com.

29. Viacom's amended complaint can be found here: http://beckermanlegal.com/Documents/viacom_youtube_080418AmendedComplaint.pdf; YouTube's reply is available here: http://beckermanlegal.com/Documents/viacom_youtube_080523AnswertoAmendedComplaint.pdf.

30. Matthew Karnitschnig, "New Viacom Deal Takes Swipe at YouTube," *Wall Street Journal*, 2007; accessed via Factiva database.

31. Pat Aufderheide and Peter Jaszi, "Recut, Reframe, Recycle: Quoting Copyrighted Material in User-Generated Video," *Center for Social Media*; http://www.centerforsocialmedia.org.

32. Joke Hermes, *Re-Reading Popular Culture* (Malden, Mass.: Blackwell, 2005), 10.

33. Joke Hermes, "Hidden Debates: Rethinking the Relationship between Popular Culture and the Public Sphere," *Javnost–The Public* 13, no. 4 (2006): 27–44.

34. William Uricchio, "Cultural Citizenship in the Age of P2P Networks," in *European Culture and the Media*, ed. Ib Bondebjerg and Peter Golding, 139–64 (Bristol: Intellect Books, 2004).

35. Patricia G. Lange, "The Vulnerable Video Blogger: Promoting Social Change through Intimacy," *Scholar and Feminist Online* 5, no. 2 (2007): n.p.

36. John Hartley, *Television Truths: Forms of Knowledge in Popular Culture* (Oxford: Blackwell, 2008).

37. Stuart Cunningham and John Sinclair, eds. *Floating Lives: The Media and Asian Diasporas* (Lanham, Md.: Rowman and Littlefield, 2001).

38. "Television Worth Talking About," *Toronto Star*, December 1, 2008; http://www.thestar.com/entertainment/Television/article/546230; Joanne Ostrow, "Vintage TV Finds Niche on the Net," *Denver Post*, May 6, 2007; http://www.denverpost.com/ci_5812946.

39. See, for example, Julian Kucklich, "Precarious Playbour: Modders and the Digital Games Industry," *Fibreculture* 5 (2005): n.p.

40. Lucas Hilderbrand, "Youtube: Where Cultural Memory and Copyright Converge," *Film Quarterly* 61, no. 1 (2007): 48–57.

41. John Hartley, Jean Burgess, and Joshua Green, "'Laughs and Legends,' or the Furniture That Glows? Television as History," *Australian Cultural History* 26 (2007): 15–36.

42. Karen F. Gracy, "Moving Image Preservation and Cultural Capital," *Library Trends* 56, no. 1 (2007): 183–98.

43. Rick Prelinger, "Archives and Access in the 21st Century," *Cinema Journal* 46, no. 3 (2007): 114–18.

44. As in, for example, the extended and as yet undelivered project of the BBC

to make its entire archive publicly available for viewing and even reuse. See James Bennett, "Interfacing the Nation: Remediating Public Service Broadcasting in the Digital Television Age," *Convergence* 14, no. 3 (2007): 290.

45. David Buckingham et al., "'Take Back the Tube!': The Discursive Construction of Amateur Film and Video Making," *Journal of Media Practice* 8, no. 2 (2007): 183–201.

46. Ang, *Living Room Wars*, 6.

47. Kirsten Drotner, "Dangerous Media? Panic Discourses and Dilemmas of Modernity," *Paedagogica Historica* 35, no. 3 (1999): 593–619.

48. Sonia Livingstone, "The Challenge of Changing Audiences: Or, What Is the Audience Researcher to Do in the Age of the Internet?" *European Journal of Communication* 19, no. 1 (2004): 75–86.

ARCHITECTURES OF PARTICIPATION

Fame, Television, and Web 2.0

Get Internet Famous! (Even if You're Nobody)
Wired cover story, August 2006

Aww Dude, I just threw up on your couch.
Kevin Rose to Alex Albrecht, *DiggNation*, episode 62

How This Kid Made $60 Million in 18 Months
Business Week cover story on Kevin Rose, August 14, 2006

At first glance, the "Internet television" show *DiggNation* appears to be two computer geeks, sitting on a couch, drinking beer, and reviewing the "hottest user submitted stories on the social news website digg.com" with an aesthetic sensibility reminiscent of *Beavis and Butthead*, Baddiel and Skinner, or Wayne's World circa its *Saturday Night Live* incarnation. By late 2008 the show had been running for three years and nearly two hundred episodes. An exchange between its hosts, Kevin Rose and Alex Albrecht, during episode 116 is certainly exemplary, if not necessarily typical. Reviewing a story about a weatherman "caught out" by pretending to fondle a pair of CGI female breasts mocked up to illustrate a breast cancer awareness week story, Rose and Albrecht giggle and snort: "Honk, honk, honk; tuning in the radio dials; this guy is fucking . . . awesome; I feel bad for this guy. . . . He might get fired for this. He had to issue a formal apology. . . . People need to lighten up; let me tell you something as working in TV. . . . When some-one puts up a CG of a gigantic, four-foot titty next to your head . . . are you not going to turn to the left and suck on it?"

Despite the hosts' lack of gender sensibilities, Rose and Albrecht have become what *The Guardian* in the United Kingdom and *The Los Angeles Times*, *The New York Times*, and other mainstream U.S. media have termed the Web's first "native" celebrities: "the most widely known web stars," largely coalescing as a "stable of Web personalities" at Revision3's Internet television studios, with Rose proclaimed as "the most famous man on the Internet," according to the technology and business magazine *Inc.*[1] While many people may not have heard of Rose or Albrecht, their digital celebrity stocks have risen considerably since the show's inception in 2005, with their fame, and Rose's in particular, a complex interplay among Internet TV, participatory culture, fame, and entrepre-neurship that the above exchange belies. Each episode of *DiggNation* achieves around 250,000 downloads, while on the micro-blogging, social-networking tool Twitter Kevin Rose has one of the largest num-ber of followers since the site launched; indeed, despite Barack Obama's election campaign creating a Twitter presence in April 2007, it wasn't until August 2008 that Obama overtook Rose at top spot on the site.[2] In late 2008, *Business Week* named Rose as one of the twenty-five most influential people on the Web—a list dominated by media moguls such as Rupert Murdoch, Jerry Yang, and Steve Jobs; venture capitalists; entrepreneurs; and (slightly more inexplicably) Jon Stewart of *The Daily Show*.[3] Rose's celebrity is not limited to the United States, with a loyal fan base having developed globally, particularly in Europe, where *The Guard-ian* described the filming of a live episode of *DiggNation* in London at the start of 2008 as "mayhem," with "more than 1,000 baying teenagers . . . yelling and laughing—it's part rock concert, part pantomime," includ-ing audience members who had flown in from Paris and Moscow for the show.[4] More aptly, noting the gendered makeup of *DiggNation*'s fans and the user community from within which they emerge, later that year the U.K.-based blog *Digital-Lifestyles* compared the reception for another live London recording of *DiggNation* as "like a boy band had arrived with mass hysteria ensuing, but it was mostly the boys in the audience that were getting excited."[5]

DiggNation is but one platform upon which Rose and Albrecht's fame is built, with Kevin Rose's emerging celebrity status in particular having as much to do with his role in online participatory culture as it is to do with fronting an online TV show. Having previously held guest and small host spots on the San Francisco local cable channel TechTV, Rose set up digg.com in December 2004, before immediately launching Internet TV studio Revision3 at the start of 2005. Following a string of unsuccessful podcasts hosted by Rose, *DiggNation* commenced in July of that year as a podcast reviewing news stories submitted to digg .com. By September 2006 it had been established as the marquee show for the studio's relaunch following the successful attraction of venture capital financing, with the success of digg and Revision3's link to the site playing no small part in the deal, as we shall see below.[6] Digg.com itself, started in Kevin Rose's bedroom with $1,000, is firmly rooted in the participatory cultural forms of Web 2.0 media, cited approvingly by Axel Bruns in his study of "produsage" and forming part of a string of social bookmarking tools, such as del.icio.us and reddit.com, which emerged in the mid-2000s (see figure 1). Digg's relationship to a changing understanding of the audience's role in media economies is perhaps best summed up by *The New York Times*, which described digg.com as the "news site with the nerve to substitute the votes of the unwashed, unpaid masses for the refined talent of professional editors," as it reported the site had now amassed $40 million of funding on the strength of its 30 million users visiting the site each month, despite the site remaining unprofitable.[7]

Digg essentially allows users to determine the shape and priorities with which news is delivered: readers "digg" a story read elsewhere on the Web—from traditional news outlets to blogs, with major news outlets from the BBC to the *Wall Street Journal* now featuring "digg" buttons—which provides other digg users a link to that story. Digg users then decide on the story's worth, either by linking to it themselves or rating the story from the digg site using the simple thumbs up or down motif familiar from TiVo. The front page of digg.com is therefore made up of the "most dug" stories—with options to view most recent top stories in any category, together with those receiving the most diggs in the previous twenty-four hours, seven days, month, or year. As Rose explained on the first podcast of *DiggNation*, espousing the user-led democratic philosophy of participatory culture, digg is a "user contributed [site] . . . but rather than an editor choose what stories go on the homepage, the users do." While it is the success of digg.com that has un-

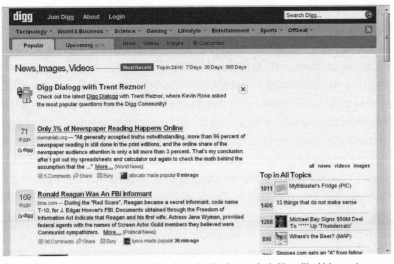

Figure 1. Digg.com allows its user community to determine the shape and priorities with which news is delivered, so stories about Kevin Rose's fame might appear on the site's "front page" provided enough users "digg" it. (Screen capture from digg.com.)

doubtedly been a major driver of Rose's fame, it is equally important to note that it is Rose's attempts to break into the public eye and move from ordinary user to both entrepreneur and celebrity that differentiate him from other Internet entrepreneurs. Indeed, his fame has become increasingly mainstream, as NBC talk show host Jimmy Fallon appeared on the podcast in January 2009 and returned the favor by inviting Rose and Albrecht onto *Late Night with Jimmy Fallon* in early March. It is the symbiosis of this movement—from user to celebrity and Internet entrepreneur—that makes Rose particularly interesting in terms of understanding the production of audiences in the digital TV landscape.

A range of cultural, media, and television studies scholars have noted the increasing trend of the media industries, particularly television, to conceive of audiences as Graeme Turner has described them: "Rather than being merely the end-user of celebrity, they can produce it themselves."[8] One of the key debates within this area has been the degree to which this "ordinarization" of celebrity—via its extension to an increasingly diverse array of people, or "DIY celebrities"—might be understood as a democratization of fame.[9] This chapter engages with this debate by exploring television's production of fame and its relationship to Web 2.0 social-networking developments, examining the changing position of the audience around the specific locus of celebrity. In particular, I examine how this role of celebrity functions in relationship to another supposedly democratizing force, the participatory culture of Web 2.0 social networks. I do so via an examination of the Internet television show *DiggNation* and, more specifically, its star and founder, Kevin Rose, as the "architect of participation" on the social news networking site digg.com. In so doing, I hope to suggest that focusing on the parallels and continuities between television and Web 2.0 fame enables us to understand some of the limitations and productivities of the audience's changing position, especially as television moves online and, in so doing, shapes some aspects of the Internet as it becomes a mass medium.

Clay Shirky's book *Here Comes Everybody* hints at the disruptive potential of fame for digital media's capacity for what he and others understand as the collaborative power of the Web. Shirky provides an interesting, if inconsistent, line of argument regarding the way the Web facilitates community and interactivity, surmising that amateur production (a consequence of widespread computer ownership) "means that the category of 'consumer' is now a temporary behavior rather than a permanent identity" as earnestly as he asserts that the "Web makes interactivity technologically possible, but what technology giveth, social factors taketh away."[10] Nevertheless, this shifting perspective does enable Shirky to question the binaries that position the Web as inherently interactive (and therefore good) and television as passive (and therefore bad). Shirky therefore recognizes that as blogging has become increasingly popular, it has also diminished in interactive value. This is not only because the blogosphere can become what Graham Murdock and Peter Dahlgren describe as a "cacophony of voices" in their critique of the political, democratic potential of blogs,[11] but also because, as Shirky puts it, "fame happens." As a particular blog's popularity increases, "no matter how assiduously someone wants to interact with their readers, the growing audience will ultimately defeat that possibility. . . . [The blogger has] to start choosing who to respond to and who to ignore, and over time, ignore becomes the default choice. They have, in a word, become famous." Far from the radical, democratizing potential of DIY celebrity or citizenship that John Hartley reads into such interactive technologies, Shirky reminds us that as the Internet or blogosphere becomes a mass medium this "is what 'interactivity' looks like . . . no interactivity at all with almost all the audience." For Shirky, the system that results starts to look suspiciously like TV, where "'interactive TV' is an oxymoron," reduced to voting in talent shows.[12] The closing down of interactivity via fame in turn challenges some of the understandings of community and the collaborative nature of "participatory culture." Moreover, as media scholars have been long aware, the result of fame is the creation of uneven power relations—between industry and star, as well as star and audience.[13] In this regard, my argument acts as a rejoinder to Mark Andrejevic's work regarding the way in which the promise of "the interactive economy to democratize production" has resulted neither in a more democratic public sphere nor the reduction of publicity to spectacle, but in a democratization of celebrity that has "disturbing implications for the democratic potential of the internet's interactive capability."[14] However, away from the lens of reality TV that Andrejevic discusses—although no less reliant on the technologies of surveillance he details—there are important distinctions to be made for the role and activity of the audience as well as the formation of "ordinary celebrity."

It is worth briefly making a note here about the framing of this chapter in terms of the changing position of the audience. As the above brief description of Rose sets out, Rose has moved from ordinary audience member (or community user) to become extraordinary in the terms set out within not only studies of stardom but also those of fans and participatory culture, which note the heightened activity of fan practices compared to most audiences. Moreover, as both a Web star and a member of the particular kinds of participatory culture I discuss below, Rose belongs—even begins to lead—what might be thought of as an extraordinary group of users: early adopters who have been termed the technocrati of the digital economy. In this sense, this study engages with what Jean Burgess rightly criticizes as a tendency within work on digital media to concentrate on the spectacular end of participatory culture.[15] However, in important ways Rose is depicted as ordinary—most markedly, he is continually aligned with the community of users on digg.com and the viewers of *DiggNation*, and he is positioned as merely their mouthpiece on the spin-off show *Digg Dialogg* (where Rose plays talk show host to celebrities and politicians, asking questions submitted and voted for by digg users). Moreover, his rise to a position of celebrity corresponds with the extension of fame to an increasingly diverse, heterogeneous, ordinary, and (some would argue) democratic populace; thus while reality TV contestants who have become famous have been discussed in terms of ordinariness and their previous status as audience, I discuss Rose in terms of a large and ordinary audience group—self-proclaimed Internet geeks—to whom this extension of fame might also apply. My positioning of this chapter in terms of the audience therefore seeks to engage in the way television—in this instance in the form of online TV—increasingly invites the audience in. Similarly to Su Holmes's work in this area, I want to suggest that the text itself is an important site for understanding these shifts; it increasingly articulates "a self-conscious relay between the positions of 'performing' and 'viewing,'" whereby the blurring of these roles becomes increasingly "central to ideas about a restaging of participation," itself "fundamentally enmeshed with the discursive construction of selfhood."[16]

IT'S NOT CELEBRITY. IT'S INTERNET CELEBRITY: ORDINARY USERS, PERSONALITY, AND PERFORMANCE

In this section I set out Rose's position as a member of the community, drawing on key understandings of performance, ordinariness, and authenticity from television and celebrity studies. I shall concentrate on the podcast *DiggNation* and its status as a text of both television and participatory culture. As a podcast released by Internet television studio Revision3, *DiggNation* clearly calls our attention to its status as "like TV": performance tropes of direct address, intimacy, and authenticity and technologies of simple front-lighting, autocues (in the form of laptops), and title sequences. As a text of participatory culture, it draws our attention to its membership of an online community and fandom: the first episode opened without a title sequence, but rather a clip from *The Family Guy* that affirmed the show's and its creators' interest in shared fan culture;[17] moreover, despite the moniker "Internet television," production values are very low, with *The New York Times* describing Revision3's programming aesthetic as "a hybrid of the polished shows created for the networks and the amateur videos that populate sites like YouTube."[18] The stress on the ordinariness of the show and its hosts—as part of what Burgess discusses as the vernacular creativity of ordinary, everyday user-generated content production[19]—is made apparent in subsequent publicity's attempts to explain the success of the show; as Albrecht makes clear, "We just did it for ourselves. The fact that people actually watched it shocked us—it's blown up beyond all recognition. Really, it's the Wild West," while Rose claims that he and Albrecht are simply doing what a "lot of geeks do . . . but don't' have a camera."[20]

FIGURE 2 The aesthetic of *DiggNation* emphasizes the authenticity of its presenters through what Henry Jenkins describes as a "vaudeville aesthetic" apparent in many user-generated videos. (Screen capture from Revision3.com.)

Of course, the success of the show—together with Rose's related rise as Internet entrepreneur—has lifted both Rose and Albrecht out of the ordinary practices of user communities and positioned them as celebrities. Studies of the increasing openness of the realm of celebrity to ordinary people have tended to focus on reality television, such as *Big Brother*, which allows audiences—as contestants and viewers—to participate in the construction of fame. As Nick Couldry has usefully demonstrated, such programming works as a form of ritual that effectively marks the boundaries between the ordinary and media worlds, with the contestants' ordinariness working at a double level, both confirming the reality of the program and signifying the "status from which the contestants compete to escape into another ritually distinct category, celebrity."[21] It is largely within the context of this apparent openness of celebrity depicted by such reality television shows, and increasingly the Web itself, that arguments regarding the democratization of fame have been waged. Graeme Turner's discussion of the "demotic turn" has perhaps best theorized the problematic of how truly democratizing the turn to ordinary or DIY celebrities is, suggesting that rather than a democratic turn, such developments are demotic, generating "the performance of endless and unmotivated diversity for its own sake," which is mined and harvested by the "major corporate structures of the traditional media conglomerates."[22] In a subsequent elaboration, Turner alternatively suggests that the demotic might otherwise prove so unruly and anarchic in the diversity generated as to be "capable of instigating but not easily organizing or managing social and cultural change."[23] I will return to these questions in my conclusion; for now I want to concentrate on the way in which it is the revelation of the real or authentic self that has been a privileged site of discourse.

Annette Hill's oft-quoted study of *Big Brother* audiences suggests that viewers look for the moments of truth that might be glimpsed through the improvised performance of *Big Brother* contestants as a key site of pleasure and evaluation of the text, particularly the contestants' relative merits to fame.[24] Hill's study points to the importance of surveillance as the key aesthetic trope in reality TV and its construction of celebrity. Both Couldry and Andrejevic have suggested how this process of surveillance has been extended beyond the confines of the *Big Brother* house, to seem natural when people are filmed for programs without their knowledge or as part of the value-generating labor exchange that underpins e-commerce's targeted marketing (such as Amazon's "customers who bought this item also bought . . ." referral feature).[25] However, both of their arguments ultimately return to reality television in order to assess how contestants' exposure to surveillance works as a form of validating and exposing the "real" self: "Being 'real' is proof of honesty, and the persistent gaze of the camera provides one way of guaranteeing that realness.'"[26] This return to reality TV makes their inquiries a question of evaluating the ordinary person's (willing) submission to surveillance, controlled by existing media conglomerates, and the construction of celebrity that results from displaying the real, authentic self. However, in the case of Rose, his role on Internet television is not one of contestant but host, and his submission to surveillance is away from television. Surveillance takes the form of exposure to, and control of, Web 2.0 platforms that track his every move: from Twittering his current activities—"having a glass of wine with @kurtsmom"—to blog entries, updating his MySpace profile, documenting his life on Flickr, and sharing his bookmarking, music, and news interests via LASTFM, del.ic.ious, and, of course, digg .com. And this relationship of control, as TV host and of self-surveillance, leads us in different directions in evaluating the relationship of fame and ordinariness—in terms of television, its audiences, and online communities.

Ordinariness in terms of Rose's television appearances therefore functions differently from that constructed around contestants on reality TV. As host of *DiggNation*, Rose occupies a role more akin to that of television presenter, although this is carefully balanced with the program's claims to be part of the wider UGC ephemera that circulate among its audience of Internet geeks. As Jim Louderback (chief executive of Revision3) suggests, the Web has increased the sense of proximity and friendship between personality and audience: "In the U.S., we [once] had television icons; people you put on a pedestal; gods. I once met Walter Cronkite and it was like meeting the president. When cable came out, it was much more down to earth—MTV VJs who you could go and hang out with in a bar. But still you felt that they'd be the ones doing all the talking. . . . [On the Web] the hosts come out of those communities and they're just like them."[27]

As Sean Redmond notes, "Being ordinary, authentic or 'real'" in this sense is a "dominant rhetorical device of fame [referenced by] . . . the onscreen and online antics of extraordinary and ordinary people supposedly *just* being themselves."[28] As I have suggested elsewhere, such notions of ordinariness have not only informed understandings of television personalities' contradistinction from film stars' extraordinariness but can also be unpicked to understand performance, authenticity, and ideology.[29] We can therefore usefully analyze how ordinariness is constructed via televisual skill in Rose's performance on *DiggNation*, particularly in terms of how this intersects with other dominant aesthetic and performance paradigms on the Web.

Just as Susan Murray details the relationship between vaudeville and the performance modes of early television, Henry Jenkins has suggested that useful parallels can be drawn between certain elements of vaudevillian performance tropes and those exhibited in what might be thought of as the early performance modes of amateur video on YouTube.[30] One of the tropes on which Jenkins focuses is the interrupted act, whereby a performer "courts a sense of the amateurish which also places a high emphasis on spontaneity—many videos are carefully staged so as to look unrehearsed. There is not necessarily a push towards liveness, but there is a push towards 'realness.'"[31]

In terms of *DiggNation*, aside from the occasional live specials filmed in front of an audience, any sense of liveness is seemingly removed by the program's status as a podcast, with audiences either downloading the show and transferring it to their iPods or portable media devices or watching on an online, on-demand video player. In *DiggNation* spontaneity is most obviously marked by the retention of the kinds of disruption Jenkins discusses in relation to vaudeville and the continual "corpsing" of Rose and Albrecht—elements that might otherwise be edited out by the prerecorded nature of the show. Karen Lury suggests that corpsing, "whereby people forget lines, giggle or in other ways break the frame of performance . . . manifests itself as the inability to sustain the look of the camera, or the other performer." However, in so doing, these moments of corpsing engender a moment where the performer "reveals him or herself as truly live, uncontrolled and expressive," which confirms the authenticity of their image to the audience.[32] The quote from Rose in the epigraph at the beginning of this chapter is but one relatively high-profile instance of his and Albrecht's regular corpsing that maintains the authenticity of their image. Indeed, for fans of the show this revelation of the authentic and real self continues to be a key source of pleasure in online TV. As one fan of *DiggNation* argued in response to *The Guardian*'s criticism of the show's rather loose format, which often leads to Rose's and Albrecht's digressing into anecdotes as well as verbal and comic cul-de-sacs, "As to the alleged incoherence of Rose's 'performance'—it wasn't incoherent but authentic."[33] Like the community of users from within which they emerge, and in contradistinction to broadcast television's personalities, Rose and Albrecht are not especially televisually skilled; ordinariness is therefore signaled by this apparent lack of a professional performance. Frances Bonner discusses a similar phenomenon, whereby an apparent lack of televisual skill is cultivated as a performance trope by particular TV presenters in order to make the audience feel the presenter is "more like us and less like them—the actual celebrities who do not become clumsy or self-conscious."[34] While there are certainly similarities in the effect on the audience achieved by Rose and Albrecht's performance mode, there is also a lack of control that signals a diminished difference between self and performance—most notably marked by the irregular length of podcasts, which can be between thirty minutes and an hour, depending on the performance of the hosts.

In many ways, therefore, the on-demand nature of the podcast further underscores the relationship of authenticity and intimacy that are the hallmarks of early television.[35] For example, just as the adoption of direct address as a performance mode by television personalities from the music hall and vaudeville served to create an intimate relationship between viewer and personality, so it serves a similar function in *DiggNation*. However, the status of the program as on-demand podcast means that it will often be watched on a handheld media device or laptop; as viewers lean forward into the screen or hold it up close to see the details of stories or expressions, a greater sense of intimacy is therefore created between viewer and host. As Louderback argues, "When you watch TV, you're seven feet away and sitting back. But when you watch on your iPod or your laptop, it's only inches away or you're holding it in your hands. I wonder whether the intimacy of our handheld devices and computers creates more of a sense of intimacy and sharedness and companionship than just sitting back and watching TV."[36]

Intimacy here, therefore, feeds back into authenticating Rose's image as part of the community: a companion for the commuter run. This is further reinforced by what P. David Marshall has noted are the importance and function of style in celebrity culture. He suggests that style can act as both a "statement of difference from as well as a statement of solidarity with the particular audience."[37] Rose's continually dressed down appearance—sneakers, jeans, and T-shirt, particularly those sporting fan boy or geek kudos—affirms his membership of the community of digg users. That this appearance rarely changes across his celebrity image—the one concession to formality in interviewing Al Gore for *Digg Dialogg* was the replacement of his trademark T-shirt with a short-sleeved collared shirt—serves as a marker of the authenticity of his persona, continually appearing "just as he is." Perhaps most central to this affirmation of his status as ordinary Internet geek is *DiggNation*'s focus on technology, with Rose continually depicted with the latest must-have gadget, reviewing technology news, or giving items away as part of the program's sponsorship deals, to which I shall return below. The ordinariness of Rose's geek style extends to the user/community philosophy he espouses, which aligns him more broadly with participatory culture, such as his promoting open-source software, championing the Pirates' Bay's move to "encrypt the Internet," and depicting the move of media conglomerates to release DRM-free mp3s as a "win" for consumers brought about by long-term strategies of avoidance, piracy, and campaigning.[38] Most important, as indicated by calling himself merely an "Internet celebrity," Rose downplays his own celebrity status in a move that both asserts his membership of the ordinary community and confirms his status as celebrity by recalling the star mythology that Holmes details, whereby media coverage of celebrities tends to express "approving attitudes towards celebrities who appear to be fundamentally *unchanged* by wealth and fame."[39]

However, the role of celebrity online is far from clear-cut and is often understood as antithetical to participatory culture and community. For example, Jean Burgess details an exchange between Daniel Meadows, the head of *Capture Wales* (a BBC digital storytelling initiative), and fellow team member Gareth Morlais that similarly emphasizes the importance of ordinariness and authenticity in how online communities might function. Here, Morlais laments the way in which "mainstream" media—such as the broadcast arm of the BBC—utilize celebrity as an a priori technique for validating and widening the appeal of content: "Why isn't there a sort of format that works in the makeover format that's driven not by celebrity but by community members? I would love to see that. Is that naïve?"

As Burgess suggests, Morlais's comment reflects a "certain amount of disillusionment, not just with the priorities of 'Big Media,' but with the extent to which 'ordinary' audiences are interested in the *authentic* stories of their fellow citizens."[40] Kevin Rose's status as star of *DiggNation* works to both confirm and complicate Burgess's suspicions: the authenticity of his membership of the community is central to his appeal (he is an ordinary geek too); however, through his podcasts and adeptness with and exploitation of Web 2.0 platforms—including the establishment of digg.com as a successful social news-sharing platform—Rose has been able to cultivate a celebrity persona and brand value that troubles the authentic, intimate relationship with the audience established here. This point returns me to the issue of surveillance and social networking technologies, which I suggested was the other site of control that distinguishes Rose from the ordinary celebrities created by reality TV and to which I want to turn my focus now.

"WHO IS KEVIN ROSE?": FAME AND ARCHITECTURES OF PARTICIPATION

Asked in the context of celebrity studies, the question of who Kevin Rose is might be used to explore the tension between on- and offscreen self, ordinariness, and authenticity. However, in the context of Rose, this question is somewhat less loaded in terms of understanding his star persona; appearing on the digg.com site as the top comment in relationship to the story on Rose as "the most famous man on the Internet," the question simply referred to Rose's comparative obscurity to the general Internet population—including active users of digg.com. What the question points to, however, is more interesting in terms of understanding Rose's fame and its relationship to participatory culture.

If Andrejevic is correct to argue that the democratizing promise of participatory media offers "publicity as celebrity" as a hybrid combination of what different camps perceive as the net's potential to foster either the "passive evisceration of publicity as spectacle" or "the revitalization of democracy," then what is missing from this equation is the question of both control and achievement. That is, extrapolating from the role of reality television in facilitating participation in media texts, whereby the end result is the celebrification of ordinary people, Andrejevic places the control and power over that new celebrity image as belonging to the existing media industries—with the fame achieved by contestants illusory or fleeting. However, if Rose's success story simply exemplifies Andrejevic's argument that reality TV and digital media mean that it will not just be important public personas, such as presidents, whose private life is the subject of scrutiny but also "the private life of the person on the street—of anyone who trains the webcam on him- or herself,"[41] then this negates the fact that Rose has had to both work to achieve his celebrity—in particular, to master social networking platforms so as to ensure people are watching and listening to him among the "chatter" of the Web—and that he himself has controlled, edited, tagged, and filtered his image.

To deal first with the notion of achievement, I want to return to Shirky's point above that in the cacophony of voices in the blogosphere and self-promotion of the net, "fame happens": some users within a community are able to master the techniques and technologies of self-publicity in order to stand out from all the people who turn the webcam, blog, Twitter, MySpace, and a myriad of other social networking tools on themselves. If these tools and techniques of self-promotion are increasingly ordinary, then one requires a degree of "vernacular skill" to master them to become famous. Wired's proclamation that anyone can get "Internet famous" seemingly corroborates the democratization of fame discourses that Andrejevic's work highlights as a possible outcome of the Net's interactivity; its August 2006 nineteen-page special declares

Julia Allison to be "the latest, and perhaps purest, iteration of the War-holian ideal: someone who is famous for being famous." Allison's rather limited fame is apparently divorced from any talent or achievement, having become well known simply through self-promotion. However, such a description belies the skill of self-promotion that has gone into achieving this celebrity status, with the article going on to not only detail Allison's mastery of a myriad of social networking tools that have made her famous—from endless Twitter updates to publicity stunts aimed at being seen in the right company at the right venue to endless blog and comment posts that at one stage led the media-gossip site Gawker to ban her for "gratuitous self-promotion that makes even the gratuitous self-promoters at Gawker blush"—but also offer tips on "how to promote yourself," "be the hero," or "boost your geek cred." The discourse here affirms the possibility of DIY celebrity, such as that explored by Graeme Turner and Nick Couldry, whereby the ordinary person feels empowered by the potential to make him- or herself famous; as Allison asserts, this "technology gives us direct power over our own brand."[42] The seemingly never-ending line of wannabe celebrities that queue up for talent show auditions or post quirky videos on YouTube or their blogs suggests that this brand needs to be worked at constantly in order to stand out from the crowd. That is, not only is the desire to become famous ordinary, but the tools with which to create celebrity are also increasingly ordinary.

The achievement of fame via the cultivation of a following across Web 2.0 platforms results in a persona that is no less mediated, nor surveilled, than those discussed by critics of reality television. How-ever, here users have greater control over the image presented and con-structed; because this fame resides largely on self-publicity, users can detail their every move or, more important, editorialize to construct a mediated self that is as exciting and interesting as possible. A familiar dichotomy between private and public self therefore continues to per-sist in Web 2.0 fame—as Rose himself admits: "There's two different sides to what we do. When I do *DiggNation*, I'm partying with the fans. It's just us being geeks and going crazy, and when I'm here at work, it's a very different environment. I spend most of my nights going to the rock-climbing gym and drinking tea. And then once a month, I go to a party, and pictures get taken, and it paints a different picture."[43]

However, because the construction of this image is a constant and interactive process—fans of Rose can post, view, or read messages on his blog or MySpace page; know his exact whereabouts via Twitter; or share his taste in music via LASTFM — this self-surveillance promises an intimacy and authenticity that is distinct from television and film. While Rose will by no means, as Shirky suggests, be able to interact with all of his audience, he can, and must, interact with at least some of the audience in order to sustain his profile — the mediated self constructed is a constantly interacting one, inviting audience members to feel part of his community and that at any point they could solicit a response from him or meet him for a beer. Arguably this is a step beyond what Bonner describes as the way in which television presenters constantly make viewers feel "let in" on their relationships and everyday lives; indeed the availability and authenticity of Rose's image seemingly blurs the boundaries between "media" and "ordinary" world.[44] It is important, therefore, that the authentic image maintained across these sites is one that is constantly open: happy to share ideas, thoughts, and criticisms on new technologies, gadgets, games, and, as a successful Internet entrepreneur, happy to be solicited for advice by fans on their potential new ventures.[45] The question regarding the democratic nature of this fame therefore turns not necessarily on Rose's achievement of fame, but how this structures his relationship with fans and the online community at digg.com. And it is here that I want to suggest that we can understand fame as structuring an architecture of participation around *DiggNation* and digg.com.

As the heading to this section suggests, Rose's fame is not pivotal to the success of digg.com, nor the reason that many millions of people use the site. However, his ownership of the site raises important questions about the relationship of celebrity and participatory culture, particularly around what Jenkins terms the "moral economy of information" that emerges with participatory culture — "that is, a sense of mutual obligations and shared expectations about what constitutes good citizenship within a knowledge community." Digg.com, as a social news site, arguably epitomizes such a knowledge community, chiming well with Jenkins's use of Pierre Levy's notion of collective intelligence by providing for a "'deterritorialisation of knowledge,' brought about by the ability of the net and the Web to facilitate rapid many-to-many communication [to] enable broader participation in decision making, new modes of citizenship and community."[46] As suggested above, digg.com allows for the collective shaping of news values and sharing of information. In so doing, it provides for a flow of ideas among users in a space designed to promote comment and exchange. However, while such communal activity might produce collective intelligence that is democratically beneficial, as Bruns's discussion of issues around copyright, reward, authorship, and communal ownership sets out, it also produces a tension: the question of financial reward for collective effort. Bruns draws on Mark Pesce to set out the fundamental problem: "If the host of the community takes the content generated by that community and realizes profit from that content, the creators of that content will immediately be afflicted with a number of conflicting feelings."[47]

The dilemma for Bruns and Pesce is clear: in order to encourage participation, all users within a community must feel valued; while this may not necessarily mean a direct call for status as a "profit participant," it does involve ensuring that no one appears to "cash in on the produsage" of the community.[48] While John Caldwell has demonstrated, contrary to Bruns's optimism, that established media companies have effectively been able to harness the power of crowdsourcing and UGC as a form of mainstream workforce bootstrapping, I want to concentrate here on how this dilemma is negotiated when the host emerges from within that community.[49] What makes this a particularly compelling area for investigation in terms of Kevin Rose as ordinary user, owner of digg.com, and star of *DiggNation* is that all three of these "iterations" of Rose's persona espouse the kind of open-source collective intelligence and fan activity that Bruns, Jenkins, and others perceive as the hallmark of participatory culture. While digg.com users do not actively create content on the digg site, by linking to news stories elsewhere on the Web, their activity can be understood as precisely the kind of value-generating labor that Andrejevic suggests is the hallmark of the online economy's reliance on surveillance.[50] Before we go on to examine his role as host in relation to the user community, it is first worth noting that a necessary corollary to Pesce's and Bruns's question of collective ownership also emerges: it concerns not simply who gets paid and how, but who takes responsibility and liability when the community is found to infringe—in terms such as piracy, privacy, or decency that have framed attempts to regulate the Web; I shall return to this corollary in my conclusion.

Clearly Pesce is referring to the hosting of Web sites, which involves the economic and labor costs of site maintenance, storage, design, and the like; however, the reference to hosting also draws our attention to its other media-related meaning: Rose's role as host of *DiggNation*. Here the differentials among Rose's status as ordinary user, digg.com owner, and celebrity become more apparent. For example, *DiggNation* opens with a series of sponsorship messages that are indicative of a more closed structure than that promoted on digg.com. It is particularly interesting that this shift trades on the authenticity and ordinariness of Rose's persona in a way that recalls the relationship between star and sponsor detailed in Murray's study of early U.S. television stardom. Spontaneity there was aligned with a performance mode that had to "exude an honesty or 'naturalness' that would engender trust in the audience," which was established via the authenticity of persona, in order to successfully pitch products.[51] For Rose, speaking honestly and openly about sponsors' products and reviewing others involves a similar negotiation built on the authenticity of his persona established through Web 2.0 communities but sold back to these audiences through television, marketed under the interactive hyperbole of podcasting, Internet television, and Revision3's positioning of itself as the "first media company that gets it, born from the Internet, on-demand generation . . . [and hosted not] from Hollywood . . . [but] from the same passionate fan base as our audience."[52] This enables Rose to sell and promote a range of products, from videogames and Web-hosting services to beer sponsorship deals and, more impressively, an online version of some episodes with a "clickable interface," whereby anything and everything in view is on sale: from Rose's Mac Powerbook to his sweater (figure 3). I don't want to moralize over what might be perceived as Rose "fleecing" his audience by continually selling it sponsors' products—certainly his tech-savvy audience is one that is not likely to be easily exploited in terms of financial capital or media literacy. However, more problematically, Rose's role as salesman extends to his position as host of digg.com; indeed in episode 1 of *DiggNation* such an exploitation of his authentic image allows Rose to feel able to talk "openly and honestly" about digg.com as if it were somebody else's site entirely.

Business Week's interview with Rose summarizes his philosophy about digg's business model as "community first, ads later," but arguably it is the authenticity of his persona as an ordinary Internet geek that enables Rose to negotiate the facilitation of the community and collective intelligence of digg while simultaneously commercially exploiting it. Describing the experience of attending a live *DiggNation* episode as akin to being in a mosh pit, *The Guardian*'s Zoe Margolis set out the im-

FIGURE 3 The authenticated persona of Kevin Rose as host allows him to act as salesman, speaking "honestly and openly" about products, or simply acting as a clickable interface to consumer products. (Screen capture from videoclix.tv.)

portance of the user community to both digg's success and the celebrity of its hosts: "Digg is not just another tech site. Because they [the users] themselves contribute to it with links and stories that they recommend to others, it's theirs."[53] As the headline quote from the article makes clear, "The Democratic Approach Is a Very Valuable Thing," Rose underscores both the democratic and commercial potential of digg as a Web 2.0 social media site. The value, therefore, of democracy is something sellable—as Rose goes on to set out; for digg this means the site "will serve as a means of gathering metrics for third party websites, providing them insights into who's digging their content, who they are spreading it to."[54] This business model has made digg.com estimated to be worth over $60 million—with Rose and co-founder Jay Adelson the only profit participants. Surveillance therefore returns to the equation, again within the control of Rose and digg.com, but this time in the form of commercially exploiting the user preferences, activities, and interactions of the community that Rose has developed.

DIGG THIS?

The possibility of constructing one's own celebrity image, persona, and brand is not a new phenomenon, nor is it peculiar to the synergies exploited by Rose between TV and Web 2.0. Both Graeme Turner's and

Nick Couldry's studies of DIY celebrity in relation to "cam-girls," who use webcams to build their own celebrity profiles, suggest that one of the important purposes toward which users put their new-found UGC power is the production of fame from one's own bedroom. Turner's and Couldry's assessments of this phenomenon, however, turn on the question of how this celebrity shapes users' relationships with existing media players. Thus, rather than such celebrity representing a democratizing trend in either fame or cultural citizenship, the interests of these girls and, in turn, the meaning of their celebrity are ultimately compromised because, as Couldry argues, "webcam producers like these have to accept that they 'have only limited control over the interpretive context in which people will encounter their site,'" while Turner suggests that the abundance and diversity of identities produced under these conditions will either be coopted by traditional media or be so contingent as to be incapable of effecting any meaningful change or control, being instead unruly, unpredictable, and irresponsible.[55] In contrast, I hope to have demonstrated that Rose has almost unlimited control over his image and important aspects of control over how the user community on digg .com is shaped and valued.

Yet one might object that Rose's celebrity is hardly relevant to his relationship to the millions of users on digg.com. Given the 30 million or more user base of that site, compared to the 250,000 or so downloads of the *DiggNation* podcast, as Rose himself notes above, his "Internet celebrity" is not all that pervasive or important. However, as I noted at the start of this chapter, the user community to which Rose belongs is extraordinary in important ways: like fan groups, it is both active and powerful, with power in this instance not limited to the ability to change storylines or save a show. Rather, it might also include the ability to affect media economies of new start-ups and, possibly, the traditional TV industry itself. Under the title "More Trouble for Hollywood," *The Los Angeles Times* reported on Rose's decision to "ditch cable [and TiVo for] Internet and Netflix," a proclamation happily coinciding with the agreement of Netflix's long-term sponsorship deal with *DiggNation*.[56] Elsewhere *The Los Angeles Times* had suggested that the cohort to which Rose belonged, the Twitter titans, "wield[s] substantial influence. With a few keystrokes, they can put a new website on the map—or they can take one off."[57]

As a leader of that community, how Rose conducts himself and runs digg.com—as both celebrity "poster boy" of Web 2.0 and Internet entrepreneur—in relationship to the "moral economy" of participatory culture is profoundly important. While Rose certainly benefits from selling his user base to advertisers, he has also been forced to engage with the moral economy of digg.com. In early 2007 users began posting and linking to stories on digg.com about the encryption key for unlocking DVDs, which would enable users to rip and burn copies of HD and Blu-ray DVDs. The story was one of those "most dugg" by users, consistently appearing on the front page of digg. Fearing litigation and aware of his own individual liability in a site that traded on collective intelligence, Rose and the digg administrators systematically removed any such postings. However, digg's actions were perceived as censorship by its community of users and not in line with the ethos of the site, which, after all, gave users the right to determine the shape of the news and what is important to the community.[58] Rose therefore responded on his blog: "After seeing hundreds of stories and reading thousands of comments, you've made it clear. You'd rather see Digg go down fighting than bow down to a bigger company. We hear you, and effective immediately we won't delete stories or comments containing the code. . . . If we lose, then what the hell, at least we died trying."[59]

Clay Shirky interprets this move by users as an instance of "civil disobedience," with digg's response recognizing the "implicit bargain that [Rose's] users assumed they had with Digg and, by extension, him." As a result, Shirky argues that this demonstrates the way that the social networking tools of Web 2.0 are marking "progress from coordination into governance, as groups gain enough power and support to be able to demand that they be deferred to."[60] While I have sympathy for such a view, ultimately this distracts us from the moves that Rose has made as the architect of participation on digg.com; most notably, this has included the continual maneuvering of the business in order to be sold to Google—the masters of maximizing value-generating labor through surveillance in the online economy. Similarly, while Rose has displayed some ambivalence toward the selling of and to the digg.com audience by delegating the task of advertising sales to Microsoft, sponsorship has continued to increase on *DiggNation*—for example, the beer sponsorship deal noted above took the form of a six-week "drink-along." Moreover, the relationship between digg.com and *DiggNation* has become more pivotal, with digg.com promoting "digg meet-ups" to now coincide with live episodes of *DiggNation* that serve as media events to confirm Rose's and Albrecht's celebrity. Meanwhile, Revision3 has laid off a large number of its staff and shows as a result of the 2008 "credit crunch," focusing the brand's identity almost solely on the affiliation of the studio with digg.com via *DiggNation*.[61]

Henry Jenkins has suggested that activities like blogging—and by extension the kind of social news sharing, commenting, and tagging that takes place on digg—are a form of social communication that forms part of what he describes elsewhere as "grassroots convergence," a "bottom up" process that intersects with the "top down push of corporate convergence." Jenkins is careful to balance the more optimistic claims of Levy regarding the way in which such cultural forms will enable the "new proletariat [to] . . . free itself by uniting, by decategorizing itself, by forming alliances." Instead, in noting the intersection of corporate and grassroots convergence, Jenkins observes that the participatory culture of blogging and emergent knowledge cultures may be coopted by commodity culture "but can also increase the diversity of media culture, providing opportunities for greater inclusiveness."[62] Such rhetoric is clearly aligned with the arguments that understand the extension of celebrity to "ordinary people" as democratic, as I discussed above, but their intersection produces troubling questions. In particular, the example of Kevin Rose and digg suggests a willingness to turn both the self, via transformation into a celebrity, and the user community, via selling the user base to advertisers, etc., into commodity culture from *within*. That is, I hope this chapter has pointed to some important questions about television's relationship to the Web and participatory culture—most centrally, is there an inevitability to grassroots convergence producing the same results as corporate convergence? If so, Andrejevic is therefore right to assert that the "lesson of reality TV for media critics is that a two-way, participatory medium is by no means an inherently progressive one."[63] In analyzing the shift to digital TV and the promise of heightened interactivity, whether by media conglomerates or co-users, we must always be acutely aware of the architectures of participation that structure the shape of that participation, interaction, and community. Fame is but one structuring logic that might work to close down the potentialities of that participation.

1. The "web stars" quote comes from Bobby Johnson, "Stars in Your Lap," *Guardian Weekend Magazine*, February 23, 2008; http://www.guardian.co.uk/technology/2008/feb/23/interviews.internet; the "Web personalities" quote comes from David Sarno, "Revision3's Web TV Runs on Star Power," *Los Angeles Times Web Scout Blog*, posted July 29, 2008; http://latimesblogs.latimes.com/webscout/2008/07/revision3s-web.html; and the "most famous man on the Internet" comes from Max Chafkin, "Kevin Rose of Digg: The Most Famous Man on the Internet," *Inc Magazine*, November 2008; http://www.inc.com.

2. Erick Schonfeld, "Barack Obama Overtakes Kevin Rose on Twitter—McCain Is Nowhere in Sight," *Tech Crunch*, August 13, 2008; http://www.techcrunch.com. Indeed despite the explosion of Twitter, during which a plethora of mainstream celebrities such as Ashton Kutcher, Britney Spears, Stephen Fry, and Oprah Winfrey have turned to the site, Rose has remained in the top fifty Twitterers with over 1 million followers; see http://twitterholic.com/top100/followers; site last accessed August 19, 2009.

3. Stewart's inclusion on the list is attributed to the distribution of *The Daily Show* on the Web by Comedy Central in the lead-up to the 2008 U.S. election; the show is credited with becoming the "place where many claim to be getting their best coverage of the election." Business Week Tech Team, "The Poster Boy: Kevin Rose," *Business Week*, n.d. 2008; http://images.businessweek.com/ss/08/09/0929_most_influential/18.htm.

4. Bobby Johnson, "Stars in Your Lap," *Guardian Weekend Magazine*, February 23, 2008.

5. Steve Kennedy, "FOWA London 2008 Review," *Digital-Lifestyles*, posted October 24, 2008; http://digital-lifestyles.info/2008/10/24/fowa-london-2008-review.

6. Donna Bogatin, "Kevin Rose: 'Kill Your Television,' and Join Me at Revision3," *ZDNet: Technology and Business News*, September 26, 2006; http://blogs.zdnet.com/micro-markets/?p=475.

7. Brad Stone, "Digg.com Digs Up Some More Cash," *New York Times Blog*, posted September 24, 2008; http://bits.blogs.nytimes.com/2008/09/24/diggcom-digs-up-some-more-cash.

8. Graeme Turner, *Understanding Celebrity* (London: Sage, 2004), 53.

9. For example, see Chris Rojek, *Celebrity* (London: Reaktion Books, 2001); Jessica Evans and David Hesmondhalgh, eds., *Understanding Media: Inside Celebrity* (London: Sage/Open University Press, 2005).

10. Clay Shirky, *Here Comes Everybody: The Power of Organizing without Organizations* (London: Allen Lane, 2008), 108 and 91.

11. Murdock and Dahlgren quoted in Sonia Livingstone, "Critical Debates in Internet Studies: Reflections on an Emerging Field," in *Mass Media and Society*, ed.

James Curran and Michael Gurevitch, 4th ed. (London: Hodder Arnold, 2005), 19.

12. Shirky, *Here Comes Everybody*, 93.

13. See Marshall, *Celebrity and Power*.

14. Mark Andrejevic, "The Kinder, Gentler Gaze of Big Brother: Reality TV in the Era of Digital Capitalism," *New Media and Society* 4, no. 2 (2002): 251.

15. See Burgess's essay in this volume; see also Jean Burgess, "Vernacular Creativity and New Media" (PhD diss., Queensland University of Technology, 2007); available online at http://eprints.qut.edu.au.

16. Su Holmes, "'The Viewers Have . . . Taken Over the Airwaves?' Participation, Reality TV and Approaching the Audience-in-the-Text," *Screen* 49, no. 1 (2008): 14.

17. *The Family Guy*'s status as cult or fan culture is evidenced by the kind of fan activism that Roberta Pearson discusses in this volume.

18. Miguel Helft, "Young Internet Producers, Bankrolled, Are Seeking Act II," *New York Times*, September 25, 2006; http://www.nytimes.com.

19. Jean Burgess, "Hearing Ordinary Voices: Cultural Studies, Vernacular Creativity and Digital Storytelling," *Continuum: Journal of Media and Cultural Studies* 2, no. 20 (2006): 206–7.

20. Albrecht quoted in Bobby Johnson, "Stars in Your Lap," *Guardian Weekend Magazine*, February 23, 2008; Rose quoted in Miguel Helft, "Young Internet Producers, Bankrolled, Are Seeking Act II," *New York Times*, September 25, 2006; http://www.nytimes.com.

21. Nick Couldry, *Media Rituals: A Critical Approach* (London: Routledge, 2003), 107.

22. Turner, *Understanding Celebrity*, 83–84.

23. Graeme Turner, "The Mass Production of Celebrity: Celetoids, Reality TV and the 'Demotic Turn,'" *International Journal of Cultural Studies* 9, no. 2 (2006): 153–66.

24. Annette Hill, "Big Brother: The Real Audience," *Television and New Media* 3, no. 3 (2002): 323–41.

25. Nick Couldry, "Teaching Us to Fake It: The Ritualized Norms of Television's 'Reality' Games," in *Reality TV: Remaking Television Culture*, ed. Susan Murray and Laurie Ouellette (New York: New York University Press), 57–74.

26. Andrejevic, "The Kinder, Gentler Gaze of Big Brother," 266.

27. Quoted in Bobby Johnson, "Stars in Your Lap," *Guardian Weekend Magazine*, February 23, 2008.

28. Sean Redmond, "Intimate Fame Everywhere," in *Framing Celebrity: New Directions in Celebrity Culture*, ed. Su Holmes and Sean Redmond (London: Routledge, 2006), 27.

29. James Bennett, "The Television Personality System: Televisual Stardom Revisited after Film Theory," *Screen* 49, no. 1 (2008): 32–50.

30. Susan Murray, *Hitch Your Antenna to the Stars* (New York: Routledge, 2005).

31. Henry Jenkins, "YouTube and the Vaudeville Aesthetic," *Confessions of an Aca/ Fan*, posted November 20, 2006; http://www.henryjenkins.org/2006/11/you tube_and_the_vaudeville_aes.html. My thanks to Jean Burgess for sharing this article with me.

32. Karen Lury, "Television Performance: Being, Acting and "Corpsing,'" *New Formations*, no. 26 (1995): 127.

33. Dominik Lukes, "Kevin Rose Rocks On," *Guardian Letters and Blogs*, comment posted December 14, 2006; http://www.guardian.co.uk/technology/2006/dec/14/comment.guardianweeklytechnologysection.

34. Frances Bonner, *Ordinary Television* (London: Sage, 2003), 51.

35. See Murray, *Hitch Your Antenna to the Stars*, and James Bennett, *Television Personalities: Stardom and the Small Screen* (London: Routledge, 2010).

36. Quoted in Bobby Johnson, "Stars in Your Lap," *Guardian Weekend Magazine*, February 23, 2008.

37. Marshall, *Celebrity and Power*, 162.

38. "DRM" refers to digital rights management systems that producers utilize to impose limits on what consumers can do with digital content and devices: for example, DRM was customarily built into music file formats, such as *.AAC, in order to prevent users from making multiple copies of the same music or video file. See *DiggNation* episodes 161 and 162, respectively.

39. Su Holmes, "'Off-Guard, Unkempt, Unready?' Deconstructing Contemporary Celebrity in *Heat* Magazine," *Continuum: Journal of Media and Cultural Studies* 19, no. 1 (2005): 31.

40. Burgess, "Vernacular Creativity and New Media," 207–8.

41. Andrejevic, "The Kinder, Gentler Gaze of Big Brother," 268.

42. Allison quoted in Jason Tanz, "Almost Famous," *Wired*, August 2008, 106–25. As the article goes on to explain, Gawker—along with other media gossip sites such as Radar Online and Valleywag—"detail her every exploit." For further discussions of the webcam girls phenomenon, see Nick Couldry, quoted in Turner, *Understanding Celebrity*, 68; Turner, "The Mass Production of Celebrity," 163.

43. Quoted in Max Chafkin, "Kevin Rose of Digg: The Most Famous Man on the Internet," *Inc Magazine*, November 2008.

44. Bonner, *Ordinary Television*, 52.

45. See, for example, Rose's posts and responses at "Forget Web 2.0/3.0, Start Something during Web 2.5," kevinrose.com, posted October 25, 2008; http://kevinrose.com/blogg/2008/10/26/forget-web-2030-start-something-during-web-2.5.html.

46. Henry Jenkins, "Interactive Audiences," in Henry Jenkins, *Fans, Bloggers and Gamers: Exploring Participatory Culture* (New York: New York University Press, 2006), 136.

47. Pesce quoted in Axel Bruns, *Blogs, Wikipedia, Second Life, and Beyond: From Production to Produsage* (New York: Peter Lang, 2008), 283.

48. Bruns, *Blogs, Wikipedia, Second Life, and Beyond*, 267.

49. See Caldwell's entry in this volume and his *Production Culture: Industrial Reflexivity and Critical Practice in Film and Television* (Durham, N.C.: Duke University Press, 2008), 336–38.

50. Andrejevic, "The Kinder, Gentler Gaze of Big Brother."

51. Murray, *Hitch Your Antenna to the Stars*, 117.

52. http://revision3.com/about.

53. Zoe Margolis, "The Democratic Approach Is a Very Valuable Thing," *The Guardian: Technology*, June 12, 2008, T5; http://www.guardian.co.uk/technology/2008/jun/12/interviews.internet.

54. Quoted in ibid.

55. Nick Couldry, quoted in Turner, *Understanding Celebrity*, 68; Turner, "The Mass Production of Celebrity," 163.

56. "More Trouble for Hollywood? Kevin Rose Ditch Cable, TiVo for Internet, Netflix," *Los Angeles Times Blogs: Technology*, posted October 28, 2008; http://latimesblogs.latimes.com/technology/2008/10/more-trouble-fo.html.

57. David Sarno, "Revision3's Web TV Runs on Star Power"; *Los Angeles Times Web Scout Blog*, posted July 29, 2008; http://latimesblogs.latimes.com/webscout/2008/07/revision3s-web.html.

58. Brad Stone, "In Web Uproar: Antipiracy Code Spreads Wildly," *New York Times*, May 3, 2007; http://www.nytimes.com.

59. Kevin Rose, "Digg This: 09-f9–11—02–9d-74-e3—5b-d8–41–56-c5–63–56–88-co," *Digg: The Blog*, posted May 1, 2007; http://blog.digg.com/?p=74.

60. Shirky, *Here Comes Everybody*, 291–92.

61. The studio's other main commitment has been to *The Totally Rad Show*, which is fronted by Alex Albrecht.

62. Jenkins, "Interactive Audiences," 151.

63. Andrejevic, "The Kinder, Gentler Gaze of Big Brother," 268.

BIBLIOGRAPHY

Abrams, M. H. *The Mirror and the Lamp: Romantic Theory and the Critical Tradition.* Oxford: Oxford University Press, 1953.

Adorno, Theodor W. "How to Look at Television." *Quarterly of Film, Radio and Television* 8, no. 3 (spring 1954).

Alvey, Mark. "'Too Many Kids and Old Ladies': Quality Demographics and the 1960s U.S. Television." *Screen* 45, no. 1 (2004): 40–62.

Andrejevic, Mark. *iSpy: Surveillance and Power in the Interactive Era.* Lawrence: University of Kansas Press, 2008.

———. "The Kinder, Gentler Gaze of Big Brother: Reality TV in the Era of Digital Capitalism." *New Media and Society* 4, no. 2 (2002): 251–70.

———. *Reality TV: The Work of Being Watched.* Lanham, Md.: Rowman and Littlefield, 2004).

———. "Tracing Space: Monitored Mobility in the Era of Mass Customization." *Space and Culture* 6, no. 2 (2003).

———. "Watching Television without Pity: The Productivity of Online Fans." *Television and New Media* 9, no. 1 (2008).

———. "The Work of Being Watched: Interactive Media and the Exploitation of Self-Disclosure." *Critical Studies in Mass Communication* 19, no. 2 (2002): 230–48.

Ang, Ien. *Living Room Wars: Rethinking Media Audiences for a Postmodern World.* London: Routledge, 1996.

Auge, Mark. *Non-Places: Introduction to an Anthropology of Supermodernity.* London: Verso, 1995.

Auslander, Philip. *Liveness: Performance in a Mediatized Culture.* London: Routledge, 1999.

Bazalgette, Cary, and David Buckingham, eds. *In Front of the Children: Screen Entertainment and Young Audiences.* London: BFI, 1995.

Beaty, Bart, and Rebecca Sullivan. *Canadian Television Today*. Calgary: University of Calgary Press, 2006.

Bellamy, Robert V. "Constraints on a Broadcast Innovation: Zenith's Phonevision System, 1931–1972." *Journal of Communication* 38, no. 4 (1988): 8–20.

Bellamy, Robert V., and James R. Walker. *Television and the Remote Control: Grazing on a Vast Wasteland*. New York: Guilford Press, 1996.

Bellamy, Robert V., et al. "The Spin-off as Television Program Form and Strategy." *Journal of Broadcasting and Electronic Media* 34, no. 3 (1990).

Benjamin, Louise. "At the Touch of a Button: A Brief History of Remote Control Devices." In *The Remote Control in the Age of Television*, ed. James R. Walker and Robert V. Bellamy Jr. Westport, Conn.: Praeger, 1996.

Benkler, Yochai. *The Wealth of Networks: How Social Production Transforms Markets and Freedom*. New Haven, Conn.: Yale University Press, 2006.

Bennett, James. "Interfacing the Nation: Remediating Public Service Broadcasting in the Digital Television Age." *Convergence* 14, no. 3 (2007).

———. "The Public Service Value of Interactive TV." *New Review of Film and Television Studies* 4, no. 3 (2006): 263–85.

———. *Television Personalities: Stardom and the Small Screen*. London: Routledge, 2010.

———. "The Television Personality System: Televisual Stardom Revisited after Film Theory." *Screen* 49, no. 1 (2008): 32–50.

———. "Television Studies Goes Digital." *Cinema Journal* 47, no. 3 (2008).

———. "'Your Window on the World': The Emergence of Red-Button Interactive Television in the UK." *Convergence* 14, no. 2 (2008): 161–82.

Bennett, James, and Tom Brown, eds. *Film and Television after DVD*. London: Routledge, 2008.

Bennett, James, and Niki Strange. "The BBC's Second-Shift Aesthetics: Interactive Television, Multi-Platform Projects and Public Service Content for a Digital Era." *Media International Australia* 126 (2008): 106–19.

Beyer, Yngvil, et al. "Small Talk Makes a Big Difference: Recent Developments in Interactive, SMS-Based Television." *Television and New Media* 8, no. 3 (2007): 213–34.

Bignell, Jonathan. "Exemplarity, Pedagogy, and Television Studies." *New Review of Film and Television Studies* 3 (May 2005): 15–32.

Boddy, William. *New Media and Popular Imagination: Launching Radio, Television, and Digital Media in the United States*. Oxford: Oxford University Press, 2004.

———. "Old Media as New Media: Television." In Harries, *The New Media Book*, 242–53.

Bodroghkozy, Aniko. *Groove Tube: Sixties Television and the Youth Rebellion*. Durham, N.C.: Duke University Press, 2001.

Bonner, Frances. *Ordinary Television*. London: Sage, 2003.

Born, Georgina. *Uncertain Vision: Birt, Dyke and the Reinvention of the* BBC. London: Vintage, 2005.

Bovill, Moira, and Sonia Livingstone. "Bedroom Culture and the Privatization of Media Use." In *Children and Their Changing Media Environment: A European Comparative Study*. Lea's Communication Series. Mahwah, N.J.: Lawrence Erlbaum, 2001.

Braverman, Harry. *Labor and Monopoly Capitalism: The Degradation of Work in the Twentieth Century*. New York: Review Press, 1998.

Brooker, Will. "Living on Dawson's Creek: Teen Viewers, Cultural Convergence, and Textual Overflow." *International Journal of Cultural Studies* 4, no. 4 (2001).

Brown, Les. *Television: The Business behind the Box*. New York: Harcourt Brace Jovanovich, 1971.

Bruns, Axel. *Blogs, Wikipedia, Second Life, and Beyond: From Production to Produsage*. New York: Peter Lang, 2008.

———. "Reconfiguring Television for a Networked, Produsage Context." *Media International Australia* 126 (2008).

Brunsdon, Charlotte. *The Feminist, the Housewife and the Soap Opera*. Oxford: Oxford University Press, 2000.

———. "Is Television Studies History?" *Cinema Journal* 47, no. 3 (2008): 127–37.

———. "What Is the Television of Television Studies?" In *The Television Studies Book*, ed. Christine Geraghty and David Lusted, 95–113. London: Hodder Arnold, 1998.

Brunsdon, Charlotte, and David Morley. *Everyday Television: "Nationwide."* London: BFI, 1978.

Buckingham, David, Hannah Davies, Ken Jones, and Peter Kelley. *Children's Television in Britain*. London: BFI, 1999.

Buckingham, David, et al. "'Take Back the Tube!': The Discursive Construction of Amateur Film and Video Making." *Journal of Media Practice* 8, no. 2 (2007): 183–201.

Buonanno, Milly. *The Age of Television: Experiences and Theories*. Trans. Jennifer Radice. Bristol: Intellect, 2008.

Burgess, Jean. "Hearing Ordinary Voices: Cultural Studies, Vernacular Creativity and Digital Storytelling." *Continuum: Journal of Media and Cultural Studies* 2, no. 20 (2006): 201–14.

Burgess, Jean, and Joshua Green. *YouTube: Online Video and Participatory Culture*. Cambridge: Polity Press, 2009.

Caldwell, John Thornton. "Convergence Television: Aggregating Form and Repurposing Content in the Culture of Conglomeration." In Spigel and Olsson, *Television after TV*.

———. *Production Culture: Industrial Reflexivity and Critical Practice in Film and Television*. Durham, N.C.: Duke University Press, 2008.

———. "Second Shift Media Aesthetics: Programming, Interactivity and User

Flows." In *New Media: Theories and Practices of Digitextuality*, ed. Anna Everett and John Thornton Caldwell, 127–44. New York: Routledge, 2003.

———. *Televisuality: Style, Crisis, and Authority in American Television*. New Brunswick, N.J.: Rutgers University Press, 1995.

———. "Welcome to the Viral Future of Cinema: Television." *Cinema Journal* 45, no. 2 (2005): 90–97.

Cantor, Muriel G. *The Hollywood TV Producer: His Work and His Audience*. New York: Basic Books, 1971.

Carroll, Noël. *Engaging the Moving Image*. New Haven, Conn.: Yale University Press, 2003.

Caughie, John. *Edge of Darkness*. London: BFI, 2007.

———. "Telephilia and Distraction: Terms of Engagement." *Journal of British Cinema and Television* 3, no. 1 (2006).

———. *Television Drama: Realism, Modernism, and British Culture*. Oxford: Oxford University Press, 2000.

Cavell, Stanley. "The Fact of Television." In Cavell, *Themes out of School: Effects and Causes*. Chicago: University of Chicago Press, 1984.

———. *Philosophy the Day after Tomorrow*. Cambridge, Mass.: Belknap Press of Harvard University Press, 2005.

Chamberlain, Daniel. "Watching Time on Television." *Flow TV* 6, no. 4 (July 2007); http://flowtv.org/?p=615.

Chan-Olmsted, Sylvia, and Louise Ha. "Internet Business Models for Broadcasters: How Television Stations Perceive and Integrate the Internet." *Broadcasting and Electronic Media* 47 (2003): 601–2.

Choi, Jaz Hee-jeong. "Approaching the Mobile Culture of East Asia." *M/C Journal* 10, no. 1 (2007); http://journal.media-culture.org.au/0703/01-choi.php.

Chow, Rey. "Listening Otherwise, Music Miniaturized: A Different Type of Question about Revolution." In *Doing Cultural Studies: The Case of the Sony Walkman*, ed. Paul du Gay et al., 135–40. Thousand Oaks, Calif.: Sage, 1997.

Collins, Richard. *The BBC and Public Value*. ESCRC Centre for Research on Socio-Cultural Change (CRESC), Working Paper 19 (CRESC, Open University/University of Manchester, 2006); http://www.cresc.ac.uk/publications/papers.html #2006.

Corner, John. "Television Studies and the Idea of Criticism." *Screen* 48, no. 3 (2007): 363–69.

Cottle, Simon. "Producing Nature(s): The Changing Production Ecology of Natural History TV." In *Media Organization and Production*, ed. Simon Cottle. London: Sage, 2003.

Couldry, Nick. *Inside Culture: Re-Imagining the Method of Cultural Studies*. London: Sage, 2000.

———. *Media Rituals: A Critical Approach*. London: Routledge, 2003.

———. "Teaching Us to Fake It: The Ritualized Norms of Television's 'Reality'

Games." In *Reality TV: Remaking Television Culture*, ed. Susan Murray and Laurie Ouellette, 57–74. New York: New York University Press, 2006.

Cunningham, Stuart, and John Sinclair, eds. *Floating Lives: The Media and Asian Diasporas*. Lanham, Md.: Rowman and Littlefield, 2001.

Curtin, Michael. "Matrix Media." In Turner and Tay, *Television Studies after TV*.

———. "Media Capitals: Cultural Geographies of Global TV." In Spigel and Olsson, *Television after TV*, 270–302.

Dawson, Max. "Little Players, Big Shows: Format, Narration, and Style on Television's New Smaller Screens." *Convergence: The International Journal of Research into New Media Technologies* 13, no. 3 (2007): 231–50.

Deleuze, Gilles. *Negotiations, 1972–1990*. New York: Columbia University Press, 1995.

Department of Culture, Media and Sport. *White Paper—A Public Service for All: The BBC in the Digital Age*. London: HMSO, 2006.

Derrida, Jacques, and Bernard Stiegler. *Echographies of Television*. Trans. Jennifer Bajorek. Cambridge: Polity Press, 2002.

Doane, Mary Ann. *The Emergence of Cinematic Time: Modernity, Contingency and the Archive*. Cambridge, Mass.: Harvard University Press, 2002.

———. "Information, Crisis, Catastrophe." In *Logics of Television: Essays in Cultural Criticism*, ed. Patricia Mellencamp, 222–40. Bloomington: Indiana University Press, 1990.

Drotner, Kirsten. "Dangerous Media? Panic Discourses and Dilemmas of Modernity." *Paedagogica Historica* 35, no. 3 (1999): 593–619.

Ebbrecht, Tobias. "Docudramatizing History on TV: German and British Docudrama and Historical Event Television in the Memorial Year 2005." *European Journal of Cultural Studies* 10, no. 1 (2007).

Ellis, John. *Seeing Things: Television in the Age of Uncertainty*. London: I. B. Tauris, 2000.

———. "Television and History." *History Workshop Journal* 56, no. 1 (2003).

Elmer, Greg. *Profiling Machines: Mapping the Personal Information Economy*. Cambridge, Mass.: MIT Press, 2004.

Evans, Jessica, and David Hesmondhalgh, eds. *Understanding Media: Inside Celebrity*. London: Sage/Open University Press, 2005.

Everett, Anna. "Double Click: The Million Woman March on Television and the Internet." In Spigel and Olsson, *Television after TV*, 224–47.

Ferguson, D. A. "Measurement of Mundane TV Behaviours: Remote Control Device Flipping." *Journal of Broadcasting and Electronic Media* 38 (1994): 35–47.

Freedman, Des. "Internet Transformations: 'Old' Media Resilience in the 'New Media' Revolution." In *Media and Cultural Theory*, ed. James Curran and David Morley. London: Routledge, 2006.

Friedberg, Anne. *The Virtual Window: From Alberti to Microsoft*. Cambridge, Mass.: MIT Press, 2006.

Fung, Anthony. *Global Capital, Local Culture*. London: Peter Lang, 2008.

Gauntlett, David, and Annette Hill. TV *Living: Television Culture and Everyday Life*. London: Routledge with British Film Institute, 1999.

Geraghty, Christine. "Aesthetics and Quality in Popular Drama." *International Journal of Cultural Studies* 6, no. 1 (2003): 25–45.

Gillespie, Tarleton. *Wired Shut: Copyright and the Shape of Digital Culture*. Cambridge, Mass.: MIT Press, 2007.

Gracy, Karen F. "Moving Image Preservation and Cultural Capital." *Library Trends* 56, no. 1 (2007): 183–98.

Gray, Ann. *Video Playtime: The Gendering of a Leisure Technology*. London: Routledge, 1992.

Green, Joshua. "Why Do They Call It TV When It's Not on the Box? 'New' Television Services and Old Television Functions." *Media International Australia* 126 (2008).

Haraway, Donna. *Simians, Cyborgs and Women: The Reinvention of Nature*. London: Routledge, 1991.

Harbord, Janet. "Contingency's Work: Kracauer's *Theory of Film* and the Trope of the Accidental." *New Formations* 61 (2007).

Harries, Dan, ed. *The New Media Book*. London: BFI Publishing, 2002.

Hartley, John. "From Republic of Letters to Television Republic? Citizen Readers in the Era of Broadcast Television." In Spigel and Olsson, *Television after TV*, 386–417.

———. *Television Truths: Forms of Knowledge in Popular Culture*. Oxford: Blackwell, 2008.

———. *The Uses of Television*. London: Routledge, 1998.

Hartley, John, Jean Burgess, and Joshua Green. "'Laughs and Legends,' or the Furniture That Glows? Television *as* History." *Australian Cultural History* 26 (2007): 15–36.

Haynes, Richard. *Media Rights and Intellectual Property*. Edinburgh: Edinburgh University Press, 2005.

Hermes, Joke. "Hidden Debates: Rethinking the Relationship between Popular Culture and the Public Sphere." *Javnost–The Public* 13, no. 4 (2006): 27–44.

———. *Re-Reading Popular Culture*. Malden, Mass.: Blackwell, 2005.

Hesmondhalgh, David. *The Cultural Industries*, 2nd ed. London: Sage, 2007.

Hewison, Robert. *The Heritage Industry*. London: Methuen, 1987.

Hilderbrand, Lucas. "YouTube: Where Cultural Memory and Copyright Converge." *Film Quarterly* 61, no. 1 (2007): 48–57.

Hill, Annette. "Big Brother: The Real Audience." *Television and New Media* 3, no. 3 (2002): 323–41.

Hills, Matt. *Fan Cultures*. London: Routledge, 2002.

———. "From the Box in the Corner to the Box Set on the Shelf." *New Review of Film and Television Studies* 5, no. 1 (2007).

Hipple, Dave. "The Accidental Apotheosis of Gene Roddenberry, or, 'I Had to Get

Some Money from *Somewhere.*'" In *The Influence of* Star Trek *on Television, Film and Culture*, ed. Lincoln Geraghty, 22–40. Jefferson, N.C.: McFarland, 2008.

Holmes, Su. "'Off-Guard, Unkempt, Unready?' Deconstructing Contemporary Celebrity in *Heat* Magazine." *Continuum: Journal of Media and Cultural Studies* 19, no. 1 (2005).

———. "'The Viewers Have . . . Taken Over the Airwaves?' Participation, Reality TV and Approaching the Audience-in-the-Text." *Screen* 49, no. 1 (2008).

Hopfl, Heather. "Performance and Customer Service: The Cultivation of Contempt." *Studies in Culture, Organization and Society* 1 (1995).

Iosifidis, Petros. "Digital Switchover in Europe." *Gazette—The International Journal for Communication Studies* 68 (2006).

Jackson, Matt. "Protecting Digital Television: Controlling Copyright or Consumers?" *Media and Arts Law Review* 11, no. 3 (2006): 252–71.

Jacobs, Jason. "Experimental and Live Television in the U.S." In *The Television History Book*, ed. Michele Hilmes. London: BFI, 2003.

———. *The Intimate Screen: Early British Television Drama*. Oxford: Oxford University Press, 2000.

———. "Issues of Judgement and Value in Television Studies." *International Journal of Cultural Studies* 4, no. 4 (2001): 427–47.

———. "Television Aesthetics: An Infantile Disorder." *Journal of British Cinema and Television* 3, no. 1 (2006): 18–33.

Jarrett, Kylie. "Beyond Broadcast Yourself: The Future of YouTube." *Media International Australia* 126 (2008).

Jenkins, Henry. *Convergence Culture: Where Old and New Media Collide*. Cambridge, Mass.: MIT Press, 2006.

———. *Fans, Bloggers and Gamers: Exploring Participatory Culture*. New York: New York University Press, 2006.

———. *Textual Poachers: Television Fans and Participatory Culture*. New York: Routledge, 1992.

Jenkins, Henry, and David Thorburn, eds. *Democracy and New Media*. Cambridge, Mass.: MIT Press, 2004.

Jensen, Jens, and Cathy Toscan, eds. *Interactive Television: TV of the Future, or the Future of TV?* Aalborg, Denmark: Aalborg University Press, 1999.

Jin, Dai Yong. "Transformation of the World Television System under Neoliberal Globalization." *Television and New Media* 8, no. 3 (2007): 179–96.

Johnson, Catherine. "Tele-Branding in TVIII: The Network as Brand and Programme as Brand." *New Review of Film and Television Studies* 5, no. 1 (2007): 5–24.

———. *Telefantasy*. London: BFI, 2005.

Johnson, Derek. "Inviting Audiences In: The Spatial Reorganization of Production and Consumption in 'TVIII.'" *New Review of Film and Television Studies* 5, no. 1 (2007): 61–80.

Johnson, Steven. *Interface Culture: How New Technology Transforms the Way We Create and Communicate*. San Francisco: Harper, 1997.

Kaplan, Debra. "Broadcast Flags and the War against Digital Television Piracy: A Solution or Dilemma for the Digital Era?" *Federal Communications Law Journal* 57 (2005): 326–44.

Keen, Andrew. *The Cult of the Amateur: How Today's Internet Is Killing Our Culture*. New York: Random House, 2007.

Kenyon, Andrew T. "Changing Channels: Media Studies, Copyright Law and Communications Policy." In Kenyon, *TV Futures*.

———, ed. *TV Futures: Digital Television Policy in Australia*. Melbourne: University of Melbourne Press, 2007.

Kenyon, Andrew T., and Robin Wright. "Television as Something Special? Content Control Technologies and Free-to-Air *TV*." *Melbourne University Law Review* 30, no. 2 (2006): 338.

Kernan, Lisa. *Coming Attractions: Reading American Movie Trailers*. Austin: University of Texas Press, 2004.

Kerr, Paul. "Channel 4 Dossier: Introduction—Thinking outside the Box." *Screen* 49, no. 3 (2008).

Kertesz, Imre. *Fateless*. Trans. Tim Wilkinson. London: Vintage, 2006; first published in 1975.

Klein, Norman M. "The Electronic Baroque: Jerde Cities." In *You Are Here: The Jerde Partnership International*, ed. Frances Anderton and Ray Bradbury. London: Phaidon Press, 1999.

———. *The Vatican to Vegas: A History of Special Effects*. New York: New Press, 2004.

Klinger, Barbara. *Beyond the Multiplex: Cinema, New Technologies, and the Home*. Berkeley: University of California Press, 2006.

Kompare, Derek. "Publishing Flow: *DVD* Box Sets and the Reconception of Television." *Television and New Media* 7, no. 4 (2006): 335–60.

———. *Rerun Nation: How Repeats Invented American Television*. New York: Routledge, 2005.

Kumar, Shanti. "Is There Anything Called Global Television Studies?" In Kumar and Parks, *Planet TV*.

Kumar, Shanti, and Lisa Parks, eds. *Planet TV: A Global Television Reader*. New York: New York University Press, 2002.

Lange, Patricia G. "The Vulnerable Video Blogger: Promoting Social Change through Intimacy." *Scholar and Feminist Online* 5, no. 2 (2007).

Lawson, Mark. "Foreword: Reading *Six Feet Under*." In *Reading* Six Feet Under: *TV to Die For*, ed. Kim Akass and Janet McCabe, xxi–xxii. London: I. B. Tauris, 2005.

Lemley, Mark A. "Intellectual Property Rights and Standard-Setting Organizations." *California Law Review* 90 (April 2002): 1889–2002.

Lessig, Lawrence. *Code and Other Laws of Cyberspace*. New York: Basic Books, 1999.

————. *Free Culture: The Nature and Future of Creativity*. London: Penguin, 2004.

Levine, Elana. *Wallowing in Sex: The New Sexual Culture of 1970s American Television*. Durham, N.C.: Duke University Press, 2007.

Lievrouw, Leah A., and Sonia Livingstone. "Introduction to the Updated Student Edition." In *The Handbook of New Media*, ed. Leah A. Lievrouw and Sonia Livingstone. London: Sage, 2007.

Livingstone, Sonia. "The Challenge of Changing Audiences: Or, What Is the Audience Researcher to Do in the Age of the Internet?" *European Journal of Communication* 19, no. 1 (2004): 75–86.

————. "Critical Debates in Internet Studies: Reflections on an Emerging Field." In *Mass Media and Society*, ed. James Curran and Michael Gurevitch, 4th ed. London: Hodder Arnold, 2005.

Livingstone, Sonia, and Magdalena Bober. *UK Children Go Online: Final Report of Key Project Findings*. London: London School of Economics and Political Science, 2005.

Livingstone, Sonia, et al. "Citizens and Consumers: Discursive Debates during and after the *Communications Act* 2003." *Media, Culture and Society* 29, no. 4 (2007).

Lotz, Amanda D. *The Television Will Be Revolutionized*. New York: New York University Press, 2007.

Lury, Karen. "Confessions of a Television Academic in a Post-TV World." *Flow* 7, no. 7 (2008); http://flowtv.org/?p=1150.

————. "A Response to John Corner." *Screen* 48, no. 3 (2007): 371–76.

————. "Television Performance: Being, Acting and 'Corpsing.'" *New Formations* 27 (1996): 114–27.

MacDonald, Keith M. *The Sociology of Professions*. London: Sage, 1995.

Manovich, Lev. *The Language of New Media*. Cambridge, Mass.: MIT Press, 2001.

Marc, David. "What Was Broadcasting?" Reprinted in *Television: The Critical View*, ed. Horace Newcomb, 6th ed., 629–40. New York: Oxford University Press, 2000.

Marriott, Stephanie. *Live Television: Time, Space and the Broadcast Event*. London: Sage, 2007.

Marsh, Jackie, et al. *Digital Beginnings: Young Children's Use of Popular Culture, Media and New Technologies*. Sheffield: Literacy Research Centre, University of Sheffield, 2005.

Marshall, P. David. *Celebrity and Power: Fame in Contemporary Culture*. Minneapolis: University of Minnesota Press, 1997.

————. "The New Intertextual Commodity." In Harries, *The New Media Book*, 69–81.

Mayer, Vicki, Miranda J. Banks, and John Thornton Caldwell. *Production Studies: Cultural Studies of Media Industries*. London: Routledge, 2009.

McCarthy, Anna. *Ambient Television: Visual Culture and Public Space*. Durham, N.C.: Duke University Press, 2001.

———. "The Rhythm of the Reception Area: Crisis, Capitalism, and the Waiting Room TV." In Spigel and Olsson, *Television after TV*.

McPherson, Tara. "Reload: Liveness, Mobility, and the Web." In *New Media, Old Media: A History and Theory Reader*, ed. Wendy Hui Kyong Chun and Thomas W. Keenan. London: Routledge, 2005.

Messenger-Davies, Maire. "Babes 'n' the Hood: Pre-School Television and Its Audiences in the United States and Britain." In Bazalgette and Buckingham, *In Front of the Children*.

Messenger-Davies, Maire, and Roberta Pearson. "The Little Program That Could: The Relationship between NBC and *Star Trek*." In *NBC: America's Network*, ed. Michele Hilmes, 209–23. Berkeley: University of California Press, 2007.

Miller, Toby. "Turn Off TV Studies." *Cinema Journal* 45, no. 2 (2005).

Mittell, Jason. "Narrative Complexity in Contemporary American Television." *Velvet Light Trap* 58 (2004): 29–40.

Modleski, Tania. "The Search for Tomorrow in Today's Soap Opera." *Film Quarterly* 33, no. 1 (1979): 12–21.

Moores, Shaun. *Media and Everyday Life in Modern Society*. Edinburgh: Edinburgh University Press, 2000.

Morley, David. *Media, Modernity and Technology: The Geography of the New*. London: Routledge, 2007.

———. *The Nationwide Audience*. London: Routledge, 1992.

Moseley, Rachel, and Helen Wheatley. "Is Archiving a Feminist Issue? Historical Research and the Past, Present, and Future of Television Studies." *Cinema Journal* 47, no. 3 (2008): 152–58.

Moville, Peter. *Ambient Findability*. Sebastopol, Calif.: O'Reilly Media, 2005.

Murray, Janet. *Hamlet on the Holodeck: The Future of Narrative in Cyberspace*. New York: Free Press, 1997.

Murray, Simone. "Media Convergence's Third Wave: Content Streaming." *Convergence* 9, no. 1 (2003): 8–18.

Murray, Susan. *Hitch Your Antenna to the Stars*. New York: Routledge, 2005.

———. "I Know What You Did Last Summer: Sarah Michelle Gellar and Crossover Teen Stardom." In *Undead TV: Essays on Buffy the Vampire Slayer*, ed. Elana Levine and Lisa Parks. Durham, N.C.: Duke University Press, 2007.

Nakamura, Lisa. *Cybertypes: Race, Ethnicity, and Identity on the Internet*. London: Routledge, 2002.

Negroponte, Nicholas. *Being Digital*. New York: Alfred A. Knopf, 1995.

Neuman, W. R. *The Future of the Mass Audience*. Cambridge: Cambridge University Press, 1991.

Ofcom. *Childhood Obesity: Food Advertising in Context*. London: Ofcom, July 22, 2004.

———. *The Future of Children's Television Programming*. London: Ofcom, 2007.

———. *The International Communications Market Report*. London: Ofcom, 2008.

————. *The International Communications Market Report: Key Points*, November 2008; http://www.ofcom.org.uk/research/cm/icmr08/keypoints.

————. *Television Advertising of Food and Drink Products to Children: Options for New Restrictions*. London: Ofcom, March 28, 2006.

Oliver and Ohlbaum Associates. *The UK Children's Market*. London: Oliver and Ohlbaum, 2007.

O'Regan, Tom. "From Piracy to Sovereignty: International VCR Trends." *Continuum: The Australian Journal of Media and Culture* 4, no. 2 (1991): 112–35.

O'Reilly, Tim. "What Is Web 2.0? Design Patterns and Business Models for the Next Generation of Software." *O'Reilly Network*, posted 2005; http://oreilly.com/web2/archive/what-is-web-20.html.

Orr Vered, Karen. "Televisual Aesthetics in Y2K: From Windows on the World to a Windows Interface." *Convergence* 8, no. 3 (2002): 40–60.

Oswell, David. "Watching with Mother in the Early 1950s." In Bazalgette and Buckingham, *In Front of the Children*, 37–38.

Ouellette, Laurie, and James Hay. *Better Living through Reality TV*. Oxford: Blackwell, 2008.

Ovalle, Priscilla Peña. "Pocho.com: Reimaging Television on the Internet." In Spigel and Olsson, *Television after TV*, 324–41.

Palmer, Edward, and Shalom Fisch. "The Beginnings of *Sesame Street* Research." In *"G" Is for Growing: Thirty Years of Research on Children and Sesame Street*, ed. Shalom Fisch and Rosemarie Truglio, 3–25. Mahwah, N.J.: Lawrence Erlbaum, 2001.

Parks, Lisa. "Flexible Microcasting: Gender, Generation, and Television-Internet Convergence." In Spigel and Olsson, *Television after TV*, 133–56.

Pearson, Roberta. "*Lost* in Transition: From Post-Network to Post-Television." In *Quality: Contemporary American Television and Beyond*, ed. Kim Akass and Janet McCabe, 239–56. London: I. B. Tauris, 2007.

Pecora, Norma. *The Business of Children's Television*. New York: Guilford Press, 1998.

Petro, Patrice. *Aftershocks of the New: Feminism and Film History*. New Brunswick, N.J.: Rutgers University Press, 2002.

Prelinger, Rick. "Archives and Access in the 21st Century." *Cinema Journal* 46, no. 3 (2007): 114–18.

Raugust, Karen. *Merchandise Licensing in the Television Industry*. Boston: Focal Press, 1996.

Redmond, Sean. "Intimate Fame Everywhere." In *Framing Celebrity: New Directions in Celebrity Culture*, ed. Su Holmes and Sean Redmond. London: Routledge, 2006.

Rideout, Victoria, Elizabeth Vandewater, and Ellen Wartella. *Zero to Six: Electronic Media in the Lives of Infants, Toddlers and Preschoolers*. Menlo Park, Calif.: Kaiser Family Foundation, 2003.

Rizzo, Teresa. "Programming Your Own Channel: An Archaeology of the Playlist." In Kenyon, *TV Futures*.

Rogers, Mark C., Michael Epstein, and Jimmie L. Reeves. "The Sopranos as HBO Brand Equity: The Art of Commerce in the Age of Digital Reproduction." In *This Thing of Ours: Investigating the Sopranos*, ed. David Lavery, 42–57. London: Wallflower Press, 2002.

Rojek, Chris. *Celebrity*. London: Reaktion Books, 2001.

Roscoe, Jane. "Multi-Platform Event Television: Re-conceptualizing Our Relationship with Television." *Communication Review* 7, no. 4 (2004).

Saen, Michael. *"Producer in Television."* In *The Encyclopedia of Television*; http://www.museum.tv/archives/etv/P/html/P/producerint/producerint.htm.

Sassoon, Donald. *The Culture of the Europeans: From 1800 to the Present*. Hammersmith: HarperCollins, 2006.

Schiller, Daniel. *Digital Capitalism*. Cambridge, Mass.: MIT Press, 1999.

Sconce, Jeffrey. *Haunted Media: Electronic Presence from Telegraphy to Television*. Durham, N.C.: Duke University Press, 2000.

———. "What If? Charting Television's New Textual Boundaries." In Spigel and Olsson, *Television After TV*, 93–112.

Seiter, Ellen. *Television and New Media Audiences*. Oxford: Clarendon Press, 1999.

———. "Television and the Internet." In *Electronic Media and Technoculture*, ed. John Thornton Caldwell, 227–45. New Brunswick, N.J.: Rutgers University Press, 2000.

Sexton, Jamie. "Case Study: Television and Convergence." In *Tele-Visions: An Introduction to Television Studies*, ed. Glen Creeber, 160–68. London: BFI, 2006.

Shapiro, Carl, and Hal R. Varian. *Information Rules: A Strategic Guide to the Network Economy*. Boston: Harvard Business School Books, 1999.

Shirky, Clay. *Here Comes Everybody: The Power of Organizing without Organizations*. London: Allen Lane, 2008.

Silverstone, Roger. *Television and Everyday Life*. London: Routledge, 2006; first published 1994.

Simensky, Linda. "Programming Children's Television: The PBS Model." In *The Children's Television Community*, ed. J. Alison Bryant. Mahwah, N.J.: Lawrence Erlbaum, 2007.

Simmel, George. *The Philosophy of Money*. London: Routledge, 2004; first published 1907.

Sinclair, John. "Into the Post-Broadcast Era." In *Contemporary World Television*, ed. John Sinclair and Graeme Turner. London: BFI, 2007.

Smith, Jo T. "DVDs and the Political Economy of Attention." In Bennett and Brown, *Film and Television after DVD*, 129–48.

Smith, Paul, and Jeanette Steemers. "BBC to the Rescue! Digital Switchover and the Reinvention of Public Service Broadcasting in Britain." *Javnost-The Public* 14 (2007): 39–56.

Spigel, Lynn. "Introduction." In Spigel and Olsson, *Television after TV*.

———. *Make Room for* TV: *Television and the Family Ideal in Postwar America*. Chicago: University of Chicago Press, 1992.

———. "TV's Next Season." *Cinema Journal* 45, no. 2 (2005).

———. *Welcome to the Dreamhouse: Popular Media and Postwar Suburbs*. Durham, N.C.: Duke University Press, 2001.

Spigel, Lynn, and Jan Olsson, eds. *Television after* TV: *Essays on a Medium in Transition*. Durham, N.C.: Duke University Press, 2004.

Steemers, Jeanette, ed. *Changing Channels: The Prospects of Television in a Digital World*. Luton, Bedfordshire: John Libbey Media, 1998.

———. *Selling Television: British Television in the Global Marketplace*. London: BFI, 2004.

Straubhaar, Joseph D. *World Television*. Thousand Oaks, Calif.: Sage, 2007.

Tay, Jinna, and Graeme Turner. "What Is Television? Comparing Media Systems in the Post-Broadcast Era." *Media International Australia* 126 (2008): 71–81.

Terranova, Tiziana. "Cyberculture and New Media." In *The Sage Handbook of Cultural Analysis*, ed. Tony Bennett and John Frow, 587–607. London: Sage, 2008.

Thompson, Kristin. *Storytelling in Film and Television: Understanding Classical Narrative Technique*. Cambridge, Mass.: Harvard University Press, 2003.

Tichi, Cecilia. *Electronic Hearth: Creating an American Television Culture*. New York: Open University Press, 1992.

Tidwell, Jenifer. *Designing Interfaces*. Sebastopol, Calif.: O'Reilly Media, 2005.

Tinic, Serra. *On Location: Canada's Television Industry in a Global Market*. Toronto: University of Toronto Press, 2005.

Turkle, Sherry. *Life on Screen: Identity in the Age of the Internet*. London: Simon and Schuster, 1997.

Turner, Graeme. "The Mass Production of Celebrity: Celetoids, Reality TV and the 'Demotic Turn.'" *International Journal of Cultural Studies* 9, no. 2 (2006): 153–66.

———. *Understanding Celebrity*. London: Sage, 2004.

Turner, Graeme, and Jinna Tay, eds. *Television Studies after* TV: *Understanding Television in the Post-Broadcast Era*. London: Routledge, 2009.

Uricchio, William. "Cultural Citizenship in the Age of P2P Networks." In *European Culture and the Media*, ed. Ib Bondebjerg and Peter Golding, 139–64. Bristol: Intellect Books, 2004.

———. "The Future of a Medium Once Known as Television." In *The YouTube Reader*, ed. Pelle Snickars and Patrick Vonderau. Stockholm: National Library of Sweden, 2009.

———. "Old Media as New Media: Television." In Harries, *The New Media Book*, 219–30.

———. "Television's Next Generation: Technology/Interface Culture/Flow." In Spigel and Olsson, *Television after* TV, 163–82.

Volcic, Zala, and Karmen Erjavec. "Technological Developments in Central-

Eastern Europe: A Case Study of a Computer Literacy Project in Slovenia." *Information, Communication and Society* 11, no. 3 (2008): 326–47.

Walters, James. "Repeat Viewings: Television Analysis in the DVD Age." In Bennett and Brown, *Film and Television after DVD*.

Williams, Raymond. "Advertising: The Magic System." In Williams, *Problems in Materialism and Culture*. London: Verso, 1980.

———. *Television: Technology and Cultural Form*. London: Routledge, 1992; first published 1975.

Wittel, Andreas. "Toward a Network Sociality." *Theory, Culture, and Society* 18, no. 6 (2001): 51–77.

Wood, Helen, and Lisa Taylor. "Feeling Sentimental about Television Audiences." *Cinema Journal* 47, no. 3 (2008).

Woolgar, Steve. "Five Rules of Virtuality." In *Virtual Society? Technology, Cyberbole, Reality*, ed. Steve Woolgar. Oxford: Oxford University Press, 2002.

Zhao, Yuezhi. "Who Wants Democracy and Does It Deliver Food? Communication and Power in a Globally Integrated China." In *Democratizing Global Media: One World, Many Struggles*, ed. R. Hackett and Yuezhi Zhao. Lanham, Md.: Rowman and Littlefield, 2005.

CONTRIBUTORS

JAMES BENNETT is head of area for Media, Information and Communications at London Metropolitan University. His work focuses on digital television as well as TV fame. His work has been published in *Screen, Cinema Journal, New Review of Film and Television Studies*, and *Convergence*. He is the editor of *Film and Television after DVD* (with Tom Brown, 2008) and author of *Television Personalities: Stardom and the Small Screen* (2010). He is the principal investigator on an Arts and Humanities Research Council two-year project on public service broadcasting, multiplatform programming, and the U.K.'s independent television and digital media industries.

WILLIAM BODDY is a professor in the Department of Communication Studies at Baruch College and in the Film Studies Certificate Program at the Graduate Center, both of the City University of New York. He is the author of *Fifties Television: The Industry and Its Critics* (1990) and *New Media and Popular Imagination: Launching Radio, Television, and Digital Media in the United States* (2004).

JEAN BURGESS is a senior research fellow in the Creative Industries Faculty, Queensland University of Technology, where she works on the politics and pragmatics of cultural participation and user-led innovation in new media contexts. Her recent work has included a major study of YouTube in collaboration with Joshua Green (Convergence Culture Consortium/Comparative Media Studies, MIT), culminating in the book *YouTube: Online Video and Participatory Culture* (2009).

JOHN THORNTON CALDWELL is professor of cinema and media studies in the Department of Film, Television, and Digital Media at the University of California, Los Angeles. His books include *Production Culture: Industrial Reflexivity and Critical Practice in Film and Television* (2008), *Televisuality: Style, Crisis, and Authority in American Television* (1995), *New Media* (co-edited with Anna Everett, 2003), and *Production Studies: Cultural Studies of Media Industries* (co-edited with Vicki Mayer and Miranda Banks, 2009).

DANIEL CHAMBERLAIN is a Council on Libraries and Information Resources digital humanities postdoctoral fellow at Occidental College, where he teaches courses on emergent media and works on projects related to advancing digital scholarship. Daniel's dissertation, titled "Emergent Media Technologies and the Production of New Urban Spaces," explored the corresponding phenomena of emergent media technologies and contemporary urban spaces, arguing that they are connected through cultural and economic emphases on personalization, mobility, and interactivity. Daniel holds a PhD and MA in critical studies from the University of Southern California and a BA in economics from the University of Michigan.

MAX DAWSON is an assistant professor in the Department Radio, Television, and Film at Northwestern University. His articles on television, new media history, and aesthetics have appeared in the journals *Convergence* and *Technology and Culture* and the volume *American Thought and Culture in the 21st Century* (2008). Currently he is working on a monograph titled *TV Repair*, which examines the history of the belief that technological innovations, ranging from the remote control to the Internet, will rehabilitate television and reverse the injuries its critics accuse it of inflicting upon American life and culture.

JASON JACOBS is reader in cultural history at the University of Queensland, Australia. He is the author of *The Intimate Screen: Early British Television Drama* (2000) and *Body Trauma TV* (2003) and runs the site screenaesthetics.com. He is currently working on the history of BBC Worldwide, and a critical study of David Milch.

KAREN LURY is reader in film and television studies in the Department of Theatre, Film and Television Studies at the University of Glasgow. She is the author of *British Youth Television: Cynicism and Enchantment* (2001), *Interpreting Television* (2005), and *The Child in Film: Tears, Fears and Fairytales* (2010). She is an editor of the international film and television studies journal *Screen*.

ROBERTA PEARSON is director of the Institute of Film and Television Studies at the University of Nottingham.

NIKI STRANGE is a digital media consultant, manager, and scholar. She is founder of Strange Digital (www.strangedigital.co.uk), providing research and strategy consulting for digital businesses and for the culture, education, and public sectors. She is also a research fellow at the University of Sussex. Her research focuses on the adoption of multiplatform commissioning and production practices in the U.K. television industry, and she is on an Arts and Humanities Research Council research project that examines multiplatform commissioning and production practices across the independent television and digital sectors. She has previously been published in *Media International Australia*, *The Television Studies Book*, and *The Encyclopaedia of Television*. Her background is in factual and arts television production.

JEANETTE STEEMERS is professor of media and communications at the Communications and Media Research Institute at the University of Westminster. After working for CIT Research and international television distributor HIT Entertainment, she rejoined academia in 1993. Her book publications include *Changing Channels: The Prospects for Television in a Digital World* (1998), *Selling Television: British Television in the Global Marketplace* (2004), *European Television Industries* (2005, with P. Iosifidis and M. Wheeler), and *Creating Preschool Television: A Story of Commerce, Creativity and Curriculum* (2010). Her work on preschool television in Britain has been funded by the Arts and Humanities Research Council.

JULIAN THOMAS is professor of media and communications and director of the Institute for Social Research at Swinburne University, Melbourne. He is a member of Australia's Centre of Excellence in Creative Industries and Innovation and the Consumer Forum of the Australian Communications and Media Authority. He writes about information law and policy and the history of communications technologies. His book *Framing Modern Intellectual Property Law*, co-authored with Megan Richardson, will be published in 2011.

GRAEME TURNER is an Australian Research Council Federation fellow, a professor of cultural studies, the director of the Centre for Critical and Cultural Studies at the University of Queensland, and the convenor of the Australian Research Council Cultural Research Network. His recent publications include *Ordinary People and the Media: The Demotic Turn* (2010). His Federation fellow project is an international study of the state of television in a post-broadcast era; the first publication from this project was *Television Studies after TV: Understanding Television in the Post-Broadcast Era* (co-edited with Jinna Tay, 2009).

INDEX

Page numbers in italics indicate an illustration or figure.

Arnaz, Desi, 126n11
art directors, 294–95
Ascent of Man, 199
Atom Films, 290
audiences/consumers, 4, 12–13, 20–22, 39–46, 80–81; as co-producers, 15, 18–21, 120, 136–37, 144–48, 153–54, 335–36; of cult television, 18, 26n56; demographic research on, 115–16; digital surveillance of, 17, 77, 80–81, 88–97, 249–50; early content-control innovations for, 52–72; family-based contexts of, 42; forensic fandom practices of, 219, 228n35; inequalities of access of, 39–41, 46; niche audiences, 106–7, 114–20; personalization of televisual systems for, 41–43, 251–52; presumed passivity of, 314–15, 321–22, 327, 336–37; shifting roles of, 337–38. *See also* DIY celebrity; everyday cultural production; user-generated content
Audio Spotlight, 92
Auge, Mark, 233–34
Auschwitz, 184, 196–99, 203n23
Auslander, Philip, 270
Australia, 31–32
authenticity. *See* intimacy and familiarity
The Avengers, 116, 119

Baker, Van, 289
Ball, Alan, 113
Ball, Lucille, 126n11
Banks, Miranda J., 11–12
Barney and Friends, 161
Barris, Chuck, 114–15
barter syndication, 123–24, 131n100
Battlestar Galactica, 113, 215
BBC, 12, 307; archive project of, 330n44; audience engagement with citizenship through, 48; Ceefax service, 61–63; interactive programming of, 147–48, 153; iPlayer

service of, 1–2, 6–7, 67, 166; preschool media of, 160, 162–63, 165, 174; public service goals of, 18–19, 132–37, 139, 148–49, 154–55, 155n8; rights and revenues policies of, 178n50; 360-degree Creative Future policy of, 18–19, 136, 150–55. *See also* CBeebies
BBC's bundled project, 132, 136–50; bundling (definition), 137–38; for *How We Built Britain,* 149; interactive features of, 144–48; for *A Picture of Britain,* 139–50, 153–54; public service goals of, 148–49
BBC Worldwide, 170
Beakley, Tim, 85
Beaty, Bart, 44
Beijing Olympics, 44–45
Bellamy, Robert V., et al., 56, 67, 139
Benjamin, Louise, 58
Benjamin, Walter, 268–69
Benkler, Yochai, 314–15
Bennett, James, 48, 154, 246
Berman, Rick, 114
Big Brother, 339–40
Big Read, 139
billboards, 85, 90–93
Blab-Off, 58–59
blogging, 272, 312–13, 336, 353
Bluetooth beacons, 88
BMW, 85
Bochco, Steven, 107–8
Boddy, William, 10, 17, 250–51
Bodroghkozy, Aniko, 115, 118
Bonner, Frances, 342, 347
Born, Georgina, 11–12, 307
brand integration, 217–18, 220, 228n33
Braverman, Harry, 306
Break.com, 290
broadband, 3
broadcast flag technology, 67–68
broadcast video colorists, 294–95
Bronowski, Jacob, 199–201
Brooker, Will, 204

McLuhan, Marshall, 9–10
McPherson, Tara, 242
Meadows, Daniel, 344
media capitals, 38–39
MediaCart, 83–84
media interfaces, 231; cultural work of scripted spaces in, 239–43; digital rights management of, 248–49; industry struggles over, 243–49; as non-place sites of metadata, 233–39, 245; personalization of televisual systems through, 251–52; surveillance and control through, 249–50
media studies. *See* scholarship on television and new media
medium specificity (means of delivery), 211, 255–77, 279n31; interruption and proximity to the present in, 258–66; television as a commodity in, 266–71, 277, 280n41; vs. open media options, 270–71
Menon, Vinay, 91
Merrin, William, 10
metadata, 233–39, 245
Microsoft: advertising projects of, 79, 93–94; home entertainment products of, 79; MediaCart shopping cart of, 83–84; Media Center interface of, 248
Miller, Toby, 13
Millimeter, 302
Mini Cooper, 85
Minow, Newton, 112
"Mint," 185–86
Mittell, Jason, 205, 228n35
Mizel, Lital, 319
mobile phones, 3, 36–37, 42, 49n17, 49n19
mobility of digital culture, 76, 81–88; diversification of industry for, 77–81; platform indifference in, 76–79
modernity, 4
Modleski, Tania, 263
Moonves, Les, 78, 79, 204

Moore, Mark, 135–36
Moore, Ronald D., 204
Morlais, Gareth, 344
Morley, David, 4, 35, 251
Muers, Stephen, 135
multiplatform production, 18–19, 132–55; in BBC's bundled project, 132, 136–50, 153–54; in BBC's 360-degree approach, 18–19, 136, 150–55; branding linkages in, 141–42; interactive structure of, 144–48, 156n23; in preschool television, 158–75; public service aspects of, 139; textual linkages in, 140–41
Murdoch, Graham, 336
Murdoch, Rupert, 333
Murray, Simone, 139
Murray, Susan, 117, 341, 349
MyCBBC, 165
MyCBeebies, 165
MySpace, 21, 286

Nakamura, Lisa, 13
National Association of Broadcasters (NAB), 77–78
National Association of Television Programming Executives (NATPE), 34
national contexts, 15–16, 43–45; of citizenship, 12, 48, 323–26, 328; in switchover projects, 3–4, 16–17, 153
NBC.com, 231, 244–47. *See also* Hulu
NBC Universal, 213–17
NebuAd, 94
Negrin, Michael, 302
Neopets, 165
Netflix, 351
networked sociality. *See* social media/Web 2.0
network television: diversification for out-of-home media of, 81–82; niche audiences of, 106–7, 114–20; online video streaming of, 244–49; periodization of, 107; post-broadcast

era of, 18, 32–33, 80–81; producer brands in, 107–14, 126n11; transformation from TVI–TVIII of, 107–26; YouTube content on, 286–87

Newcomb, Horace, 42

The Newlywed Game, 115

new media studies. *See* scholarship on television and new media

News Corporation, 286

The Next Generation (TNG), 114, 120–26, 131n100

niche audiences, 106–7, 114–20

Nick Junior, 158, 161–63, 165, 167–68, 171–72

Nicktropolis, 165

Nielsen, Jakob, 65

Nimoy, Leonard, 116, 125

Noggin, 158

non-places, 233–39, 245

Non-Places (Auge), 234

Nowhere Man, 220

Nuit et Bruillard (Resnais), 197–99

Nutley, Michael, 148–49

Obama, Barack, 333

Ofcom, 155n5, 155n8, 162

The Office, 213–14, 216, 217, 222

"*The Office* Is Closed," 216–17

off-network syndication, 122–23

online games, 273–76, 279n35–36

online tracking boards, 299–300

online video streaming, 244–49

On the Lot, 290–91, 309n13

ordinariness, 16, 25, 337, 347–54, 359. *See also* intimacy and familiarity

O'Reilly, Tim, 315

Orr Vered, Karen, 148, 156n23

Oswell, David, 160

Ouellette, Laurie, 10

Outdoor Advertising Agency, 85

out-of-home media: advertising in, 81–88, 90–97; audience surveillance systems in, 77, 80–81, 88–97; East Asian mobile television markets, 37–38, 42, 49n17, 49n19; penetration of, 82, 85–86

Out-of-Home Video Advertising Bureau, 85

Page, Don, 111

Panasonic, 297

Paoletti, Rebecca, 288–89

Paramount Pictures, 123–25

Parks, Lisa, 16, 18, 252

Patel, Mark, 295, 309n19

Paterson, Richard, 6

Paul, Trey, 124

pay TV (cable and satellite), 32, 39–40

PBS preschool programming, 158, 160–62, 166

Pearson, Roberta, 6, 18

Peña Ovalle, Priscilla, 13

penetration of digital media, 2–3, 82, 133, 155n5

periodization of television, 18, 107, 123

Pertierra, Anna, 32

Pesce, Mark, 348–49

Philco Mystery Control, 58

A Picture of Britain, 139–50, 153–54

Pixel Corps, 291

Playhouse Disney, 161, 163, 165, 167–68

playlist mode of consumption, 41–43

The Plot to Kill Hitler, 184, 193–96

political potential of media, 44–48; generation of cultural citizenship in, 324–26, 328; national identity formation in, 43–45; surveillance and control in, 249–50

Pompei, Joe, 92

Pontin, Jason, 89–90

post-broadcast era, 18, 32–33, 80–81

Poster, Mark, 10

post-network era, 18

post-production work, 294–95

power. *See* political potential of media

Prelinger, Rick, 325

James Bennett is head of area for Media, Information and Communications at London Metropolitan University.

Niki Strange is the founder of Strange Digital (www.strangedigital.co.uk), providing research and strategy consulting for digital businesses and the culture, education, and public sectors. She is also a research fellow at the University of Sussex.

Library of Congress Cataloging-in-Publication Data
Television as digital media / edited by James Bennett and Niki Strange.
p. cm. — (Console-ing passions)
Includes bibliographical references and index.
ISBN 978-0-8223-4887-0 (cloth : alk. paper)
ISBN 978-0-8223-4910-5 (pbk. : alk. paper)
1. Digital television — Social aspects. 2. Digital media — Social aspects.
3. Technological innovations — Social aspects. 4. Information society. I. Bennett,
James II. Strange, Niki III. Series: Console-ing passions.
HM851.T465 2011
302.23'45 — dc22   2010038073